Promises Kept

To David with Love, 12/6/13

We hope you are inspired
by our story of love and life.
Remember to always keep your
promises and believe!

Luanna Rugh
Leonard Rugh AKA 'Rough'

Promises Kept

How One Couple's Love Survived Vietnam

Leonard and Luanna Rugh

iUniverse, Inc.
New York   Bloomington

Promises Kept
How One Couple's Love Survived Vietnam

iUniverse books may be ordered through booksellers or by contacting:

iUniverse
1663 Liberty Drive
Bloomington, IN 47403
www.iuniverse.com
1-800-Authors (1-800-288-4677)

ISBN: 978-0-595-52018-3 (pbk)
ISBN: 978-0-595-50758-0 (cloth)
ISBN: 978-0-595-62113-2 (ebk)

Printed in the United States of America

iUniverse rev. date: 1/7/2009

Luanna Rugh is co-author of *Snowflake Secrets*,
published in 2008 by Whiskey Creek Press

This book is dedicated to the
brave men and women
who fought in Vietnam,
especially the men in
Bravo Company, Fourth Platoon
199th Light Infantry Brigade.
You will never be forgotten.

ACKNOWLEDGMENTS

Lu and I want to thank all those who have had a strong impact on our lives:

Our family was always there for Lu and me. I'm not sure we would have made it through all the trials we had to face without their assistance, encouragement, and love.

My doctor at the Naval Hospital Camp Pendleton, Frederick Jackson, MD, who gave me back my life and then was tragically killed in an airplane crash a few years later.

My comrade in Vietnam, Marty Glasgow, who was very important to the outcome of my life and this book. May God be with you. You must be in heaven as you've already spent your time in hell.

My father-in-law, Walt Brush, who died in June 1995 of cancer. Walt and I spent many great hours going places and doing things, more than most natural fathers and sons. He was always there for me if I needed a ride or just someone to talk to. He was my sidekick, or maybe I was his. He taught me a lot about living life with purpose and dying with dignity. I truly miss him.

My lieutenant for my last few months in Vietnam, Don Bratton. You set the story straight about what happened the day I was wounded. Thanks to you, the nightmares have stopped and I've been able to look myself in the mirror without the guilt I lived with each day for over thirty years.

Lu and I both want to thank the special people from the Community Presbyterian Church who took us into their hearts with love and support.

Julie, Christie, Margie, Steve, and other members of the Lagunita Writers Group who gave me the courage to continue and the help to make my words come alive. They taught me about sentence structure and punctuation, as English is not my forte. Martha, you're the greatest hostess.

Larry and Lorna Collins for their patience, encouragement, editing skills, time, wonderful meals, determination, and all-around pushiness, just what we needed to see this dream become a reality.

This book would not be complete without a special thank you to my wonderful wife, co-author, and friend, Lu. She made sure I had time to write what I wanted before she ever became involved in the writing process. I thank her for keeping all the letters I sent home and allowing me to use them for this book. They helped me remember important details and the chronological order of events. This is actually our story about our love and the promises we kept to each other, turning tragedy into triumph.

Leonard Rugh, 2008

Introduction

This book is about a courageous couple who have overcome overwhelming circumstances and odds. It is about a loving, devoted wife who demonstrated a great deal of strength and loyalty as she stood by her husband as he returned from the battlefield with a horrendous wound. It is about a brave soldier who shows everyone of which he is made. Together this couple defies what everyone expected, and accomplished far more than everyone thought possible.

This story is about a soldier who was wounded in battle, and his devoted wife who is there to encourage him, and provide the strength and love needed for him to recover. This is an exceptional couple, who signify the sacrifices our military men and women endure to protect our liberty. It does not matter which war, conflict or campaign the soldier may be involved; the battlefields, and dangers are the same.

I have the honor to have this couple as my friends, and I have the highest respect for them. I served with Len Rugh in Vietnam, and I was with him when he was wounded. I salute Len and Luanna Rugh.

Donald C. Bratton

Contents

Prologue

May 2000, Washington, DC

Thirty-one years after my time in Vietnam, I stand before the black granite gash in the ground. The morning feels humid with dark clouds threatening rain at any moment, very appropriate. *How many days and nights did we live in the rain during that damn war?*

I'm heavyhearted, walking with the aid of a brace and cane; but I'm alive! It's time to confront those faces that only my mind can see, because I was the one who got them killed. An accident, but still … my fault.

Over fifty-eight thousand names of the brave who didn't come home confront me. I know I'm responsible for some of them. I must say I'm sorry and good-bye. We weren't best friends, but we fought together. They died there. I made it home.

I only knew them by their nicknames. I didn't want to get too close or too personal; they might be gone in the next breath. But now I have to find them.

Rat! Yes, I remember his given name. The black panel he should be on is listed in the directory. I open the book slowly, searching the pages. *What? No entry for Rat? He and the rest of my squad were killed that horrible day.*

Joe! He and I were closer than anyone else. So, I turn the pages again, hoping his name won't jump out at me, even though it should. *Damn! No Joe listed with the 199th.*

Am I crazy? Am I confused? Has my head injury caused me to forget? What the hell is going on?

My mind races back. I still remember every moment of that hellish time like it happened yesterday, especially that disastrous night.

I still see, feel, and live with the consequences of the six months and eighteen days I spent in that godforsaken place. The memories never fade even though I try to seal them away. It's a hell I've carried with me all these years.

This is the hardest; I cost the lives of some good men. I stand here, rain pouring down my face like the tears I've shed so many times. Seen through nature's tears, the book before me becomes a blur.

A hand has been on my shoulder the whole time, adding its support as it always has over the last thirty-one years.

"Len, there must be some way to find out why the names aren't here," my wife whispers in my ear as she puts her arm around me. She leans closer to be sure her umbrella covers us both. "Maybe it means that those men didn't die. Could you be mistaken?" she asks quietly.

My solemn moment at this monument to death is suddenly shattered when a busload of kids, aged twelve or thirteen, head for the wall. The path in front is wet and slick, and soon becomes a Slip 'n Slide™. Jumping from the top of the wall to the ground below must look like a great game.

These names carved in the granite mean nothing to them. Men and women who died in a long-forgotten war that even their parents are too young to remember.

It's raining harder now. The children have gone, and all is quiet. In the distance, thunder booms, and I hear it as it rolls across the memorial. It sounds like artillery in the jungle. *This is the year 2000, isn't it?*

In an instant, I'm transported back, back to August 1968 and the letter ...

BOOK ONE -
THE WAR

Chapter 1 - The Beginning

From: The President of the United States
To: Leonard W. Rugh
Greetings: You are hereby ordered for induction into the Armed Forces
of the United States ...
It was signed by a member of the Selective Service Board.

* * *

Wait a minute; I'm too old to get drafted.

I looked again, but there it was in black and white. I had to report
to the induction center in Los Angles, California, on 20 August 1968.
I was going to be drafted into the army!

My twenty-third birthday was only a few days away and I had been
married for almost two years. But this afternoon the letter I had hoped
would never come, arrived.

Many thoughts crashed through my mind: *This must be a joke! But,
no, it's the real thing. Hey, I was just discharged from the navy. How can
the army draft me? Oh, God, how is my wife going to take this news? How
am I going to break it to her?*

Walking back into our apartment, I called to Lu, "Hi, kid, I got
the mail."

She came out of the kitchen with a big grin on her face. She always
smiled, but my news was about to change that. "What do you want for
dinner? I forgot to take anything out of the freezer this morning. Hey,
why so serious?"

"Sit down; we have something to discuss."

"You're really scaring me," she exclaimed as she sat on our new couch.

"I received a notice from the President of the United States asking me to join the army."

"Well, just tell them you can't go. You're married. Besides you're going to be twenty-three next week and that's too old!"

"Honey, you don't understand. I've been drafted. I have to go. I don't get a choice."

"No, I won't let you go! Damn, we're just too happy; I knew it couldn't last."

"Come on, kid, we need to make plans. I'm going to be gone for two years."

"I know I'm being unreasonable, but this just can't be happening."

"That was my first thought, but it's reality, and we have to deal with it."

"Hey, weren't you in the navy before we met? I thought you got a discharge."

"Yeah, but I didn't serve actual time except for basic training in the Naval Reserves. When the unit was called up, I failed the physical because of my migraines and my shoulder dislocation problems."

"Well, then, the army won't take you either."

"Honey, we have to assume they will."

"Okay, we'll do it your way, but I don't have to like it!"

"That's my girl. We've always worked together, and we'll get through this. Just have faith."

* * *

The two weeks passed quickly for Lu and me. The morning I had to leave for Los Angeles came all too soon. Lu was being a real sport, trying hard not to let me see how upset she was.

The long drive to the United States Army Induction Center in Los Angeles went far too quickly. I knew the trip home alone for Lu would be tough.

I hoped they'd find some reason to not take me; that the discharge papers in my pocket would keep me from going. But I was only kidding myself.

Lu waited around just in case like I knew she would. She still believed I was coming home with her.

We were given a so-called physical check-up. My migraines and shoulder problems were of no consequence. The war in Vietnam was escalating, and the army needed bodies.

Unfortunately, I only had a few minutes to say good-bye. I walked out and placed my hands on Lu's shoulders. Her big blue eyes held a question, but she already knew the answer. I took her in my arms and held her close, trying to give her strength and all my love.

"You know I'm on my way, don't ya? It's going to be a long time, but we'll make it. I love you. I'll write and call when I can. Now give me a kiss."

She let out a long sigh and hugged me tighter. Her kiss was deep and full of so much love. It would have to last me for at least two months. "Now say good-bye. I'll see you soon, I promise," I said. I tried not to look back as I headed toward the bus.

Chapter 2 - Basic Training

We arrived at Fort Ord, California, about three hundred miles north of Los Angeles. All the way there, I still couldn't believe it was happening. I was scheduled for a total of sixteen weeks of training, starting with eight weeks of basic, followed by another eight weeks of advanced individual training, or AIT. At the height of the Vietnam War, the largest number of draftees ended up in the infantry, becoming "grunts" or "ground pounders."

When we pulled in late that evening, we filled out reams of paperwork. A mean-looking sergeant took a quick glance and put them in a folder. He handed me my file and said to always keep it with me. He emphasized that losing it wouldn't get me out. I was given my dog tags to wear at all times. I was really in the army!

"Okay, maggots," the sergeant bellowed as we arrived at our sleeping quarters, "might as well get some sleep. The lights go out at twenty-two hundred hours; for you ex-civilians that's ten o'clock PM."

We were no longer men; we were "maggots," "dogs," "kiddies," or even worse.

The next morning we were awakened at zero-five-thirty. Right after breakfast, we went to our company area. There, waiting for his new recruits, was one tough-looking banty rooster. He looked about nineteen years old and around five-six. Though short in stature, he was all muscle under his tailored army OD (short for olive drab) uniform. What hair we could see under his Smokey-the-Bear hat was in a buzz cut.

Since we were scheduled for haircuts, we'd all look like that soon. This was still the time of the hippie rebellion. Many of the other guys had very long hair, soon to fall to the floor of a barbershop along with a few tears.

This kid would be our drill sergeant for the next eight weeks.

"For you maggots, the name is Sergeant Rose, but you will call me Drill Sergeant. You will remember I work for a living. I am not a sir!"

Officers didn't get much respect. They were also referred to as sixty-day wonders, shake and bakes, and other disdainful names.

"You will do nothing unless I tell you to do it. You will not even think unless you ask me first. Do I make myself clear?"

We all quietly answered, "Yes."

"You will address me as 'Drill Sergeant' and sound off when speaking. Do I make myself clear?" he boomed.

We all shouted, "Yes, Drill Sergeant."

"I still can't hear you."

This time everyone yelled as loud as possible, "Yes, Drill Sergeant!"

"You maggots might get it right one of these days. Leave your bags where they are and follow me," he continued. "You will not walk in my company area. You will run at all times unless told otherwise."

We were off and running to get our new uniforms and footwear, compliments of the taxpayers and the government of the USA. We were issued basic OD T-shirts, boxer shorts, socks, pants, shirts, a baseball cap, and black army boots.

The boots were to be kept polished to a very high gloss, spit-shined so you could almost see your face in them. Everything had to be stored in our footlockers in the prescribed military way. Then we were assigned our bunks and issued bedding.

"Forget how your mommies taught you to make your beds! This is how the army makes a bunk. As you can see, there are no wrinkles. If I drop this quarter in the middle and it bounces, it's made properly. Otherwise, it ain't."

I'd heard old GIs talk about this trick with the quarter but thought it was a joke. It wasn't. This guy actually bounced a quarter off our bunks to see if we'd made them properly!

It had been a long day, so we climbed into bed and slept, hoping when we woke the next morning it would all vanish like a bad dream.

At zero-five-thirty, the lights came on and a metal trashcan rolled down the middle of the barracks between the two rows of bunks making a hell of a racket. We were startled awake. In addition to the noise, the drill sergeant bellowed, "Get your lazy asses out to the company street, like five minutes ago."

I'd been warned by friends who'd gone though basic training and was prepared. I'd slept in my fatigues, so all I had to do was put on my boots, and I was out the door. Some of the other men had been forewarned, too.

"I see I have some Clark Kents in my company," he hollered, referring to those of us already dressed. "So, do you men want to do some PT while we wait for the rest of the maggots to get their butts out here? This morning maybe we'll do a simple twenty pushups. Now drop!

"I want to hear you sound off during this drill, and do it like this," he said, as he dropped into the pushup position. "First it's down; your body will not touch the ground. Then you will come up and sound off. 'One, Drill Sergeant,' 'Two, Drill Sergeant,' and so on until I tell you to come to attention."

We managed to complete twenty pushups while waiting for the rest of the men. The whole company had to do fifteen more. So, those of us who were prepared ended up doing a total of thirty-five pushups. We learned we couldn't outsmart the drill sergeant, but we continued to try.

The process of molding us into men who could follow orders and kill the enemy had started. The military used the term "enemy" or another label when referring to those we would be fighting. In past wars, we'd fought Japs, Nips, Krauts, and gooks, all dehumanizing names. We were being trained to fight the VC, the NVA, or gooks, but never flesh-and-blood people.

The psychological remaking of our thinking from "thou shalt not kill" to "kill or be killed" also began. We were trained to open fire on the enemy when given orders without question or hesitation. We knew it meant the difference between life and death on a battlefield.

That morning, we had our first breakfast in the mess hall. We were surprised to see two chin-up bars just outside the door.

"Do ten pull-ups before entering," yelled the senior drill sergeant. He positioned us at attention.

"Yes, Drill Sergeant!" we responded.

Man, we sure do a lot of yelling!

I quickly found out that SOS, or shit-on-a-shingle, was creamed dried beef on toast. But it wasn't something I'd have cooked, served, or eaten if I'd had a choice. The stuff looked like someone had vomited all over my toast, and it smelled almost that bad. I was a picky eater and would rather go without than eat something I didn't like. If this was any indication of things to come, it was going to be a very long two years.

Right after breakfast, we were asked to volunteer to be squad leaders. It was a chance to get out of KP, and I really hated doing dishes, especially the amount of stuff the army dirtied. I decided I might as well take a shot at it.

We reported to the sergeant's room one at a time to be interviewed.

"I say, Private, aren't you a little old to be here?" he asked.

"My sentiments exactly, Drill Sergeant. Maybe you could tell that to the top brass and have me sent home."

"Just what I need in my platoon, an old man and a smart-ass to boot. What makes you think you can keep up with these kids? The squad leader runs at the front of the formation at all times."

"Well, Drill Sergeant, I figure being at the front of the formation makes it easier to keep going. When you lead, you can't lag behind."

"I still have to see a few other men who want the job. I'll know by tonight at dinner."

With that, I was dismissed.

We reported to the company street to begin our training in how to march. We marched, we marched, and we marched some more. After lunch, it was more marching. We must have marched halfway to San Francisco and back, all on a street about a hundred meters long.

At this rate, I'll need new boots before I ever get out of basic, I thought.

* * *

"Privates Simms, Rugh, Colby, and Bruno, get your maggot asses over to my dayroom right after dinner," our drill sergeant bellowed as we got into formation.

"Yes, Drill Sergeant," the four of us yelled in reply.

After chow, we got word that the four of us were the new squad leaders.

"You may think you're getting out of work, but I expect you to be my hands and my eyes. You will be sure each man, his area, and the entire barracks are ready for inspection every day. Rugh, you have first squad. Simms, second. Bruno, third. Colby, that leaves you with the fourth. Any questions?"

"No, Drill Sergeant," we answered in unison.

I made it. Great, no KP. All I have to do is keep up with these young kids and hold it together. I'm only twenty-three and in pretty good shape, so what could be the problem?

* * *

After roll call each morning, we headed out for our mile run, but I know we ran more than a mile. We would then have breakfast, eaten in a big hurry since the drill sergeants were yelling at us the whole time to get our maggot butts out the door to physical training or PT.

"Rugh?"

"Yeah, Simms."

"Do you feel like we're learning a foreign language? Using initials for just about everything is sure strange. We need to understand KP, PT, and CO. Words and phrases are shortened whenever possible, but not always. Why is A Company known as Alpha Company? It doesn't make sense."

"Don't ask me. It's the military way. I'm sure there's a logical reason for everything."

"Yeah, who are you kidding?"

* * *

I finally had time to write my wife to let her know I was surviving.

Hi honey,

Please send letters since I can't make or receive telephone calls. I wrote the return address on the envelope.

It's only been two days and already I miss you so much. This is really a different life. I'm fine and I'll survive, although the PT is demanding, especially with my shoulder. PT is physical training for you non-military types. Ha! Ha!

I have good news; I've been made a squad leader. The best part is I get out of KP. You know how much I hate washing dishes.

My drill sergeant is already calling me "the old man." He and the rest of the platoon are between seventeen and nineteen. You wouldn't think a four- to six-year difference would be a big thing, but when running and doing PT, it really counts. I wouldn't admit this to anyone, but I'm a little out of shape.

Well, we have inspection in a few minutes and I need to spit-shine my boots again. Don't laugh; we really do that. I'm looking forward to seeing you in eight weeks. I love you with all my heart and miss you a whole lot. Be a good girl and write soon.

Love, Len, your husband and lover

* * *

We were at the mercy of every drill sergeant in the company. If you so much as sneezed, they were waiting to make you do push-ups. It was all part of following orders no matter what. If we were caught walking when we should be running, it was, "Drop and give me twenty."

Our mornings were spent in classes which ranged from basic first aid to hand-to-hand combat.

"Private Rugh! Front and center."

"Yes, Drill Sergeant."

"One of your duties is to keep your men awake during training!"

"Yes, Drill Sergeant!"

"Why is that man asleep in my class? Kick him in the balls and get his attention. What he's here to learn may save your life as well as his!"

"Yes, Drill Sergeant!"

It was difficult for any of us to imagine that in a few months we'd be in a war fighting for our lives.

* * *

A week after my arrival, I was introduced to a rifle. A lot of us were raised in the city, so firing a weapon was new. I'd never been hunting in my life. But I was probably heading to a place where someone would shoot at me. I had to be taught to kill if I was to protect myself and those around me.

9

The army was using M-14s in basic. We carried the heavy rifles in our hands diagonally across our chests while running the mile and a half to the rifle range. The dirt path, mostly downhill, wasn't too bad on the way there.

The target at the rifle range was the silhouette of a man. It suddenly hit me: *We're being trained to shoot at flesh-and-blood people.*

The drill sergeant warned us, "This rifle has a real kick to it, so hold it properly or you could break your shoulder. Tuck it in tight. Lay your cheek against the stock, sight down the barrel, lining up the target. Then gently squeeze the trigger."

Holding the rifle, staring at the target, and firing was hard the first time. The deafening sound of the M-14 going off just about scared me to death. I'm not sure where my rounds went, but they didn't hit the target. However, before the day was over, most of us managed to make a few holes in the paper; some even hit within the outline of the man. *This will definitely take practice.*

Afterward, we ran, not walked, back up the hill. What a pain! If someone in the company did the unthinkable and dropped out of this uphill race, the rest of the company ran in a circle around him until he was able to get up and finish. The drill sergeant kept yelling at him to join the company. "You're making your buddies run while you're sitting on your damn lazy ass resting!" The humiliation was to force him to push himself past what he thought was his breaking point.

"We never leave a fellow GI behind for any reason," the drill sergeant emphasized as we continued back.

Later that night, we squad leaders discussed how things had been going. Part of our responsibility was to set the fire watch. We assigned men to walk the barracks all night, one man per hour on each floor.

"Shit, they ran our asses off today; that's when we weren't in PT. I guess they're trying to get us in shape," said Simms.

"Yeah, in Vietnam we want to be in the best shape possible," Colby replied.

"Right now, we'd better set watch. Everyone needs to get some sleep," I said as I headed for my bunk.

* * *

That was pretty much the routine for basic training. Day after day after tedious day, we ran, did PT, fired our weapons, ate meals, policed the barracks, marched, and had classes. The time went slowly. I wanted it to be over so I could see Lu. Finally, it was graduation day.

The night before, we sat around reflecting on our first two months in the army.

Simms laughed as he said, "Remember the first time we ran the hill to and from the firing range? I thought we'd all die carrying that fucking heavy M-14. Yesterday it didn't seem as steep coming back."

"Yeah, and when I had to fire at that paper target, and I saw the silhouette, I just about puked. Now, it doesn't even register there's a man there. I only want to get my shots close together and get my good marksmanship badge," Bruno added.

"I'm in better shape now than I was even while playing football and baseball in college. My wife'll be happy about that. The PT does have its rewards," I chimed in.

Simms continued, "I've also noticed the guys are really paying attention. I guess they've finally realized this is real. We'll most likely be sent to Vietnam."

"Lu and I have come to the same conclusion. When I'm in 'Nam, it'll be tough on her. But she's a trooper and she'll be fine."

"I'm looking forward to seeing my family at graduation."

"Me, too, Colby. Most of them are coming, but I think my dad will have to work. The Simms men are steelworkers. I will be too after I'm discharged. It's just about impossible for him to get off, especially during a war."

"Well, tomorrow can't come soon enough. I need to hold my wife and give her a big kiss. It's been way too long!" I declared as I headed for the sack.

* * *

Lu and her family drove up for graduation in her dad's camper. Boy, did she look good to me. The minute she stepped out of the truck, I grabbed her and kissed her, then held her tight. I didn't want to let her go. God, I missed my Lu!

I finally greeted the rest of the family. We ate a picnic lunch together at tables near the barracks.

Lu helped me put on my dress uniform for the parade.

"You sure look handsome. You know what they say about falling for a man in uniform," Lu said as she stepped back for a better view.

"Honey, we've been married almost two years and this is the first time you've seen me in uniform."

"Well, maybe I'm falling in love all over again. You sure look fit and trim. Just, look at all those muscles. I've missed you."

"I'm so happy to see you. The days were long and the nights even longer just thinking about you."

"Stop it. I'm embarrassed. No, don't stop; I love hearing your voice. It seems like eight months instead of only eight weeks," Lu said smiling.

"Well, I'll see you after the ceremony. Love you."

"Love you, too."

"Hold still so I can use your dark glasses for a mirror while I put on my cap. Bye, beautiful."

* * *

The battalion marched in formation, we saluted, the flags waved, and everyone felt a sense of patriotism.

When it was over, I met Lu and her parents and sister. We drove into Monterey to Fisherman's Wharf. I only had a four-hour pass, not much time to spend with them.

Everyone else ordered fish for dinner, but I wanted steak. It was the biggest T-bone I'd ever seen, covering the entire plate, and man, did it taste good!

After dinner, Lu's dad slipped me the keys to his camper with a big grin. Then he announced they'd walk around on the pier for an hour or so. I didn't know how to thank him.

I took Lu's hand, and we ran through the parking lot. We had one wonderful love-packed hour. Two months of separation to make up for, and who knew when we would see each other again. We'd just gotten dressed when we heard her dad and mom talking very loudly as they approached.

I had less than an hour before reporting back to base, so our time together was almost at an end. It was way too short. We didn't even have a night together, and I'd start another eight weeks of training immediately.

Chapter 3 - AIT

I would complete my second eight weeks of AIT at Fort Ord. The next morning we discussed our next assignment.

"Hey, Rugh, this is crazy. I've been talking to some of the other guys. A lot have plans to go to college after this tour. They want to become teachers, businessmen, or professionals. Of course, the army is sending them into the infantry to become grunts," declared Simms.

"Yeah, and they sent a man who can't read or write to clerk's school. Now that's really dumb," Colby added.

"Maybe they plan to teach him to read and write. It might be good for him," I responded.

"You're staying here for ground-pounder school, too, aren't you, Rugh? Man, I thought you had some college before being drafted, so why didn't you go to Officer Candidate School? Rumor has it your test scores would have gotten you in," Simms asked.

"Sure, I could have gone to OCS, but it would have meant another year added to my tour. Two years is enough. I have a life at home. I want to go back to my wife as soon as I can."

"Yeah, I understand."

"Well, good luck, Simms, and the rest of you guys. Maybe we'll meet up in 'Nam."

"'Bye," Simms said as he walked out the door heading to his new unit.

* * *

Hi honey,

I am glad you and your family made it up for graduation. Thank your dad for taking the time off work and for letting us use the camper. It was wonderful; just what I needed.

Our new drill sergeant is taller but just as mean. It looks like I'm not going to be a squad leader in AIT and we'll be working long hours, six days a week.

Would you believe, we sat most of the day on the bleachers in the pouring rain? They brought chow out to us, but have you ever tried to eat a peanut butter and jelly sandwich in the rain? I don't recommend it.

They were teaching us about small weapons. We'll learn how to fire the mortar tube, the light anti-tank weapon, or LAW, the fifty-caliber, and the new M-60 machine guns. Hey, they even outfitted us with the M-16 which they're using in 'Nam; no more heavy M-14s.

I was talking to a couple of fellows. We were all thinking the same thing. We should have been at home watching TV in front of a cozy fire with our families, wives, or girlfriends. Once again, the small things seem to come to mind when we think of home.

Honey, last Friday was so much fun. I'll be able to handle the next few weeks since I've had a chance to hold you and talk to you. I hope it will make it easier for you to wait until I can get a pass to come home.

I may not be able to write often or call, but I will send my love on the wind and in my dreams.

I just found out we're getting up at 4:30 AM for some dumb reason. Sometimes I would like to tell the army to go to hell, and the sergeant along with it.

Well, enough griping for now. Good night, kid.

Your husband and lover, Len

* * *

Mark Franklin was a little older than the rest. He was twenty-one and also married, so we had some things in common. We ended up in the same platoon and were bunked close together. He was a tall, lanky kid and easy to like. One day, after about a week in AIT, we had a few minutes of free time. He and I got to talking about wives and home.

"I have it all planned. During AIT, I'm going home on leave as often as I can," I said.

"We'll only get weekend passes and can't travel more than fifty miles from base or it's 'brig time.' I thought you lived in Orange County. How are you going to get home? It's south of LA, isn't it?" he asked.

"I need to see my wife! I'll fly, take the bus, or hitch a ride, just to spend a few hours with her. My map shows the distance between Fort Ord and Buena Park is less than fifty miles. Of course, it could be a little off."

"Yeah, off by about three hundred miles!" Mark pointed out.

"Well, I did say it was *my* map. I might have drawn it a little screwy. And just how far do you have to travel to get home to see your wife?"

"Uh … about fifty miles. Rhonda lives in Reno. I think I had the same mapmaker you did."

We laughed at the leave policy. The army knew we'd travel outside of the limit, but nothing was said if we were back at the base Sunday night by eighteen hundred hours. As long as they didn't ask us where we had been all weekend, we sure as hell weren't going to tell them.

* * *

We settled into a routine, much like that of basic only more intense.

"This getting up at 0500 is starting to get to me, especially when we don't get back to the barracks until after 2100 every night. Then we have to clean our rifles and boots before we can get any rack time."

"Hell, it's almost midnight and we're due for more escape and evasion tomorrow night. That means map-reading classes and night maneuvers in the hills in this damn cold," Mark complained. "How do you stand it, especially since you're from sunny southern California?"

"It isn't easy! It's getting colder every day. I thought I was going to freeze my butt off when we went out to the beach range this morning. The sky was beautiful and clear, and then the wind came up, blowing in from the sea across the bay and hit me like a knife. The army didn't give us any cold weather gear."

"We have two more months of winter here, and it feels like it could snow, so I guess we'd better get used to it, Len."

"Man, last night when we were in that blasted foxhole overlooking Salinas, I kept thinking the only good thing about Vietnam is that it's tropical and warm."

"Len, that is *not* a fuckin' good enough reason to go to that damn hellhole. I don't want to get shot at in Vietnam. My wife and I have plans which don't include me going off to war."

"Well, since we'll probably be sent there, we should try to make the best of it and get as prepared as possible. The guys training us have been there and survived. I want to learn all they can teach. It could save my life."

"I can't think that way. I'm still hoping for some other duty, maybe even here in the States."

"You can pretend all you want, but we're most likely going." I wanted Mark to concentrate on what was ahead.

"You're right, but I still don't want to be out in the fucking cold playing at war," Mark grudgingly acknowledged.

"Maybe the E and E will be cancelled since men in black pajamas could be seen in the snow." I was referring to the "enemy" in our escape and evasion tactics classes.

"You must be joking; they won't cancel. I've heard that if we're captured by these guys, we'll suffer through some realistic torture, including being thrown in a pit full of shit. No thank you. They aren't going to get me, not without a fuckin' good fight," Mark said as he headed for his bunk.

"You got it," I replied as I slipped under my blankets for some much-needed sleep. I was more tired than I wanted him to know. All the early morning wake-ups and late nights were starting to take their toll. *One of these days I'm going to tell the army to buzz off,* I thought.

"Okay, all you maggots, hit the street like right now," bellowed our senior drill instructor at 0500 the next morning. At times, depending on how our drill sergeant felt, the day started even earlier, but always before the sun came up.

This must be a nightmare. This asshole is standing at the door of the barracks yelling at us to get up and dressed. I feel like I just closed my eyes. It's still pitch black outside and, I'm sure, colder than an arctic night.

"Okay, kiddies, we will grab a quick breakfast, then go on a little hike. You've been getting soft, so no more truck rides. We'll be running from now on. First Platoon, move out," he ordered.

He led us on what turned out to be a twelve-mile speed march into the hills to our training area. The first stop was the hand grenade pits. We practiced tossing the real things so we wouldn't be afraid to touch them once we got to the war.

Our drill sergeant asked, "How many of you guys have played basketball?"

Most of us raised our hands.

"Well, lobbing a grenade is like throwing the ball from the basket to half court on a fast break."

He continued, "And, unless you have steel teeth, don't use 'em to pull the pin like you see in the movies. The correct way is to hold the grenade firmly in your right hand. Grab the ring holding the pin in place with your left hand and give a firm pull. You have ten seconds before it explodes. As the handle pops off, start counting. At seven, toss the damn thing at the target. This only gives the enemy three seconds to react, not very much fuckin' time before it blows 'em to hell."

We each took a grenade. One at a time, following instructions, we threw it down the range.

"I told you, you stupid asshole, you're supposed to pull the pin *before* you throw it at the target! Okay, let's try it again, maggots, and get it right this time."

After a few more practice throws, we ran on to the radio area. There we had instruction on the proper way to handle a PRC twenty-five, more commonly called a prick-twenty-five by the troops. It was the main radio used in the field. After our training, we could all operate one to call in artillery support, report enemy locations, or call for a medevac chopper. Without the proper codes, procedures, or frequency, we'd be useless.

"I don't want to be carrying one of these prick-twenty-fives if we go to Vietnam. That damn whip antenna might as well have a red flag on it for every sniper in the field," I heard someone say.

"Yeah, my buddy just got back from 'Nam. He told me to never volunteer to be an RTO," another trainee replied.

17

We stored those words for future reference. None of us wanted to be a target in Vietnam.

"Whether you ever carry one or not, knowing how to use it might save your life," the instructor informed us.

We also had classes in setting booby traps and spotting the ones set by the enemy. We were taught how to disarm them by instructors who had been in 'Nam.

These guys were living proof there really was a war going on. They had first-hand knowledge about fighting and how to survive. Everyone paid attention. The war was getting closer.

During one of the short breaks between classes, Mark and I were sitting around talking.

"Boy, Rugh, it sure got my attention today when we were learning how to set up and spot booby traps. That stupid bastard, Nelson, was working on putting a booby trap together when the instructor pulled him to his feet. He yelled at the kid, 'I had a buddy get fuckin' blown away because he was moving too fast! Slow down and do it right the first time 'cause you won't get a second chance in 'Nam.' I felt kind of sorry for him," Mark said.

"The sergeant wants me to be squad leader. He said Nelson isn't working out. I sure wouldn't want him leading my unit in combat. He's likely to get us killed."

"Shit, Rugh, I didn't think you wanted the responsibility."

"Well, when the sergeant orders you to do it, there isn't much choice."

We were joined by several other guys. "Today on the range, didn't those machine gun rounds seem damn close as we low-crawled under that fuckin' wire?" Roberts asked.

"I felt the same way. My fatigues were full of dirt and sand I'd plowed up. The range instructor didn't need to yell, 'Keep your heads down.' I must have been half way to China by the time I reached the other side," I answered.

"If this is anything like 'Nam, I can do without it. But there's no way around it except going AWOL to Canada or Mexico. My wife and I discussed it and decided it would be hard to look my kids in the eye if I did something that stupid," Mark added.

"You're like me. We were raised to do our duty. I have a wife and someday we hope to have children. I have a responsibility to them and to my country. I may not want to be here, but I am, so I need to do the best job I can." I think a lot of us felt the same.

"We'll just have to get through this fuckin' shit."

"I'm sure you're going to make it. Mark. I've watched you in training."

"I sure as hell hope you're right. I've finally accepted that I'll most likely be heading for Vietnam, but I plan on coming home. My wife will kill me if I don't.

"Lu and I have lots of plans when my hitch is up. We want to buy a house and start a family."

"Okay, kiddies, nap time's over. March out for E and E, now. We'll eat cold tonight."

"Yeah, everything's cold," someone muttered.

* * *

Hi honey,

First and most important is I love you! I hope to come home next weekend. I should know by tomorrow. I'll call and give you my flight info as soon as I know for sure.

Guess what, I'm a squad leader. Nelson, the guy I replaced, decided to swing on me, so I pulled his pass. He went AWOL and is now out of the company. He won't be missed. He didn't fit and was always messing up.

I've been playing football every night. We won last night and tonight, so we play again tomorrow. We're getting close to the end of the playoffs. If we lose the next game, our team is out. Playing football gives me a chance to let off some steam. I have a few bumps and bruises, but it's a lot of fun.

I spent two nights after football in a foxhole freezing my ass off. This last week has really been a pain and it's really cold. Now I know where the term "a cold day in hell" came from.

I miss you very much. I didn't realize how lonely a person could be in the middle of eighty GIs. I love you.

Love, your husband and lover, Len

* * *

Time went faster in AIT. We could call home on Sundays, and some of us traveled home to our families. We finished fighting our war games early Saturday afternoon. With my twenty-four-hour pass in hand, I headed for the nearest airport. Lu picked me up for a few hours together before I had to fly back. Recharged, I could handle the next six days of torture.

* * *

Christmas 1968 was special. I was home with Lu for twelve days. She had to work, but I filled in as an extra cook so I could be with her. I made more money in those few days than I made in two months in the army.

Christmas Eve we both worked the late shift and didn't finish until 2:30 AM. We walked out and got in the car. I turned the key. Nothing.

One of the officers who visited the restaurant was still in the parking lot and realized we had a problem.

"Hey, Len, what's the matter?"

"Darn it, Roy, I left the lights on and the battery's dead. You know it'll be hours before the Auto Club gets here at this time of night on Christmas Eve."

"Let me see what I can do." He got on the radio. "A tow truck should be here in about ten minutes. I'll hang out with you until he arrives. Have your wife get into the patrol car where it's warmer."

"Roy, you're a lifesaver!"

"So, you're heading to Vietnam? I lucked out. Police are exempt for the most part, but my brother was just drafted. He'll most likely go there."

"Yeah, well, I'm not looking forward to it, but it's something I have to do."

"If it means anything, I'm proud to know you. Good luck and come back safe."

"Thanks, Roy. I intend to," I said as the tow truck pulled up.

The holidays were wonderful but over way too soon. It got more difficult each time I had to go back to Fort Ord.

* * *

Hi honey,

The next two weeks will be our hardest training yet. They are really trying to get us combat-ready. Last night we set up a landing zone and had to hold it against an enemy assault. It was very realistic. We had to dig foxholes. I know you'll laugh at the mental picture of me with my little army shovel digging a hole in the ground while freezing to death, bullets flying around and big 105 rounds overhead. Ha! Ha!

Today we are practicing a "fire and movement" exercise where we move out and fire at targets at the same time. No more blanks; we are using live ammo too. They're being careful about our safety, so don't worry. Yeah, right, you not worry.

I can't wait until we can go for a walk by the beach listening to the waves roll in, drive wherever we want to go, work at the kind of job we choose, and have our kids when we want. That's what I'm here for.

Our life together has been the best. I don't know if anyone has ever been happier than you and I. Living in a free country makes that possible.

I love you very much. See you soon.

Love, Len, your husband and lover

* * *

I received my orders. I'd known what was coming, but seeing it on paper, in black and white, hit me hard.

"Happy second anniversary!" Lu greeted me on the phone. "How is my favorite army guy?"

"Yeah, happy anniversary to you, too! Sorry, I can't be home to celebrate. I got my orders today. I report to Travis Air Force Base in two weeks. It's Vietnam."

"Oh damn, I kept hoping you'd end up somewhere in the States or Germany."

"Me, too, but that's not the case. I'll call and let you know when I'll be landing at LAX."

21

I was given the next three months' pay in advance to spend on my leave—all of three hundred dollars in cash. Going to the jungles of Vietnam, I wouldn't need it.

I hitched a ride home the same day. My wife had no idea I was on my way as I wasn't due until a few days later. She was at work when I arrived. I walked into the restaurant in my uniform. I wanted to surprise her and have something to eat. It had been a long trip home. I got the desired effect. She let out a scream and ran to give me a big hug and kiss. Everyone in the place gave us a standing ovation. I'd never seen her that shade of red before.

After she served me my dinner, I left her the biggest tip she'd ever received as a waitress—all three hundred dollars under my plate. I was almost killed before I got into the war!

"What were you thinking when you pulled a fool stunt like that? How could you leave that much money lying around? What if someone else took it?"

"Ah, honey, I was where I could keep an eye on it the whole time. I wanted to see the look on your face. It was great! I'll bet the two little ladies from Pasadena would have had a good laugh." At that she smiled.

I remembered it well: When we were first married, she worked at one Pasadena restaurant and I worked at another in the same chain, about two miles away. She would take me to work at 4:00 AM and then drive to work for her shift. I used to walk to her store and sit on her station while waiting for her to get off work.

One day the two little ladies, who used to come in every afternoon, told Lu they were very upset with the young man who always sat on her station.

"Martha and I are going to say something to that nice looking 'cheapskate.' You always give him very good service and we've noticed he never leaves you a tip. It's just not right!" she exclaimed.

"That very handsome young man is my husband and since the money goes into the same budget, he probably didn't think to leave one," she replied.

"Oh, how dreamy! He comes here to visit you every day. How romantic. He must love you very much."

How could she remain angry at her wonderful, dreamy, romantic husband?

* * *

We spent the next week moving Lu to her parents' home and the following week we took a short vacation in the camper. We had a wonderful, loving time together. I made a promise to Lu that on my honor, one way or another, I would return. Even though I'd vowed, both of us knew it might be the last time we'd spend together.

I took a little longer than two weeks. In fact, I took a whole three weeks.

The last night before I reported to Travis was tough for both of us. We stayed awake most of the night, clinging to each other. We'd said everything there was to say and done everything there was to do. We were prepared, just not ready for me to leave.

The day dawned clear on that early March morning in 1969. Lu took me to LAX. She put on a brave front, but we knew the next year would be hell for both of us.

The time came for me to board my flight. I held her in my arms and kissed her deeply. It was so hard to let her go. She was crying. I just wanted to stay and comfort her, but I had to walk away. All the way down the ramp, I wished I could turn around and go back, but my responsibility to my country kept me moving forward.

Chapter 4 – Travis

When I arrived at Travis, the sergeant looked at my orders and said, "I see you are seven days overdue checking in, Private. You didn't miss your flight to 'Nam, but you'd better have a damn good reason for being late!"

"I decided if the army's going to send me to some godforsaken country where I might be killed, I deserved more leave."

"Damn nice of you, asshole. So what's your fuckin' story?"

"Two weeks wasn't enough time to spend with my wife before going to Vietnam. The government owed me that extra week."

"What?" he bellowed. "Well, jerk-off, you were wrong, and it's going to cost you; that much I can guarantee. In the morning, report to the OD (officer of the day). He'll determine your consequence. The army does not take its solders being AWOL lightly."

"Sergeant, it was well worth it, whatever the punishment."

"By the way, you dumb shit, formations are at 1800 and 0530. You *will* be there! Do I make myself clear?"

"Yes, Sergeant, I'll be there," I snapped.

After my reaming out, I found the sleeping quarters in a converted hanger with some four to five hundred other men. I spotted another soldier and asked, "Hey, man, what's there to do around this base at night?"

"Well, Rough," he said, mispronouncing my name stenciled on my uniform, "there isn't much except waiting until your number's called for your flight."

I figured we should introduce ourselves so I told him that it was Rugh or Len. His name was Ron.

"I've been here for two days just doing the same thing: going to formations, doing paperwork, getting shots, and picking up all the shit the army issues us to fight this fuckin' war."

"I just want to get through this next year, come home, and get on with my life," I answered. He looked like a kid and had probably just made the eighteen-year-old age limit for being shipped to Vietnam.

"Yeah, I guess that's all I want, too. Hey, at mess it's best to stay towards the front of formation. The sergeants usually start at the back pulling guys out for KP."

"Thanks. Do you know the penalty for being a week late?"

"You were AWOL for a week? I don't know. What are they going to do, send you to 'Nam? We're already on orders to go there," he chuckled.

"I don't know either, but I'm sure I'll find out tomorrow morning."

* * *

It was the same old military routine: hurry up and wait. As Ron said, at mess that night the sergeants got all the men they needed before they got to me. *Whew, I really hate KP.*

After dinner, it was back to the bunk to wait for lights out. Except the lights never went dark. Flights left around the clock and the loudspeakers constantly blared call numbers.

"Attention: the men on United Airlines charter flight number fifty-five, that's five-five, report to hanger number three. Your flight will leave at twenty-two thirty hours."

Zero-five-thirty came cold, dark, and early. Too soon it was time to see the OD to find out my punishment for being AWOL. The OD checked my records for what seemed like an hour; then he looked up.

"There must be some judgment for your lack of regard for military discipline. I'm giving you an Article Fifteen on your record, punishable by fourteen days restriction to the base and fourteen dollars from your next paycheck."

No big deal. I was already restricted and the fourteen dollars was the best money I'd ever spent. The Article Fifteen, one of the lowest forms of military discipline, would show up on my 201 file. No sweat. I was only going to be in the army for the required two years, not a lifetime occupation.

My next stop was the medics. They examined my records for any missing vaccinations and added the extra ones required for Vietnam. They were using the new shot gun; it was easier and faster when processing hundreds of men.

The GIs standing in line looked like kids to me. The thought crossed my mind: *How many of us will be returning in a year? How many lives will be permanently changed, damaged, or lost? Where do I fit? What will happen to me? I could be one of those statistics of war. I could be killed! Enough of that kind of thinking, Rugh. Concentrate on the good things in life; what I have to come back to. I made a promise and I mean to keep it.*

Next we were issued uniforms the government thought would beat the heat and humidity of South Vietnam.

I checked back for my orders, hoping they had been misplaced. Just wishful thinking. The waiting got more difficult every hour.

Then they started calling names. I heard, "Private Rough."

Darn, they still can't pronounce my name.

Even though I thought I was prepared, it still hit me in the pit of my stomach like a lead ball. "You will leave at 0600 tomorrow."

I called Lu to let her know I was shipping out early the next day. I told her how much I loved and missed her, and promised her again that I'd come home. Now all I could do was hope and pray the time would pass quickly and without incident.

I didn't sleep that night. I picked up my orders and 201 file and was sent to a holding area to wait for my flight number to be called.

The military did not have enough planes and ships to get all the manpower into the war quickly enough, so they paid civilian air carriers as charters. I was on an SAS passenger jet. This was the last day my feet would touch American soil until R and R in Hawaii with my wife. I was on my way, but I'd return. I promised Lu. Somehow I knew that death did not await me in Vietnam.

Chapter 5 - On My Way

"Good morning, gentlemen and ladies. My name is Susan, your head flight attendant. This is SAS flight twenty-two with stops in Hawaii, Guam, and South Vietnam."

It all sounds so normal, like we're just heading for a vacation!

"Boo," "Hiss," "Hiss," the replies rippled through the plane, along with some more obscene remarks.

They went through the regular safety routine, but no one was paying attention. The guys were checking out the flight attendants.

After the plane left the ground, I decided to look at my 201 file and see what this Article Fifteen looked like. I went through it all and could find nothing showing any action taken against me. I heard later, anyone having any military discipline had his records carried by one of the officers.

My guess is my Article Fifteen had ended up in the circular file. The major who was my judge must have understood my reasons and let it go. Lu would be especially happy it was not going on my record. She'd been worried about me getting into trouble.

First stop: Hawaii, to take on more fuel and a few soldiers on their way back from R and R. We couldn't see much, but there was a sweet flowery smell, which began as soon as the door to the plane was opened. I was already looking forward to a time in seven or eight months when I would be back for R and R with my wife. We'd be able to spend a week here in this tropical paradise.

Our next stop was Guam. Then we were back in the air for the final leg of our trip to Vietnam.

After what seemed like days, the plane started into Long Binh Air Force Base.

It was not a typical approach. In fact, we dropped so fast that anyone standing would have hit the ceiling and then been thrown to the floor.

"Damn, that was some air pocket," someone commented. The plane was speeding toward the airport and we were all wondering if it was going to set down before crashing into the runway or plunging off the end into the water.

"Sorry, guys," came the announcement. "This is the way we land to keep from taking ground fire from the VC."

There really wasn't much to see, only rice paddies surrounding the base, looking like a blur of green and brown as the ground quickly passed by.

While taxiing down the runway, we heard the flight attendant say, "From the crew on SAS flight twenty-two, thanks and please take care of yourselves. We want to see all of you on your way home in a year!"

"You can be damn sure I'll be doing just that," one of the guys said, none too quietly. He voiced all our hopes and prayers.

Everyone was trying to get a look at what was waiting for us, and soon it was chaos. One of the stewardesses made a plea, "Stay in your seats until we come to a complete stop."

We were typical airline passengers. The message didn't get through. One impatient GI muttered, "Get your damn face out of my window."

A sergeant yelled, "Knock it off! There'll be enough fighting once you get on the ground. No sense doing Charlie a favor without even getting a chance to fight him."

Finally, the door opened. The heat, the humidity, and the smell hit us. It was a hot, earthy odor, one that stuck in our nostrils and began to cling to our skin and clothing.

Welcome to Vietnam!

Everyone stood around. No one was in any big hurry to get off the plane. An officer, who had gotten on in Guam, took charge. "Okay, all you mean bastards, it's time to see your new home, so get off this damn machine."

We found out these planes were nicknamed the Freedom Birds by those returning from the war unscathed. We all wanted to ride the Freedom Bird back to our families and home.

Out we went; no air-conditioned terminal greeted us. We walked into a blazing hot, clammy afternoon. Every breath carried the stench of this country deep into our lungs. It was especially tough after being cooped up for the long flight.

"Hey, Sarge, what in the hell is that god-awful smell?" one GI asked.

"Something you'd best get used to. What you smell, besides the rotting jungle, is the burning of shit cans. The military has gone back to outhouses in this fuckin' place, and the cans are burned for sanitation at least once a week."

Talk about air pollution, this really makes LA smog smell like roses, I thought as we moved down the stairs.

The officer took charge and marched us a safe distance from the plane. A clerk roared up in a jeep and jumped out before it came to a stop. "New arrivals, your bags will be off the plane any minute. Hang loose in the shade until then."

We milled around, trying to take in our surroundings. We retrieved our stuff and followed the clerk to a small reception area off the field. As we marched, we saw another group of GIs leaving for home. When they passed us, someone shouted, "Hey, you bunch of FNGs, don't you wish you were headed to the World instead of the damn war?"

"You bet your ass," someone from our group yelled back. We found out later what FNGs were: fuckin' new guys.

Watching the returning GIs, something struck me. It was the faraway, eerie, haunted look in their eyes, as if they were staring at something we were unable to see. They had endured things no human being should have: too many deaths, too much destruction, too many buddies lost. They were going home, but for many, not leaving the war behind.

I hoped when my time came to take the Freedom Bird, I wouldn't carry these burdens.

We marched away toward our destiny in Vietnam.

* * *

We received more papers to be filled out, and then our assignments. I was assigned to the 199th Light Infantry Brigade and told their truck would arrive later that afternoon. Until then, we were to wait.

I glanced at my two new buddies. One looked Italian with a Roman nose, olive complexion, green eyes, and black hair, probably curly if not cut so short. The other man reminded me of a younger version of one of my college professors, a real studious type. He was about my height with sandy brown hair and blue eyes covered with wire-rimmed glasses.

"Hey, Perini, is that how you pronounce your name?" I asked.

"Yeah, but I go by Joe. How do you pronounce yours, Rug?"

"Nah, its Rugh, like it was spelled R-U-E, but my first name is Len."

"I'm Dan, nice to meet you both," responded the other GI.

"Do you feel strange? Here we are in a war zone. I feel naked without a weapon," the guy named Joe said.

"Luckily, it's only for a few hours," Dan answered.

Joe responded, "You bet your ass!"

* * *

Our truck arrived and the driver yelled over the noise, "Throw your bags in the back and climb aboard. We're headed to Redcatcher, the distribution point for the brigade."

We could tell the war was at hand. Sandbags lined the floor of the cab and the bed in the deuce 'n half, as this two-and-a-half ton truck was called. Chicken wire covered the cab windows.

Oh God, I'm really here in Vietnam! I just wanted to throw up.

Dan asked, "We aren't far from the city of Saigon. Are the chicken wire and sandbags really necessary?"

"It's like this," the driver answered. "Anything can happen and usually does, so better safe than sorry. You can't even trust the kids. While you're feeling sorry for them, they could drop a grenade into the gas tank. Not all of them are like that, but we don't take chances."

The truck jolted forward. It wasn't long before we were at the outskirts of Saigon. The driver only knew how to use the gas pedal and the horn. We did our best to hang on and not be thrown out of the truck as we sped through the narrow streets.

The people of Saigon had gotten good at dodging military trucks. We managed to get through the city without hitting any of the pedestrians, mopeds, bicycles, and other vehicles. We careened towards our new way of life in this war-torn nation of sights, sounds, smells, people, customs, and food so foreign to us we could have been on another planet.

I'd been dreading this time, this country, this war, and now I was in the heart of it. More than I've ever wanted anything in my life, I just wanted to go home.

Chapter 6 - Redcatcher

After a harrowing ride, we arrived at Redcatcher, the reception center for the 199th Light Infantry Brigade. The truck dropped us off in front of a wooden building where a clerk met us.

"Welcome to Redcatcher. Only three of you? Shit, Bravo Company lost more than that last week. How am I supposed to keep our manpower up to strength when they only send me three FNGs?"

"We noticed a lot of Vietnamese in uniform with weapons on base. What's the deal? How do you know the good guys from the bad guys?" I asked.

"There are a lot of gooks running around here carrying weapons. They're ARVNs, or Army Republic of Vietnam, and they are supposed to be on our side. They've been approved to be here, so don't get shook up over it."

Joe muttered, "A gook's a gook. I'm not fuckin' trusting 'em."

The clerk continued. "Fill out these forms, and then I'll show you where you'll spend the night." He reminded us we each needed to have a minimum of two hundred dollars in the company safe for R and R. Then he took us inside another building with a bunch of empty tables. He told us to remove all of our uniforms from our duffel bags. Another GI handed us razor blades with instructions to cut off all tags, shoulder patches, names, and rank identifications.

"Wait a damn minute. I paid good money to have this stuff sewn on, and now you're telling me it was wasted?" Joe asked what we were all thinking.

"That's the way it's got to be. Some other GI's most likely going to be wearing them at some point, and you will be using another guy's gear.

32

You'll only need one set of fatigues in the field. This makes it easier for them to be stored."

So we set to work cutting off all the tags, stripping away the last of our identity. Now we were just nameless GIs. We were then ordered to change into our OD green fatigues and to turn in the extra boots and uniforms we were issued at Travis. They were used to replace worn-out gear. We didn't know or care who ended up with these uniforms as long as we had one to wear when our time came to go home.

Our next stop was the barracks, where we found three empty cots. We unpacked and settled in. I took the opportunity to write my first letter home.

> Hi honey,
> Well, I'm here. I'm really in Vietnam. The scariest thing is ... I'm in the war! I want to be home with you in my arms, loving me and telling me that it was all just a bad dream.
> Nope, I've opened my eyes and pinched myself. Yes, I'm really here at a base called Redcatcher.
> It's the in-country distribution point for the 199th Light Infantry Brigade. There's a mess hall with hot chow, enlisted and officers clubs, and even a small post exchange.
> I'm only here for a few days, but I'll be back when I head for R and R in about eight months and when I come home next year.
> God, I miss you. I've never felt so alone and lost. Being ripped away from my life and my wife is hell. I only have 364 more days to go, but who's counting? Ha! Ha!
> I'll write more when I know my address. I will love you always.
> Love, Len, your husband and lover

* * *

The first night, the three of us, Joe, Dan and I, took advantage of the enlisted club. The place was air-conditioned and smoke-filled like any bar back home. There was the stench of alcohol, unwashed bodies, and fear. There was cold beer for those who were old enough (you had to be twenty-one) and cold soda for those who weren't. We all thought it was stupid. Men were fighting and dying every day for their country, but couldn't have a beer to celebrate living through this hell.

There was a Vietnamese band playing live music. A version of "California Here I Come" and everybody's favorite, "I Want to Go Home," seemed to be the only two songs the band knew.

"Let's get out of here," Dan yelled over the blaring music.

"I'm tired of these same dumb songs. I sure as hell don't want to be reminded we have a whole fuckin' year before we can go home," Joe shouted back.

"Besides, these vets won't mix with us. We kind of stand out with our white skins and clean uniforms," I hollered across the table.

Dan took another swig from his Bud and swallowed. "Yeah, there's not much to talk about. We don't want to hear their stories about the war, and they don't want to hear about how we miss home."

A bottle crashed and beer drizzled down the wall. We froze, but the band played on.

"You sumabitch, I tol' you to keep your shit togeder in the fuckin' field," yelled the drunk who'd thrown the bottle.

The recipient of his tirade, equally drunk, screamed something about doing his job. He was so out of it that we could barely understand his slurred comeback, but the bottle he held by the neck made it evident he was about to bash in the skull of the first loudmouth.

He threw, missed his mark, and glass smashed against the bar. The fight was on. We all stepped back to give the combatants room. After all, it wasn't our fight.

I thought these guys would have had enough fighting during the past year. Then it hit me: *Maybe they just need to let off some steam before boarding the Freedom Bird in the morning.*

The MPs arrived as the three of us headed out the door and back to our sleeping quarters.

"Hey, man, I sure hope we're not that screwed up after we've been here a whole damn year!" Joe complained. "All I wanted was a cold beer, but could I get one? Hell, no! I could only get a coke and even that was fucked up by two stupid drunks."

"Well, Joe, beer isn't good for you young guys anyway," I kidded.

"Yeah, it'll stunt your growth or put hair on your butt, or something like that," Dan added.

"What the fuck's going on? Did I hook up with two preacher's kids or something?" Joe asked.

"Believe it or not, I am. I don't know about Dan."

"Not me. I like my Bud, thank you, but in moderation. Getting sloshed isn't my style."

* * *

We slept in a wooden barracks with steel-framed cots stacked against the wall. The bottom six feet or so were reinforced with sandbags, but still so flimsy the mosquitoes could have carried it away.

We didn't have mattresses, just rusty springs and a sheet - something about jungle rot and bugs. I took out my poncho liner, a small lightweight quilted blanket, and attempted to cover the metal. It was too hot to use a blanket anyway.

We had mosquito netting for protection, which kept some of those flying monsters off our bodies. They were so big and plentiful they sounded like F-4s as they dive-bombed trying to get through.

We not only heard the mosquitoes, but we heard the real sounds of war. Big guns fired at some unknown enemy target. Let me tell you, it was frightening. We were totally exhausted and slept, but it was a nervous sleep.

* * *

The next morning, we went to our first class. It was on the customs, habits, language, traditions, and differences of the Vietnamese people.

The instructor told us, "They're smaller in stature, but it doesn't mean the VC or NVA are weak. They can go all day, half the night, and still have some fight left in them. Don't get the idea that their size makes them any less fighting men."

He went on to tell us what we could expect from them, and what was expected of us as representatives of the United States.

After lunch, it was back to the room for another class. It was taught by a forward observer whose job was to spot for one of the artillery companies.

"It's important to understand just how effective the artillery can be. If you're unlucky enough to be without one of us, you can do your own spotting. Just be sure you give the right coordinates. The 105s are deadly and can bring a lot of destruction on the enemy when used correctly. That's why it's important for each of you to learn how to call a fire mission."

* * *

A few days later, I asked the other two, "Have you heard when we'll be shipped out? I'm not in any big hurry to get out in the field, but this waiting makes me nervous."

"Hell, Len, I guess the military is in no hurry to get us into the war, which is fine by me," Joe replied. "I'm scared shitless about fighting in this fuckin' mess."

But Joe had spoken too soon. When we returned for class that afternoon, one of the clerks announced, "Okay, you FNGs, report to the armory this afternoon. It's time to get your weapons."

"Well, Len, it looks like we won't be here much longer," whispered Dan.

The clerk continued. "Perini, Rugh, and Mays, you're with Bravo Company. Whitley, Christensen, and Collins, you're with Charlie Company. Pick up your 201 files at the office and report to your company area after lunch. They'll issue rifles to you here at Redcatcher."

We had time before lunch to locate Bravo Company, so we asked where they were. When we got there, we met a sergeant sitting in the shade. He was getting ready to process out for his ride with the Freedom Bird back to the World. We were surprised to find he was willing to talk to three FNGs after our treatment at the club the night before. He wanted to know everything about the home he'd left a year before. We told him as much as we could in the short time we had.

"So you guys are headed to Bravo Company?"

"That's right, Sarge," Joe answered. "Now, can I ask you a dumb question?"

"Kid, there ain't no dumb questions. In this place, answers just might save your life. Always ask. So, what do you want to know?"

"Just how fuckin' bad is it out there?"

"Bad enough is all I can say. It's really screwed up most of the time. Since you answered my questions about home, I have some advice for you. When I left the company the other day, the Fourth Platoon was short of men. If the commanding officer asks if anyone wants to go to the mortar platoon, take a shot at it. It will mean less fuckin' night ambushes and more time at the base. The CO uses the mortar platoon not only for night firing but base security as well. So keep your damn heads as well as your asses down!"

I looked at my watch, "It's about time for lunch. Nice talking with ya'."

"Yeah, you'd better get some good chow while you can. Once you're in the fuckin' field, its C-rats three meals a day."

"Thanks, Sarge. Have a great trip home."

* * *

When we returned to the company area, the clerk greeted us. "So you three are the only new guys being sent to Bravo Company? Damn, this is not going to make the CO happy! Have you checked out your M-16s yet?"

"That's what we're here for. Where's the armory?" Joe asked.

"It's the third building behind this office. You can't miss it. Just look for the sandbags and razor wire. Then head to the rifle range and get them zeroed in. You'll be choppered out to your unit at 0800 tomorrow morning."

As we walked toward the armory, Joe remarked, "Shit, guys, this means we'll be heading out to the firebase too fuckin' soon." We just nodded.

At the armory, we picked up our assigned M-16s and were directed to a dried rice paddy.

We were greeted by a Rosie Grier double. He was big enough to have played pro football and had a mellow attitude which made it hard to believe he was the sergeant in charge of the rifle range.

His voice rumbled when he spoke. "You men just come from the armory with your pretty new M-16s? You take care of 'em, keep 'em clean all the time, and they'll become your best friends. Now let's see how they shoot."

He took his job very seriously and explained how and why we had to zero our rifles.

"Now you men set your M-16s to semi and fire at the targets, one at a time. Let's get these weapons zeroed."

We decided to split up for the afternoon and rest, go to the enlisted club, or write home. I chose the latter as I really needed to talk to my wife.

Hi honey,

I'm still at Redcatcher. It's pretty nice for being in a war zone. We're enjoying the hot chow and showers.

I'm still waiting for your letters to catch up to me, so I haven't had any word from home yet. I hope you are doing okay. I know it's tough, my being in this lousy war.

I can't keep your letters. They must be burned so the VC won't be able to write lies and send propaganda home.

We get paid in military paper (MP). The guys here call it "funny money" as we can't use American dollars. The US Government doesn't want the real stuff to fall into the hands of the enemy.

Two guys from the flight over are also being assigned to Bravo Company. Joe and Dan are younger than I am. I think Joe is only nineteen and Dan is twenty-one. It sounds like we're going to be stationed in the Delta. It's mostly rice paddies.

So far the mosquitoes aren't too bad for me; others are having a lot of trouble. They are enormous and deafening. The army issues us repellent, but the odor is so horrible no one will use it.

Well, I want to get this on the chopper this afternoon. I'll write as soon as I get settled in and tell you all about my new home and my address.

I love you and I miss you so much already. This is going to be one very long, miserable year.

Love, Len, Your husband and lover

* * *

"Well, Len, what do you think about volunteering for the mortar platoon?" asked Dan while we sat in the club that night.

"I'm not sure yet. Usually volunteering for anything in the army's a bad idea," I replied.

"Shit, I'm for any fuckin' thing to keep us out of the field." Joe said animatedly.

"You've got a point there, Joe. I'll give it more thought before making my decision," I nodded at Joe.

"I've been giving it a lot of thought myself."

"Dan, you give everything a lot of thought. Your mind's always working. Don't you ever just act first?" Joe grinned at him.

"Yeah, you kind of remind me of my trig instructor at Pasadena City College," I added.

"Yep, you are a real professor, Professor Dan." Joe had tagged Dan with the nickname that would stick throughout his tour of duty.

Unlike our first night at the club, we were left in peace. It was a solemn evening. We would be in the war tomorrow.

* * *

The next morning, we headed out with our duffel bags and rifles. We saw a Chinook helicopter. These workhorses of the army, nicknamed shithooks by the GIs, were big mothers with two rotors, giving them lifting power to haul men and equipment, even trucks.

We checked in with the crew chief. This was his bird. He did everything except fly the thing. He was a tall, but muscular, cigar-chewing staff sergeant.

"Okay, guys, put your shit by the ramp and keep your asses out of the way. We're leaving in zero five mikes."

The three of us set our bags near the open rear ramp as ordered and got our first glimpse inside.

"Would you look at that! It's a damn hangar," Joe exclaimed.

"I'll bet it could carry a whole company and all of its equipment at the same time." Dan had probably calculated the square footage for cargo and lifting power of the craft to carry it to the base.

"Len, you don't think it's only carrying just us three guys, do ya?" Joe asked.

Dan responded, "I'm sure there must be a lot of other stuff going out to the firebase besides us."

Dan was right. We watched as about a ton of supplies and our bags were loaded. There were cases of C-rations, ammunition, mailbags, and who knew what else.

When we were given the okay to board by the crew chief, we looked for a seat. But guess what? No seats! There was only some webbing near the wall with a pull-down rack.

"Welcome to America's finest transportation this side of the Pacific." The chief yelled at us over the noise. "Put your asses in the slings or put them on the floor, makes no difference to me, and hang on."

The rear door slowly closed on Redcatcher. The whine of the engines grew louder as the big bird started to move up and forward.

Talking was impossible. These choppers were built for work, not for comfort. There was absolutely no insulation in the cargo area, only the outer skin separated us from the engine noise. A couple of porthole-style windows let in dim light. We had nothing to do but sit back and let the shithook take us out to Bravo Company.

It wasn't very smooth, sort of like riding in my wife's Mix Master, but it beat walking. We weren't in the air long before we felt the vibrations and heard the change in pitch, meaning we were on a downward path. The supplies shifted some, and we worried about how well they were secured to the floor.

We wanted to get a look at our new home, so we stood at the windows. All we could see were rice paddies, not a landing zone in sight. I thought: *The pilot isn't going to try and land this monster on the narrow strip of dirt passing as a road, is he?* Sure enough, that's what he did.

The blades kicked up so much dust and debris, the bird was almost hidden from those on the ground. The back door lowered, the three of us picked up our gear, and walked down the ramp into the war. The heat from the exhaust and the March humidity hit us full force.

We got about ten yards when we noticed one tough-looking sergeant headed straight at us. He was not smiling as he strode toward the rear of the chopper. The crew chief was right behind us waiting to greet him.

Chapter 7 - Meeting Bravo Company

"Yo, Top," the crew chief greeted the newcomer. "Brought you some new guys."

Top was the name used for a first sergeant. He stood about five foot eight and was built with more muscle than I expected from someone his age, since he looked like he should have been retired. His skin was burned to a deep mahogany. His buzz haircut didn't hide the fact that he was graying. However, he commanded authority, and not just because of his rank. His presence alone demanded attention.

"Welcome to your new home, Fire Support Base Jeanie." Top smiled at us. It was a nice greeting.

We turned to pick up our bags thinking to follow the sergeant back to the compound.

"Just where the hell do you cherries think you're going?" he bellowed over the whine of the chopper's engines. The smile had changed to a snarl. "Get your asses back in there and get all the shit off that bird now!"

"Yes, Top," I answered, being careful not to call him "sir."

We assumed "shit" meant all of the supplies on the chopper. It was back through the dust and backwash of the shithook's engines, and into its belly.

A few men from Jeanie came to help. Everything had to be offloaded quickly so the chopper could get back into the air. It wasn't safe sitting on the ground for very long.

We left the supplies in the middle of the dusty road to be picked up later. Then we grabbed our bags and followed Top through the gates.

Top grumbled loudly, "Well, I see the damn REMFs still don't know how to count. The CO requested fourteen replacements and they send us a grand total of three cherries. I guess we'll just have to fuckin' make do."

We weren't positive what a cherry was, and had no clue about a REMF, but figured we'd find out. We sure weren't going to ask Top.

"We're now cherries. Is that better than FNGs?" Joe asked.

Dan and I just shrugged our shoulders.

Later we discovered that a new man was a cherry until he came under fire by the enemy.

REMFs took more explaining. It seemed there were those GIs who spent their entire time at a rear base. They were cooks, secretaries, and supply clerks. They filled our orders, issued our pay, and sorted our mail, but never fought.

They only had to worry about inspections, how clean their uniforms and rooms were, and if the hooch girls got their boots spit-shined. Or, what club they should go to at night for a steak and cold beer. These were the "rear echelon mother fuckers," as those on the front lines called them.

"Wait here. The CO should be right out."

The sergeant stuck his head in the doorway of a building and said, "Captain Scott, our replacements are here."

The commanding officer was only about thirty, rather young to be a captain, but in war, promotions came faster than during peacetime.

"I see we've been screwed again," were the first words from the CO. "Only three, huh? Is there a chance any of you three have an MOS of Eleven Charlie?" he asked.

Eleven Charlie was the army's military occupation specialty code for trained mortar men.

"No, we're Eleven Bravos," we all responded.

"Is there anyone who might like to give mortars a try?"

This was what we'd been waiting for.

"Well, sir," I said, "we'd all like to." We held our collective breaths waiting for his answer.

"Since you are in such a big hurry, take your gear over to the mortar pits and report to Lt. Abajian," he said as he pointed to the middle of the firebase.

"Yes, Sir. Right away, Sir."

"You at least know what a mortar tube is?" he asked.

"We do, Sir," we answered as we started to salute the CO.

"Get those goddamn hands down! Out here in the field saluting is forbidden. It's a good way of getting one of my officers or me killed. This is a frickin' war zone. Snipers are everywhere and always on the lookout for a target."

We found out later that during Captain Scott's first tour of duty, his mortar platoon kept his firebase from being overrun. They dropped mortar rounds so close to the outer berm that the VC weren't able to get inside. This was his main reason for keeping a mortar platoon as base security. We figured this would be our ticket to remain in base.

We decided to explore the area until we heard from the lieutenant, since he was still out on patrol. We discovered there was a good chance of pulling night guard duty, night firing assignments, and going out on patrol. So much for our "staying in base camp" theory. It looked like we'd be doing double duty.

Finally, the lieutenant sent word for us to meet him in five mikes (five minutes).

He ordered everyone in the mortar platoon to form up at Gun One. Contrary to our training of never being in groups of more than two or three, we followed his direction.

"Okay, let's see … The CO sent some cherries to Fourth Platoon. Let me guess, none of you are Eleven Charlies," he said while looking right at Joe, Dan, and me.

"I'm afraid you're right, Sir," I responded, "but we'll do our best to learn. Right, guys?"

For some reason, I'd become the unofficial spokesman for the three of us.

"Sure enough," the other two responded.

The lieutenant introduced himself. "The name is Lieutenant Abajian, but in the field, 'LT' will do. I'm really easy to get along with."

A couple of guys snickered.

"I won't have any loafing or goldbricking in my platoon. Which means every swinging dick in the Fourth will pull his fair share of weight around here, or he's in deep shit, whether an FNG or one of you old-timers."

He was a young man, fresh out of OCS. But I had a bad feeling about him, not my normal reaction to someone new. He seemed to have let his authority go to his head, and I sensed the men resented it.

"Okay, let's find out who we have here. Which one of you is Rough?"

"The name is Rugh, Sir," I said. *You wouldn't think a simple four-letter word spelled R-U-G-H would be so difficult to pronounce!*

"That's what you think. From now on it's 'Rough' just like it is in this damn war."

The nickname stuck. I became a soldier named "Rough." Very few men were called by their given names or even their last names. Nicknames just happened. In my case, the lieutenant tagged me.

"Now we know who Rough is, which one of you is Pa ... Per ... ah, Perini?"

"That would be me, Sir," Joe spoke up. "You got it right."

"Which means you must be Mays," he said as he nodded to Dan.

"Roger, Sir," Dan acknowledged.

"You'll begin your training with Wild Bill today after lunch. He's the tall, skinny Texan." The LT pointed to the man next to Joe. "He'll show you where we bunk. Get your stuff set up before dark."

"Howdy, y'all, we'll be meetin' about 1300 for trainin'."

Did he really say "howdy y'all"? He should have been wearing cowboy boots and a ten-gallon hat.

The rest of the men welcomed us. We were now officially a part of the Fourth Platoon.

I had time to write Lu about my new home.

Hi honey,

Well, I'm finally at a firebase in the rice paddies. It's called Fire Support Base Jeanie. I'm not supposed to tell you exactly where it's located, but we are somewhere in the Delta, not too far from Saigon.

I'm in a mortar platoon. I volunteered for something in the army! There was a good reason for it. I had been told they spend more time in the firebase than out on patrols, which sounded good to me.

I've been here all day observing the operations. The guys are great. Joe and Dan came in with me and I like several that I just met today. I'm not sure I like the lieutenant, but I'll wait and see.

I need to get some lunch and go to mortar training. This will be my first taste of C-rations. Gee, I can hardly wait. Yeah, right.

I sure miss you. It seems like I've been gone a long time already, but it hasn't even been two weeks. A lot has happened in that time. I will write often so you'll know I'm all right. I love you so much.

Love, your husband and lover, Len

* * *

"All right, listen up y'all. The mortar pits are laid out with Gun One in the middle, Gun Two is on my left, and Gun Three's on my right. These here are 81mm mortar tubes. I'm gonna' teach y'all about aimin' and firin' this fuckin' thang.

"First and most important rule is only the head gunner is allowed to drop the rounds! Aimin' the tube so the rounds hit the target is tricky and takes a lot of practice. The mortar crew is made up of the head gunner, assistant gunner, and two ammo bearers who are responsible for makin' sure the rounds are prepped to fire. Rat will explain the procedure."

Rat was a small guy, maybe five foot seven inches tall with his boots on, and 145 pounds soaking wet. He didn't have any rat-like features. Actually, he looked more like a surfer to me. *It'll be interesting to find out how he got his nickname,* I thought.

Rat continued, "The more packets, the farther the distance. Unused packets, for shorter distances, are tossed into that empty ammo box to be disposed of later."

We spent the rest of the afternoon learning the specifics of aiming and firing. Dan picked up the mathematical part very quickly and was asked to be a part of the FDC (Fire Direction Center) crew. Wild Bill assigned Joe and me to Gun Three. It was the one most shorthanded.

Just before the sun went down, we got word that the night supply chopper was on the way in and we should be ready to unload when it put down. After the dust had settled and the rear ramp was down, we formed a bucket-brigade line. The supplies, crates of mortar rounds (three rounds to a crate), cases of C-rations, and other stuff, had to be moved about fifty yards into the firebase. Unfortunately, and much to Top's displeasure, no more replacements were sent.

Our first night was hectic. We were called out on a fire mission at 2200. We got everything set up and ready to fire. The FDC radioed Wild Bill and cancelled it. He told us to head back to our beds for more sleep as we could get called again.

We were too nervous to sleep and could easily hear the chatter on the radio. At midnight Wild Bill yelled, "Hey, Mugs, Rat, get your asses out here. Fire mission."

Everybody, from all three guns, went to watch Gun One. It was the best way for us new guys to learn what it was really like. Observing the precision and timing of this crew gave us a better idea of what Wild Bill was trying to teach us.

They fired about forty luminous rounds over the next hour for an ambush patrol. As one would slowly drift to the ground on its small parachute, another would be fired off to constantly keep light above the enemy's suspected location.

The First, Second, and Third Platoons went on a search mission while Fourth had guard duty the rest of the night. Joe, Dan and I had been welcomed to firebase Jeanie in a big way.

* * *

One thing I learned very fast was not to make close friends. Even though the three of us had come in together and could have become good buddies, we didn't. We each held something of ourselves back; it would be easier to accept if one of us were killed or maimed. Yet, we relied on each other as fellow soldiers to do our jobs.

The days turned into one work detail after another, mostly filling sandbags between practice drills conducted during the cooler morning hours.

A week later we were sitting around eating C-rats when I commented, "I can't sleep with all the mortar firing, but I guess we'll get used to it like the old-timers."

"Old-timers! Shit, Rough, these guys have only been here four to six months and they're old-timers already?"

"You bet, and they can teach us a lot."

We were continually training, fine-tuning the speed at which we could get our tubes up and ready to fire. There was competition between the three mortar teams. This helped develop teamwork among the individual gun crews. It sometimes caused friction, but a healthy rivalry was good and increased our speed, our most important objective.

We couldn't escape from the sun beating down and temperatures rising into the triple digits. We crawled into our bunkers to rest during the hottest part of the day, but the heat was relentless.

* * *

The firebase had one jeep with a small trailer used to bring supplies back when battalion sent our re-supply by river instead of the shithook. There were two small bridges on the way. Unfortunately, they had to be checked for booby traps both ways by those left in the firebase.

New men always asked, "Do we really need to check everything in both directions?"

The answer was a resounding, "YES, if you want to stay alive." Better to be safe than go home in a body bag. This was made very clear to us on Good Friday.

Dawn broke as the Tiger Alphas (trail ambushes) were on their way in. The morning routine began. The mortars had stopped firing. All we could hear was the shuffling of tired feet on dirt and the humid breeze as it caused the tarps to flutter on their poles. There were a few moans and groans as men stretched their muscles after a night of attempting to sleep.

"Shit, eleven more months of this and I'll never be able to fuckin' stand up straight again," Joe mumbled.

"If you live so long," Dan responded.

Then there was silence.

The FDC's radio came to life: "Bravo-Two-Two-X-ray, Tiger-Alpha-One requesting permission to return, over."

Any group entering the base knew they had to identify themselves if they didn't want to be hit by friendly fire. The base had to protect itself against possible attack by the VC at all times. The incoming personnel popped a colored smoke canister. The RTO called the color of the smoke to identify the returning patrol.

The army was afraid the VC might capture an American radio tuned to our frequency. If the base called for a specific color, the enemy would know the color of the smoke asked for, allowing them to pass through the gate.

"Tiger-Alpha-One, pop smoke," crackled through the radio.

"Tiger-Alpha-One, we see goofy grape, over," the RTO responded.

"Roger, goofy grape it is, over."

"Tiger-Alpha-One, bring it on in, over."

The TA started to emerge through the purple smoke. The morning's silence was shattered as an explosion bruised our ears, and gray and black smoke mingled with purple.

"Medic! Dammit, we have a man down," blared the radio.

"Mugs, Rat, move it," Doc yelled over his shoulder as he raced toward the wounded man. The rest of the company jumped up, facing the smoldering area, rifles at the ready, hoping we would get a chance to retaliate. Our guts told us we wouldn't. There was no doubt about what had happened. A booby trap and a wounded GI, way too close to the base.

It wasn't long before we saw Doc leading Mugs and Rat as they ran back toward the safety of the firebase carrying the wounded man on a stretcher. It was the lieutenant from First Platoon. He was wounded in several places, and blood soaked his flak jacket and fatigues. The jacket had most likely saved his life.

This was my first bloodied man. It was a scary sight and brought the reality of war closer.

"Damn, that's Lieutenant Bratton," I heard a soldier standing near me tell his buddies.

"Aw, man, he's one of the best officers," another replied.

"Yeah, LT Don always looks out for his men. Hey, here comes Smitty."

I glanced up as another man joined us.

I listened as Smitty breathlessly reported, "Doc just told me all the blood was from superficial wounds. He'll be okay, but they're sending him to the hospital at BMB (Brigade's main base) to treat him for infection. LT should be back in a week or so."

One of the men responded, "That's great!" We all agreed.

I didn't know it at the time, but it would prove lucky for me that Lieutenant Bratton survived the attack.

The medevac chopper, called for as soon as Doc left the firebase, arrived. Bravo Company quickly secured the LZ (landing zone), and the lieutenant was on his way to the hospital in just a matter of minutes.

The new guys, me included, had been indoctrinated.

* * *

When the evening supply chopper came in, arriving around 1500, it brought precious mail from home. Everything stopped until the mail was handed out and read. We didn't do a thing until we finished.

I finally received one from my wife. With all the moving around, one finally caught up with me. It seemed like forever since I'd last heard from her.

> Hi, Husband and Lover,
> You have only been gone a few days, but it seems like months. I really miss you a bunch!
> I know by now you should be with your unit and at a firebase. I hope it's someplace safe and not in the middle of too much fighting. I worry about you a lot. I know you told me not to, but you would in my place.
> I looked in an atlas and realized when I go to bed at night you're waking up the next day in Vietnam. It seems strange to me, but it's a time when I feel closest to you. So when you get up, listen to the wind for my words to you. I will be sending you my love.
> Please take care and remember your promise to me and return home safely.
> All my love, Lu

* * *

Jeanie was a permanent firebase, though not very large, and had a couple of outhouses. This meant the shit cans were burned once a week for sanitation. It was one nasty job. They were cut-off fifty-five-gallon drums filled part way with lye placed under the single hole in the seat of the wooden outhouse. We had to drag these drums about fifteen feet or so using empty sandbags as gloves. We filled the can with gasoline, struck a match, and tossed it inside. After burning the contents, we added a new batch of lye and pushed them back. They were good for another week.

I'd never smelled anything as awful as one of those things on fire. I don't know if the VC recognized the smell, but it was very noticeable in the air of the surrounding area. The duty usually fell to the Fourth Platoon as we spent the most time in base.

There was one funny incident involving the outhouse, a dud 105 round, and me. The shell had landed about two hundred meters from our perimeter. On this particular day, Top and the CO decided they were going to destroy the stupid thing before it could be used against us. In their hurry to dispose of it, they forgot to inform Fourth Platoon, or I had missed the word. I never did figure out which.

I was sitting in one of the outhouses. It was a quiet morning with no day firing going on. Then, into this peaceful, tranquil moment came one very loud, ear-splitting explosion. My first thought was, *What a lousy time for Jeanie to come under attack. Boy, I sure didn't want to die here with my pants down!* With my helmet on my head, I flew out the door of the wooden structure, reached for my rifle with one hand, and tried to hold my pants up with the other. I hit the ground looking for a place to hide.

Our rifles went everywhere we went. We carried them to the stream for our rinse-off. We even took them to bed.

Well, anyway, I looked up and there was the rest of Fourth Platoon laughing their dang fool heads off, as if this was the funniest thing they had ever seen in their lives. It just might have been at that!

"Thanks, guys. Sure am glad I was able to give you something to laugh at. I was just lightening the mood," I uttered, trying not to look too embarrassed as I lay there mooning the sky.

"Shit, Rough, you would be laughing, too, if you'd seen the way you came flying out, grabbing at your britches. The look on your face was fuckin' priceless."

"Darn it, Joe, I could just see me being caught with my pants down around my feet and no place to hide during the first attack on Jeanie in God only knows how long."

No, to me it wasn't funny at all!

* * *

It seemed I was always being singled out to lead. I hadn't been in the mortar platoon more than a couple of weeks when the lieutenant appointed me as squad leader for Gun Three. I took to the job quickly. I had worked in management and I'm sure my age helped win the respect of the men. None of the other guys wanted the responsibility, so there were no complaints about my being appointed. I promised the LT I would whip Gun Three into the best of his crews.

We found out the former squad leader was the sergeant we had met at Redcatcher who told us to volunteer for the mortar platoon. So here I was, an FNG, in charge of getting this crew in shape.

Chapter 8 – Words From FB Jeanie

Hi honey,

How are you doing? I miss you so much even though it has only been a month since we were together. I'd rather be home with you.

As you know, I am at Fire Support Base Jeanie. The base is circular, laid out like a clock face. We have machine guns atop fighting bunkers built at the four major points of the clock. A road bisects the base north to south. Actually, it's more like a large, flat, dirt pathway, which rises about eighteen inches above the surrounding ground. It's just barely wide enough for a military jeep. Our mortar pits are off-center and just to the three o'clock side of the road.

There is a village called *My Phu* about two miles from the base. The Song Ben Lac River is perpendicular to the road, and the village is at the junction of the two. This country is rice paddies and streams with low-growing palm trees, not more than five feet high but real thick and close together, called nipa palms. For some reason, the rice paddies nearest the river and surrounding the firebase sit empty and dry. It could be a pretty area for farming if it wasn't located in this war-torn country.

Those of us in the mortar pit have a front-row seat watching the farmers from the village walk through the firebase to their rice fields. They're still trying to work the land, even with the war going on and the VC demanding most of their rice harvest. The villagers and their families have always been farmers and fishermen. We're close at hand so we keep a security watch during their working day, helping to preserve their way of life.

The homes of the village line the river on both sides, so close to the banks they hang over the water. I use the word "homes" in the broadest sense of the word. They remind me of some villages we've seen in Mexico. Some are made out of mud, wood, and straw with palm leaves for roofs. Others are made of just about everything the Americans throw away—sheet metal, C-rat boxes, wooden crates the mortar rounds were packed in. Anything we discard, they use.

The men of Bravo Company recognize the villagers going through the base. We suspect everyone, even the children.

I feel sorry for these youngsters; they never get to just be kids. From the time they're old enough to walk and comprehend, they're working. You should see them when we give them candy. I thought I was going to be mugged while I was trying to pass some out. They were all over us. It isn't just candy; they try to get anything they can, even soap. They scrounge for everything. No wonder they think of us as odd. We eat only what we want and throw the rest away.

When I stop and think about this land and these people, I realize those who are our age have known nothing but war since they were born. Their faces are lined with apprehension and fear.

How many times have you heard a plane diving down towards the earth and dropping bombs, or have artillery go off at different times day and night where we live? Have you seen what a shell can do to a rice paddy or a canal? Can you picture a woman who looks sixty or seventy carrying water in five gallon cans back and forth from the canal to the village? I can; I've seen it.

These people don't have much to live for.

There's one villager, an old man, who's probably one of the elders. He's humped-over and shrunken down, and looks a hundred years old. His skin is tanned dark and leathery dry with wrinkles around his eyes from years of squinting into the sun, which is very bright, reflecting off the water of the rice paddies. I'm sure he's spent most of his life plowing the fields from dawn to dark, plodding behind his water buffalo.

I watch him come and go each morning and evening. He shuffles through base leading a procession of children, some riding on the buffalo's back. They pull on its large head and horns or push it from the rear. It's very docile with the old man and the kids.

When this guy and his followers pass through the entrance to the base, at least one of the men on guard bows and asks him if he's off to check his booby traps for any dead GIs, a question the old man obviously doesn't understand. He slows his shuffle, bows his head, and smiles. Through the jibes, he keeps on shuffling, bowing, giggling, and smiling his toothless smile. I think some of the guys are convinced he really is setting out booby traps during his daily trips to the rice paddies.

Most of the young men are gone from the village now. They are either in the army of the south or have been forced to join the Vietcong.

What I've seen makes me so thankful for my home. Just the luxury of taking a bath in clean water and having a meal not heated over C-4. Man, I can't wait to get back!

Speaking of bathing, you should see the water hole we have to use. We always go in groups and take our M-16s as it's about two hundred yards outside the perimeter. The brackish water level seems to be based on the tides, but we've yet to figure out where the water goes or comes from. It is really warm, so it doesn't cool us off, just removes a layer of dirt and some of the sweat. It's like taking a bath in a dirty ocean. Oh, what we wouldn't give for a few extra gallons of clean water for a shower. We can't even brush our teeth in fresh water; it's way too precious.

I've got to say good-bye, but I'll write again tomorrow.

Love, Len, Your lover and husband

Chapter 9 - The Chaplain

One Sunday we went down to the river to get the supplies. They were sent out on an LCM (landing craft military) being used to move men and supplies up and down the river to bases nearby. It wasn't much of a river, more like a flowing, muddy sewer.

A curious sight met the detail when the boat arrived. When the ramp was lowered onto the bank of the river, an immaculate green uniform strode off. He was a chaplain, so clean we could tell he hadn't been out in the field before. We were almost blinded by the sun's reflection off his spit-shined boots. He'd come to Firebase Jeanie to see to the needs of the men.

It was rare having a chaplain; everyone wanted to attend services. We had to go in shifts to avoid a large concentration of GIs in a small space.

We didn't have any permanent buildings, so we used plywood to make enclosures, covered on the outside with sandbags. Sometimes we even found corrugated tin for a roof. The large structure used for the CO's headquarters had a canvas tarp over the top. A chapel would have been a luxury, but most of us were good at praying on the run.

Our chaplain of the day held services standing inside the mortar pit, using the blast wall for his pulpit and communion table. The men stood outside facing him. He read from the Bible, gave a short non-denominational sermon, served communion to those who wanted it, and prayed for us all.

It was dusk when the chaplain finished. He needed to return to his base, but it wasn't safe. Daytime trips were dangerous; after dark could be deadly. The few navy men who had accompanied him that morning weren't enough security for an evening run down the river to the navy base about ten miles away.

"Gun Three, you're security detail for the trip. Dan, you go with them and drive the jeep back. You do know how to drive?"

"You bet, LT."

"Rough, you're in charge."

"Roger, LT."

The bridges had been checked, so we headed for the river. We boarded the LCM with our guns at the ready. The trip was uneventful and without any contact with the VC. The problems came after we arrived at the navy base.

We were told we'd have to spend the night and return to Jeanie on the morning run. We were stuck. Thank God.

We had all missed dinner, so it was off in search of some chow. That's when the trouble started. We found a mess hall, but the mess sergeant said he was closed. I was in charge according to the LT. It was my duty to be sure my men were taken care of.

"Shit, Rough, it looks like we're fucked again," Joe said. "I guess we go without food tonight."

"I don't think so," I said.

I turned to the mess sergeant, who looked like he hadn't missed a meal since he'd been brought into this world. And he had the nerve to stand in front of four tired, battle-weary, hungry soldiers and tell us his mess hall was closed for the night.

I wasn't in the mood to be nice at that point. "Hey, jerk, my men and I haven't eaten since this morning."

"Yeah, so what?"

"I think it would be a great idea for you to find some food in this kitchen of yours, don't you?" The safety on my rifle just happened to snap off. The sound of an M-16's safety being set is a very loud and very distinct metallic click, especially in the close quarters of a quiet kitchen.

"I'm sure sandwiches would be just fine, don't you?" Boy, I had gotten his attention, or maybe it was my M-16, but that sergeant changed his mind quickly.

"Ah, maybe I could find some sandwich fixings," he stuttered as he opened his kitchen.

We feasted on thick roast beef sandwiches, fresh fruit, and all the cold milk we could drink. Best of all was the real chocolate milk, which made me think this must be heaven. Mmm, I loved it! And no C-rats!

Then we had to find a place to sleep. This problem was solved much easier than the food. The sergeant in charge of the LCM told us we could sleep on the boat. He dug up some air mattresses. Navy personnel slept on nice cots and didn't need them. We finally got eight hours of uninterrupted sleep. The navy was in charge of security, so no night duty.

The next morning we went to the mess hall for breakfast. No need for the rifle. It was, "Come right on in and help yourself to the real eggs, pancakes, cold milk, cereal, fresh fruit, or anything else."

"Hey, I'm taking some of this fruit back. I haven't had any in months," Rat said as he stuffed another apple into his fatigue pockets.

He kind of looked like Mr. Universe with bulging muscles. We all grabbed some fruit for the road.

"Boy, Rough, wouldn't this be great to come back to after a night out on a Tiger Alpha?" Ole asked as he stuffed an orange into his pants.

"A body could get used to this kind of food in the morning; sure beats the hell out of the damn C-rats any day, and we wouldn't even have to carry them on our backs," Rat added.

"No, just in our pockets," I kidded him, and we all laughed.

We agreed with Ole. After long hours on patrol, it would really be great to come back to this type of base with its amenities. It could have made our lives almost bearable.

Later that morning, we reported to the LCM for the return trip to Jeanie. Our one night out of the war had come to an end.

We helped unload the supplies onto the trailer for the trip back through the gates. The usual group of Vietnamese boys watched and waited for any handouts we might throw their way. We'd learned to never fully trust them, though. One could be a messenger of death.

"Okay, just where the hell were you guys last night?" Mugs wanted to know as he met us at the mortar pit. He was a short, good-looking kid with brown curly hair, a mustache, and chocolaty brown eyes that would impress any girl.

"Don't try to tell me Abitchie sent you on a flippin' Tiger Alpha, because I know better. I heard you were security for the chaplain. So, just how was the navy base, anyway?"

"You really don't want to know. How those guys live would just piss you off," Ole said.

"If you say so, but tell me anyway. I don't think I could get any more pissed off than I already am," Mugs replied.

Ole explained, "It has a mess hall, regular barracks with cots, almost no Tiger Alphas, and warm water to take showers."

By the time he'd finished the last word, everyone from Fourth Platoon was there to listen.

"Boy, what I wouldn't give for a warm shower and food that didn't come from a can. When I get home to Texas, I plan on eatin' all the hot chow I can get my mama to fix. I can almost taste a big juicy steak with all the trimmins."

"You know, Bill, those damn guys should relieve us once in a while. They'd find out what the real fuckin' war is like. I bet we'd get better support if they spent time in the field."

"Great idea, Joe, but it'll never happen. They'll serve their time in a nice secure base camp, then go home and brag about fighting in Vietnam. Just one more screw up in this fuckin' war," Rat replied.

"Hey, Rough," Mugs remembered, "LT wants to see the crew chiefs."

"Roger, Mugs." Darn, I had been thinking it was time to get a letter off to the home front. Lu wasn't going to believe we practically held that poor cook at gunpoint to get dinner. Well, it would have to wait until later.

Chapter 10 - Friendly Fire

"Hey, LT, you want to tell us the war is over, right?" Mugs started when we got to HQ.

"No such luck. What I called you here for is something you're just going to love."

At this point the lead ball hit my stomach.

"Well, the fun and games are over for you guys." He was referring to our overnight detail. "Now its time to really earn your fuckin' pay."

"I didn't know any of us didn't earn our lousy pay, LT!"

"Careful, Rough, you're a squad leader now."

"Hey, LT, what did you call us for?" Mugs changed the subject.

"We have a sweep mission tomorrow. The choppers will be here at 0600 to take the company out for a short patrol."

"If the whole company is going, does that also include the Fourth Platoon?" asked Mugs.

"I said the whole fuckin' company which includes the Fourth Platoon, except for Gun One. Wild Bill, you and your crew will remain for base security. Pass the word to your men to pack light, only two meals and water for one day."

Mugs and Wild Bill were old-timers and knew what happened on one of these sweep missions. On the way back to the mortar pits, they filled me in. After I told my crew to get ready for the patrol, I went back to my hooch to pack and write a letter to Lu.

* * *

Hi honey,

Tomorrow I go out on my first patrol into the rice paddies. We'll only be gone a day, so I won't write tomorrow.

We haven't seen much evidence of the VC but we're going out to look for them anyway. I guess it's better to know where they are than to be surprised.

My nickname here is Rough. We all have them.

I love you and I miss you so much. My year here can't get over too soon. I need to get back to my wife and my life as a real person named Len, not Rough!

Love, your husband and lover, Len

I put my writing stuff in my ammo can and closed it tight to keep it dry and away from the rats. They were bigger than cats and would chew on anything in sight.

I lay down on my cot intending to get some rest when Wild Bill hollered, "Hey, Rough, y'all hidin' in your hole?"

"What the heck do you want, Bill?" I asked as I crawled out.

I liked Wild Bill. He was about three inches taller than me, a thin 170 pounds, with light brown hair and piercing green eyes. He was a no-nonsense guy like me. When we were in charge, we did our jobs efficiently.

"I need a coupla thangs. As y'all're not goin' to be here tomorrow, be sure your gun is set for defensive firin' before leavin' in the mornin'."

"Roger, Bill. What's the other thing?"

"Y'all were at Fort Ord for trainin' like me, weren't ya?"

"Yes. Why?"

"Well, there's a guy in Second Platoon that looks like the feller that was a part of the instruction cadre for search, escape, and evasion. Did you recognize him?"

"I thought he looked familiar, I just couldn't place him. I think his name is Marty Glass ... something-or-other. They called him Glass, right?"

"Yep, that's the guy. Over here, though, he's called Drill Corporal. He showed up right after you did."

"I figured he'd stay stateside rather than volunteer to come to 'Nam."

"You'd a thunk. Well, y'all git that gun ready."

"Roger, Bill," I said and headed toward my pit, calling, "Hey, Joe, you, Ole, and Rat get out to the mortar tube, like right now!"

"Dammit, Rough, I knew there would be no friggin' rest this afternoon!" Joe grumbled.

"There's always tonight, if you're lucky."

"Big joke, we're on guard duty tonight or have you forgotten?"

"I didn't forget, Joe, but Bill needs our gun pre-plotted for defensive firing in case it's needed while we're on patrol."

"You guys don't need me for that. I'm headed back to sleep," Rat said as he turned around.

"Get your butt back here. We're going to prep some rounds and you guys are going to practice setting up on target. I want Gun Three's crew to be the best. Then maybe next time we'll get to stay and guard the base."

"Yeah, you're right, Rough."

We practiced for about an hour. If the base came under attack, all Wild Bill and his crew would have to do was step to our gun and drop the rounds into the tube.

With night fast approaching, I told Joe, "Get your chow and hit the rack. I'll let you know when it's your turn."

I continued giving directions, "Rat, you need to eat now, you're on guard in an hour."

"Okay, Rough."

I assigned the rest of the schedule and headed back to my hooch to open a can of C-rats. After my dinner, I'd lay down until it was my turn.

* * *

The choppers arrived at dawn. We climbed aboard quickly. I could feel it shudder as the pilot pulled away from the dusty landing zone. The nose dipped then started a fast rise headed toward the cloudless sky. We had been in the air about ten minutes, watching the farmland and countryside pass beneath us, when we started our descent.

We had passed over many dry paddies on our way to the drop zone. Now we were over some that were water-filled. *Where are we going to land?* I wondered. We started down right above the standing water.

The chopper came to a hover. *We're not going to land?* It was a good ten-foot drop. *They've got to be kidding! We're going to jump! Man, John Wayne never did it this way!*

The crew chief started yelling, "Out, out, let's go, everybody out!"

There was no time to think, just jump. I managed to land feet-first in thick gooey mud that sucked me down. I found myself knee-deep in muck and ooze. *How are we supposed to walk in this stuff?*

I thought I'd fallen into quicksand, but it was only a Vietnamese rice paddy. What a way to start my first patrol.

The choppers took off, their job completed. They'd hauled us in, dropped us off, and headed out for another mission. I looked up as they disappeared over the horizon. It was a cold LZ for them at least, no enemy fire.

They had no sooner disappeared when a sound that no veteran can ever forget seemed to zero in on us. It was the loud whistle of an incoming round followed by an ear-shattering explosion. Dirt, mud, and water went every which way. Even before the sound from the first explosion died away and the water and mud had settled back into the paddy, we could hear another round on its way. Death was in the air and raining down on Bravo Company!

"Go! Go!" Top was yelling, as if it was necessary to get us moving. Most of us headed toward the nearest bit of protection. For some, it was a blade of grass or a stalk of rice, just something to make us feel safe. A few of us were trying to find a rice paddy dike that might give us cover. I learned just how thick the buttons on my uniform were while trying to melt into the ground. I wanted to make myself as small as possible. Hard to do when you're six feet tall and weigh about 180 pounds.

Two new guys just stood there. Top yelled again, "Go, go, go," trying to get them to move. We'd been trained to react immediately to an order. Still, they were frozen in place. Finally, some of the old-timers reached up and yanked them down into the mud.

Top was on the radio. "Arty One, this is Bravo One. Shut the God damn firing down! You're fuckin' firing on Bravo Company's position! We're taking incoming!"

Arty replied calmly that they were not firing in our area. We must be mistaken.

Top let the idiot know exactly what he was going to do as soon as the operation was over and we got back to base. That is, if our own 105s didn't blast us away first.

While he was passing this bit of info on to Arty, another round landed not far away with a deafening explosion. We heard the Arty officer say, "Wow, I guess you are taking incoming."

"No shit, asshole. What the fuck do you think I've been trying to get through that fuckin' thick head of yours?!" Top yelled into the hand mike.

They finally got the message and the firing stopped. We were very lucky. There were a few bruises and abrasions from flying debris, but no one had been killed. Mud covered everything and filled every crevice of our fatigues and boots.

"Shit, this is one incident I do not want to fucking repeat!" Joe declared. "I've never been so damned scared, and I sure as hell don't want to experience it again!"

"You'd better believe we'll get fired on again; we're in a damned war. I just don't want it to be friendly fire from our own artillery! That's way too scary!" Mugs replied.

"I've lost ten years off my life today!" I felt the urge to pinch myself to make sure I was still alive. I checked for blood, then thanked God I had not been wounded.

Now that the firing had ceased, our hearts stopped racing and it was time to get on with the patrol. We had been given a few minutes to get our minds cleared, then we were moving, but we felt like we were in slow motion.

"My legs feel like Jell-O."

"The feeling will soon pass, Rough. It's the adrenalin pumping. You'll get back to normal after a while," Mugs reassured me.

The day went slowly as we walked through the wet paddies, checking out anything suspicious. Thank God the rest of the patrol was uneventful.

We spent the night in the field and headed back into base with the early morning light.

This mission was one I'd never forget. Now, how could I tell Lu we'd been fired upon by our own 105s without sounding like I'd been in danger? Yeah, right!

Chapter 11 – The Trained Eleven Charlie

A few days after we returned, the supply chopper brought out a couple of new men for the company. One of them was a true Eleven Charlie who'd actually been trained as a mortar man!

We found out he'd been stationed in Germany, playing some peacetime games for about a year. He learned all about firing a mortar in a pretend war. He was to spend twelve months in Fourth Platoon fighting in Vietnam where the enemy would be shooting at him with real bullets.

The fully-trained mortar man made Abitchie happy, and all the squads wanted him as a part of their gun crew. But his very first night, Mac jumped right in with both feet and almost got blown away.

We were standing around observing the night firing so Mac could get an idea of how we did things. Gun One, Wild Bill's crew, was firing a mission. A night patrol needed illumination rounds. We had them timed so that as one round's light faded, we dropped another. Because of the unstable ground in Vietnam, we had to realign and level the gun between rounds to hit the same mark.

Not knowing our procedure, Mac, thinking to keep the illumination in the air and trying to impress us, ran over, jumped into the gun pit, and dropped a round right down the tube. That was wrong, with a capital "W"!

Wild Bill almost lived up to his name when the round came blasting out like the rocket from hell.

"Boy, I'm glad I'm not the new guy. Bill's gonna kill him!" Mugs said.

Bill was mad enough to make Mac a killed-by-friendly-fire statistic, only this time it would have been from Bill's M-16. After talking our fool heads off, we finally got him cooled down a little before he could get his hands around Mac's throat. We thought it better to send the new man on guard duty at one of the bunkers. It was a sure bet he wasn't going to end up on Gun One's crew.

I'll never figure out why Mac did such a stupid thing. On our squads, only one man, the gunner, was allowed to drop rounds down the tube. Through hours of training and teamwork, he knew where everyone would be. Safety was the rule, and someone could have been killed. So much for our trained mortar man.

At morning formation, the LT grumbled, "Dammit, Bill, you know every Eleven Charlie we've ever gotten, and we haven't had many, thank God, needed to be retrained."

Bill just glared at the LT.

"Fuck it all, Bill. What in the hell were you thinking when you went after this guy? Do you want to burn shit cans for the rest of your stay in this damn war?"

"I just wanted ta strangle the bastard, LT!" He glanced down at Mac. "He coulda gotten us all killed with his stupid stunt."

Mac sat there, his head hung in contrition. I felt kind of sorry for the guy.

The LT continued, "Remember, you didn't know a goddamn thing when you got here. You just about screwed up during your first week, too. We had to educate you, and he needs to be retrained the same way."

For the first time since I'd arrived, I agreed with the LT.

"Don't put him on my crew. I might just kill the varmit yet, 'specially if he tries ta help again! Y'all give 'em to one of the other crews. Rough on Gun Three can whip the son of a gun inta shape; I'd probably geld 'em." Bill drawled.

I started to reply, but the LT turned to Mac, "Okay, come with me," as he headed back to headquarters.

I had mixed feelings about having Mac on my crew.

A short time later, the LT stopped at Gun Three. Mac followed close behind. We were in the middle of practice. Everything came to a halt. I walked over to the two men. Bad news stood there facing me.

"Rough, Mac is now in your squad. Get him shaped up, but don't kill him."

"Right, LT, we'll do our best to make him a good crew member."

He was going to be a pain, but I understood. This skinny, auburn-haired man had the reddest, bushiest mustache I had ever seen.

"My name is Len, but the guys call me Rough. Grab your stuff and put it over there." I pointed to our squad's bunker a few yards away. "Then step into the mortar pit and meet the rest of the guys."

"Sorry about the mistake last night," Mac started. "I just thought you wanted rounds going up. I didn't know only the gunner was allowed to drop them in. I won't make that mistake again."

"If you fuckin' want to stay alive, you won't," Joe said as he gave the new man a disapproving look.

"Mac, you just met Joe, our smart-mouthed assistant gunner. That little guy sitting over on the blast wall is called Rat. He got his nickname when a big Vietnamese rat bit his hand while he was asleep one night."

"I killed the bastard. He won't be chewing on me again."

Everyone snickered.

"The big brute with the beer belly over on the ammo box is Ole."

He grumbled an unhappy, "Aloha."

No one seemed pleased about having Mac on the team.

"You've met everybody. As you can see, Bravo Company's under-manned, so get used to doing a lot of work."

"Yeah, we have night guard duty, day guard duty, and night firing. Once in a while you'll get a chance to go out on patrol, a trail ambush, or Tiger Alpha as they're called," Rat commented with his usual sarcasm.

"The best part is, when we're not practicing, we fill sandbags. I just love shoveling dirt into those little green mesh bags," Ole added, flexing his muscles. "We do get to eat, and sometimes we even sleep a few hours."

"Your first lesson is to forget everything you've learned. There's a whole new set of rules here," Rat added.

"We do our best to keep the gun pits flat but with all the firing, they never stay level. The gunners and assistant gunners readjust the tubes before each round." I wanted Mac to be aware of our problems.

He nodded, listening intently.

"All right, guys, we'll practice later this afternoon. Mac, you can bunk next to Ole for now until we can build another hooch."

"Sure enough, Rough," he replied.

"As you can see, we don't have a mess hall here at Jeanie. We have C-rats, though. There are no showers but we have a water hole where we can wash off the sweat. We always go in groups of three or more."

"Thanks for pointing out the great things about the base."

"Yeah, it's not much, but its home."

After getting Mac set up, I headed towards my hooch to get a letter off to Lu. I just had to tell her about this new guy.

> Hi honey,
>
> I have a good-news, bad-news story to tell you. We got this new trained mortar guy. Boy, he is one crazy mixed-up kid. He didn't wait to see how we did things, but started dropping mortars down the tube. I thought Bill was going to beat him up, but now he's a part of my team. With lots of training, I think I can whip him into shape.
>
> Our gun has about had it. The thing needs so many repairs its ridiculous. Then Mac, the new guy, comes here and tells us about having new mortar tubes in Germany. It's really frustrating. In Vietnam we need the guns badly, but who gets them? The men in Europe who are only playing at war.
>
> Even the ARVNs get newer weapons than we do. I think it's to help the Vietnamese build a better force from within to eventually take over the fighting. It probably looks good on paper in Washington, but I don't think these guys will ever be able to fight this war by themselves.
>
> This year cannot get over soon enough. Say hello to everyone at home. I love you and I miss you so very much.
>
> Love, your husband and lover, Len

Chapter 12 - Rice Paddy Patrol

"Y'all, the LT wants everybody to meet at his hooch in five mikes," Wild Bill announced one morning.

At the meeting, the LT explained we would all head out on an Eagle Flight mission, except the crew from Gun Two. This would be a three-day drop.

The company would patrol during the day, be picked up in the late afternoon, flown to another place to set up a night ambush, and the next morning be choppered again to a different location to start the second day's patrol—repeating this process for three days and nights before returning to Jeanie.

On the way back to the mortar pits, we were discussing the meeting.

"So now I know what an Eagle Flight is, I just don't understand the fuckin' reason for it." Joe looked to the group for answers.

"It's one way ta make fifty soldiers seem more like several hundred. Them good ole boys at Command are tryin' to scare the VC into thinkin' we have a lot more men in Vietnam than we do. After this mission, y'all will be able to understand it better," Wild Bill enlightened us.

"Well, we have one problem. Joe and I and a couple of the other guys haven't been out on this type of patrol before. What do we take, and how do we pack?" I asked.

"Do I have to nursemaid y'all? Hells' bells, what kind of GIs are ya anyway? I'll explain this one time only, so don't forget!"

Bill told us how to pack and what to take for three nights. He also explained to us about how to walk and where to walk and where not to walk while on patrol in the rice paddies.

"Do y'all want me to come tuck ya in and sing ya a lullaby, too?" Bill laughed as he headed for his hooch.

"Naw, we got Rough to do that for us, but thanks anyway," Joe said to Bill's retreating back, with such a straight face, anyone might have believed him.

There were times Joe could be a pain in the butt.

* * *

At 0630 the next morning, five Huey helicopters picked the company up and headed out to our first day's patrol area.

"Ah, man, it's going to be walking in muddy rice paddies again," I complained.

"Yeah, after our first short patrol I was hoping I'd never have to hump in this shit again," Joe grumbled.

Rat reminded us of what Bill told us, "Do not walk on the dry paddy dikes, as the fuckin' VC will most likely have them booby-trapped."

"Shit, we've got to suffer the heat and exhaustion of walking in the muck and crap," Joe bitched. "Not my idea of fun, no damn way."

"Having the knee-deep water and gooey mud filling my boots is the part I hate most. It adds more weight to my already overloaded body, making each step a struggle."

"I know what you're talking about, Rough. Just thinking of the distance Command wants us to cover each day makes me realize how impossible this war is," Ole complained. "I'll never get used to it."

"Well, it's not like we have a fuckin' choice. After all it is our stinking job," Rat reminded him.

Ole had to have the last word, "It doesn't mean I have to like it. Uncle Sam doesn't pay me enough."

Our packs and flack jackets were going to kill us in the heat before the VC could take potshots at us. We'd only been on the move for about an hour. Our shirts were soaked with sweat and fatigue had already set in.

Thank God, the day's patrol turned out to be quiet. There was no VC contact. We had a day to get into the patrol routine. It was a lot different than what we'd learned in basic or AIT.

We made it to our LZ with time to spare and had a few minutes rest before we were picked up.

* * *

As soon as we arrived at our destination, the LT ordered us to set up our night defensive positions. "Okay, guys, this is how the CO wants the NDP set up. The command group in the center with each platoon responsible for a quarter section of the perimeter."

"Hey, LT, what else do we do?" Joe asked.

"We put out several trip flares and Claymore mines in our section, and arrange our watch schedule. Then we wait for the VC and blow his ass back to Hanoi!"

We were hoping they wouldn't show. No one wanted to be a statistic.

We ate our meager C-rat meals in shifts while the men on duty sat with their rifles facing out. Then we switched, letting those men eat while we sat in the defensive position.

I pulled the 0200 to 0400 watch and decided to have a little snack. Each C-rat box had a tin of crackers. I thought they would be easy to eat while on duty.

Everyone was on edge waiting for what might be an all-out firefight with the VC. No one really slept. We were waiting for the telltale rustle of the bushes or the snap of a dried stalk of rice, any little sound to alert us to the presence of the enemy.

You can't begin to imagine how loud crackers can sound in the middle of a very quiet night! After my first thunderous bite, I expected to feel the rounds from fifty M-16s tearing through my body.

Then I heard Mugs mutter, "Shit, Rough, use some damn peanut butter to muffle the sound of those fuckin' crackers!"

I was sure it would be funny in about twenty years or so, but right then it was damn scary. I wouldn't soon forget the lesson.

We all got our wish that night. No VC appeared, just a lot of very hungry mosquitoes. The army issued us mosquito repellent, but its odor was so strong, the VC could smell it a mile away. We refused to use it.

"Hey, y'all, cover your arms and any other exposed skin with mud. After rootin' like armadillas in the muck today, you should have a bunch," Bill told us.

"It seems to work," I whispered. "The mosquitoes are leaving me alone."

"Well, what are you worried about? You haven't been bothered by these damn flying bloodsuckers since you've been here," groused Joe.

He'd been having a terrible time with mosquito bites, to the point where he'd gone to Doc for some anti-itch cream.

Between spending the day struggling through the gunk of the watery paddies and being too afraid to close our eyes in sleep, we were totally exhausted by morning.

The choppers were there early to take us to our second day's patrol area. It was another day of walking in the sweltering heat and humidity.

We'd been traveling for several hours when I looked up just in time to see Joe almost bump into Rat who was only a couple feet in front of him. The company had slowed down and everyone was dragging their butts, trying to conserve their strength.

"Fuck it, Joe, get back into this damn patrol," Rat hissed as he looked over his shoulder and saw Joe too close behind.

"Sorry, Rat, I guess I can't drift off like I did in basic," Joe apologized.

"No shit! Wake up. This is fuckin' war. We need to be alert and ready to act instantly," Rat admonished.

"I know. I know. My mind just wandered. It won't happen again."

"Damn right it won't!"

"I just got word we're going to get a ten-minute rest break," I informed everyone.

"Son of a bitch, we finally get a break?" Joe asked. "Man, it's a good thing, too, as I'm about done in."

"I'm as fresh as a daisy, myself," spoke Rat with all the sarcasm he could muster as he took a deep whiff of himself. "Whew-ie, maybe I'm wrong about that."

The company as one stopped and dropped their packs, as well as their bodies, on the nearest dry dike.

"Did any of you guys look before you put your fucking butts down?" Top barked. "No? I didn't think so! Remember this is the VC's home turf, and they just might have had a *Chi-com* grenade set to fuckin' go off right up your asses. You got away with it today, but you might not luck out next time."

"Shit, Rough, I was so tired I didn't even think about a damn booby trap," Joe mumbled.

"I know what you mean, Joe. I didn't see a lot of old-timers check out the dike before they dropped either. We've been lucky so far on this patrol."

"Yeah, but can it continue?" Joe questioned.

"Sure hope so," I answered. It was almost a prayer.

The ten minutes passed all too quickly. We only had time for a drink of warm water. Our canteens couldn't compete with Old Man Sun in trying to keep anything cool. We could only dream of icy cold glasses of clean water.

The day dragged slowly by as we searched for any sign of the VC. They were masters at hiding and evading the US Army. Our presence in the area was to keep them in check so they couldn't operate openly, spreading terror and domination over the South Vietnamese people.

We finally got the word we were taking two-five mikes for lunch.

"Point team, find a good spot. There will be a fifty percent alert." We heard the CO call to the point team on our RTO's radio.

"That's the best thing I've heard all damn day," Joe admitted.

"You mean it's only lunchtime?" I groaned, exhausted.

Our last break seemed like hours before. The fatigue from keeping up the pace in the swampy area was playing tricks with my mind.

This time everyone checked out the dry paddy dike before they dropped their packs. Brush and tree lines were about fifty meters on either side of us.

A few minutes later I heard, "Hey, Rough, that area would make a good spot to set up a Tiger Alpha." Joe whispered as if speaking aloud might cause the VC to appear.

"Roger, Joe, I've been sitting here thinking the same thing for the last few minutes. We're not in a valley, but this situation gives a Bible passage from the Twenty-third Psalm new meaning. 'Yea, though I walk through the valley of the shadow of death, I will fear no evil for Thou art with me.' To tell you the truth, Joe, I'm terrified of what might be out there," I said, pointing my M-16 toward the brush.

"I'll tell you now, this little Italian boy is scared shitless. I don't want to fuckin' be here, and I don't want to die here!"

"None of us does. If anyone claims he's not afraid, he's a damn liar. We have to do our jobs and hope everyone else does theirs."

"Thanks, Rough. Sometimes it's nice to know you feel the same," Joe said.

"Come on, Joe, it's time to eat," I said trying to get into a comfortable sitting position. "Boy, it sure feels good to sit down and get the load off my back for a while."

As I turned to my pack to dig out a can of ham, Joe asked, "Hey, Rough, you have a P-38 with you?"

"How else am I going to open this can?"

"Good, I forgot mine."

"Am I your mother?"

Joe looked at me, disgusted, "No damn way, you're too tall and way too ugly to be my mom, that's for damn sure."

Chuckling, I asked, "I hope you have some C-4, or do you need to borrow a pinch of that too?"

"Shit, Rough, even I know to carry C-4."

"After you chew open your can of C-rats, at least you'll have something to heat it with," I replied.

Some bickering helped us relieve tension when our bodies were as tight as phone wire.

I looked for three golf ball-sized rocks to use as a stove. On the dike, they were easy enough to find. Placing them in a triangle, I put a small piece of C-4, about a quarter of an inch square, in the middle of the rocks. I opened my can of ham and lit the C-4. The ham was cooked in about a minute as the C-4 burned hot and fast.

With Ole to my right and Rat to my left, both facing the tree lines, rifles at the ready, I ate my lunch. Then I heated some water and made hot chocolate. I preferred it to the stuff in the C-rat box called coffee. That stuff was lethal, more like the proverbial battery acid.

I finished lunch and took up my rifle, facing the tree line. I was on security now. The more eyes the better. It was quiet all around except for the low murmur of voices in guarded conversation. We were all bushed and not at our best. Even the old-timers weren't very observant.

Then I noticed the bugs had stopped humming. No noise. It was too quiet. Danger! Everyone became alert at about the same time. We could feel the threat.

Exploding rounds from enemy AK-47s shattered the silence. "Oh, God, what's happening?" I heard someone scream.

Off to our right about fifty yards, the spot where Joe would have set up an ambush, a Viet Cong patrol had seen us and opened fire on our position.

Lunch be damned! Cans and food went everywhere as we dove for cover, if you can call a rice paddy dyke cover. We grabbed our M-16s and returned fire while trying to keep our heads and butts down. Red and green tracers crossed paths as firing continued from both sides.

The CO snatched the mike from his RTO and yelled into it, "Arty Bravo-One, this is Bravo-One-One, requesting airburst at grid Gulf-8, over!"

His RTO turned and hollered at the company, "Heads up, incoming!"

We continued to fire while waiting for help from above. Within moments, we heard the screeching whistle of the 105. A burst of white phosphorous exploded above grid Gulf-8, raining down on the VC.

The CO was on the radio instantly, "Arty Bravo-One this is Bravo-One-One. Right on target. Fire for effect HE."

Death and destruction rained down upon the enemy from above as high explosive round after deadly round came crashing to earth. Brush, trees, and VC body parts were thrown skyward. The smell of cordite, fresh dug mud, and death hung in the air. The AK-47s were silenced. The enemy was dead.

For some of us, this was our first firefight head-to-head with the VC. I was petrified and I'm sure Joe and the rest of the men were, too. The VC were either lousy shots or God was protecting us. Other than a few shot up backpacks, several C-rat cans with direct hits, and lots of dirt kicked up, we were unscathed.

Before we could continue, we had the gruesome job of canvassing the area where the VC had been. We were looking for papers, maps, diaries, or letters to give us clues about their activities.

There was blood, lots and lots of blood. And bloody body parts were scattered everywhere. None of us could have imagined just how horrible this task was going to be. I didn't know if I was looking at a pile of garbage or a torn and broken human being. Searching through shirt pockets was a ghastly job. We found nothing useful among the carnage.

I was beginning to realize part of the reason the veterans who were returning home the day I arrived had such a vacant look. Seeing the results of this firefight could give anyone nightmares. No one could be unaffected. I know I'll carry the images for the rest of my life.

* * *

The CO called for First Platoon to be point team. Then we heard, "Move it out." We were glad to leave that hideous place. There was no time to dwell on the fear.

This firefight was considered a success for two reasons. First, a number of VC were killed, and second, we had no casualties. There were a few minor cuts, scrapes, and bruises, but nothing needing more than a bandage.

"Fuck, Wild Bill, how do they know how many VC we killed this afternoon? All I saw were torn bodies?" Joe wanted to know.

"I was sick the whole time I was trying to check pockets. Some were so bad I just couldn't do it. I heard a lot of guys upchucking," Mac gagged out.

"Like y'all, I'm sure some pockets were missed. I know I missed some, but I went as far as I could make myself go." Wild Bill's face almost matched the color of his eyes—green.

"I couldn't tell how many men we killed. I wasn't up to counting the number of arms and legs scattered around to figure it out!" I was feeling sick myself.

"I couldn't care less, just so long as we weren't asked to pick up the body parts," Rat said.

"Yeah, you're right," Joe agreed.

The company needed to get back on track. We were all nervous and upset about the firefight. We had to be alert. If there were more VC in the area, they'd probably heard the 105s and might come to investigate.

We had to go another twenty-five hundred meters to our LZ, where we would be flown to another spot to spend the night. Several hours humping through the mud helped take our minds off of the sight we'd witnessed.

We'd hoped we might be sent back to Jeanie. But no such luck.

We moved as fast as we could while trying not to overdo it in the heat. We hoped to reach our LZ with a little extra time to get some rest.

At 1500, we heard, "Attention all Bravo stations, this is One-One-X-ray, taking one-zero mikes. Assume defensive perimeter, over."

I knew One-One-X-ray was the CO's RTO. All radiomen had a designation of X-ray added to the call sign of the officer they carried the radio for.

The company started to form a circular defensive position around the CO and his command group. The point team had found some dry rice fields making it easier to form our defense.

While we were resting, I heard Mac exclaim, "Hey, you guys, wouldn't it be great to take off our boots and let the damn sun dry our feet?"

"You bet. But I'm not risking the VC taking pot shots at us and catching me without my boots on. No fuckin' way. These feet will have to stay wet," Joe answered.

"Even if you do get your feet dry, you're just going to put them back into wet boots. They're never dry either." I hated to upset the kid with facts.

"Hey, Mugs, how do you stand it? I need to know."

"Let me tell you the bad news, you never get used to it. You just do the best you can to live with the conditions and hope you survive. Things are going to get worse during the rainy season."

"Thanks a lot, you turd."

"Mac, you sleep with your boots on like the rest of us, I presume?" Rat asked.

"Do I look like some kind of idiot? Be careful how you answer. It's just when I was in Germany, things were different. We had chow halls, showers with hot water, and we could sleep with our boots beside our beds, not in them. And we never went out on patrols carrying the world on our backs."

"Hey, I've got news for you. You're not in Kansas anymore, Toto," Joe kidded Mac.

"I don't see any way around wet feet and boots," Mac finally acknowledged.

"Yeah, well, when I get back to the World, I'm going to find a nice warm sandy beach to lie on and let the sun dry my feet for the rest of my life." I began to daydream about being on a beach with Lu. It was my favorite pastime.

"Can it, boys. Is anyone watchin' the damn tree line or are we gonna have Victor Charlie shootin' at our asses again?" Wild Bill asked, trying to get our minds back to the war.

Well, so much for my daydream. "Hey, you dopes, we should be looking for them instead of letting them take us by surprise."

"Wilco, Rough," they replied.

"After the firefight, I'd think y'all would be a lot more on guard."

"Got it covered, Bill," I said pointing my rifle at the tree line.

Our ten minutes passed too quickly. As word traveled through the company to "Get it on," there was a collective groan.

We traveled through some dry rice paddies, and the going was a little easier. We were near exhaustion, so this was a welcome change.

We arrived at the LZ with about fifteen minutes to spare and set up security before sitting down to rest.

"Rough, isn't Wild Bill beginning to sound a lot like the LT?" Joe mumbled.

"Just a little, but as much as I hate to admit it, he was right. We were lucky the VC didn't get any of us today. We'd better pay attention if we want to get back to the World alive."

* * *

The choppers took us to our NDP. We were supposed to engage the VC while on patrol, but most of us would have been happy never to go through another firefight. Thankfully, that night there was no contact.

Chapter 13 – Patrol Day Three

The morning started out cool, but we knew it would get very hot and humid as the sun rose. We moved out as fast as the mud and water would allow.

We watched, listened, searched, and moved, hoping to avoid another firefight with the VC.

"I'm already tired, and we've only been on the move a couple of hours," I complained to Joe.

"Mugs and Wild Bill seem to be having as much trouble pulling themselves through the frickin' paddies as we are," Joe observed.

I checked my Timex. It was only 0900. "Shoot, this means we won't get a break for at least another hour, unless the CO feels we need one earlier."

"I sure as hell hope he does."

"I'll bet it gets over one hundred degrees with the humidity at 99.9 percent today."

"Yeah, Rough, and there's no shade in sight."

"I don't think I've seen a decent tree since we got here. I guess we just keep humping 'cause griping won't do us any good."

"It's just the life of ground-pounders. Besides, who'd care anyway?" a more mature Joe commented.

* * *

The day grew steamy long before the sun had reached its zenith in the sky. Our bodies dragged, our feet stumbled and our minds reflected on the events of the previous day.

We ate our lunches in shifts again. There wasn't much talking as fatigue numbed our minds. We rested and waited, always looking for the VC.

"LT, the CO wants to talk," Ole said as he handed the mike to the lieutenant.

"Dammit, Rough, I have a bad feeling about this. It's not going to be anything good."

Joe was right.

"Rough, the Fourth has point for the rest of the day. You and Joe start."

"Roger, LT."

I turned to Joe, who was right behind me, "Okay, get the compass from First Platoon and let's move out."

"No problem, I have it right here," said Ole as he tossed the compass to Joe.

"Rough, I guess I'm the point man, and you're my back-up," Joe said, stepping past me.

We sloshed our way through the water-filled paddy toward the front of the company.

"I'll take over point in an hour."

We'd learned that an hour on point was all one man could endure. He had a lot of responsibility, checking to make sure we were on the right heading, watching for the enemy and booby traps which might be in our path, and he set the pace for the whole company.

Soon we were headed toward the pickup zone. The choppers would move us to another night defensive position.

It seemed like only minutes later when I heard, "Hey, Rough, my hour of torture is up. Time for you to lead this damn mess."

"Joe, that hour was quick. I guess I've been daydreaming," I said.

"Well, stay sharp and focused," Joe reminded me.

"I know. I need to pay attention or I won't last long."

"Yeah, and your wife would be unhappy if something happened to you!"

"I know. I made her a promise."

It seemed the sun was never going down. I tried to conserve water, but one canteen was empty, and my second was a long way from full. The heat and rough terrain took a lot out of us.

* * *

My hour was about up when we got word to stop for one-zero mikes.

"Rough, the CO says to pick a spot out of the goddamn muck if possible," Joe said.

"Just in time, I'm about done in," I mumbled.

Joe and I found a good place, a dried-up paddy with room for the whole company to get out of the water. We checked the area and moved into a defensive perimeter.

"LT, the CO wants all platoon leaders at his command point in zero-two mikes before we start moving toward the pickup zone," we heard Ole call to the lieutenant.

He was only a couple feet away. "On my way," he answered.

The LT was gone briefly. "Okay, guys, Fourth Platoon is now pulling rear security," he said when he returned. "Our pickup zone should be only an hour or so away."

"Hey, LT, what's wrong with this spot? We have a nice dry secured area for the choppers."

"Don't ask me, Rough, I just follow orders like you, but hang on for a minute." With that he headed toward the CO's group once again.

He was smiling when he came back.

"I have some great news. The CO thought our idea of not moving anymore today was a good one. He called the rear with our suggestion. They also decided we'll use this as our NDP. The choppers will pick us up in the morning."

"Roger, LT. Y'all mean the assholes actually took an idea from us grunts and fuckin' agreed?" Wild Bill asked.

"It helped that the captain didn't want to move, either. Wild Bill, set our night defensive positions and a guard duty schedule."

"Roger, LT."

It was hard to sleep knowing the VC might be close. I wasn't ready to put my trust in a guard who was as tired as I was.

We set up before it got too dark to see what we were doing. Even with a sliver of moonlight and all the stars shining, it was still as dark as a tomb. We could see millions of stars, many more than back home in the World.

Knowing the area and its features during daylight didn't help after the sun went down. Things changed, becoming very eerie. The terrain took on ghostly shapes and our imaginations ran wild. Objects which had been rocks, bushes, and shrubs by day, now became the enemy in some form or another, all creeping towards our NDP. Adrenaline pumped and we felt panic in our bellies. Anyone who said he wasn't terrified was lying.

* * *

"Thanks, Joe, for getting me back on track today," I said while heating my meal.

"Hey, you know, we've all had moments when we're not in the war."

"Yeah, but it could have been deadly."

I found myself thinking: *I hate the mud. I hate the humidity. I hate the heat. I hate the water. I hate the mosquitoes. I hate the VC. I hate the army. I hate this war. I hate being away from my wife and family and I really hate Vietnam. God, when did I become such a hating person? It's not in my nature to hate at all; maybe I've become this person called Rough.*

"Wild Bill, got a minute?" I asked.

"Damn straight, pardner."

"I have a simple question. When did you start hating where we are and what's happening to us, or do you?"

"I'm not sure when 'xactly, and yes I do hate all of this. Why?"

"Well, I keep thinking that I hate this and I hate that. I didn't realize I could hate so many things at one time. I have a church background and I was taught to 'love one another' and of course the Ten Commandments. Where does all the hate come from?"

"This fuckin' war changes y'all, Rough. No way 'round it. You're not the same person anymore, or ever will be again for that matter. Y'all have to change after seein' what we've seen and doin' what we've done, fightin' in this goddamn war. No fuckin' way y'all can remain the same."

"Dammit, Bill, I don't like it!"

"Like it or not, Rough, that's how it is."

"Maybe I'll understand what's happening in a couple of months, but right now it's confusing."

"I think it is for everyone who's fightin' in this stupid war."

"You're right, Bill. It doesn't make it easier, but I'm glad to find I'm not the only one with questions and frustrations."

"Rough, it's your watch," Ole told me. "Rat's on your right; he takes over after you."

"Roger, Ole. Where's the Claymore clacker?" In case I would have to blow a mine, I'd need the trigger.

"It's just to the right of the radio. There are a couple of grenades there as well. Remember Rough, you only have to squeeze once to detonate the mine."

"Wilco, Ole."

I checked. I didn't want to be searching in total darkness if the VC attacked. They wouldn't wait. They'd move right through, killing everyone.

The company had a couple of the new starlight scopes. They were a definite help to those of us on guard duty. They took any existing light and magnified it forty thousand times. We could observe the terrain and detect movement through a green tinge. We couldn't distinguish between an American or Vietnamese soldier, but if they were in the wrong place, too bad. This was a free-fire zone.

* * *

The next morning, after an uneventful night, Ole took a call. "Hey, LT, the CO wants to see all platoon leaders in zero-two mikes."

"On my way. Fourth, get the night stuff in and be prepared to move out."

Most of us were ready to go as daylight brought relief from the frightening night. Once again we could see what was around us. The terrain was back to rocks, shrubs, and bushes.

"Dammit, Rough, I hope we're headed back to Jeanie soon. I was so scared last night, I couldn't have taken a piss if I'd wanted," Joe confided.

"I know what you mean, Joe. I was too frightened to even need to pee," I mumbled.

We'd gradually learn how to survive the pitch-black nights on patrol. But fear and uneasiness were our constant companions.

* * *

"Okay, Fourth, time to set LZ security; choppers due in two-five mikes. The CO wants teams searching the ground for any surprises."

"Roger, LT."

The squad headed off in search of the VC who might have slipped into the area. The guys were careful, probing the ground. Things like spider holes couldn't be detected until you were right on top of them. Even then, they could be missed.

I had been curious about the term "spider hole" and asked the lieutenant about it.

"There's a type of spider which finds a cavity in the ground and builds a door made of twigs, leaves, debris, and web which blends in with the landscape. The spider hides in the hole, and when unsuspecting prey walks by, he springs out and captures dinner. Well, the VC hide in holes with a trapdoor made out of dirt, rice stalks, and other stuff to make it look like part of the environment. When we walk by, he's able to sneak out and kill us."

Rat and Ole were punching at the ground with their rifles, about fifty meters from our position. Ole stood erect and pointed his M-16 at a spot in front of one of the dikes. He made a few gestures, and Rat shook his head in the affirmative then started back.

"LT, we need to blow up a spider hole out there."

"So, do it, Rat."

"Roger, LT."

He turned and ran back to Ole, then said something we couldn't hear. They both pointed their rifles at the ground and emptied a clip of M-16 ammo. Ole put his rifle on the ground and took a grenade from his belt. Rat lifted the edge of the cover using the muzzle of his rifle while Ole pulled the pin, counted to seven, and tossed it in.

"Fire in the hole," Ole yelled.

He and Rat turned and ran about five feet and dove to the ground, landing face down. They got as flat as they could. The grenade exploded and the ground shook as smoke and dirt hurtled skyward.

A thorough search proved there were no bodies. However, we did find a cache of supplies, which we destroyed.

"Bill, keep the patrols out for another five mikes and be sure they check the dikes carefully."

"Roger, LT, after what Rat and Ole found, I'm sure they will."

"The choppers are due in ten mikes. I don't want one shot down, because we screwed up."

"Roger, LT."

We picked up our gear and checked for places where Victor Charlie could hide.

"LT, all's clear," Bill called back five minutes later.

"Roger. Ole, get me the CO."

"Bravo-One-One this is Bravo-Two-Two-X-ray, over."

"Two-Two-X-ray this is One-One-X-ray, go."

"Area clear, over."

"Roger, out."

The CO's RTO called the choppers. "Bravo chopper, this is Bravo-One-One-X-ray, LZ clear, ready for pickup, over."

"One-One-X-ray, pop smoke, over."

The RTO pulled the pin on one of his smoke grenades and tossed it at the landing zone. There was a soft bang, then a hissing sound, as the grenade spewed forth yellow smoke across the rice paddy and skyward.

"One-One-X-ray, I see banana yellow, over."

"Chopper one, Roger, banana yellow it is; bring it on down, out."

We could tell by the sound of their engines they were the smaller Hueys. They came out of the sun, making them difficult to see. Ten men would go on each chopper. Even here in a secure LZ, we didn't want the choppers on the ground longer than necessary.

They touched down and we jumped through the open doors. I took my place next to the door gunner, facing out with feet hanging over the edge. The chopper left the ground in a forward motion, and before we knew it, we were wrenched away from Mother Earth. The pilot pulled the nose toward the sun, drawing us faster and faster into a clear blue sky. We were going back to Jeanie.

The view was great as the bird lifted off. I could see the quilted pattern of the wet and dry rice paddies we had been patrolling. It didn't look as menacing from up here.

The exhaustion seemed to fade as we were whisked away. The wind rushing through the doors washed the tension from my body and my mind.

We weren't in the air very long before the feel of the chopper changed. We were on our way back to earth. Jeanie was in view. I never thought this base, with its green sandbag bunkers and the razor wire, the dirty pond, and the narrow road, could be such a great sight.

All of the choppers put down on dry ground, unlike our leap into the water-filled paddy at the beginning of the patrol. Our backpacks seemed lighter; whether it was the absence of water and C-rats we had consumed or because we were home, I'm not sure.

I couldn't believe how much mud was caked on my uniform, in my boots, and on my body. I looked like a statue made of clay. I couldn't wait to take a few minutes at the bathing hole to wash off the muck.

Chapter 14 - Back to the Routine

The only things that kept me sane were the letters and packages from home. Lu could brighten my spirits with just a few words. She had a way of describing life that really made me laugh.

"Hey, Joe, you've got to hear this!"

"From your wife?"

"Yep. She says ..."

... The weather here is beautiful. The sky is blue, the birds are singing, the flowers are blooming, and spring is in the air as we head into May. I hope it's spring with birds and flowers and stuff where you are. I don't like the thought of you in an ugly war zone....

"Only my Lu would expect flowers in this stinking hellhole. When was the last time you saw or heard a bird sing, Joe?"

"Birds? I don't think there are any birds left in Vietnam. They've all flown away."

"Aw man, listen to this."

... I'm so mad at these war protesters! A bunch of servicemen on leave in civilian clothes joined a demonstration march in New York. Just who do they think they are? Nixon's only been in office for three months and they're already complaining about the bombing in Vietnam.

These guys must be doing really hard duty stationed here in the US. I'm sure they have no idea what war is like. They should be sent to Vietnam or given dishonorable discharges for being anti-American!

I'm proud of you and all the guys over there putting your lives on the line for our freedom. I love you....

"Well, the rest is rather private."

"I agree with your wife about sending those bastards over here. Just let them protest to the VC."

"I'd give anything for leave at home with Lu," I said, tucking the letter in my pocket to read again later.

Bill called out, "Rough, y'all finished with the mail?"

"Yeah, I'm done."

"Good, the LT wants a platoon meetin' in ten mikes. Get yer crew."

"I was talking to the CO, or I should say he was yelling at me and the other platoon leaders," the LT greeted us. "He's downright pissed at the way the VC got a drop on us the other day. We need to figure out what happened. We were just damn lucky we didn't have casualties. I want all of you to get home alive."

We agreed.

"It's time for you to fuckin' wake-up! My squad leaders have to do a better job of overseeing your men. You can't let anything slide, even in base."

"Roger," we responded.

"I'm no good at writing letters home telling someone their loved one was killed."

I thought about the devastation it would cause if Lu got one about me. That was the shock I needed to get my mind focused.

As we were leaving, I heard the LT call out, "Bill, wait one ..."

* * *

Bill stopped by my pit. "Rough, Gun Three will pull guard tonight. Oh, yeah, the LT said I could borrow one of your guys."

"Roger, Bill. I'll adjust the guard times so you can have a man. When do we get some rest?"

"Shit, y'all rode back to Jeanie and didn't have to hump it, right? Why do y'all need rest?" He asked sarcastically. He was exhausted like everyone else.

"I know, Bill. Quit the bellyachin' and git ready for tonight," I mocked his Texan accent.

I was sure he was giving me the one finger salute as he headed off to his pit.

"Joe, you and Mac get the gun set for defensive firing. We have LPs out tonight, and Guns One and Two will be covering them. As usual we have guard; short one man since Rat's helping Bill's crew. I'm headed over to the FDC to see Dan."

I turned around, and Dan appeared as if he'd been reading my mind. "Rough, here are your numbers for tonight."

"Thanks, Dan. It's going to be a long one."

"No shit, Rough. Hopefully we'll get a reprieve and it'll be quiet."

"I wouldn't bet on it."

"It would be a nice change," he replied as he walked away.

I gave the numbers to Joe and went back to my hooch to make up the guard rotation.

We were back to the boring routine of running a firebase: guard duties day and night, and constant practice on the tubes. As crew chiefs, we'd catch the flak if anything went wrong with the guns. My guys had done a good job, and I told them so. I reminded Rat to head to Gun One before dark.

"Mac and I needed a little more practice on the gun," replied Joe. Mac was turning into a first-rate member of the team. He'd finally relaxed and the other guys were beginning to tolerate him. Joe was determined to whip this Eleven Charlie into a war-qualified mortar man.

I intended to get some rest, but the temperature in the sun was hotter than a summer day in California's Mojave Desert, and the humidity was like a sauna. The droning of the ever-present mosquitoes and the sounds of my guys practicing made sleeping impossible.

After a half hour or so, I sat up and brushed the mosquitoes away from my face and neck. We had learned it was dangerous to hit mosquitoes while on a Tiger Alpha. The sound traveled far into the night, alerting the VC to our presence. While in base, we trained ourselves to follow the same habit of not slapping them.

I went to see my team.

"Shit, Rough, being a crew chief must be a bitch."

"Yeah, it's a pain, Joe, but someone has to do it."

"I know for a fact that Rat didn't want it; neither did Ole. Besides, you were the perfect choice seeing as how you're the old man."

"Gee, thanks for the vote of confidence, Joe. Now strip two powder charges on ten more rounds, then you and Mac get some rest. Got it?"

"See, there you go being the crew chief, again," Joe said. I walked away thinking, *Like the job or not, it's mine. They are my men, my responsibility and I worry about them.*

* * *

A week later, I walked over to Gun One to see about night duties, and I saw Top talking to Wild Bill. He always brought bad news.

"Come on over, Rough," Top motioned. He turned to Bill, "As I was saying, the lieutenant's on his way. Get the other squad leaders here so we only have to go through this once."

"Roger, Top."

Bill left to get the others.

Once everyone arrived, Top began, "Lieutenant, the company's been given a mission starting in a couple of days."

"Dammit, Top. It seems like we just got back."

"Not my call, LT. Bad news for your platoon, though. The Fourth is going to have to take one of their tubes and ammo on this patrol."

The men moaned and groaned.

"You've got to be shitting me, Top."

"It's not a fuckin' joke, LT. The company is setting a cordon around a small village to the north. We'll be choppered part way, but we'll have to hump it the last two thousand meters before we can set up."

"Fuck, do you know what it's like walking a couple thousand meters carrying the mortar and ammo?"

"Again, LT, it's not my call. It's a bitch, but the orders came from headquarters. The CO will give us more info later. I thought you'd like some advanced notice."

"Thanks, I appreciate the heads-up," the LT acknowledged as Top headed back to HQ.

LT continued, "Gun One will go on this cordon, but we'll take the mortar from Gun Two since One is pre-plotted. Get everything ready to go. I'll tell you more as soon as I get word from the CO."

"LT, can't I take my mortar tube?" Bill asked.

"Yeah, I'm used to mine," Mugs added.

"You both know how difficult it would be to change all the plots. No, we'll do it like I said, and that's an order."

"Roger, LT, we'll be ready. I'm gonna need to use the rest of the platoon to help carry rounds," Bill said gritting his teeth.

The LT kept on, "I expect we'll need some HE and illumination rounds. Gun Two's crew will be staying at Jeanie using your gun, but you'll have Rough's men to help."

"My crew will be real happy to hear that, LT," I said sarcastically.

* * *

The sun would be gone soon and it was cooling off. The sky had turned navy blue. Dark would quickly follow. I gathered the men around Gun Three and gave the assignments for the night's guard duty. I took the last.

"Rough, you just love the 0400 to 0600 shift to watch the sun come up in the morning."

"It's the time of the day when I feel closest to my wife, Joe. She says a prayer before going to sleep and I feel her caress my face with her love."

"Fuck it, Rough, all that mushy stuff. Yuck! I know it's really because you get to hear 'Good Morning, Vietnam! What a fine, fine super fine morning,' from that idiot at battalion headquarters," Rat said giving me a bad time.

"Yeah, the bastard just loves letting us know it's time to get on the move while he sits in his cushy chair in his private room in his air conditioned building," Joe added mockingly.

"I'd have a few choice words for that son of a bitch if he ever got out here in the real war," Rat swore.

"All right, everybody, lets get back to the guard schedule. Now, I know all of us are tired, but don't mess with your buddies tonight."

"Are you talking about us not doing the full two hours of our shift?" I heard a chorus of innocent replies.

"Don't BS me, guys; I know better. I do not want to be awakened early. Got that?" Everyone had shortened their shift by waking up the next guy ten to fifteen minutes early to take over. I'd even done it a few times myself. "I strongly suggest you fix your chow and get some sleep," I continued.

* * *

The night passed quickly. The sounds from the mortar crew were filed away in our subconscious as part of the night noise. It should be there. Besides hearing the firing, I was listening to be sure the men were changing guard at the right times. I could see the dial on my watch in the dark if it was up close and I strained my eyes. Being a crew chief wasn't fun, but I took it seriously.

I heard Ole wake Joe. My last thought before dozing off again was, *I have two more hours of sleep.*

"Rough, time for guard," I heard Joe say as if we were in an echo chamber.

"Darn it, Joe, you just started your watch," I mumbled.

"Sure, two hours ago. It's 0400. Get your ass on duty."

I looked at my watch; sure enough it was 0400. I'd slept fully clothed with my boots on. All I had to do was toss the mosquito net out of the way, roll over, swing my feet off the cot, and onto the ground. I reached under my cot for my M-16 and donned my helmet I used as a pillow. It took less than a minute to crawl out of my bunker, ready to go. This preparedness could be a matter of life or death in case of an attack.

The sky wasn't a pitch black anymore. Daybreak wasn't far off; less than an hour away.

The tranquility of the moment was broken when I heard Wild Bill shout, "Hang," then as he dropped another round into the mortar tube, the final command, "Fire."

A couple of seconds passed as the round dropped down the tube and hit the firing pin at the bottom. The explosion was deafening in the predawn quiet. Another illumination round was being sent skyward. It hung from its parachute spreading light for the troops on patrol. The burning white phosphorous flare gave the illusion of morning as it drifted slowly back to earth.

I knew it was our gun firing, but I still had to catch myself before diving to the ground. I don't think anyone can ever get used to hearing the rounds exploding out of mortar tubes.

As I watched the sky change through the colors of daybreak, my mind washed back to all those early mornings when Lu and I drove to Huntington Beach. The sun came up behind us as we gazed out over the ever-changing color of the waves rolling up on the shore. Those were some of the happiest moments of a better time and place. I wished I was back there with her in my arms, watching the waves again instead of here protecting this miserable piece of real estate.

Another night of no contact, another night of safety, another morning I was still alive.

* * *

"Rough, do you know how heavy these fuckin' rounds are?"

"Dammit, Rough, Rat's right. They weigh a ton."

"Joe, you and I both know it's more like ten pounds each, not a ton, and we're only assigned three each."

"That's thirty extra fuckin' pounds!" Joe complained.

"Yup," I replied, "about the same as carrying the tube, the legs, or base plate. Only the aiming device weights less than thirty pounds. I know it's lousy, Rat, but its orders."

"Yeah, I know," Rat acknowledged.

The discussion was interrupted when Wild Bill called, "Hey, Rough, the LT wants us at his headquarters now."

The LT's office was a small space with a cot and a makeshift desk of ammo boxes. Not much different from the bunkers his men slept in.

"I don't know any easy way to put this," the LT started as soon as we gathered. "The CO wants at least twenty illumination and ten high explosive rounds. Each man will carry three rounds apiece plus food, water, and sleeping gear, and twenty clips of ammo for your M-16s."

Bill said rather sarcastically, "We'd already figured that out, LT."

"My RTO has enough extra weight, with the radio, so no rounds for him. Dan and the FDC crew can help; besides it's only two thousand meters."

"Through them marshy rice paddies, LT? That's bullshit."

"Bill, those are the orders!"

As he dismissed us, I could tell the LT was pissed.

On the way back, Bill commented, "Damn him. He knows nothin' about walkin' through the crap of wet rice paddies carryin' more'n half our body weight. He never does it."

"Bill, calm down, we knew it was coming. Besides, two clicks is better than walking a three or four-day patrol carrying the mortar and rounds."

"Yeah, I guess yer right, Rough, but he just bugs the shit out of me at times."

"I know. He gets to all of us," I said.

"Well, y'all, Brigade made their damn decision." Bill looked at the platoon. "It's just like we figured."

"This war belongs to the ARVNs more than us. I think they should be doing the fighting." Rat voiced what we'd all been thinking.

"Ain't gonna happen! Those lily-livered excuses for soldiers ain't never gonna be able to protect thar stinkin' country." *Man, the Texan slang really shows up when Bill's angry.*

"Well, I think …," Joe started.

"Y'all don't get paid ta think, just ta do your goddamn job!"

"If you say so, Bill. But I still think carrying ninety pounds of shit on our backs is pushing it."

"Fuck it, Joe, there you go thinkin' again." He glared, shook his head, threw his hands in the air in frustration, and stomped off.

As I stood to leave, Joe asked, "Heading out to write to your wife?"

"I try to keep her up-to-date and warn her if I'll miss writing for a few days. I don't want her to worry any more than necessary."

"I bet this fuckin' war is hard on her, too."

"You're right, Joe. You know the news always makes things sound worse than they are. When I write, I need to be specific about what I'm doing. The trick is not letting it sound like I'm in danger."

"You mean you told her what we've been up to? Fuck it, Rough, that's just plain stupid!"

"Well, until this last time out, a lot of what we were doing was guarding Jeanie and pulling some short patrols, not much to worry about. Now things are changing big time, but I don't want to alarm Lu unnecessarily."

"I see your point, but you need to let her know everything. You wouldn't want her to find out you lied."

"It's not exactly a lie; it's more of an omission. But you're right."

I walked to my hooch and started another letter.

Hi honey,

I love you and miss you so much. How is the new job? Tell me about what's happening at home.

I had a talk with Joe. Today he sounded older than his nineteen years when he reminded me to keep you a little better informed about what Bravo Company, and especially what the Fourth Platoon is doing. We're going to be spending more time out on patrol. Now, don't get worried. Yeah, you not worry, sure.

I'll let you know when there will be a long break between my letters, like now. This may be the last one you'll receive for four or five days. The company is being sent on a cordon to watch a village the VC has been terrorizing. We will sit and wait for someone to show, then kill or capture them.

I'll be carrying so much weight that adding a pen and paper would be too much. We'll be able to receive mail when they bring out supplies, so keep writing. Since it takes seven days for you to receive this, I'll be back in base before it would matter anyway. Your letters from home make the days pass easier.

I'll start the letters home again as soon as possible. Say "Hi" to everyone, and tell them I'm okay.

Love, your husband and lover, Len

* * *

The next morning dawned bright and clear. I got my crew up and working. Looking up, I saw Bill coming toward us. I hoped he only wanted to see how the guys were doing.

"I came to tell y'all the LT wants the squad leaders in zero-five mikes."

"Roger, Bill, zero-five mikes," I acknowledged.

There was bad news coming; I could feel it in my gut. There'd be last minute instructions and I didn't want to hear what the LT had to say!

Chapter 15 - The Cordon

I was the last to walk into Abitchie's office. Every face was downcast.

The LT announced, "We leave for the cordon in the morning."

Loud moans were our response.

"I told you it was coming."

"We hoped the cordon had been cancelled. You know, good news for a change," Dan said.

"Well, it's not. The choppers will be here at 0630. The hamlet has jungle on one side and rice paddies on the other. Victor Charlie invades the village, threatens the inhabitants, takes their food, and moves on. The villagers try to resist, but the VC are vicious. The high command has decided to send us to put a stop to it."

"Wouldn't this be a job for the ARVNs?"

"Are y'all kidding, Rough? They're damn useless, kinda like a steer in a cow milkin' contest." *I just love Bill's Texas humor.*

"It'll be simple," said the lieutenant, putting us back on task.

"Come on, LT, in this war there's no such thing as simple," I protested, leaning against the only solid wall in his office, the sandbag part anyway. "So how does this work?"

"We keep everyone from going in or out of the village after dark. A free-fire zone will exist. Anyone moving is shot, no questions asked. They'll most likely be VC."

I had to know, "Will this really succeed?"

"Well, it has before and it should again if all goes as planned."

"Okay, LT, what's our job?" Bill asked.

"Our mortar will be ready to fire at all times. The company will be deployed around the village, similar to a night defensive perimeter. Each platoon will have a quarter-section to guard. We'll be spread pretty thin, so keep in constant contact with the man on either side of you. There'll be an evening supply drop after we determine what's needed."

"Glad to hear that, LT, 'cause the thirty rounds we'll be a-carryin' won't go too far in a firefight."

"The brass realizes that, but we don't want to start without any rounds."

"That makes sense. My guys will handle the extra weight, LT."

"Of course they will, Rough. Now, get packed. Mugs, have your crew do night firing tonight at Gun One's position. Bill needs to pack yours this afternoon. Dismissed."

"Well, Mugs, y'all wanted to be number one so here's yer chance."

"Yeah, yeah, and we'll do a great job of it too." He walked off shaking his right hand in the air as if dismissing the whole thing.

"What did the LT have to say?" Joe asked when I returned.

I explained, but my crew looked skeptical. "Get ready, we leave at dawn."

I had faith in my guys; they'd do their jobs, carry the extra weight, and be just fine.

I had time to write another letter to my wife.

Hi honey,

Once again here is the news from Fire Support Base Jeanie. As I told you, we're off on a cordon. We'll surround this village and keep everything in from getting out and everything out from getting in.

We leave in the morning, to where, we don't know. Remember, this means no letters for a few days.

This is my first cordon and I have to admit to being a little nervous. I try hard not to let the guys here know just how scared I really am. I'm older and more experienced, as Joe is always pointing out, so a lot of the guys look up to me for support. I often feel like a dad to these "kids" and have to appear in control which can be very stressful.

I'm so glad I have you to talk to. I need your voice telling me everything will be all right. I pretend I can hear your words of wisdom and advice, even though it's not really a two-way conversation.

Honey, I want to be able to hold you in my arms right now. I love you so much! God, I wish I was home! It seems like forever before we can be together on R and R. It can't come soon enough for me.

Well, I've got to get packed. I just wanted to make sure this got in the mailbag going out on the evening chopper.

All My Love, Your husband and lover, Len

* * *

Watching the sun slowly appear over the horizon, we waited in the dry paddy for the choppers to arrive, our heavy packs at our feet. They were awkward with the ammo strapped on and there was no center of balance, no matter how many times we packed and re-packed. Throwing it in the door would be easier and faster than climbing aboard the chopper with our gear on.

Five landed, one per platoon and one for the CO's group. We loaded quickly. Each man had been assigned to a particular spot which made it easier to account for everybody. We were away in only few minutes.

It seemed we had barely lifted off when we were at the LZ. We touched the ground in a dry rice paddy and offloaded. The thought of jumping the last six to eight feet with the heavy packs had our stomachs in knots.

The patrol headed towards the village, crossing water-filled paddies most of the way. We were all hoping and praying we would be able to set up our perimeter in a dry area. It would be a nightmare to place a mortar tube on muddy ground and try to level it.

Walking was so difficult that at times we were on our hands and knees sloshing through muck, mire, and slime. No one wanted to be left behind, not even for a second. The CO kept pushing us since he wanted to be at the village by noon.

We'd been on the go for about an hour. Joe was ten feet in front of me. I looked up; he was trying to pull his right boot out of the mud. I watched as he started falling to his left, throwing his arm out to stop his fall. I moved to help, but couldn't get there in time. His arm sank and disappeared into muck up to his shoulder. His rifle was in his right hand, and it and his other arm went straight up, trying for balance. I grabbed his pack and yanked.

"Dammit, my watch was fuckin' sucked right off," he yelled looking at his slimy, watch-less arm.

"It couldn't have gone too far. Reach back in the hole," I tried to sound encouraging.

Joe searched. "I can't find it! Damn! It's gone until some gook farmer digs it up."

"Come on, Joe, we've got to get moving!" I hollered at him.

"Son of a bitch! I guess my $7.95 Timex isn't worth getting left behind for," he muttered as he finally got to his feet and started moving forward again.

He mumbled and grumbled the rest of the day about losing his stupid watch.

* * *

By early afternoon, we were finally just outside of the village. It had been a long walk with only one rest break and one lunch break. We were ready to drop, but we had to set up the perimeter around the village before we rested. Nightfall came quickly in the countryside.

Since very few of the company knew any Vietnamese, battalion had sent one of their *chi hois* to translate. A *chi hoi* was an ex-VC who had turned good for a price: his freedom and his life. These *chi hois* were called Kit Carson scouts by our battalion. Kit, as we nicknamed him, was sent into the village to talk to the headman and let him know the Americans were there to help.

Wild Bill found a dried paddy for his mortar tube. "Y'all are not gonna believe my good luck, LT. All the way here, I've been runnin' ideas through my head of how to set this damn thing up on wet ground."

"Oh, I guess I forgot to tell you about this area. It's why the Fourth Platoon has this sector to secure. Since yours is the only mortar, the CO wanted to make sure you could hit a target."

"Thanks a lot, LT." Then Bill mumbled sarcastically to himself, "You bastard! One of these days I'm gonna ..."

"Hey, Bill," I interrupted, "need help?"

"Thanks, but my crew can do it. Have your men drop off the rounds they was a-carryin'. Put 'em over there; HE on the left," he said pointing to a large clump of dried rice stalks.

Dan yelled to Bill, "You're going to have fun firing tonight without the aiming stakes. I can't find them."

"Son of a bitch, how'd I do somethin' so damn stupid. I left 'em on the fuckin' chopper. I guess the FDC and me will be doin' a lot of guesswork."

"Bill, guessing is not the smartest idea in the best of circumstances," Dan complained. "The illumination rounds aren't a problem, but the HE rounds need to be right on target. You could blow away the village or worse yet, hit one of our own patrols. Let's hope we won't have any contact until the supply chopper comes tonight."

"I'll go let LT know I fucked up."

There was no movement that night, therefore no need to fire, making Bill happy.

* * *

The sun came up with a vengeance. There was absolutely no shade. It was even hotter than at Jeanie. At least there we had the bunkers to escape some of the sun's intense rays. We tried making a cover using our ponchos, but they only seemed to intensify the heat.

I tried to conserve as much water as possible, but it was a lost cause. I sweated it out as fast as I poured it in. We were all glad when we heard water would arrive on the evening chopper.

* * *

We received our mail in the field, which was great most of the time, but the dumb REMFs also sent our packages. We were already carrying extra weight and they sent us packages! In the firebase, these were welcome, but not here.

I had written home and asked Lu to send some books to help pass the time in base. Like the good wife she was, she put about fifty Louis L'Amour westerns in a box for me. Was this great gift delivered at the firebase? Of course not! This wonderful, heavy package was delivered while we were out in the field.

Great! Now I had books to read. Great! Now I also had fifty books to carry. They were just too priceless to dump, so I had to think of a way to get them back to the firebase. How could I get the men to help?

I was trying to come up with something, when I heard Joe ask, "Hey, Rough, can I read one of those books?"

"Why, sure," I said, "but there's one condition." *Here goes my plan.*

"Yeah, what is it?" he asked.

"It's no big deal. You can read the book but you have to hump it back to base. By then we shouldn't have to carry mortar rounds."

"Hey, why don't you put out the word you have books? I'm sure other guys would like to borrow one."

"Great idea, I wish I'd thought of it," I said smiling. *My plan's working!*

Word got around: Rough had a library. It didn't take long before the books were out on loan. Lucky for me, boredom won out over a few ounces of extra weight. While some were pulling security, others sat reading right in the middle of the war.

* * *

It was a slow afternoon and an even quieter night. With all the so-called intelligence from headquarters, there still had been no contact in two nights. Tiger Alphas were sent out, but they never saw a soul.

"Dammit, Wild Bill, we carried all of these fuckin' rounds out on this patrol and we haven't used one yet! I thought there were supposed to be *beaucoup* VC in this area," Joe complained the next morning.

"Y'all're right. It's been too damn quiet! I got this itchy feelin' somethin' bad's 'bout to happen. I don't like it a'tall."

"I sure as hell hope you're wrong! If it wasn't for the fuckin' heat, this could almost be a vacation."

"Joe, this is war. Stay alert," I yelled at the kid.

"Don't I know it? But, it just seems strange we haven't had any contact," Joe continued.

"Yeah, my crew's really gettin' edgy. I don't want a firefight or nothin', but firin' some rounds would keep 'em sharp."

"I'm afraid we're being lulled into a false sense of security. We need something to keep us in focus." I looked up as Rat joined the group.

"Rough, Bill, the LT wants to see you."

The LT began, "It looks like our intelligence was wrong, but Brigade wants to give it one more night. We'll set out Tiger Alphas, so Bill, have your crew ready."

"Right, LT. Any chance of gettin' in some practice today?"

"You can practice this morning while it's cooler, but rest this afternoon. I want you ready for tonight."

"Wilco, LT."

"Meeting dismissed. Hey, Rough, do you still have one of those books I can borrow? I understand your wife sent you a ton."

"Sure, LT, I have a couple left. You can borrow one under the same conditions as the rest of the guys—you carry it back to base."

"It won't be a problem. Thanks."

I guess even lieutenants get bored when nothing's happening.

The waiting and watching was as deadly as any firefight. Our concentration waned. We became lethargic and vulnerable. But, danger was always present.

Night finally arrived. A TA stumbled across one VC. We never understood why he was out there alone. He might have come out of a hole for some fresh air and a piss. He might have been wandering through the area lost. He might have even been out looking for female company. Whatever the reason, he was in the wrong place at the wrong time and was obliterated. The TA fired so many rounds into the poor gook he was hardly recognizable as a human being.

Bill's crew fired off numerous illumination rounds toward the TA's position. The sky and the surrounding area were lit up like high noon. We needn't carry that ammo back to base!

After a thorough search, we couldn't find any more VC. The CO decided to keep the TAs out until dawn, just in case someone should show up. We were mentally back in the war.

Just before dawn, we heard another explosion. Had we found more VC? No, it was a water buffalo. The dumb thing walked into one of the ambush positions and was blown away.

The CO was pissed! This was going to cause a lot of trouble!

The animal was important and valuable to a poor family. Nothing mechanized could handle the mud and water required in growing rice; it was the farm tractor. It provided much needed fertilizer and didn't need gas or parts to keep it working.

Killing the animal created a problem between the village and our troops. The CO demanded to see First Platoon, the ones responsible, NOW!

We could hear him shouting, "You really fucked up! How could you not distinguish that huge animal from the VC? Shit, even a REMF could tell the difference. You know better than to harm a water buffalo! When we get back to base, you will be the shit burning detail for the next month. Now get your asses out of my sight."

LT later told us it would cost the army two hundred and fifty American dollars to placate the farmer and the village chief.

We were all glad we hadn't been the ones to make the mistake. The lesson for the day: Do not kill water buffaloes!

* * *

"Okay, pack up the trip flares, mortar rounds, and Claymores. Police the area and pack up all trash," LT ordered the next day.

"How far are we going to carry the damn mortar?" Mugs started, and I finished, "And the leftover rounds?"

"It's only a short walk, since the choppers are picking us up just outside the village."

They were on time. Everyone quickly loaded the gear and we took off.

I just had to tease Bill, "Hey, did you remember the aiming stakes?"

"Fuck it, y'all go ta hell!"

The laughter released the tension of the previous three days.

We'd only been in the air a short time when we could feel the descent. They dropped us off near the road, a good two hundred meters or so from base. It seemed a long way back since we still had a few mortar rounds, the mortar itself, our packs, and, of course, our prized library.

* * *

Figures for the cordon operation were: one dead VC, his AK-47, no papers, one very dead water buffalo, some pissed-off farmers, and one bill for two hundred and fifty dollars, American.

Was it a success? Who knows? At least we didn't lose any men. I considered any time we were out in the field a total success when it cost us nothing but firepower and sweat.

Chapter 16 - Gun One

"Welcome back," I heard Mugs say to Wild Bill. "This three-night stint as head gun cured me of wanting to ever be number one. We did a good job," he said in defense of his team. "But I'm glad we don't have to do it again. I like my pit better than yours. Besides, now I can sleep while you do all the firing," Mugs razzed Bill.

Early that evening, Dan dropped by. "It should be a quiet night. They're only sending out one LP and no Tiger Alphas. Boy, those listening posts are so important. They're our extended eyes and ears, letting us know of VC movement."

"Yeah, sometimes we forget what they do for us," I remarked as I headed back to my hooch.

I lay on my bunk listening to the sounds around me. I heard the call for an illumination round. When the LP thought they saw or heard something, they'd call and hunker low to the ground, not showing profiles. As the glowing flare cast its light upon the countryside, the VC would startle and be easy to spot. They'd become targets for the LP.

Gun One was firing as usual. I heard Bill and his crew locate the round and prepare to drop it in the tube. Bill yelled, "Hang," followed by, "Fire," as he dropped the round.

I expected an explosion when it hit the bottom of the tube, but all I heard was silence.

Then Bill yelled, "Son of a bitch!" He then shouted over to Gun Two, "You're up. I've got a hang-fire!"

Suddenly, everyone was up and running towards Gun One.

Bill hollered, "Turn the fuckin' thang upside-down, and beat on it with that damn shovel handle. I'll catch the round when it comes back out. It shouldn't go off." I heard him mutter under his breath, "I hope."

We all watched at a safe distance. I'd never had one hang before, so this was a good learning experience—if we didn't get blown away.

"How did you fuck things up now, Bill?" the lieutenant grumbled as he ran from his hooch, fastening his pants and trying to put his helmet on at the same time.

"LT, I think y'all should stand back 'til we get this damn round out of the fuckin' tube."

"We can't afford to lose a tube, Bill, so get that misfire out in one piece!"

"Thanks for carin', LT," Bill muttered sarcastically.

Finally, the round slid out of the tube and Bill caught it like he was delivering a baby. He carried it to the other side of the blast wall and put it down very carefully. It would be disposed of in the morning. The excitement for the evening was over, and we all headed back to our places while Gun Two finished the fire mission.

* * *

Hi honey,

I'm back from the cordon and everything is okay.

I just finished my last roll of film and sent it to Kodak yesterday. Boy, sending the rolls in to be processed, postage free, and having the pictures sent directly to you was a great idea. Bring them on R and R and I'll explain who everyone is.

We started this morning under clear skies and a blistering sun. No clouds means a hot day—usually over a hundred degrees and ninety percent humidity. It's a good thing three hundred gallons of drinking water is sent out every day as there isn't any on this base. Our Coke and beer rations, which come out each week, disappear very fast. I still trade my beer rations for Cokes. I get more to drink that way.

Rumor is, we'll be off in a few weeks to a place called the Fishnet Factory, brigade's forward headquarters. We'll be turning this base over to another company.

The LT called a formation this morning just after we started drill. Believe it or not, he actually had some brooms. We had to sweep the dirt in the platoon area. Yeah, I said sweep the dirt! How stupid in this heat. It was a complete waste of our time.

I'm beginning to hate this LT and I'm not the only one. Almost all the guys think his rank has gone to his head. He rotates home very soon; not soon enough for me.

You know what? I've been thinking I miss your smile the most. It would melt the heart of a stone man. Added to your laughter, it shows that you are so full of love and just plain enjoy living. You light up my world and I love you.

Thanks for the news from home, but don't get so upset about the anti-war stuff. I know it's hard to understand the protests taking place on the college campuses. Their demands seem unreasonable and uninformed about what we're doing over here.

I must confess I'm disappointed with Canada. How can they allow American military deserters to settle there? All the guys were really pissed at the news! I'm glad I didn't choose that way. I'd never be able to look you or our children in the eye if I had avoided my responsibility to my country.

I wanted to let you know I was safe and send all my love. God, I really miss you! Be a good girl while I'm away, and I promise, I'll be home before you know it.

Love, Len, your husband and lover

* * *

Now, we struggled out of our cots, ate breakfast, practiced, swept our area, slept, and tried to keep cool. It would be a long two weeks before we left for brigade headquarters.

Chapter 17 - The Fishnet Factory

Our orders were to pull security at brigade's forward headquarters. It was housed in an old building on the outskirts of Saigon, which had once been a fishnet factory.

Our last night at Jeanie turned out to be really bad! At dusk we sent out several TAs. One ran into a booby trap, a *chi com* grenade. The explosion caused multiple shrapnel wounds on arms, legs, and faces. Their flak jackets had protected their torsos.

The TA returned to base with their wounded. A medevac chopper was called for three of the more seriously injured men who were flown to the military hospital at Binh Hoa AFB. It shook us out of our complacency and reminded us we were fighting a war.

The next morning, we cleaned the area and packed our company's equipment. Everyone was looking forward to the move, hoping things would be better there.

Five Hueys arrived at 1330 to transport us, and then a large Chinook came to move our mortars. Since everyone and all of our gear could have been sent on just the shithook, we figured it was all for show. The VC would think a large company with lots of men and equipment had moved in.

We set down on the landing zone in front of the gates to the compound. For safety, only one chopper landed and unloaded at a time. The other four circled the area searching for VC. After the last Huey took off, the big one landed to offload our equipment.

The front of the factory faced the road to Saigon. There were about 150 meters between the front gates and the road itself, enough room to land the large Chinook. Supplies, new men, and weapons could be delivered right to our front door.

I had a slight misconception about helicopters before being in Vietnam. I thought they all took off straight up. Not so. Some needed room for forward movement, and the walls around the fishnet factory didn't allow for this type of takeoff.

The company chopper had to be parked outside the gates. Men guarded the bird day and night. This assignment wasn't difficult during the day, but nighttime was a different story. Too many people moved about, and the chopper was exposed. Why the VC didn't take it out with an RPG, or move in and blow the thing away with a grenade, we never figured out.

The main building stood about three stories high with a multitude of radio antennas on the roof. It had the name of the factory in big red neon letters, spelling out *"Khai-Vinh"* across the top with a large 199th insignia above the gates. It was an impressive building, considering the rest of the permanent structures in Vietnam.

The compound at the back of this old factory was about four hundred square meters. When it was in production, fishnets were laid out to dry there before being shipped for sale.

Three walls and the back of the building enclosed the area. The top of the ten-foot-high wall had a layer of broken glass covered by razor wire, in case the VC got by the listening posts and the night ambushes. It had one drawback: the VC could get close to the unprotected sides of the building if the guards weren't always alert.

Our portion of the compound had plenty of room for the fire direction center, three guns of the mortar platoon, and small sleeping hooches along the wall. We lived near the guns so we could get them on line as fast as possible. We had to be ready for anything twenty-four hours a day.

Security was set up with fifty-caliber machine guns at the four corners. There were three two-man platforms in the middle of each section with M-60 machine guns.

After the open spaces of Jeanie, it felt like a prison. Were we safe? I liked to think we were more protected than at Jeanie, but we were in a war zone, and it was still the VC who ruled the nights. No one was ever truly safe.

* * *

"Aw, man, look at our new mortar area," Bill said as we walked around the compound.

We stopped and stared at the spot where we were to set up our guns.

"I need ta talk to the LT." Bill pointed at the existing mortar pits as he walked away, "Y'all dig out our shovels and start ta work."

When Bill returned, the look on his face wasn't encouraging.

"I'm damn sure we won't like what he's got to say," Joe whispered.

"You bet your sweet ass y'all won't like what I'm gonna say!" Bill must have overheard. "The CO wants to start inspections in the mornin', along with all our other duties."

"This is a fucking joke," Joe complained. "That means we have to be in our mortar pits by 0630 with weapons, ammunition, a canteen of water, wearing a flak jacket and steel pot!"

Bill continued quietly, "This crazy-ass inspection is just one of the dumb things we have to do while we're here. So get used to it."

"You were gone a long time. What else did you find out?" I asked.

"Talk about gettin' screwed," Bill said, "I heard the army's payin' the owners of this buildin' a nice tidy sum so brigade could use this stinkin' place for its headquarters."

"Well, I think it fuckin' smells like dead fish," Joe complained. "Whew!"

"What do y'all expect it should smell like, yella roses?"

"Like in the Yellow Rose of Texas, Bill?" I heckled, humming the melody.

"Rough, don't git on my bad side, ya hear?"

Everyone chuckled.

We never understood why it smelled like fish, since the nets made here had never been used. Maybe it was just our imagination.

"I got some good news, too. We'll have hot food three times a day, good clean water to bathe in, movies, TV, and some light inside at night."

"Hey, now we can write more letters home. You got that, Joe?" I reminded him of our conversation on keeping the family informed about our situation.

"Yeah, I'll write my mom tonight," he replied.

Wild Bill continued, "Okay, y'all git to work on this fuckin' pit. We need it done 'fore dark."

It took us all afternoon to get the mortar pit and the ammo bunker in passable shape. Several weeks of work would be required to get the area the way we liked it.

Taking turns, we had our first taste of hot chow in more than a month from a real mess hall. I don't think we even cared what we were eating. It just tasted great.

The best part was the shower. We used fresh water instead of dirty salt water. I was really clean for the first time in over a month. Too bad I only had my dirty, sweaty, smelly clothes to put back on. We hadn't yet received clean clothing for the week. Even those reeked with the stench of Vietnam.

* * *

The compound was a permanent base of operations, so another company was stationed there with us. This allowed free time, even though we were confined to the area. We couldn't go into Saigon. It was off limits. However, across the road, there were the usual businesses, one of which has followed military men throughout history: the ever-present whorehouse. It was doing a thriving business this close to a large group of horny American GIs. The local females were taking advantage of the opportunity to earn money selling their bodies.

Even though the area was officially off limits, many soldiers would sneak across the road for a visit. This was a diversion, a break from the war. They planned ways to keep from getting caught, but were willing to take the chance for a half hour of pleasure. Even the known dangers of venereal diseases didn't deter them.

The brass knew and worried about the VC capturing soldiers while in a passionate moment. They tried to put a stop to it, but the guys were determined.

Of course, the guards never saw anything. The MPs kept the jaunts across the highway under watch, but many of them were waiting their turn. I guess they were human, too.

Doc had been giving out *beaucoup* penicillin pills, and too many guys had been sent to the hospital for shots. That wasn't for me. The cure wasn't guaranteed, and who knew if that crap would ever go away.

It would be ironic to get through this miserable war unscratched and come away with some disease which could kill you years later.

* * *

Brigade came up with a brilliant idea. Unfortunately, they weren't the ones who had to put it into practice. They had a searchlight installed at one corner of the factory. The idea was to give more light to the LPs and TAs if they saw or heard any suspicious movement. It could also be used if headquarters came under attack.

We put the searchlight out each night, shining it at different spots outside the base when requested. It was a good idea unless you were the one behind the thing. The light was a perfect target, and so were the men manning it. We pointed it in the general direction we wanted the light to shine and then got the hell away from it.

Those of us on guard detail also had starlight scopes. We could keep a close watch on the whorehouse after dark, affording the GIs some protection from Charlie while they were inside. But we had to be very careful not to cross the bright searchlight; multiplying it forty thousand times could temporarily blind a guy.

"Well, Rough, I guess it must be working," Dan said, referring to the searchlight guard. "I haven't heard of any of our guys not returning from the whorehouse. I know we're supposed to be concentrating on the TAs and LPs, but I try to give the house as much attention as I can."

"I know what you mean. I sure as hell don't want to lose a man to some gook just because he's stupid enough to visit the ladies."

Brigade Headquarters was a semi-secure base out of the field. It was close to civilization and, therefore, subject to all of the evils of society of the time. In addition to the whorehouse, we had our first encounter with drugs. Where they came from was only speculation, but a good guess was the house across the street.

In the field, the use of drugs was way too dangerous. Mixing them and contact with the enemy could be lethal. This was the only occasion when Bravo Company had the opportunity to get involved in any of this mess.

Smoking cigarettes was a common practice as long as it was out of sight. The guys could scoot down behind the light on the roof and hide the bright orange glowing tip of a cigarette. No GI wanted to become a target for some VC's AK-47 or rocket propelled grenade.

Since E (Echo) Company was also assigned to the security of headquarters, our duty was often mixed with GIs we didn't know. One night, Joe and I pulled searchlight guard with an Echo guy. About fifteen minutes into our shift, he lit up what we thought was a cigarette.

We soon noticed a strange odor. "Hey, Len, is that the shit I think it is?"

"I've never smelled pot before, but I think that's it. It's certainly not a cigarette!"

"What do you fuckin' think we should do?" Joe whispered.

"I'll talk to him first and let him know we won't tolerate it on duty, see if it makes a difference. If not we'll go from there."

I approached him between smokes. "Hey, guy, we need to have a little talk."

"Yeah, what's your problem, asshole?" he started out.

"Wait a minute; it's you who has the problem. We both know it isn't a Camel you're puffing on. It's a stinkin' marijuana joint!"

"So, what's it to you anyway? You and your buddy want to get some?"

"Hell, no!" Joe said emphatically. "It's one thing to screw up your own mind and put yourself in danger. Just don't mess with our lives. While you're on duty with us, you will be fuckin' clearheaded. Understood?"

"You are also putting the guys out on listening posts and ambushes in real danger when they need this light," I added.

"Do you really think you can do a good job while smoking a friggin' Mary Jane, you sorry bastard?" Joe continued.

The man glared at us defiantly.

"Let's look at this from a different angle," I tried to explain. "You might be out there tomorrow night and need this light. The enemy could be sneaking up on you or this base so you call for light. What if the three guys manning it are stoned? From what we've seen, they wouldn't be able to help. They'd hardly be able to find the light, let alone point it in the right direction. Get the picture?"

Of course he didn't get it. He was too far gone to be able to understand anything.

"Hey, Rough, we aren't getting through to this son of a bitch. The two of us can handle any calls. We'll do our job so this jerk won't put the TAs and LPs in jeopardy," Joe continued, "When Top makes his rounds he'll see this asshole and frickin' straighten him out. Then we won't be responsible for him."

"It just might work, but will Top get on me for not reporting him sooner? I don't need him angry at me."

It was my responsibility to tell the sergeant of the guard. Joe said he'd handle the gun while I took a leak and looked for the sergeant.

On the way back, I passed Top.

"Rough, aren't you on searchlight?" he asked.

"Yeah, but we have this problem."

"It had better be important for you to have your ass this far from your post."

"Well, Top, we need you to make your rounds a little early and start with the searchlight."

"Okay, out with it, what can't wait until my regular check time?"

"One of the guys from the other company on duty with us has some Mary Janes. He's been smoking since before he came on duty and is really out of it."

"What the hell! Get back to your post, and I'll take care of this fuckin' asshole. No one does drugs while I'm on duty!"

"Thanks, Top. Joe and I weren't sure what to do.

"It's okay, Rough, you did the right thing. It may save lives, including his own, the stupid bastard. I'll be there in about ten mikes."

"Roger, Top."

When I returned, I explained to Joe what was about to happen.

"He's going to be in deep shit. Man, that stuff stinks. I'm getting high just sitting here," Joe grumbled.

"He needs help before he endangers all of us." I was really ticked off.

As luck would have it, he was lighting up another joint as Top walked up behind him. The first reaction was a solid slap across the back of the kid's helmet to get his attention.

"Wa …," he came up swinging, but Top grabbed his arm before he completed the punch.

"What the fuck have you got there, asshole?" Top asked in a loud stage whisper. Normally he would be shouting at the top of his lungs, but there were always VC waiting for someone to kill. Anyone shouting would definitely be a target.

The dumb guy was so out of it, he had no idea what was going on. Top was really pissed. Joe and I figured this kid would be pulling shit can burning detail for weeks to come and maybe some loss of pay. We hoped he would get the point, but Joe and I both felt he was a lost cause.

Top almost threw the stupid kid off the roof and then marched him away. We spent the rest of our watch quietly thinking about the problems some of these GIs would have when they returned from this war.

* * *

"Well, how many days until R and R for you, Rough?" Joe asked one morning.

"Heck if I know, but its way too long. Man, I can hardly wait to be with Lu. I really miss her."

"You know, Len, you're so damn lucky to have someone back home in the World to think about and to look forward to seeing. I know it's been tough on both of you, but I would trade places in a heartbeat."

"I guess being an old married man has a few advantages," I kidded. "Well, I need write to her before guard duty. Hey, when was the last time you wrote home, Joe?"

"All right, pappy, I'll go scribble a note to my mommy before my nap."

"Smart-aleck kid!" I muttered as he turned and grinned at me over his shoulder when he walked away.

* * *

Hi honey,

I sure miss you. I haven't had much of a chance to write to you since we moved to the Fishnet Factory, our brigade's forward headquarters.

I pulled all night guard on the searchlight. The three of us on duty keep awake listening to the radio for requests of assistance.

The light makes a good target. Of course, if the VC try and hit this place, they won't find me anywhere near it. I don't know what I did to make the LT mad, but this seems to be my assignment.

I received the second package of books today. They sure got here fast. The *Playboy* is wild this month. The guys said to tell you thanks for sending it and the books! The westerns are good, but the war stories didn't go over too well.

The food here is fair and hot most of the time. It's a real break from C-rats. We even have cold milk at breakfast. It seems like the little things are sometimes the most important.

I have to get to guard. Yeah, it's the darn light again.

I love you very much and miss you with every breath. I was just talking to Joe about R and R. Boy it seems years away. I pray to see you soon. I need some of your sanity in this crazy mixed-up war.

Love, Your lover and husband, Len

* * *

Rat and I pulled guard with a couple of guys from the other company that night.

We sat quietly talking, "I heard the VC decided it was time to let everyone know they were at war. Or else the guys in Delta Company pissed off the local villagers after we left Jeanie. A few got hit when they went out to our old bathing hole a few days ago," I commented.

Rat shrugged. "Yeah, I heard it had been booby trapped. They must not have swept the area."

"It looks like Top was right. He was always bugging us about keeping a close watch on things. I guess it kept us from ending up like those guys."

"You know, Rough, I always hated that miserable excuse for a bath tub …," Rat muttered as the radio came alive with a call.

* * *

"Y'all know the CO wants this base in great shape when we leave."

"Well, Bill, we've been working on it every day. It's better than it was when we got here," I said.

"Now you can see why we're here, we are the 'Bravo Company Builders' after all. You should have seen Jeanie when we first arrived there," Mugs explained. "It was almost as bad."

"The lieutenant in charge of fishnet didn't do anything with the mortar pits. The blast wall isn't finished. The ammo bunkers, where we store our mortar rounds, are supposed to withstand a direct hit from an RPG. We've got a lot of work to do," I replied.

We had to tear the old structures down and rebuild them. And we needed to finish before the VC attacked and the rains began in earnest.

We leveled the ground for the floor, then filled mortar boxes with sand for the walls, and protected them with hundreds of sandbags. Corrugated sheet metal covered by more sandbags formed the roof of the ammo bunker.

Each day began with our stupid inspection. Then it was sandbag filling detail. We didn't have sand, so we dug up the dirt in and around the compound. It was a lot of work, but when we were finished, we'd be proud of our accomplishment.

* * *

"I have some news about Delta Company," LT started our morning meeting. "They had contact with a VC sniper team last night. Two VC were killed and another three captured. Delta had two wounded, not seriously."

"Shit! That could have been us! I guess luck is still with Bravo. I hope it stays for a long time."

"Me too, Mugs, me too," I agreed.

The LT frowned when Joe interrupted. "Scuttlebutt has it we're getting more men for Bravo Company."

"Yeah, we got two more for the mortar platoon, seven more for the line platoons, and four will return from the hospital today," LT informed us.

"Hey, this'll help a lot!" I was excited. Maybe I'd get another man for my squad. Rat was going on R and R soon.

"It probably would have, except First and Second Platoons were on an all-day operation yesterday. Our luck finally ran out. They had six men injured."

"How? Did they get hit by rifle fire?" I asked.

"No, booby traps. No one killed, but two are going to a hospital in Japan and then home. The other four are in the forward hospital. They'll be back soon, I hope." The LT looked as upset by the news as we were.

"We never seem to get up to full strength. Just when we get more men, we fuckin' lose others," Joe was frustrated like the rest of us.

My luck's still holding. I wasn't on the patrol. Of course there's more than luck to it; God's keeping an eye on me. I have a promise to keep to Lu, and I won't let her down.

"You've probably already heard there's going to be another patrol. Men from Fourth might be assigned to one of the other platoons. Since losing the injured men, they'd like some with experience to replace them, not these FNGs we're gettin' today. I'll make assignments later."

"Roger, LT," Bill answered for the rest of us.

My thought of being lucky was crushed when I found my name on the list. Damn!

As I sat down to write to Lu. I realized how much I'd been writing recently. I was afraid and needed her strength to carry me through. *Oh, Lord, I just want this nightmare to be over so I can go home,* I prayed.

* * *

Hi honey,

I'll be leaving in the next day or two for a seven-day patrol. So don't worry if you don't hear from me.

There's a lot of action around the Fishnet. The VC are attacking everywhere, getting their last licks in before the rainy season hits.

I'm doing fine, just counting the days until R and R with you. I'm very lucky to have you in my life. Thank you for being my wife. I love you and miss you so much.

I received the football in the mail a couple of days ago. I was sore yesterday after our first game, but I really enjoyed playing again. It brings a little bit of home here and takes our minds off of this lousy war for a while. We have another game this afternoon on the back lot. The guys said to tell you thanks. I think they're all jealous of me and a little in love with you. I know I love you.

We went to the rifle range at Firebase Stephanie today. We fired all of the old ammo. In this heat and humidity, it rusts and has a tendency to stick together, causing our rifles to jam. Not good in a firefight. If it jams on the range, no one's in danger.

Then we came back, thoroughly cleaned our weapons for inspection, and loaded fresh ammo in our magazines.

Say hi to everyone for me.

Love, Len, your husband and lover

Chapter 18 - The Long Patrol

"Rough you and your crew are assigned to First Platoon for this next patrol; they're short experienced men. It'll mean about a week in the rice paddies south of here, where American troops haven't patrolled before."

"Virgin territory, huh, LT?" Rat asked.

The LT ignored him. "You'll set up a cordon around a large village at night and go out on patrols during the day. But it will be different from the one we took part in while at Jeanie. There's supposed to be a large concentration of VC in the area."

"Yeah, we've heard that before."

Before he could respond, Joe asked, "LT, are we taking our mortar and rounds with us?"

"You'll carry your packs with all your supplies and ammo, but since you'll be a part of First Platoon, you won't be taking your mortar tube."

"Okay, LT!" Joe was a happy guy.

"It doesn't sound like we'll get much sleep."

"Sleep, well, ah … Rough, there will be … ah time, I'm … I'm sure."

"Thanks, LT," I grumbled.

"Do we hump enough food for a week?" Rat asked. He was always worried about his stomach.

"The chopper will send out meals and water. Only carry enough C-rats for two days."

"When do we leave?" I asked.

"The choppers will be here at 0800 tomorrow. Check in with Lieutenant Bratton from First Platoon. Ask him how he wants to use you guys."

"Roger, LT."

* * *

I'd met Lieutenant Bratton before. I was glad to see he'd recovered from his bloody encounter with the VC at Jeanie. I admired him. He always went about his duties with purpose and determination, and treated his men intelligently and with respect.

"Lieutenant Bratton, PFC Rugh reporting. My squad's been assigned to you."

"I've been expecting you. I understand you work well together as a team, so I'm not going to break you up. You'll be my fourth squad. Have you been briefed on our assignment for this sweep?"

"Yes, sir. What time do you want us here in the morning?"

"Meet at the LZ at 0730, and I'll give you your chopper assignment then."

"Roger, Lieutenant Bratton."

"Just call me LT."

"Roger, LT. I go by Rough."

* * *

The day turned out to be a wet one. The rain had come in the night, and there was still a light mist. It would be a miserable week if we had to endure this weather every day.

The choppers arrived and the LT assigned us to the fourth Huey. It was a short trip to our area of operation. After our arrival, we spent the day organizing our gear, laying out our cordon positions, and familiarizing ourselves with the terrain we were to guard.

Lieutenant Bratton explained his expectations of my squad and pretty much left us alone to accomplish it. We completed our duties efficiently and felt like responsible humans again. He appreciated our training, experience, and ability.

The first day was quiet. We hoped the report of the large concentration of VC was an exaggeration. We set up for the night cordon and heated our evening C-rats. Those of us not on guard, on listening posts, or the Tiger Alphas took advantage of the opportunity to catch up on sleep.

The day may have been quiet, but the night was something else. It seemed most of the VC movement in this part of Vietnam was between 2000 and 2400 hours. After midnight, the VC settled in and didn't travel much.

On this first night, the Tiger Alphas caught several small VC patrols. They came walking down the path toward the village and right into our ambushes. A few shots were fired, but no one was injured.

We called in a Huey the next morning to pick up eleven VC prisoners. None had any papers or maps on them, but interrogators might come up with some information. The team thought it a very successful night.

The next morning, a hot breakfast was sent out.

"Hey, Rough, can you believe hot chow? Man, this makes my stomach happy, and it beats the hell out of the fuckin' C-rats."

"Rat, don't you think of anything but food?"

"Yeah, like getting out of this damn war alive!"

"Amen to that!" I answered.

After breaking camp, we walked about three clicks out and around the southwest corner of the village. We looked for evidence of the VC. It turned out to be a quiet day with no results.

The CO found another good spot for an ambush. We set up our night defensive position and he assigned Squads One and Four for the Tiger Alphas.

Squad Four? Blast, that's us.

"I'm ready to be on a TA tonight; I want some damned action."

"Joe, you're an idiot. Why, in the name of all that's holy, do you want to go on an ambush?" I asked, "These guys are using real ammo and they want to kill us for God's sake!"

This young guy wants action. All I want is a nice warm bed and a quiet night. I must be getting old, and I hope to get much older.

Food and water were brought out by chopper. It seemed dumb to us. Wouldn't it give our position away? Oh, well … We needed to get the ambushes set before the VC started their movement, so the two TAs were sent out about 1830.

At 2130, a VC patrol came stumbling through Squad One's position. After the first volley of shots were fired by both sides, seven VC were captured, two of whom were slightly wounded. Everyone on the TA was safe, but scared. Thank God my TA hadn't encountered anyone.

"I'm kind of glad we didn't have company last night," Joe said at breakfast the next morning.

"What happened to the guy who was 'ready for some action'?" I asked. "Did you forget your rifle or something?"

"Aw, screw you, Rough!" Joe grumbled. "I forgot my damn ammo clips."

I had a good tension-easing belly laugh. It felt good, but I was sure Joe didn't appreciate it.

* * *

We were getting to know the area well. We looked for anything that might seem out of place or different from the day before.

On our fourth day, some of the guys went into the village to get water. The locals caught the rainwater off the roofs in large earthen urns. As we filled our canteens, each man dropped in a purification tablet. I don't know if they did much good, but the army thought so.

While there, our Kit Carson scout was approached by one of the village elders. He told us to set up our ambush in a particular area where we would find *beaucoup* VC.

We didn't always believe this source of information, since the VC often controlled the villagers. However, this elder confirmed some of our own reports.

Command told us to set up our night defense and several Tiger Alphas there in hopes of finding the large numbers of elusive VC.

The patrol was to head into the area the village elder had suggested. I didn't want to go home in a body bag because I ran out of rounds for my M-16, so I took five extra magazines giving me five hundred rounds and three hand grenades. I wasn't taking any chances, not with my life. I also bugged Joe about not forgetting anything. He had a few choice things to say to me as a thank you.

On this operation, the CO ordered Second and Third Squads to set up two ambush positions, each manned by twenty men.

Whew, my squad would stay back; but I kept the extra supplies in case the TAs missed and the VC attacked us.

The terrain was best suited for an L-shaped ambush. Each TA used the short side of the L to let any VC pass them and walk into the major killing zone along the long side. They could then take out any enemy who tried to retreat in their direction. That's the way it was supposed to work, but sometimes the gook army wasn't on the same page of the playbook we were using.

Fourth Squad was happy to pull night defense at the company's position. While setting up our NDP, the LT stopped me. "Rough, set up a guard rotation and be prepared to help either of the two TAs. From what your lieutenant had to say about you and your crew, you can do this job without my needing to tell you every move."

"Roger, LT," I replied.

Our LT actually had something good to say about us? I was in shock!

"Hey, Rough, when and where do you want me to stand guard?" Mac asked, shaking me out of my reverie.

"We're pulling two-hour shifts tonight, so how about taking the first one at nineteen-hundred? Then wake the man to your right. And, Mac, I said two hours."

"Shit, Rough, I wouldn't short my shift."

I assigned the rest of the guys and sat down to eat.

"Man, I hate this warm, rusty, shitty-tasting excuse for water. I plan to keep large pitchers of pure, clean, cold stuff in the refrigerator when I get home," Joe said taking a drink from his canteen.

"Yeah, I keep telling my Lu it's all the little things I miss."

"Your wife must be some kind of woman. I envy you, Rough," Joe continued. "I thought I had lots of time to meet the right girl, but Uncle Sam had other ideas. Before I could catch my breath, I was on the bird with you heading here."

"There'll be time to find the right one when you get out, you'll see."

I hope and pray I'm right.

I went to my assigned spot for the night and checked my watch. It was 2030. If the VC kept to their usual timetable, movement would begin in the next hour. The men were trying to catch a few minutes of sleep, but we were all too anxious to relax.

I felt alone as I stared into the void. The night was inky dark and rain clouds covered the stars and the moon. It reminded me of the trip Lu and I took to Carlsbad Caverns in New Mexico. At one point on the tour down through the bowels of the earth, the lights were turned off. We found ourselves in a scary world totally without illumination. It was an unsettling experience.

On this still and quiet night, there was only the constant drone of the mosquitoes. No one spoke or moved. There was just the loud beating of our own hearts in our ears, thumping, thumping away at a frantic pace.

Fear waited with us. Deep-down-bone-chilling-sweaty-palms-made-you-want-to-puke fear consumed every man. We knew this could be our last night on earth. None of us wanted to die in this horrible, god-forsaken country, so far away from home and family.

The dying part was something we rarely talked about. To speak of it just might bring it too close. You know the old saying, "from my lips to God's ear." Well, we didn't want the idea anywhere God might think it was a request or a prayer. The only prayer we wanted Him to hear was that we all got home safely.

The quiet was shattered when one of our Tiger Alphas detonated a Claymore mine. It was followed by the sound of their machine guns opening up. It was Tiger Alpha Two to our right about three hundred meters.

The radio came to life. "Zero-One, Tiger-Alpha-Two, we have contact, about fifteen Victor Charlies," an excited voice boomed. "Most were taken out by the Claymore and M-60s. The rest threw down their weapons and were captured, over."

"Tiger-Alpha-Two, Zero-One-X-ray. The Charlie Oscar wants them live. Bring prisoners in come morning."

"Roger, bringing in prisoners come morning."

"Roger, Zero-One, out."

The radio became silent and so did the night. Our hearts pounded and our breathing was labored. It was over in a matter of minutes, but it had seemed like hours.

We tried to sleep, but the adrenalin was still pumping.

We didn't have more than an hour until the radio crackled alive again. "Zero-One, Tiger-Alpha-One-X-ray, over," whispered the RTO.

"Tiger-Alpha-One, Zero-One-X-ray, over."

"Zero-One, we can hear a large group of VC moving through the water-filled paddy to our right between our positions. They must think they're out here alone since they're talking and laughing and not attempting to keep quiet."

"Tiger-Alpha-One, give us the coordinates for Victor Charlies, over. Backup is on the way."

"Roger ..."

We knew a Cobra gunship would get the coordinates and arrive in one-zero mikes. Arty was also given coordinates and directed fire on the enemy position. After the firing stopped, it was a bloody mess. We killed seventeen VC and captured another thirty-five, some wounded.

When we searched the bodies in the light of the next morning, we found lots of valuable information. It had been a successful night.

We had one casualty and several wounded from Tiger Alpha One. I didn't know the man who was killed, but I'd seen him around base and while on this patrol. He'd seemed like a nice kid. I felt guilty about being glad it wasn't me.

One medevac chopper arrived and took the injured men and the body of the young soldier back to the forward hospital. Two Chinooks with a dozen MPs transported our fifty-seven captured prisoners to wherever they went for interrogation and incarceration.

Our morning meal arrived on one of the choppers. However, very few of us felt like eating. A somber mood hung in the air.

The CO issued orders for us to break camp and start on patrol. We did some mop-up where the big firefight had been, and then we were off again.

The next few days were very quiet. We didn't encounter any VC. The platoon was exhausted when we received orders to return one day early. We were close to Fishnet, so we humped back. It gave us time to reflect on the big firefight and to give thanks that we were still alive.

We'd taken out over eighty VC, a quarter of them dead. The six-day patrol was successful, I guess, but it cost us one man. Two more sustained major wounds and were headed home. Seven had minor injuries and would be treated and then sent back into action.

When the protective walls came into view, we all dreamed of hot showers and much-needed sleep. We wouldn't have duty for twelve hours. I just wanted to clean up, get some sleep and write home. Thank God there were several letters from Lu.

* * *

Hi honey,

Well, we're back and I have lots of stuff to tell you. I'm sorry I didn't write to you yesterday, but after our long walk back to base, I took a shower and laid down for a nap. The next thing I knew it was dark, and I had missed dinner.

I'll tell you about the patrol in another letter. I need to do some thinking about what happened before I put it into words. It's enough to say I'm back in one piece, so don't worry about me, love; I'm fine, really.

The monsoons have started. It only rained thirty minutes last night, but the way it works over here is funny. As the days pass, it rains earlier and earlier until it comes down all day and night. This goes on for five to six months. Of course the heat doesn't let up until evening, and then it gets downright cold.

I'm sure you heard Nixon's speech today. Even though he said he would be pulling troops out of South Vietnam, it won't be the 199th. There are only three main elements south of Saigon: the Ninth Infantry, the Twenty-Fifth Infantry, and the 199th with a few supporting groups. It would be nice, but not likely, so don't get your hopes up.

You have probably also heard on the news things have been popping all around Saigon. You needn't worry; the VC seem to keep out of our way.

I did get to the PX in Saigon this morning. It'll be the last time in a long while. I was there for about thirty minutes, just enough time to buy a box of envelopes, writing paper, and a case of A&W Root Beer. Our CO likes it, too.

Saigon is one big mess. It's even worse than what I remember of "TJ" in Mexico. Most of the buildings are really run down. Quite a few places have been blown apart. It's not a nice place to visit except to get away from here for a short time.

Well, I need to get ready for guard. We haven't had any kind of duty for a while, but the time has come.

I love you so much, and I will hold you and love you for the rest of my life. Whoever wrote "war is hell" can't even imagine what hell war can really be if he never fought in Vietnam. I'm sorry to lay this on you, but sometimes I just need your strength and your love to get me through the days and nights.

Knowing you are at home waiting for me makes me the luckiest man on earth. I love you and I won't forget my promise to you!

Love, Len, Your husband and lover

* * *

"I've been screwed again! My friends, my buddies have screwed with me for the last time!"

"What are you talking about, Joe?" I asked.

"You're not going to believe this, but when we were out on the patrol with First Platoon, our buddies from Fourth stole our Coke rations. That's what I'm talking about!"

"Joe, calm down, we should get a new ration tomor …"

"I don't give a damn. First of all, I can't have a fuckin' beer and now my buddies have stolen *my* fuckin' Cokes, the damn buddy fuckers."

"Hey, you're just tired from the patrol. Take a day to relax. We'll get the new week's ration and everything will be okay, you'll see." I tried to put things into perspective.

"Yeah, well from now on I'm going to think of me as number one, and to hell with anybody else. I've just figured out my nickname for this damn war. From now on call me 'Buddy Fucker' because that's what I'll be doing. I'm going to pay those guys back for screwing me over. They've messed with the wrong Italian."

He took off mumbling to himself, kicking at the dirt as he headed back to his hooch. I was glad he wasn't mad at me.

* * *

A few days later at our morning meeting, Wild Bill said, "Hey, LT, I've heard brigade is thinkin' about movin' Bravo somewheres else."

"Yes, the CO told me that last night. Word sure travels fast."

He had my attention.

"We need to be ready to go by the end of the week."

"Roger, LT," Bill replied.

* * *

At 0800, Saturday morning, we were loaded onto trucks for the move to the Binh Dien Bridge. It was located southwest of Saigon and very close to Fire Support Base Jeanie. Guarding a bridge over a major river would be a different and, we hoped, interesting duty.

Chapter 19 - The Bridge

We heard Top over the roar of the truck engines, "Move it out!" Lurching into motion, leaving a dusty trail of red dirt, our time at brigades' main headquarters at the Fishnet Factory ended. Once out the gate, we were on a paved but potholed road. The trucks dodged to avoid them. When we weren't swerving, we were treated to some body-jarring bumps. The trucker managed to avoid humans, bikes, mopeds, and everything else straying in front of him. When we slowed down, the ever-present boys were there hawking their sisters as "the best fuck in Saigon" and "the number one whore."

Finally, we crossed the Binh Dien Bridge over a nameless, muddy, dirty sewer of a river.

Everyone had been informed of the rules of engagement for the bridge. There were businesses and some small hamlets along the road in either direction. People moved about at all times, day and night. We couldn't shoot at anything that stirred, but we also had to be watchful for anyone or anything which might be a threat.

Fishnet and Jeanie were mostly free-fire zones. Anything moving after dark could be blown away. The only exception was the street side of Fishnet, but we had our lights to illuminate the area.

"Great, not only do we have to keep an eye out for the bad guys, but now we have to wait until someone takes a shot at us before we can return fire," Mugs complained.

"Damn ROE," Wild Bill muttered.

The LT heard the comments. "None of us likes the idea of letting some gook take a free shot, but you will abide by the rules." Abitchie glared at us. "Do I make myself clear?"

"Roger," we reluctantly acknowledged.

He continued, "Sandbags will be trucked out here tomorrow to rebuild our blast walls and sleeping bunkers."

"That's good, because these things are in shitty shape," Joe pointed out.

"For tonight, you'll just have to make do with minor repairs," the LT said as he walked away.

"Minor repairs! Now that's a joke," Mugs complained.

"We ain't got much time afore dark so y'all'd better get your asses in gear," Bill ordered.

"I'll bet there are a lot of fuckin' rats in this shit hole."

"What's the matter, Rat? Don't you want another run-in with your good buddies?" Joe asked with a little laugh.

He was referring to the time at Jeanie when Pat (his given name) had been bitten by one of those big suckers. He'd spent a couple of days getting rabies shots at brigade's hospital, hence his nickname.

"You won't think it's so damn funny if one of those suckers takes a liking to some part of your anatomy. Those fuckin' shots were a pain. Time out of the field wasn't worth all the hell I had to go through in the hospital. You can be sure my forty-five will be close."

"Where did you get a forty-five? Are you planning to carry the radio?" Dan asked.

It was standard procedure for the RTOs (radiotelephone operators) to carry a 45-caliber pistol. It weighed less and was easier to carry with the PRC-25, its extra batteries, food and water. He didn't always have two free hands to fire his M-16. Still, most RTOs elected to carry the heavier weapon in favor of better firepower over the pistol.

"It's none of your fuckin' business where I got it. But, I found it lying in the shower room back at brigade. No one else was around, and it looked like it had my name on it, so beware, rats!" Rat shook his fists at the absentee rodents.

"You're an idiot," I yelled.

We argued often as an outlet for our nervous energy. But just let someone outside try to mess with anyone from the Fourth or Bravo Company, and then there'd be hell to pay. We'd stick together like red Vietnamese mud.

We found a large sleeping area, which was to become known as the Hotel. Whoever built it had done extra work using empty ammo boxes filled with dirt for the walls and added sandbags for further protection. It was an easy way to build and provided a cool place during the day.

However, our first night exposed a major design flaw: when the rains came, the roof leaked like a sieve.

* * *

We were all standing around after breakfast the next morning assessing what part to work on first when Wild Bill walked into the group. "Hey, y'all, the LT has called for a platoon meetin' at HQ in ten mikes."

The LT began the meeting by giving us our assignments and duties. "This is an important road into Saigon. We're to make sure nothing gets to the bridge which can blow the damn thing to pieces.

"I know the river is dark and muddy, not clear enough to see anything below the surface. During the day, we'll get in a little target practice using up old ammo to blow away anything larger than a tennis ball floating down the river. After dark, we'll drop a few grenades just to be sure there aren't any VC underwater with explosives. Questions?"

"Are we going to have round-the-clock guard duty on the bridge?" I asked.

"The company will, but since we're expected to be standing by the mortars for orders to fire at night, Fourth Platoon will only supply a few men, mostly during the day."

"What about the FDC? Are we still plotting the TAs?"

"Don't worry, Dan, the FDC will be reconstructed and you'll do your job."

"Who'll schedule the guard rotation?" I asked.

"Bill will do it. He and I will discuss the requirements."

"Ah ... LT," Joe spoke up, "I passed Top on the way here. He told me our sandbags will be at the command post around 1400 today. We'll need men there to help unload and to pick up our share."

"Rat, Mugs, and Rough, go with Joe to get our supplies."

"Roger, LT," I answered for the others.

"Remember, these are civilians, the ones we've been sent here to protect. So act accordingly!"

"Right, LT," we all mumbled.

"Dismissed."

* * *

"Man, if I could get my hands on Alpha Company, they'd be in a world of hurt," Rat said.

"How could they let their AO get so out of shape?" Joe stood looking around and shaking his head.

"We'll need to start at the foundation and work our way up. Might as well have started from scratch, at least then we wouldn't have to tear it down first," I complained.

The men argued almost the whole time about how the work should be done. We bickered and complained, cussed and discussed, but we knew our jobs. When we finished the rebuilding, it would be the best.

As we walked to the command post to get our supplies, Mugs said, "I'm glad we're finally getting filled sandbags. I can't believe we're not doing that job."

"Mugs, how long have you been in Vietnam?" I asked.

"Eight months, twenty-one days, and …," he looked at his watch, "four hours and thirty-two minutes. Why?"

"And in all that time, has brigade ever sent out filled sandbags to any base?"

"No, this will be a first."

"No, this will not be a first … the bags are empty. WE have the pleasure of filling them!" I chuckled.

Mugs walked ahead of the group to hide his chagrin.

"The friggin' rain last night proved how much work the Hotel needs," Joe said.

"That was rain? I thought we must have been transported under Niagara Falls the way the water came through the roof," I added.

"You know, Rough, I remember seeing something just laying around back at the Fishnet, which might solve our leaking problem." Joe looked around to be sure he wasn't being overheard.

"I know it won't be long before Doc needs to go there for supplies," Dan reminded us.

"Doc, when you go back to Fishnet, ask for Rough and me to go along for security. It'll be a good excuse for taking us."

"I feel like you're up to something. Could you be thinking about picking up some building supplies while we're there?" I innocently asked.

My answer was his devilish grin.

"In fact, I need to go next week. I'll let you guys know when the trip is scheduled."

"Thanks, Doc," Joe said with a smile.

* * *

Meals were a challenge. We thought anything would be better than C-rations. We were wrong. Our meals were trucked in. Large corrugated metal containers were supposed to keep things hot or cold (more like warm and cool).

The contents weren't always easy to identify by taste, appearance, or consistency. We thought for breakfast we had scrambled eggs and some type of meat. Lunch was a sandwich. We all debated whether it was chicken, tuna, or deviled ham. The bread was smashed together and stuck to the filling. We had only water to drink, as our rations of Coke and beer hadn't arrived. And this was only the first day!

Brigade had to send out tanks with drinking water since no amount of purification pills would make the river water safe. Even the people living there got their drinking water from the rain runoff they caught in large urns.

* * *

Hi honey,

We left by truck for the Binh Dien Bridge two days ago. I think its on the map I sent you. The VC would like to knock out this main artery leading into Saigon.

There's a lot of building for us to do. Boy, this place is a real mess. There isn't a bunker or mortar pit that doesn't need to be taken down and rebuilt.

I was on guard when Apollo 10 came down. We get the news without TVs to watch. It's really fantastic what the US is doing. We heard everything went very well.

I was sent as a shotgun for a chaplain going to Jeanie yesterday. The base had gotten into a firefight the night before and needed some spiritual help. It looked like it had taken a real beating. I was glad we'd moved.

Duty at the bridge is supposed to be a good job, but so far I have my doubts. We are lucky enough to be on the good side of the bridge. The platoon on the other side gets a terrible smell from the sewage in the river.

About 2:00 PM today it started raining again. We hadn't had a shower since leaving Fishnet, so about fifteen of us stood out in the downpour. It was really a sight!

How's my number one kid? I love you and I worry about you taking care of yourself. I don't understand why two people with so much love have to be separated. It makes it hell for both of us. There are so many things we could be doing together. It's such a waste.

Only four months until I can hold you and love you on R and R in Hawaii. I'll come back to finish my tour here, then its home for good.

I send my love to you every night. I wish I could reach out and take you in my arms and hold you. When I snuggle next to you, I find a heat that warms more than just my body. It goes down to my very soul. God, I love you.

Remember my promise.

Love, your lover and husband, Len

* * *

A few days later, Doc wandered over. "Hey guys, I've been thinking."

"That could lead to trouble, Doc!" Joe said, ribbing the kid.

"Since there's water close at hand, I was just wondering ..."

"You don't mean the river?" Mugs asked.

"Keep your fly traps closed for a couple of minutes and hear me out," he said.

"Go on, Doc. What's your idea?" I asked to encourage him.

"We don't have a pool of water like we had at Jeanie, but we get lots of rainwater every night. I think we could make a stall shower right here in the platoon area. It would take work, though. We'd need some pallets for a floor, and two-by-fours and plywood from the mortar crates for walls. I saw some large empty drums just sitting near the bridge. We use them to catch rainwater, let it heat during the day. We dump the warm water into a drum with holes poked in the bottom, set on a high platform above us, and guess what? We have a shower!"

That's the most I ever heard the kid say at one time.

"Sounds better than showering in the rain," I replied.

"It would also be a lot of fuckin' work," Rat said, complaining as usual.

"I think a little work would be well worth the chance to get really clean. Let's do it," said Joe.

"All right. First we need to rescue some fifty-five-gallon drums. We might as well keep them from disappearing into the village and put them to good use for ourselves," Dan suggested.

Doc reminded us, "They're down by the bridge."

"Let's get the pallets and mortar boxes. And we'll look for any other supplies we need," Mugs said, as he picked up part of a packing crate.

Joe took off with Mac and Dan to rescue five or six drums.

"How about a hand here," Joe called out as the men returned rolling three metal containers.

Of course, being smart asses, we clapped and cheered.

"How 'bout a standin' ovation for these brave men?" Wild Bill shouted out over the noise.

"Okay, assholes, you're the last animals who get to use it. No work means no showers," Joe yelled back.

"All right, don't get so uptight. You asked for a hand. We threw in the cheers and the ovation for free," Mugs said with a laugh as he moved to help.

"Hey, guys, scuttlebutt has it that LT is going on R and R in a few days. So I was thinking, if we waited until he left, we could do the work then and no one would know."

"Doc, you are an absolute genius!"

"Thanks, Rough, I need to hear a compliment once in a while," he said as he glanced at the rest of the platoon.

"Anytime, kid, anytime," I said, remembering he was only eighteen. *God, was it nearly six years ago I was that age? Where had the time gone?*

We set to work hiding the drums. Joe and his crew of scroungers returned with two more and also supplied two-by-fours and the hammer and nails. Where they came from I wouldn't venture to guess, and didn't care.

The shower was going to be very welcome. The rain had produced lots of red, sticky, stinky mud. It clung to everything we owned and every part of our bodies. Washing with soap and clean water would be heaven!

* * *

With all the movement after dark, everyone was on edge. We found it hard to fault Mac the night he opened up on someone running across the road about a hundred meters from our bunker.

"Just who the fuck is taking pot shots at this time of night?" the LT yelled, climbing out of his hooch trying to stick his helmet on his head.

Mac had popped off about five rounds. Thankfully, he had his M-16 on single shot and not automatic. The LT was really pissed when we found the poor gook hiding behind a clump of palms. Mac had ruined his night of amour. Bet he wouldn't be running around after dark again.

The next morning, the CO called in our lieutenant. We could hear him yelling, "Don't you have any control over those guys in the Fourth Platoon? One more fuck-up and it will be a long while before they see anything but Tiger Alphas. Do I make myself clear?"

"Wilco. This will be the last time. I guarantee it," we heard LT reply.

After this dressing down by the CO, the LT called the platoon together. "My butt's on the line. You assholes screw up one more time and we're all in deep shit! Top needs men for Tiger Alphas and you could all be out there. As most of you know, I'm leaving tomorrow afternoon for my second week of R and R. I expect this area to be rebuilt and brought up to my usual standards while I'm gone. I've vouched for you guys. So don't screw me!"

"Roger, LT. We'll wait 'til someone shoots at our asses. Then can we blow the bastards away?"

"Stop being a fucking smart ass, Bill, and get this area in shape."

After the meeting, Joe whispered sarcastically on the walk back to our area, "A whole week without Abitchie. I don't know if I can stand the separation."

Everyone chuckled.

* * *

Doc scheduled his trip to Fishnet two days later. The VC had been firing on American vehicles, so Top told him to take two men for security.

"Okay, Joe, your plan's in motion. We'll leave right after lunch. You and Rough have been assigned to ride shotgun."

"We're ready," Joe said with a grin.

Doc drove through the streets of Saigon like it was the Indy five hundred. He didn't want to be in the city any longer than necessary.

When we arrived, Joe told Doc, "We'll see you right over there." The place wasn't far from the gate, but out of sight of the guards.

"How much time you gonna need, Joe?"

"Twenty-five minutes ought to do it. Can you give us that long?"

"No problem. That's 1400 by my watch," he replied.

"Well, 1400 it is. Let's go, Rough." Joe and I went one way while Doc went another.

As we walked, I asked, "So what now?"

He just smiled and took off. It soon dawned on me we were headed to the chopper parking area.

"Great, its still here!" he said pointing off to one side at a rolled-up rubber landing pad. "Luck's on our side once again. The chopper's gone so there's no guard on duty out front. It hasn't moved an inch since last time I was here. I don't think they're planning to use it, so ..."

"Are you thinking what I think you're thinking?"

"You bet your green ass I am, and I can't think of a better use for it. Can you?" he questioned. "After all, it's just sitting there rotting in the sun, and we wouldn't want that to happen, would we?"

"No, of course not," I answered his rhetorical question.

"Now all we have to do is go over, pick the thing up, and take it back to where we're meeting Doc. Just act like we're doing something we've been ordered to do, Rough, and no one will even think twice about us carrying the thing away."

He was right. Not one person gave us a second look. We were just some dumb jerks on some stupid detail, or we wouldn't be carrying the heavy thing on our own, would we?

"Hey, Rough, here comes Doc. Get ready to toss this thing on the jeep. We'll cover it and his supplies with the tarp and just drive out the gate. No problem!"

Doc came to a stop. With a great heave, we tossed the pad up and onto the jeep.

"Let's get the fuck out of here," Joe yelled at Doc.

We tried to cover the pad with a tarp while flying down the road. It must have been a funny sight, but amazingly none of the guards paid any attention to those who were leaving.

We got the attention of Bill, Rat, and Mugs when we arrived back at the bridge, though. "While we were guarding this vehicle, something fell onto it and needs to be removed now. We wouldn't want Top to see it," Joe said.

It didn't take long before the pad was out of the jeep and into the Hotel where it was safe from prying eyes.

The next morning, we began repairs on our sleeping quarters. We figured there was no need to take it completely apart. We pulled the old sandbags from one side and started the mat there. As we unrolled it over the top, we covered it with the old bags we'd removed. When we finished the process, the whole thing was hidden, and the roof looked like it had before we started. It took four hours with everyone working. The idea of being dry while sleeping that night was a great incentive.

To finish the Hotel, we'd add another row of sandbags to the roof. But for now, we needed to begin work on the mortar pits and ammo bunkers. Our very lives could be at stake from either the VC or an angry LT if they weren't completed.

* * *

Morning came too early. We had to be up, dressed, fed, and in our places at 0600. The crowd of human flesh was already lined up to cross the bridge and backed up for a quarter mile or more. They were waiting for the blockade to lift so they could descend upon the streets of Saigon.

We knew there had to be some VC mixed in with the regular citizens, but we didn't know who they were. Most of these people looked like the enemy to us. The ARVNs weren't any better at detecting the VC than we were.

The Americans would stand off to the side of the road while the ARVNs walked though the crowd, looking for anything suspicious. It was a rare situation when someone was stopped, checked closely, and a VC suspect weeded out. But even this was done haphazardly. Our job was only to help the ARVNs, when asked, and keep it orderly. We wanted them to do their jobs without our assistance. It was their country; it should have been their war, not ours.

Masses passed over the bridge, on foot, on bikes, and on mopeds, inbound in the morning and outbound in the afternoon. The bridge closed at sundown, except for some military traffic.

Horns honked, engines revved, and people yelled, impatient to get through the gates and into the city.

Finally, at 0800, an ARVN officer yelled, "Open the gate!" over the roar. It was like the start of some marathon as the roadblock was lifted. We held our breaths until the last of the mob was on the other side.

No VC had been able to plant any explosives during the night, so the bridge was safe for the start of one more day, and life went on as usual for these people trying to eke out an existence in Saigon.

Chapter 20 – Bored at the Bridge

While the LT was on R and R for a week, we finished two smaller ammo bunkers, two of the three mortar pits, and had the roof and one side of the large sleeping bunker completed.

We also managed to build the shower, much to Doc's delight, and it was great! The water warmed in the black drums sitting in the direct sun all day. It felt good after our hard, sweaty workday, and worth the extra time and energy needed to get the water up to the shower drum.

It was amazing how much we could get done when we didn't have the constant harassment from the LT. We hadn't realized how much of a pain he was until he was gone.

* * *

"Rough, have you had a chance to talk to the young girl always near the water urns?" Joe asked me one day during a downtime around the platoon area.

"Yes, I spoke to her just this morning. From what I could understand with my pidgin English and hers, she's thirteen years old. I think she said, 'If only the Americans would go back to America and the commies go back north where they came from, maybe the war would go away.'"

"Not very fuckin' likely," Joe responded.

"I know. What hurts most, here's a girl of thirteen who has known nothing but war all her life. A life of being afraid the VC could come at any time to kill her father, rape and kill her mother, and maybe even rape her. We're the only protection she has. It's crazy!"

"I know, Rough. If there's any reason for the US to be in this fuckin' war, this is one of them," Joe added.

"As much as I hate this war, if we could give this country back to its people without communist domination, it would be worth it. I worked with kids before being drafted and the thought of any child, any person, living in constant fear is enough to piss me off."

"I'm glad you feel the same as me," Joe commented. "Well, I've got to get to guard duty, talk to you later."

* * *

One thing I really hated was the monotony as the days crawled slowly by. There was little action at the bridge, nothing like we had been told to expect. We were only assigned to firing the mortars and hadn't received a call in over a week. Except for the boredom, it would have been okay by me to go without any action during our stay.

It wasn't long before Bravo took up target practice to replace the monotony. We justified shooting at anything floating toward the pilings of the bridge, by our original orders from the LT. We fired during the day and at night. With generator-powered lights, we could see well enough to hit stuff floating downriver.

One afternoon, about a week after he got back, the lieutenant called us all together. It seemed some of the residents had been complaining to the CO about our target practice. "You damn boneheads, Top was on my ass about you taking potshots off the bridge. He said, 'Since you characters have so much time to waste, I need to conduct an inspection around this fuckin' place.' His words, not mine. By tomorrow at 0900, you'd better have everything, including your rifles, ready for inspection."

"Roger, LT. We'll be ready," Bill answered.

"Roger, LT," Joe mimicked while he walked away. "What a fuckin' nightmare!"

"Can you believe this shit? Inspections in the middle of a goddamn war," Mugs grumbled.

"Not a damn thang we can do about it, but I know Top. He thinks he'll have enough men for the shit can burnin' detail come 0900." Bill put into words what we all thought.

"You don't think he expects Fourth Platoon to pass, do you?" Joe asked.

Bill replied, "We're gonna have to work our tails off, so let's get started, and that includes cleanin' our M-16s."

"I haven't cleaned my rifle since we got to the bridge. I'm not sure I remember how," I kidded.

"It's like riding a tricycle; you never forget," Mugs clowned, and we laughed.

"We'll do the best we can and hope he's in a good mood," I replied. "Remember, no firing off the bridge tonight. However, we can still drop a couple of grenades to keep Charlie in his place and out of the river."

We'd all be in for it if we didn't pass the stupid inspection.

I removed the rounds, opened up my rifle, and took a good long look down the barrel. It was dirty, and rusted as well. *Oh, God, I fired it this morning.* "Joe, you ought to see inside this thing. It looks like it has jungle rot."

"I know what you mean. We've all been lucky one didn't blow up. You can be sure I'll take better care of mine from now on," Joe mumbled.

"Maybe it's a good thing Top called for this inspection," I replied. "I need to keep things in better fighting shape."

The day passed quickly as we worked side by side. We must have done a creditable job, as Top passed us, although we all suspected he was disappointed. No guys from Fourth for his lousy detail.

* * *

The next night was busy as Gun One was called on for four fire missions. We also had two timed tests to see if we could get the gun up and ready to fire fast enough. LT wanted to make sure we were still in top form.

A couple of calls were for H & Is. We were attempting to harass and interrupt the flow of the VC in the area. It took two hours to fire both sets. We fired several rounds, waited ten to fifteen minutes, and fired three or four more. With the irregular pattern of firing, the gooks wouldn't know when it was safe to move.

No one within a couple hundred meters could possibly have slept through all the firing. Even though we stuck our fingers in our ears, when the round went down, they would ring for hours afterwards.

The next morning, Dan stopped me. "Rough, the LT wants you to learn the job in the FDC."

"Roger, professor, I'll report after dinner tonight."

"You might want to get some sleep this afternoon; you'll be working all night," he commented as he walked away.

The LT wanted everyone to be able to do each and every job. We never knew when it might be necessary for one of us to fill in for a fallen member of the platoon.

* * *

Hi honey,

I get a pay raise in July to $155, which includes my regular pay, hazardous duty, and overseas pay. Wow! Well, at least I can send you more to put away for R and R and to live on.

I've been working in the FDC and sleeping during the day. I learned enough in two nights to work in there if needed.

We pull four hours of guard a night and are on 100 percent alert until 11:00 PM. Last night I slept a whole eight hours. I really miss your body next to me when I sleep. I just can't get used to being so far away. Time passes slowly. When I look to the future, it seems like forever before we'll be together again.

During the day I look forward to mail call. After that, I sleep until dinner and then get ready for the night.

The weather is hot, mucky, and rainy. All of it comes at one time.

My wish list for the next package: tape recorder, film, cans of peaches, tuna, small jar mayonnaise, potato chips, razor blades, powdered milk, instant breakfast, beef jerky, jelly beans, M&Ms, peanut M&Ms, and other kinds of snacks, you, your love, and anything else you can think of to make life bearable.

Honey, I can hardly wait to get home to hug you. I want to buy a house, start a family, and change jobs. I hope we get started on either Jeff or Sandra during R and R. Think about the area we want to live in and have your brother send me info on the police force there. I've decided to become a cop, if you agree, of course.

We'll talk about our future together while in Hawaii. It's still looking like R and R will be October, so give me the best dates.

I've been getting some good pictures. I try and get myself in as many as I can. I think that's what you want. I'll tell you about them when I see you.

Thank you for the flag and the reminder of Flag Day coming up on the fourteenth. It will proudly stand over every firebase from now on. Well, at least over the mortar platoon.

I'm sure you've heard about the men being pulled out of Vietnam. Since the 199th isn't one of the units going home, don't get your hopes up that I'll be home soon.

We're still having a quiet time around here. It's funny though, we can sit on our bunkers watching and listening to the choppers in other areas having contact. Of course I'm not going to complain.

Well, that about does it except for one thing. It's about time for me to let you know how much I love you. I do love you with all my heart. Knowing that, we can make it through anything, even this separation.

I'll love you always and forever. Remember my promise to you.

Love Len, Your husband and lover

* * *

"Quack, quack, quack," I said.

"Quack, quack, quack," Joe echoed.

"Quack, quack, quack," Ole added.

"Quack, quack, quack," Mac joined the chorus.

"Quack, quack, quack," Rat completed our ensemble.

All of us were being smart asses as we walked past the guys on Gun One.

"All right, you fuckin' assholes. We was just followin' orders," Bill yelled at the parade of hecklers. "We didn't make no damn call to fire on a bunch of blips on radar. It twern't our fault it turned out to be a bunch of ducks! It was them stupid REMFs! They cain't tell the difference between a gook and a duck."

We weren't about to let Gun One forget about firing on the ducks. We finally had something to hold over their heads and quacked every time we walked by.

* * *

One day at lunch, I started thinking of home. I imagined Lu fixing some real food like she did before I was sent to this hellhole. It wasn't C-rats. It was delicious, and she made it from scratch. She's a great cook, and time couldn't pass fast enough for me to get back to her loving arms and wonderful meals.

"Rough, you're thinking too hard about something, or should I say someone?" Joe sat down next to me on the mortar pit blast wall. "It must have been a sexy thought of your wife with that grin plastered on your face."

"You're probably not going to believe this, but I was daydreaming about Lu's cooking."

"Was she naked while in the kitchen?"

"I'm not going to answer that question. And no, I'm not going to leave it up to your imagination either!"

"Got it, Rough, private, hands-off stuff!"

I changed the subject. "I was sitting here wondering about R and R in Hawaii. I hope the bigwigs haven't taken all the spots for themselves."

"I'm sure your wife's looking forward to meeting you in that tropical paradise. By the way, have you told her about your little plan of extending for thirty days in Vietnam so you can get an early out when you get back to the World?"

"No, I'll wait until we're together in Hawaii."

"Yeah, sure! Who are you trying to kid?"

"I do need to talk to her about it. She's still a little miffed at me for turning down OCS before discussing it with her. I'll make sure she knows this time."

"You wouldn't want to lose your happy home."

"Joe, I just can't see putting up with all the bull of six months' stateside duty. By staying in this hellhole for an extra thirty days, I'll be processed out of the army at Travis. I dream of the day when I walk off the plane into Lu's arms to stay forever."

"Is your plan to get a position in the rear and become a REMF for those thirty days?"

"You bet. I'd do anything to get out early, though I'm not sure Lu will see it that way. She'll probably want me home where it's safer."

"Good luck, but, you can't blame her for wanting you out of Vietnam."

"I know you're right." I looked at my watch. "I have guard. Talk to you later, Joe."

* * *

"Hey, Rough, the LT wants to see all the crew chiefs ASAP," Dan said one afternoon about four weeks after we arrived at the bridge.

"Maybe this will be good news," I said as Wild Bill joined us.

"With our luck the word'll be that we have to get ready for a cordon or somethin'," Bill replied.

The LT began, "On June eighteenth, Bravo Company will have a stand-down at BMB. Three days out of this fuckin' pit. No night firing, no Tiger Alphas, and no guard duty. We need to heal some of our wounds and try to get the company up to strength."

Our CO, Captain Scott, was rotating home for the second time. We would miss him. He was smart and usually had our safety at heart when making his decisions. Unfortunately, our LT would remain a few weeks longer.

"Our new CO doesn't want you getting too soft, so there will be some jungle training."

Moans and groans followed that statement from LT.

"Dan, we'll have TAs out the next two nights. Tell your crew they can pack up the FDC as soon as the TAs are targeted tomorrow evening. See my RTO for the coordinates on the ambushes."

"Roger, I'll get right on it, LT," Dan replied.

"We'll have to wait until the following morning before dismantling and packing the mortar tubes, Bill."

"Roger, LT," Bill acknowledged.

* * *

Hi honey,

Happy Birthday! I haven't been anywhere to get a card or a present, but I didn't forget. I love you, and I'm still fine. Those are the two best gifts I can give you. Someday I'll make up for all the things we've missed.

Well, I have some good news. We are going to brigade's main base or BMB on the eighteenth for a stand-down and a little jungle training. It means no war for three whole days. BMB is at Long Binh, about ten miles north of here, but out of an immediate war zone.

It's really protected so we can get some sleep and, better yet, some hot food. Believe me, I am ready for both! I wish I was coming home or even on R and R so I could hold you, but that time will come soon.

I hate to make this short, but we have a lot of work to do before we leave, and I want to be sure this goes out in the mail. It's getting dark, and we have to get ready for night practice. Time is sure moving slowly.

I didn't get this mailed, so here I am two days later finally finishing it.

Yesterday we left at 0700 for another firebase being given to the ARVNs. Our company spent the whole day cleaning up the mess another company left. Most of it was filling the trash hole with sand bags. We didn't get back to our camp until 1830. All we had to eat for the whole day was C-rations. By the time I finally had dinner, it was time for guard. I was just too tired after guard to write.

This is our last night at the bridge. We are supposed to have a general inspect the area before we leave tomorrow. We'll be up early again as we have to police our area. I guess they want everything perfect for the ARVNs when they move in. As for me, I don't care if the whole place falls down and the trash is three feet deep. The ARVNs haven't done a thing for us or their own country.

It seems like a lifetime before I'll be on my way home for good. Then I can hold you and tell you in person just how much I love you. Even though our country means a lot to me, I hate this separation. You are my first and most important love.

I miss you.

Love, your husband and lover, Len

* * *

Most of us didn't feel like packing C-rats when we left. There were always a few children around, boys mostly, ready to retrieve discarded items, and especially C-rations the American GIs didn't want. They'd gone without much food most of their lives, so even C-rats would be a grand meal. We opened the boxes and tossed out those items we wouldn't eat before we left. To them, it must have felt like Christmas in June.

They really liked what we call the lifer candy bar. This chocolate bar was a part of all C-rat boxes. To those of us used to a Hershey chocolate bar, this substitute tasted more like brown wax with enough preservatives to keep it a hundred years. It had probably been around since WWII. Only a lifer or these starved kids could enjoy them.

The next morning, we were up by 0500. We had our tubes down and all of our equipment packed and ready to go, and the area ready for inspection at 0900. The general took all morning and part of the afternoon. Why, was a mystery to us.

The ARVNs arrived to take over. What surprised us most was that they were on time. But, what was more astonishing was where they placed the equipment and beds. Their mortar platoon moved into the area we had just spent four weeks rebuilding. Instead of using the Hotel for sleeping, we watched as they put extra gear and supplies in our old quarters. To them, keeping the equipment dry and out of sight was better than their comfort.

They were using smaller mortar tubes than the US Army used. They took up less space. So they put their sleeping gear in the open area near the pits and ammo bunkers Bravo had used for mortar rounds.

There wasn't a changing of the guard ceremony at the Binh Dien Bridge, more like, "It's yours now," from our CO to theirs.

As soon as the inspection was finished and the ARVNs had possession, we bid farewell and climbed into the trucks for the trip to BMB.

We'd store our entire stock of ordinance while at BMB, but some of us still had grenades attached to our packs. We should have waited and added them to the company's stockpile. But, our first thought was to rid ourselves of them quickly.

Now American GIs are just boys at heart, and boys can quickly get into trouble with live weapons. All along the route, on both sides of the road out of Saigon, were rice paddies. We started lobbing the grenades into those that were water-filled. It gave us some gratification to watch them explode, sending water, muck, and little green plants into the air. What a sight!

This probably wasn't the smartest thing to do, but we were having way too much fun. That was, until Top found out. It's hard not to recognize the sound of grenades going off, even under the water. Top stopped the convoy.

"Goddamn mother fuckers, what in the hell are you doing?" Top asked as he rounded the corner of the truck. "Do you all have shit for brains? Do not, I repeat, *do not* lob grenades off the back of this truck! Do I make myself clear?"

"Roger, Top!" we reluctantly replied.

"Do I need to climb in there and baby sit your asses to make sure you don't detonate any more grenades?"

"No, Top!" we yelled.

"Boy, what a killjoy," Joe mumbled.

I wondered if Top was angrier because we were lobbing grenades or because he couldn't join us in the deed.

Chapter 21 - BMB

Wow, three whole days of rest and free time. Top told us the only things we had to do were get plenty of sleep and visit the barbershop. The first morning, we took Top at his word and slept until 0800 ... and almost missed breakfast.

It was definitely time to get a haircut and shave. We didn't have the facilities for a real haircut in the field. Once in a while, one of the locals came by with a pair of scissors and did the job.

The haircut at the barbershop only cost twenty-five cents, but the best part of the visit was the neck massage for a whole nickel more. The barbers were middle-aged Vietnamese men. *What, no exotic women to cut our hair and give us a massage? Lu would get a good chuckle at the whole thing. God, how I miss her laugh ...*

I finally got a chance to read the last of the second batch of Louis L'Amour westerns. Between the heat, humidity, and everyone reading the books, they were getting pretty ratty. We decided to leave the poor things behind in the barracks when we moved out.

* * *

"Hey, guys, we've got jungle training in about ten mikes," Joe announced, sticking his head into the barracks after lunch.

"What the hell are you taking about? We're on a rest break here, right?" Mugs asked.

Rat crossed his arms over his chest, in disgust, "Yeah, and I'm not moving!"

"Don't bother me, I'm sleeping." I turned over facing away from the door and tried to regain my dream of Lu and me on a beach in Hawaii.

"Not now, you're not. The new CO's decided its time we got jungle training. Remember, LT told us to expect this, so get your asses out of your racks and in fuckin' formation ASAP. Those are his orders."

"I'm hoping this is just general training. Fighting in the jungle would not have been my first choice of places to be, Joe."

"Agreed, Rough. Now grab your helmet and flak jacket and let's go."

"Yeah, yeah, yeah," I muttered as I pushed past him.

One of the sergeants from headquarters addressed us. "Today you will be learning how to prepare a chopper LZ in the jungle and how to insert in from a helicopter at one hundred feet above the canopy. You will learn to rappel down ropes into the jungle. Today we will practice off a platform. So get your gear and follow me."

"I told you, I heard this fucking CO wants to make Rangers out of us. Now, he's got us jumping out of choppers! What's next?" Rat grumbled.

This had us all worried. The jungle seemed bad enough. But this new CO had us scared.

* * *

Hi honey,

We are now at BMB. I told you about it in my last letter. We arrived in the late afternoon, put everything away, then ate chow and saw a live show. I just took a hot shower and got to bed at 9:30 PM.

We met our new CO. Even on this stand-down, he has us doing jungle training. We're all hoping our next firebase won't be in the jungle! Ugh! That's the worst area for patrolling, according to the guys I've talked to. We'll know in the next day or so.

We've finally finished reading the last books you sent. They really got used a lot. I think just about everyone in Fourth Platoon and some in the other platoons read them. We need more, but wait until after we move to ship another box.

This is a quiet time and I'm getting rested and eating good chow, well, better than C's. We don't even have to pull guard duty. Except for the training exercises, it's almost like being out of the war. I can dream, right?

I think I miss you more now than when I'm out in the field. I have a lot of time to think about the fun we had. Wow! It's only three and a half months until R and R. I can hardly wait to hold you in my arms again. I love you so much.

Love, Len, your husband and lover

* * *

The second night at BMB, the company held a barbeque. Everyone was treated to a real steak dinner and live entertainment. No, it wasn't Bob Hope, but the band, from Korea, sounded pretty good.

No one wanted to miss the steak dinner. It would be the first and probably our last while in Vietnam. Our company paid for the meat out of its recreation fund. The little strip steak was as tough as leather, but for us, it was a great meal.

There were a lot of suspicions about food orders. We'd heard the REMFs charged the company top price for our supplies, but bought cheap and put the extra cash in their pockets. We figured that's probably what happened with our steaks.

It really burned our butts to realize they could buy a nice steak dinner at one of the clubs any time they wanted it. But our biggest gripe was how slow they re-supplied the troops in the field.

Everyone knew there were shady dealings going on, but nothing was ever done. It added to the rift between the men in the field and the rear echelon mother fuckers.

They were also responsible for holding our money for R and R. It took seven or eight months for us to save enough, but when we got ready to go, we were often short-changed, and there wasn't anything we could do about it, either.

If these base camp bunnies had spent even one day out with us, they might have developed an appreciation for what we went through. Twenty-four hours a day, seven days a week, we placed our lives on the line fighting this nasty war, affording them the opportunity to sit on their fat keisters back in their safe area.

* * *

The three days passed by all too quickly. Right after dinner on our third night, we stopped the lieutenant. "Hey, LT, just where in the hell are they gonna truck us to tomorra?" Wild Bill asked.

"Get the other squad leaders and meet at my headquarters in twenty minutes. I'll tell you together."

"Wilco, LT," Bill and I answered.

I had an awful feeling in my gut.

Sure enough, it wasn't what we wanted to hear, but it wasn't unexpected either. "Tomorrow morning we're going to Fire Support Base Libby. It's located in the jungle about fifty miles north of here."

God, I'd hoped I was wrong. I moaned along with the others…

The LT continued, "It's a new base, so we'll build most of it from scratch."

"Well, of course, we are the Bravo Company Builders, right? I've spent so much time rebuilding firebases since being in this stinkin' country, I'm thinking of going into construction when I get home," Mugs said. The vision of Mugs with a mouth full of nails, holding a hammer, made us laugh.

"Are we goin' by truck or are we bein' flown out by choppers?" Bill asked.

"I have good news and bad news on that," the LT began. "Tomorrow, we'll be trucked most of the way, but I've been told we will have to hump it in the last six thousand meters. It should only take two days, so pack light. The CO wants us to get a little taste of working in the jungle before we make base."

He looked at us, then continued with the bad news. "The mortar platoon is going to become a foot platoon, but just for this patrol."

"Yeah, right, I knew this was gonna happen. So, what's up with the mortar tubes?" Wild Bill asked.

"The chopper will bring the heavy equipment, including the mortars, and the rest of our supplies to Libby."

"This is not going to be an easy stroll in the woods is it, LT?" Dan asked.

"That's for damn sure." He spread a map out on his desk. "We'll be trucked to this spot right about here," he said pointing to a location along a winding highway. "The company is going to be sweeping this jungle area on its way here, Firebase Libby."

There was a lot of very green territory between the two points. The legend said "dense jungle."

"Tell your squads, it's flak jackets and steel pots on this little hump."

"Roger, LT," Bill answered.

"Is there any good news?" I asked.

"Yes, there's a battery of 105s based at Libby to give us close support. If there are no other questions, you're dismissed. Get packed."

We headed back to the barracks. "Oh, hell, I've heard really bad thangs about jungle fightin' which scares the shit out of this little ol' Texas boy."

"Yeah, it's not going to be good," Dan said.

"That's the way life is. Some of us are always getting shit on."

I lightly punched Mugs' shoulder and said, "That's really philosophical."

"One more thing," Dan continued, "I've heard the heat and humidity there are worse than the rice paddies."

"Thanks, we needed to hear more good news," Mugs said sarcastically.

"Well, we'd better git our crews ready for tomorra's mission."

"Roger, Bill," we acknowledged.

We were about halfway back when the LT caught up.

"I forgot to ask, have you and the other crew chiefs been over to the armory and cleaned your mortar tubes yet?"

"Not yet."

"Goddamn it, why don't you have those fucking mortars cleaned? You knew it had to be done. I don't want them shipped out to Libby dirty."

"They've been trainin' my ass to fight in the fuckin' jungle!"

"That's no damn excuse, Bill. Now all of you get over to the armory at first light and get your jobs done!"

"Roger, LT, we'll have the tubes cleaned before we leave," I stepped in front of Bill before he completely lost it and punched the LT. He was that mad.

"The trucks will be here at 0900, so be done and have your shit ready to load by 0830! I want everybody and everything standing there when they roll in. The CO and Top are going to be pissed if we aren't, and so will I," he said as he walked away.

"Sure thing, LT." I was still trying to hold Bill off.

"There are times, I just wanta beat the shit out of 'em and then kick the bastard's fuckin' ass."

"I noticed, Bill." He was angrier that I'd ever seen him.

"It would'a been almost worth it, but thanks for not lettin' me make a stupid mistake." He began to calm down.

"No problem, Bill."

"Do you really think those guys at the armory will be to work at first light?" Mugs asked. "If I have to get my butt out of bed early, they'd better be there."

"You bet your sweet ass they will! I'm goin' over there ta let 'em know Fourth is gonna' arrive at 0600. Someone'd better be available to give us our fuckin' tubes and cleanin' supplies," Bill drawled.

"I'll go with you," I offered when we got back to the barracks.

"Naw, I'd rather go alone, but thanks. Shit!" Bill yelled as he slammed his locker closed a few minutes later. "I don't need this jungle crap. I'm too far into my tour of duty!"

Now I knew what was really eating him. He only had ten weeks left before catching the Freedom Bird back to the World. I'd be upset, too.

After his comment, Bill was off to talk to the men at the armory.

"Rough, don't you think you should go along anyway to be sure we don't lose a crew chief?" Joe asked me.

"Bill knows what he's doing. He'll get through to those guys. I'm staying out of it."

It wasn't long before Bill was back.

Joe asked, "Are we cleared for an early morning at the armory?"

"You betcha! Now, y'all'd better be there on time to clean mortars or y'all are in deep shit with me!"

"Right, Bill, 0600," we all responded.

* * *

Before leaving, we received a new order: in the field every platoon would carry a radio.

Being a squad leader had its advantages, not being an RTO was one. But, I did have the job of figuring out which man was capable and would give me the least amount of trouble. Ole was my choice.

He had carried the radio for a week back at Jeanie while our regular RTO had been on R and R. He was a big, strong guy who, I felt, could handle the extra weight. I approached him. We spoke for a while and he begrudgingly accepted the assignment.

"Well, Rough, at least I won't have to walk point with the Prick-25."

"Okay, Ole, the job is yours." *Whew! What a relief.*

"I've notice the humidity doesn't seem to bother you much, what's your secret?" I asked.

"I was born and raised in Hawaii. This humidity is worse here, but I manage just fine."

"I didn't realize that."

"Yeah, Ole is really short for my Hawaiian name which is too long to spell or pronounce. I bet you thought it a nickname from my last name, Olsen, huh? My mama and daddy did it as a joke, I think."

"It worked," I chuckled.

"Hey, I'll give you names of some great restaurants and stuff you and your wife might like to do on your R and R."

"I'll take you up on the places to eat, but I think we can figure out what to do."

I just had to laugh when this big Hawaiian blushed a lovely shade of pink.

The evening was spent putting together our backpacks. Besides the two days of C-rats and water, we added four blocks of C-4 explosive, one shrapnel, and one smoke grenade. Also, a couple of trip flares, twenty magazines of ammo for the M-16, poncho liner and poncho for bedding, flak jacket, steel pot, and, of course, our M-16.

I had time to get off one last letter. Pencils and paper were weight and not considered necessary on a short hump like this. We were only going to be in the jungle for two days.

Hi honey,

Have you ever tried to write a letter in a room full of drunks? It's not an easy thing to do! It's our last night here at BMB and while I was showering, everybody was drinking.

We're moving tomorrow, headed for the jungles about fifty miles northeast of Saigon. We'll be traveling fast and light so there isn't any way for me to write. It's only a two-day hike to reach Firebase Libby.

Once we get there, we'll be spending very little time in base as we'll be out most of the time on operations. When I was in the south I was safer, as the mortar platoon stayed mostly in the firebase. Now we are being transferred to a line platoon and there's a lot more fighting.

One more thing, I will always let you know what's happening as often and as best I can. I won't try and hide anything from you.

I'm a little scared. I guess going into something new always leaves a guy with this feeling. Everyone is frightened. You can see it on their faces.

I made you a promise and I will keep it. I am not going to play war hero, but I won't be any coward either. I'll do my job. Our love is stronger than anything that lies ahead, and with that knowledge I should be able to withstand what's to come.

I love you so very much. With you waiting at home and the strength and support you send in your letters, I'll be fine. I may get down, frustrated, angry, or whatever, but one word from you and the sun comes out, even in the pouring rain. Your letters are like the promised rainbow after a storm. Our love is greater than the distance which keeps us apart and better than what most couples have, always remember that. I will come home to you no matter what! I promise. Remember, I love you with all my heart.

Love, Len, your husband and lover

Chapter 22 - A Taste of the Jungle

None of us wanted to go back to the reality of war. When the trucks arrived, we loaded up in the morning sun. The temperature was already nearing ninety and the sun hadn't even begun to cast its searing heat straight down.

This would be the end of our stay in the delta region south of Saigon. Bravo Company was on its way northeast, up into the mountainous jungle areas as a blocking force along the Ho Chi Minh Trail. The Ho Express was used by the NVA to transport supplies to the south through Laos and Cambodia, a safer route as the jungle helped to hide their movements from American planes.

Our nerves were strung tight as guitar strings. Tensions were high, and we hadn't even left BMB. We'd had two days of jungle training, all the preparation we'd get. Now we faced the unknown. Were we ready? We'd soon find out.

Word came; time to move out. Black smoke belched from exhaust pipes as the engines roared to life and our small convoy of five trucks lurched into motion.

It wasn't long before Saigon and all signs of civilization were far behind as we headed up Highway 13. Our rifles were locked and loaded. We were ready to counter an ambush if one came while on the road north.

And then it engulfed us ... growing on both sides of the highway. As far as the eye could see up and down the road ... it was the jungle ... green hell.

This was not the fire and brimstone picture of hell we had been taught in our Sunday school classes back in the World. No, this was a living, breathing, hot, humid, wet hell, with death lying in wait behind every leaf.

We made it to a spot on the map where command had decided we'd start our patrol toward Firebase Libby. How far we traveled, I'm not sure, but it didn't seem long enough. And yet, it had taken forever to get here.

However, it was not the same spot the LT had been shown. Instead of being only six thousand meters from the firebase, we were at least forty miles out. It dawned on us: this wasn't going to be any two-day walk in the woods. Hell no! It was going to be a long, dangerous, and exhausting patrol.

We grumbled to each other about this change of plans as we climbed out of the trucks. Bravo Company was screwed again.

The CO wanted to see the LTs and all the squad leaders ASAP.

"Command has changed our orders," he began the meeting. "There's reported to be a large concentration of NVA between here and Firebase Libby. We're going to sweep this entire area and clean out any bunker complexes we can find of supplies and men.

"It will be a longer patrol, but I've been told Bravo Company can handle it. I want each platoon to cut a path through the terrain so we can spread out and cover more area. If you find anything, call my RTO. Get your men ready to move out. We leave in ten mikes."

* * *

The jungle was so dense it was impossible to move forward without cutting our way through it. The machete was quite loud, as it rang out with each blow, breaking the stillness of this green barrier. Our enemy had to know where we were. God, we sounded like a herd of elephants.

The CO had ordered us to fight our way through the stinking jungle with platoons abreast. Each was separated by about twenty meters with the command element in the middle of second platoon. There he could control the company and be better protected. That meant all four platoons had to have their point teams hacking through the jungle. It was four times the effort, four times the blood and sweat, and four times the noise.

We were never sure if this was to scare the NVA into thinking we were a much larger force chasing them north, or if this gung-ho CO just wanted to see what Bravo could do.

"Rat and Mugs you'll start as Fourth's point team. There are machetes stacked by the truck. Here's the compass heading. I'll switch you off with Rough and the professor in about an hour. Now let's head out."

"Shit, I haven't walked point since I arrived in Vietnam, and dammit, I don't like it," Dan complained. I knew Dan must be extremely upset; I'd never heard him swear before.

This first day brought me into contact with the steamy humidity, the intense heat, and the earthy smell of the jungle. I thought I'd gotten used to the climate, but this was bad stuff. It drained my energy fast, and I was dragging by the time the CO called a halt for lunch.

"I hate this fuckin' jungle already, and we've only been humping in it for three hours." Joe dropped his pack and followed it down to the wet, spongy ground. He and Mac had taken the third shift at point.

We were all too tired to check for booby traps or mines. Besides, we were in the path we'd just carved out of this stinking monster.

"Man, I should have stayed in Germany. It was nice and cold there," Mac commented.

"I think any of us would jump at the chance to trade for that duty," I said. "What's more, I could have had Lu with me." I thought of her a lot. It helped keep my mind off the rotten conditions.

The lunch break didn't last long. The rest of the afternoon passed in an almost trancelike state. I had to push my tired body; I had to keep going.

Finally, the CO stopped the company for a ten-minute rest break. Thank God. I couldn't have gone on much longer. It was difficult hiking through this treacherous terrain.

"Doc!" The panicked voice scared us.

Most medics were called Doc, even though they weren't doctors. Our medic had been given sixteen weeks of training in basic field first aid.

"Hey, come check me out!"

It was Mugs, and the way he called, there must have been a crisis. Against our training, we all moved to see what was going on. We hadn't hit any booby traps or been in contact with the enemy, so what could it be?

We were disgusted by what we saw. There sat Mugs with his shirt and flak jacket pulled open. Attached to the middle of his chest was one huge, ugly-looking, fat, black, blood-sucking leech! The black color was due to all the blood it had sucked out of Mugs's body.

I remember being told in one of the classes back at Redcatcher about these creatures. Leeches start out as thin, brown, twig-like, inch-worm looking things, but grow in size and change color as they become engorged with their victim's blood.

Mugs reached for the ugly black mass. Doc hollered, "Don't pull that off!" His warning came too late.

"Damn it, I just had to get the fuckin' blood-sucking bastard off me!"

"Now I'll have to cut the head out. I need to talk to Top and let him know we'll need a little extra time on this stop. Ole, get Top on the radio."

"Sure, just a sec ..."

Doc turned to the rest of the platoon. "Don't any of you guys pull a leech off! There's no way to remove the whole thing by yanking at them." He'd made his point.

Ole lifted the hand mike to his ear. "One-Two X-ray, this is Three-Two X-ray, Doc needs to talk to Top, over."

"Roger, wait one," came the voice through the speaker.

"Okay, Doc, Top's on the radio," Ole said, handing him the mike.

"Top, I have men with leeches."

"Yeah, so what?"

"I have a problem. An echo mike pulled one off his chest, but the head and the sucker are still under the skin. I'll need about two-five mikes to cut it out, over."

"Understood, Doc, wait one."

After a short pause, Top returned. "Charlie Oscar says you have one-five mikes, so get moving. The company will set up security and hold, over."

"Roger. Out."

"Hey, guys, pass the word to set up security. We have one-five mikes. I don't want any of you getting some nasty infection out here. I guess you all must have skipped or didn't pay attention to the leech class back at Redcatcher."

We were given a quick refresher on the subject while we watched Mugs in pain. This time we listened. We didn't want what was happening to him to happen to us. We could tell it hurt like the devil.

Opening his medical bag, Doc pulled out a bottle of peroxide. He poured a generous amount onto a scalpel, sterilizing it, then he turned to Mugs. "This might hurt, but it's nothing to the pain you'll suffer later if we don't remove it now." Doc then poured some of the liquid on Mugs, which bubbled profusely, killing the germs on his chest.

"Damn it, Doc, is this really necessary?"

"It sure is so button up your mouth, Mugs. Leeches seek heat and a nice warm GI's body is perfect." Doc turned to the group of morbid onlookers. "Everybody check yourselves and then examine each other. Any of you characters have a dry smoke?"

"Aw, come on, Doc, this is no time for a cigarette break," Mugs complained.

"Just watch and learn, fellows," Doc replied.

After lighting up, he cut open the skin behind the head and placed the glowing end close to the leech. The head backed out. Doc knocked it off and stomped it into the ground. He poured on more peroxide. It bubbled again as it cleansed the wound, killing more germs. He probed the wound with his scalpel to verify all parts of the leech were gone, then covered it with a field bandage to keep it clean. The surgery was finished in the allotted fifteen minutes.

As crazy as it sounded, the heat from the hot end of a cigarette caused a leech to let go of its victim. We could remove the offending little sucker in one piece. It was enough to make anyone want to take up smoking—almost.

Now, we not only had meal breaks, but also leech checks. This was to be the procedure for the rest of our patrol in the hideous jungle.

Doc had finished checking us out when the radio came to life. "All Bravo stations, time's up." We were in no hurry to get moving again. Our packs felt like they were full of lead as we lifted them into position. But, we started hacking our way through the green hell once again.

Mugs complained as we headed out, "Hey, I'm a wounded man, maybe I need a stretcher. Do you think I'll get a Purple Heart?"

"I don't think the army considers a leech the enemy," Doc said, with a weary, half-hearted laugh.

* * *

Many of us had played sports where we had to move fast with the extra weight of uniforms and equipment. We'd gone through the running and physical conditioning during basic training and AIT and the months spent in the rice paddies here in Vietnam, but nothing had prepared us for this. We already felt beaten down, and this was only the first day.

It seemed more like a week. Our packs became lighter as we ate our food, drank our water, and discarded items we no longer felt necessary, such as cameras and personal radios. We were not able to walk upright as the weight on our backs kept us bent at the waist just to keep moving. We carried our rifles over our shoulders like shotguns, or let them hang from our hands at the ready. If our point team missed the enemy, we'd be in real trouble.

The sun was relentless, beating down on the canopy of the jungle. What it created was a sauna.

We took quick drinks of water on the move, no time to stop. The liquid in our canteens was lukewarm and not very refreshing, but it replaced some of the fluid lost from the sweat rolling off our bodies like small rivers. These were streams of hot, smelly, salty sweat, which did nothing to cool us. I'd never sweated so much or smelled so bad.

The company was moving fast and it was obvious we wouldn't be stopping for another break. The CO wanted to reach the selected NDP and get set up before dark.

Around 1600, we broke out of the jungle into an area of elephant grass. Wild Bill announced, "Charlie Oscar is settin' up here for the night."

According to the map, we had walked over three thousand meters on our first day. We'd just have time for dinner before sending out our listening posts.

When the dreaded night approached, no light from the moon or stars could penetrate the dense foliage making our starlight scopes useless. For our safety, there would be no movement after our positions were set.

Our artillery-forward observer, shortened to Arty-FO, called in our NDP. At the same time, he called for a marking round. We didn't want to be at the wrong coordinates if we had to call in firepower on the enemy.

Arty-FO called out, "Be on the lookout for an airburst. It should be on our right about a hundred meters."

The call came in over the FO's radio. "Shot." The round was on its way.

Then, "Splash," to let us know when it should explode.

It did all right, a good two hundred meters from our position and on the wrong side.

"Hell, we're not where we're supposed to be!" Wild Bill complained.

"No, the FO called in the wrong dang position," Dan answered. "He needs to find our NDP on the map and radio the corrected coordinates."

"Well, gee, it makes me feel really good to know we could get accidentally bombed by our own 105s because our FO can't read a fucking map," Joe said, his voice rising with each word.

"Yeah, once was enough," I muttered, thinking back to the friendly fire incident while at Jeanie.

The FO called in our corrected position. The 105 Battery could now find us if we needed them for support during the night. This time the test round was right on target.

Now it was time to set out our defenses. Everyone helped chop down the elephant grass so we had a clear line of fire, then we took turns going out to the edge of the clearing to set the trip flares and Claymores. The rest of us either kept on the alert or started dinner. We were relieved when the night chopper brought out precious water.

We were near the enemy and everyone was fatigued, a combination which could spell disaster. We had learned quickly how to sleep with our sixth-sense wide-awake, tuned in to any change. If the bugs or night creatures became quiet, we'd immediately be wide-awake. A feeling, a smell, a noise, a movement, anything at all would alter our alertness. But, we never felt safe enough to really relax and fall into a deep sleep.

* * *

We were up and moving on our second day. Another chopper was supposed to be sent out to pick up our water containers, but none showed, so we had to pack them with us. Just what we needed, more weight!

Our short night's sleep didn't give our bodies much of a break. But, as ordered, we put on our packs and continued plodding through the jungle looking for signs of the NVA.

Suddenly, everyone was on alert. The radios came alive with chatter about movement to our right and just in front. A small group of NVA soldiers was reported. We began moving as quietly as we could to intercept this small patrol before they could report our position.

"Rough, how can we see to fight in this fuckin' jungle? How do we know we're firing on the NVA and not some of our own men?" Joe mumbled.

"I don't know yet, but I think we're about to find out," I whispered just as all hell broke loose. We heard loud gunfire coming from about seventy-five meters to the left of us, First Platoon's side.

It lasted only a few minutes, and then all was quiet once again. There were only five men in the gook patrol, and none survived the assault. We had one man injured, although not seriously. He was just grazed by a bullet on his leg, but he would be sent to brigade's hospital. In the jungle, we couldn't take a chance of infection.

The bodies were searched, and then we began to move on, wanting to get as far away as possible. We were sure other NVA had heard the sounds and would come to investigate.

* * *

It would have been easy to follow the company's forward progress through the jungle since we had not learned how to move silently. That would come with time. We were new to the jungle, but our lives depended on mastering the skill quickly.

The CO called for us to set up our NDP at about 1700.

After we had everything ready, we took turns fixing chow.

"I'm having a big dinner since we didn't have time to eat breakfast and not much of a lunch," Rat said setting up his stove.

"Aw, Rat, always thinking of your stomach," I teased him.

"I had heard we'd be getting hot chow. Yeah, sure. I think C-rats are better anyway." Rat smacked his lips as he took out a lifer bar. He was the only one with the stomach to eat the things.

"Yeah, well, I thought we were only supposed to move 1200 meters today, but it was another three thousand-meter day," Dan complained, after he checked his map.

"It's the new CO's idea. That damn gung-ho bastard!" Bill grumbled.

"You know, this jungle patrol isn't as bad as I had expected. It's a whole hell of a lot worse! How has my life gotten so screwed up?"

"Mugs, you're fucking right. As usual, we're all screwed!" Rat said.

How many months of this can I endure? I thought. *I'm more exhausted than I've ever been in my life and it's only the second day. Oh, God, please give me strength.*

* * *

The next morning, we were choppered to another part of the jungle. From the air, we got a view of what we had been hacking our way through.

There were open spots where the elephant grass grew six to eight feet tall. We had to jump from about five feet up, but the blast from the rotor blades at least parted it so we could see the ground.

That night we stopped at a place where a herd of elephants had been. On a closer look, we realized the NVA had also been there. They were using these huge beasts to carry supplies down the Ho Express. Top estimated they'd been gone at least twenty-four hours.

We hadn't seen an elephant, but they left lots of evidence. The look and smell of elephant dung would be burned permanently into our memories. Ugh!

"Hey, Rough, do you know what the hell's going on tomorrow?" Joe asked later that evening.

"All I know is we're supposed to be moved north to help the First Cav. I heard it's a two-day operation."

"Yeah, well this was supposed to be a fuckin' two-day operation, and we're going on day five with no end in sight."

"You've got a point there, Joe, but I don't know what to tell you."

"Well, you're not a lot of help."

"That's too damned bad! I'm as pissed about all this crap as you are, but there's still not a thing I can do about it! I just want to be out of this friggin' war and back home with my wife!"

"Is that any way for a preacher's kid to talk?"

"Yeah, we weren't allowed to swear when I was growing up. I learned it all from you."

"God, Len, you're beginning to swear almost as much as me!" Joe said, "You'd better clean up your language before you see your wife in a couple of months."

"Joe, thanks for the reminder. I'll definitely work on it before R and R. Lu wouldn't be happy, that's for sure."

I waited until I finally calmed down, realized he was right, and took a few minutes to write Lu. I borrowed a pen from Ole and paper and an envelope from Joe. I'd requested writing supplies and hoped they would be coming out on the next chopper.

Hi honey,

Sorry it has taken so long to write. Let me explain. We thought when we left BMB we would be trucked directly to our new firebase right up Highway 13. Boy, were we wrong. We started up the highway, but we took a detour and we were let off only a short way into the jungle.

I don't know how much I'll be able to write as it's hard to keep the paper dry. I have on the same clothes I started with on Sunday. We do get a dry pair of socks when the chopper comes out, then we put on our wet boots. Between sweat, crossing streams, and rain, we're never dry.

Our equipment weighs at least fifty pounds, more than it should for this type of terrain. We pack up every morning and move from 2,500 to 3,000 meters a day. The jungle is hot, humid, and very close. All I can say is it's HELL!

We had an Air Mobil today. It's where the choppers pick us up and move us to another spot. I got a good look at the area we've covered. Boy, was it a lot. It's so dense you can't see the jungle floor in most places, only the tops of the trees. From the chopper's view, it doesn't look as deadly as it does at ground level.

We came here to disrupt the flow of supplies from the north to the south. We're also looking for any bunker complexes, which might store supplies for the NVA patrols. Our duty is to prevent them from building up supplies and men to escalate the war.

Well, we're getting ready to move out again and the supply chopper is leaving so I need to finish this.

I love you with all my heart.

Love, Len, your husband and lover

* * *

"Hey, Rough, did you get any sleep last night? I know you had two watches with only two hours in-between. That's rough duty. Ha, ha, I just made a joke. Rough … duty, did you get it?"

"Yeah, I got it, Joe. The pun was just too funny for words."

"What a grouch you are this morning. Where is your usually sunny personality?"

"What is it, the seventh day for this patrol and this uniform? We haven't been shipped out clean stuff this whole patrol," I grumbled. "I'm wet, I stink, I'm tired, and I want to go home. Why should I be cheery?"

"I guess I've depended on you to be in a good mood to help keep my spirits up. When you're like this, it just makes it harder for me to get motivated for another day."

"Sorry, Joe, I'll work on a smile, but that's the best I can do for you."

The morning chopper finally brought our first change of clothes after seven days. Personal hygiene really suffered on patrol; only the constant rain made us bearable, even to ourselves.

I'd only been able to shave once—not enough water to spare and no way to trap rainwater. The evening chopper dropped our water supply down from above the trees in rubber tubes. We each received about five quarts which half-filled our bladder canteen. Not nearly enough, but we had to make do until the next evening.

* * *

"Rough, pack it up. We're moving again in one zero," Joe broke into my few moments away from the patrol. All morning I'd been thinking about our conversation. "Hey, Joe, thanks."

"What'd I do this time?"

"Just reminded me of who I am."

"Yeah, well, time's up and we gotta go. We'll talk later."

"What's the big rush?" I asked burying my C-rat can.

"The major just radioed. He spotted some movement to our front and wants us to set up a blocking force. He ordered Arty to take some of them out and turn the rest back towards us."

"Damn, I knew those jerks would get us into another firefight before we got to Firebase Libby."

"God, Rough, I hope it isn't a large company of NVA. I'm too bushed to put up much of a fight."

"We all are, Joe, but if we get help from the 105s and Cobra gunships …"

"Don't bet on the gunships. That's asking a lot, especially the way things have been going. Well, here we go into the fires of hell. I only hope we survive."

It took only a few minutes to pick up the trail of the NVA the major had spotted. Command set up a plan using the 105s to zero in on the enemy patrol, killing as many as possible. Then they began driving them back toward our position. We set up an ambush to intercept the remaining NVA as they came down the trail. We hoped we were prepared and the plan would work.

Even though I knew the 105s were going to open up, I still jumped as the silence was broken with the horrific sound of the rounds screeching overhead. The explosions caused the ground to shake, along with my knees.

The enemy was being bombarded right on target. We were all hoping every one of the NVA would be annihilated. We knew we'd be firing at whatever was left. There wasn't a man who didn't have sweating palms and a sinking feeling.

We could hear crashing through the jungle as they headed our way. Our weapons were cocked and ready and we waited for the word to fire. We wanted them to be in the killing zone before we opened up. The M-60 machine guns fired a burst taking out many of the enemy. We were then given the order to take out those remaining. We killed or captured over fifty NVA. Unfortunately, one of our men was killed and two received serious wounds.

The company located an open area to land a medevac helicopter. We carried the dead GI and the two wounded soldiers on stretchers to the LZ. In a matter of minutes, they were on their way to the brigade's hospital. The body was going home. It was a solemn time.

No matter how often we fired our weapons at the enemy, there was no thought about taking another human's life. We were doing our jobs as we'd been trained.

When one of our own died, the first thought of every GI was, "Thank God it wasn't me," followed by the deep sadness of losing a comrade and the ramifications of his death.

* * *

Later in the day, we finally stopped for a fifteen-minute lunch break. Joe and I talked about what was happening to the platoon.

"We're losing too many men on this patrol, mostly from exhaustion," I observed. "I was surprised when Mugs had to be taken out by a medevac chopper, but he just couldn't have taken another step."

"Damn, I'm pissed. Who thought we should carry more weight every time we lose a man? Why couldn't they transport his pack, too? It sure isn't my idea of how to keep men well in this fuckin' jungle, Rough."

"If this is what a short patrol is like, God help us on a long one! I'll be ready for R and R before we ever see a firebase again," I said to Joe.

"No shit, Rough. How many men has Doc sent to the hospital?"

"Too many. The Fourth is down to eleven. We started with seventeen. If I'd let Doc have his way, he'd put me on a chopper to Firebase Black Horse, too. I should have a real Doc look at my feet and this damn ringworm. On top of it all, a cold has caught me. Well, at least I haven't had to cough too much out here. It could be fatal if the NVA heard me."

"Damn it, Rough, give yourself a break. Let Doc put you on a chopper and get the fuck out of here. Anyone else would do it if they had the chance."

"Sure, Joe. Do you really think the CO and the LT are going to let me go?" I argued.

"If Doc says you need better medical attention, yeah they'd let you go. Like it or not, they'd have to."

"Well, when I get to Libby and into some clean clothes and dry my boots out, I should get better."

"Uh huh."

"God, I really hate this rain. There's no way to get out of it. We have to eat in it, walk in it, sleep in it, and we even have to fight in it. I hope to heaven, I don't have to die in it, too!"

"Hey, man, where'd that come from? You must really be in bad shape to even think the damn word, let alone say it. You know better."

"I'm sure that's what the guy from First Platoon thought before that gook killed him this morning."

"Rough, you need to get out of the field and get yourself in better physical and mental shape, too. Take Doc up on the flight out of here."

"Thanks, Joe, but I'll be fine. We should be getting to Firebase Libby soon, and I'll have time to get back on track. I just haven't heard from Lu in a few days. I really need her words of love. She's my steadying force. Bet there'll be a bunch of letters when I get to Libby."

"Man, you are one lucky asshole. I envy you. Of course had I been an old man when I was drafted, I might have had a wife back home in the World to write to me, too."

"What the hell's up, guys? What are you talking about?" Rat asked as he, Dan, and Ole joined us.

"We're just talking about this patrol," I answered.

"Yeah, this jungle is some thick shit. I'm sure even Tarzan would find it impossible if he wasn't swinging from tree to tree. Can you imagine a whole platoon, with full packs, swinging on vines through the canopy?"

We chuckled at the vision.

"Ole, you amaze even me with your deep thinking." I loved to kid him.

"Trying to swing from tree to tree would be difficult. There isn't much room between them," Rat pointed out.

"This place stinks of rotting and decaying plants. I'm sure my mother would have compared it to my smelly socks a few years ago."

"I don't think your dirty socks can even come close, Joe. It's a very distinctive smell and will always make me think of this miserable time in my life. Hey, we better get going or the CO will come down on our necks but good."

"Yeah, Rough, I guess our little break is over," Joe answered as he headed out. He and Mac had point for the next hour.

Chapter 23 - Two-Day Patrol—Bullshit!

One night, a bunch of us were sitting around, talking about the new CO. We all knew he thought he should have gotten a Ranger company and was trying to convert Bravo Company into one.

Someone used the term "Ricky's Rangers" to describe Bravo Company. I'm not sure where "Ricky" came from since it had nothing to do with this CO's real name. It just started out as a joke, caught on fast, and stuck.

* * *

"Hey, Rough, you have one of those fancy watches with the date don't you?" Joe asked.

"If it's correct, it says 30 June."

"That's what I thought. This is our ninth day out and I'm fuckin' tired!"

"Yeah, I hope we reach Firebase Libby someday soon, Joe."

"What's this deal about not sending our friggin' mail out?" Mugs complained as he joined us. He'd returned that morning from the hospital.

"I hope you're making that up. Letters from Lu are the only things keeping me going."

"Rough, I really enjoy listening when you read them to us. It gives me something to look forward to. I'm thinking about finding a girl like yours when I get back home. What did she say when you told her about sharing her letters?" Joe asked.

"Well, ah, you see, ah, Joe, I, ah, haven't exactly, ah, told her. She might be a bit upset. She's a very private person and I'm not sure she'd appreciate me sharing them. I'll tell her someday."

"What! You haven't told her?" Joe had an incredulous look on his face, "One of these days you're going to be in deep shit."

"Only if she finds out!" I exclaimed.

"Good luck!" Joe said, grinning like a hyena.

"Just be sure you tell her it was censored," Rat added. "You didn't read the juicy parts."

"Thanks, Rat, I'm sure it's going to make a huge difference in her reaction."

"Good luck!" Rat mimicked Joe and smirked like a baboon.

"It's nice to know I have such supportive friends."

I had a few minutes before the supply chopper took off. I needed to let Lu know I was okay. That is if I could find something dry to write on.

Hi honey,

I'm fine, just very tired. It's our ninth day on patrol. The conditions are terrible, really sapping our strength.

I'm taking care of myself as best as I can in the jungle. I will be home as I promised. You can count on it!

I miss you and I want to hold you in my arms. I need to make sure you're real and not just a dream.

You asked what we have to carry in our packs. Well here goes. We each carry a Claymore mine: ten pounds, a trip flair: one pound, a LAW: five pounds, a large knife: four pounds, about 5 quarts of water: 14.7 pounds, our C-rats, four meals: ten pounds, the rifle-cleaning kit, the pack itself, ammo, a rifle and our sleeping gear: seven pounds dry or twelve pounds when wet. Whew! It all adds up to a ton.

I get clean clothes every four to six days, but I'm wet all the time. I smell like sweat and the jungle. The real problem is the leeches. They only take a little blood and cause no harm if I take them off quickly. Doc showed us how.

Sorry, but this C-rat package was the only paper dry enough to write on. I trimmed it to fit in the envelope. I need to get this on the chopper to you. Just remember I'm fine and I love you with all my heart!

Love, Len, Your husband and lover

* * *

On our twelfth day out, the company was picked up by choppers and taken to the edge of the jungle. We would be working with the Seventeenth Cav, a mechanized unit, so we wouldn't be doing much walking, and none of it humping through the jungle, thank God!

Our company and the Seventeenth were set up as a blocking force while the ARVNs tried to push the NVA our way. We weren't sure if they'd make it. We had little faith in their abilities.

We sat and waited to spring the trap. It took a bit of doing. Ever try camouflaging a huge armored personal carrier? Even though they were muddy and OD green, they were immense. We had to blend them in with the undergrowth so the enemy couldn't detect them. What a job!

"Hey, professor, how do we make an APC look like a tree? Isn't there some formula we can use besides breaking our backs cutting bamboo?" Joe teased Dan.

"You know, Joe, there isn't one for making an APC disappear, but I might find one for a moron like you to go away."

"Ha! Ha! You son of a bitch, I really needed a laugh!"

"Yeah, we all did," I added. "Want some good news? The LT says we're going to be here for a couple of days."

"Just think of it, two whole days out of the stinking jungle!" Dan remarked.

"Does the CO really think they're going to make this trap work?"

"Well, Joe, we should know by this time tomorrow if it's a success or a bust! My money's on the latter," I said. *I can't understand why we're here bleeding and dying for people who aren't interested in fighting for themselves. I hope the South Vietnamese care enough about their own country to do the job. But I don't have much hope,* I thought.

Too bad I didn't have real money on the bet. We sat and waited all the first day and into the night. The next morning, we were still waiting. By late in the afternoon, it became very obvious, there would be no NVA walking into our trap.

I don't know about the Seventeenth's CO, but ours was so pissed he almost turned purple! Of, course, he took it out on us. We'd sat for two days ready to spring the trap, but you have to have someone to spring it on to make it work.

"I told you guys yesterday, it wasn't going to happen," Joe gloated.

"Well, I didn't want to get into another firefight with a large group of NVA anyway," Rat said.

"Still no action. Our luck's holding ...," I smiled. I'd gotten some long-overdue rest and couldn't have been happier. My crew looked better, too.

The next morning, it was back into the jungle to move in on a reported NVA unit. Command didn't let Bravo Company sit in one place very long.

We'd already cut out a field of fire and put up our sleeping quarters. The foxholes were almost finished when the major flew over. He decided we were to head to another spot. All that work for nothing.

We moved another one thousand meters and started to set up again. Once more the major wanted us to move another five hundred meters. The CO argued for what seemed like hours and finally said we'd move, but we stayed put. By the time we set up and ate, it was dark. Then the rains came.

The next morning we moved the additional distance and positioned for the trap, but the NVA had other ideas. It was another day of no contact and rest.

We were all glad we were on the perimeter and not near the CO after this failed trap. He'd argued with us yesterday; and now he was way past pissed. Thank God there wasn't much more he could do to us; we were already marching on a fast pace through hell!

* * *

The days plowed on, one after another. Each day seemed like the one before. Special days came and went without us even being aware. We were still on patrol and missed the Fourth of July celebration.

Mac returned from a few days in the hospital and filled us in, "You guys should have seen it. The sky was lit up with enough flares to make a summer night at Disneyland seem dull. I watched as tracers pierced the sky every which way. It didn't last long, though. The officers in charge decided it should come to an end before someone was hurt or killed."

This wasn't the first Fourth of July Americans had spent in Vietnam. I could only hope it would be the last.

We moved again by chopper back to where we started a few days earlier. It was now the fifteenth day of our two-day patrol. We were headed to another LZ, to be moved again.

Those of us still remaining in the field were so tired, it was all we could do to stand upright. Our brains were numb and our bodies were on automatic. None of us would last much longer without a break.

I muttered to myself, "Next time I stop, there's no way I'll able to get moving again."

Joe had heard me. "But we do have to get the fuck up and move. We sure as hell don't want to get left behind in enemy territory." He tried to put things into perspective.

"I don't think I can go on."

"Rough, remember all you have to live for: your wonderful wife, a home, and a life. So don't give up!"

I felt like I was in a daze. "God, I must have dozed off while walking, Joe."

"You scared me, man. Don't do that again. Okay?"

"Yeah, I'll try." I hoped I sounded like the normal me. I resettled my pack on sore shoulders, put my head down, and began moving again.

It was hard staying upright and not falling behind. All my energy was focused on putting one foot in front of the other while staying alert for potential danger.

I had never in my life been so physically and mentally exhausted. Only the thought of my Lu kept me from just sitting down and dying on the spot.

Oh, God, give me strength and help me through this, I prayed over and over again to myself. It became a litany I used as a cadence to keep my feet moving, always moving, in the line of humanity snaking our way through hell.

Chapter 24 – Ah, Libby at Last

It was day fifteen. We had been patrolling ever slowly toward Firebase Libby. Those of us still in the field were so tired we could have dropped in our tracks and slept for a week. If we had many more days like these, the whole company would be in the hospital.

Granted, the CO had covered the same amount of ground, but he hadn't swung a machete walking point. He hadn't carried more than a canteen of water and a meal or two weighing a couple of pounds. And he certainly never carried an M-60, any Claymores, or trip flares, and never, never ever did he carry a PRC-25!

We were constantly burning the leeches off our bodies. Thorns pierced us even through our uniforms causing infections. Many of us had developed a fungus on our feet from being constantly wet from the incessant rain and humidity. Those same conditions allowed ringworm to invade our bodies. And to top it all off, some of us had colds.

God, I hate this jungle!

* * *

Hi honey,

This is probably going to be a gripe session so I want to apologize in advance. I'm fine, just very beat from the past two weeks. It's amazing how much one person can take. The body goes on even when you think you've reached the limit.

My hands are cut from all the prickly bushes, elephant grass, and bamboo I've had to hack through. I have huge blisters from the machete.

My God, I thought FB Jeanie, Fishnet, and the bridge were bad, but not at all like this hell. I don't want to ever be in this kind of place again. Give me the sunny beaches of southern California. Hell, I'd even take the freeways and the smog, anything, just get me out of this godforsaken jungle!

I draw on your strength and your words of love to give me the reason to go on in this stinking hell. Letters from home are very important. Please get everybody writing.

I've had a lot of time to sit and think at night since it's too wet to sleep. Home will be like heaven with a table to eat on, a shower with hot water, ice-cold milk to drink, a bathroom, and a dry place to sleep with you every night. I dream of our home. I hope we can buy our own house and start raising a family as soon as I get out of the army.

I'm fine, so don't worry. I can hardly wait for R and R so you can see for yourself. I've lost some weight. Everybody has. Lots of exercise and very little food can do that. You wouldn't want a fat husband would you? Besides, when I get back and eat some of your good home cooking, it won't take long before I'm back to normal. I love you and I miss you so much.

Love, Len, your husband and lover

* * *

For those men who were out fighting in the rice paddies, jungles, and mountains of this pathetic little country, it was one dangerous day after another. At any moment we could come face-to-face with death. What a hellish way to exist!

All most of us cared about was getting out of the Vietnam War alive and back to the real world, if there was still such a thing. Maybe our reality was skewed. Maybe the war was real, and what we thought of as home was just a fantasy. Our minds were so tired we could believe almost anything.

The company was down almost twenty men since we left on this damn patrol. Oh, guys would be medevaced out and then return a few days later to do it all again, but we never caught up.

Command wanted us to get a taste of jungle fighting. Well, they got the desired effect. We were now seasoned jungle fighters and it only took a little over two weeks to do it. We had stopped living like civilized people. Out here, survival by any means was all that counted.

* * *

We got word that we were only 3,500 meters from Firebase Libby and would be humping our way there the next day. This horror would finally end.

"Just think, by tomorrow night we should get hot chow, a shower, a dry bed, clean clothes, and a little breather from this fuckin' jungle," Mugs said as we finished setting up our NDP.

"I wouldn't bet my ass on it." Joe looked around before he continued, "We aren't there yet."

"Yeah, we still have another full day's walk tomorrow," Ole added.

"You know, Rough, the Charlie Oscar wants a promotion, so what he really needs is a big body count," Joe said as he watched his dinner cook.

"That's true, Joe. I just hope we won't have to pay the price," I said. "We've already had two men killed."

"Ricky is a gung-ho jerk with some really bad ideas. I'm surprised we haven't lost more than that."

"You're right, Dan. He thinks nothing of ordering us to cut our way through dense jungle, hump sixty pounds or more, go with little food and water, and cover four thousand meters in a day. Someone's going to shoot the bastard one of these days," Joe said, with a mouthful of food.

Watching, Rat licked his chops like Wile E. Coyote looking at the Road Runner.

"I'm glad to know I'm not the only one who feels that way," I commented.

"Dammit, here comes more trouble," Joe said as Top approached.

"All right, let's get this cluster spread out. I want the NDP set before dark."

"Wilco, Top, don't worry, we're done," I responded.

As Top turned to leave, Mugs asked, "Top, are we really going to finally get to Libby tomorrow?"

"If things go according to plan, the CO wants to be there by mid-afternoon."

The news sounded really good to us, but we didn't entirely trust it.

I finally had time to heat my meal. I'm glad they labeled everything, because sometimes we couldn't recognize what we were eating. We wondered if some of the C-rats weren't left over from WWII or, at the very least, Korea.

* * *

Night came swiftly in the jungle. It wasn't a gradual light-to-dark, more like a black shroud being thrown over the sun. And, as usual, the rains started soon after, never allowing anyone to rest.

The blackness slowly lifted and morning arrived. The radio came to life with what else, but ... "Good Morning, Vietnam. What a fine, fine super fine morning."

"Someday, I'm going to shoot that bastard if I can find his fine, fine super fine ass. He needs to shut the fuck up!" Joe shouted.

Most of us had been awake early in anticipation of this patrol finally coming to an end. Hopefully, the enemy would not make his presence known today. All we wanted was to get to Firebase Libby and stay at least a week or two.

Breakfast was a quick cup of hot chocolate and a package of crackers. We did our morning leech check. At least the rain kept the mosquitoes away. They were the lesser of two evils in our minds, but we had to live with both of them. We were invaders of their territory.

The word to, "Get it on," was passed through the ranks. What was left of our breakfast was quickly dumped, and the cans buried. We didn't want to leave anything lying around which Charlie could use to figure our numbers.

The CO gave the order to march back in single file. The point platoon to start was the First, followed by the Third, then Second, and finally the Fourth. We began by pulling rear security. If we were lucky, we would be at the firebase before we had to walk point.

We stretched out a long way, but it was much easier to travel. We could hear First Platoon's point team hacking through the thick jungle. We plunged ahead, plodding, one foot in front of the other, not really thinking about anything but getting through the next couple of hours.

There would be a lot of calls for Doc tonight. Among the usual leeches, ringworm, and bites, he would also be cleaning minor cuts and infected punctures. The jungle was unforgiving. Every tree and bush seemed to be covered with long, sharp needles and thorns, all aiming for our hands, arms, and faces.

* * *

"Rough, the lieutenant has decided you and Rat will be Fourth Platoon's first point team," Ole said after lunch.

"Fuck, how'd we get so lucky?" Rat complained.

"You two are about the only ones still standing. Everyone else is just too beat!"

"Yeah, well I'm going on pure determination at this point. My body is just moving out of habit and my brain is dead. I'm about as beat as anyone else."

"Well, Rough, you guys are the chosen ones, so go do your job."

Rat and I moved past the rest of the company. I knew who was going to end up with the machete. Rat had beaten me to the front and was holding the compass.

"Let's get this mess moving," Rat said from about eight feet behind. "From reading the map, we're about a click or more from our new firebase."

"Where am I headed to from here?" I asked.

After Rat took a look at the compass, he pointed at a very large tree. "We should be heading that way. The tree's in the right direction."

"Okay," I respond. "Just keep me going close to the right Alpha Zulu, Rat. I want this day over so we don't get stuck out here again tonight."

"Roger, Rough."

I looked for the top of the tree and tried to plot the easiest way. There was no easy way! It was thick jungle everywhere. Right in front was a big clump of bamboo with no way around it. I needed a really sharp blade to cut through this, the tallest, fattest grass I had ever seen. Unfortunately, I only had this miserable dull excuse for a machete.

I had been on point for about twenty minutes when I heard a panicked, "Rough, freeze, don't move a muscle."

I froze in mid-stride, afraid to put my foot down. But I had to, very, very slowly. When my foot touched the ground, nothing exploded. I let out a breath, which I hadn't realized I'd been holding.

"Rat, just what was all this freeze shit about," I asked, still frozen in place.

"Dammit, Rough, didn't you see that fuckin' two stepper?"

We had been told about the Bamboo Viper at Redcatcher. It's a snake, nicknamed two-stepper because it's said if bitten by one you'll only get about two steps before death. I didn't want to find out firsthand if the stories were true.

I wasn't expecting to see one of those things come flying out of a stalk of bamboo, but, according to Rat, one did. I was lucky. The snake took off away from me or else they might have needed a chopper to carry my dead body out of the jungle.

"I guess we'd better inform Top and the command group to remind the company to keep an eye out for things that slither through the bamboo," I said, my voice quivering.

"Right, I'll pass the word back." Rat turned and hollered to the GI behind him.

My voice had stopped shaking and my breathing was almost back to normal after the scare. Man, it was bad enough being attacked by gooks, leeches, and mosquitoes, but now snakes; it was just too much. "God, I hate this stinking jungle!" I looked skyward and yelled.

The new point team had been at work for only about half an hour when we heard, "Libby's in sight!"

As the point team prepared to break out of the jungle, a call went over the radio to the firebase: "Bravo base, this is One-One-X-ray on our way in, over."

"Pop smoke! Over," came the reply.

The CO's RTO popped a grenade and green smoke billowed out of the hissing canister.

"Bravo One-One-X-ray, we see jolly green, over."

"Roger, firebase, jolly green it is."

"Hold position. We will deploy a man to lead you through the mine field, over."

"Roger, hold position, out."

The company followed the security man out of the jungle right through the green smoke. We moved slowly over the blackened red dirt barren of any growth. The black was due to the constant burning of the jungle foliage done by the security force stationed with the 105 Battery already at the base. The jungle was continually trying to reclaim the open area.

One of Bravo Company's duties now would be to keep the hundred meters between the firebase and the jungle devoid of vegetation. We wanted a clear field of fire. Detecting any movement by the NVA would be vital to our safety.

This base was new and would require a lot of work to finish, but this piece of naked red dirt in the middle of the hideous green jungle was now home.

Our first patrol set the tone for the worst duty imaginable, and this was only the beginning. Our days of staying in the firebase when the rest of the platoons patrolled were at an end. There'd be many more patrols for Bravo Company, Fourth Platoon in this green hell.

Chapter 25 - Firebase Libby

Trucking us to Firebase Libby would have been easier than the hellish sixteen-day slog through the jungle. Much to our relief, we never ran into the expected contingent of NVA. However, the experience gave us a horrifying taste of what future patrols would be like.

Firebase Libby was close to the Ho Chi Minh Trail. US B-52s bombed parts of the trail, but not long or hard enough as far as we were concerned. Our military wanted to release a whole passel of bombs right on Hanoi, but there were reports of American prisoners being held there. This was North Vietnam's way of protecting the city.

The firebase was isolated from the South Vietnamese population. So Bravo Company would have very little contact with the people we were here to help.

* * *

There was an artillery battery of 105s assigned as support when we were out on patrol. This was a larger base and, with the presence of the Arty company, qualified for a field kitchen.

The exhausted men of Bravo Company were given no time for rest. Listening posts began the first night. Four men comprised each LP. They were sent outside the perimeter three to four hundred meters, where they sat and waited very quietly, listening for any movement from the NVA. If contact was made, they'd radio back to base, and we'd drop several mortar rounds on the enemy's heads. These LPs were our extended eyes and ears.

The supply choppers had delivered our mortar equipment. After a night's rest, we spent most of our first full day setting up new pits. They were very primitive with just temporary blast walls. We had to level the base plate area and get the aiming poles set in their correct positions. We attached flashlights with red lenses to the aiming poles. They were left on all night, so the gunners could find them in the dark. This was SOP for all our bases with mortars. The US Army sure used up a lot of batteries.

The army engineers had been informed what our requirements were. A scraped-off area waited for us to build on. It was nice to have a lot of room for the mortar pits, bunkers and our sleeping hooches. They'd left some corrugated sheet metal, which made a good start for roofing since we couldn't find any helicopter landing pads. We'd reinforce everything with sandbags.

Our first priority was constructing sleeping bunkers, then the mortar pits and ammo bunkers. We needed protection from the rain. The heat and humidity were nearly unbearable. There was no place out of the direct sun. Much to Top's dislike, we discarded our shirts and helmets while working. He could accept the shirts coming off, but the helmets were one item he insisted we wear at all times.

"This place is too close to the enemy. Those helmets won't do you any good if they're in your bunker or lying around," he boomed.

We tried to comply, but for the most part we just kept them close at hand. We understood the importance of wearing them, but it felt like our heads were boiling under these conditions, and we just wore our floppy jungle hats to keep the sun off.

* * *

At our daily platoon meeting, Bill grumbled, "From what I hear, LT, the 105s plan to do very little illumination firin' when we're in base."

"You've got it right, so we'd better be ready." The LT continued, "Dan, set up the FDC."

"Roger, LT," Dan answered. He'd become the unofficial head of the FDC. This was due to his knowledge of math and his time in country. We were old-timers now.

"Joe, you'd better get to work," I suggested.

He just winked and walked off, whistling. He was a scrounger. His work was to take a stroll around the base looking for anything we could use. Good stuff would most likely be found near the 105 company area.

What made Joe our best scavenger was his boyish appearance. He sort of blended in and didn't look like he'd be up to anything if spotted—perfect for the task.

Since bright lights were required while doing their calculations, the guys from the FDC would be totally exposed. We'd build a small enclosure in the days ahead to keep the light from being seen from the outside, protecting them from a sniper's bullet and, of course, from the weather.

"I'll need tables and maybe a couple of tarps to use for a cover tonight," Dan began his list.

"Joe wants to get into the FDC and off the mortars for a while. This might be the incentive he needs," I whispered to Dan.

Dan nodded at me and asked Joe, "Are you interested in training with me?"

"You betcha."

Dan offered to speak to LT. With that incentive, off Joe went in search of something to make a temporary center for Fire Direction Control.

It must have worked. In less than an hour, there magically appeared: a rubber ground tarp, some two-by-fours, a large piece of plywood, and a couple of sawhorses to build a temporary shelter and table, provided by an eager Joe.

* * *

The 105s fired most of the night, supplying defense for other companies working around the area. The noise of these big guns made it difficult to get any rest. Sure, we'd heard them before, but they'd been in the distance. Here they were firing up close, at times right over our heads. As with everything else in this war, we had to get used to it. It was the quiet from the artillery company we noticed the most.

* * *

Libby's kitchen was set up in a tent in the middle of the base. The cooking and eating structure consisted of upright two-by-fours with a large OD green canvas top. The cook stoves were lined up in the back of a couple of jeeps parked along one side. Tables were plywood laid atop sawhorses. (*Hmmm ... where had I just seen that set-up?*) Everyone had to eat standing up since there were no chairs. We were looking forward to eating there.

We soon found out everything wasn't as it seemed. The food in our fantastic kitchen, although hot, was horrible. We would rather have had C-rats than this slop. These cooks were probably draftees who'd had six weeks of training before coming here. It wouldn't have been so bad if they were just heating food out of cans, but these guys tried to make homemade stuff from scratch. Yuck!

Our first night, they tried to cook chicken. Now you wouldn't think it would be too difficult, but it was undercooked inside and burnt outside, not to mention, tasteless. No amount of salt and pepper would help. The scrambled eggs were from powder and the SOS was worse than ever. These guys couldn't even cook potatoes by boiling them. They came out almost raw or like soup. The only thing cooked well was the Spam.

This was nothing like the kitchens we had sampled at Redcatcher or BMB.

* * *

Hi honey,

This is going to be a long letter to make up for the last two weeks.

Well, we made it. We're at Firebase Libby. They brought us in yesterday after sixteen days of pure hell. No one knows how far we patrolled. We started about forty miles from where we are now, but, we've circled around, doubled back, been moved by chopper and truck, and zigzagged all over the place. We humped three thousand to four thousand meters on all but a few days. It was a damn long way.

Our company is really down in strength. We lost six men to wounds, mostly minor, and twelve men to exhaustion. They were sent to the hospital. Two men were killed. We started with ninety-four and ended up with seventy-four.

Many were sent to the hospital with exhaustion, but were returned after a few days rest.

I'm really tired, but I'm holding up. The sores from the leeches are healing, my ringworm is going away, my foot fungus is getting better, and my cold is almost gone.

I know you're worried, but please remember I will keep my promise to come home. It's really not bad as long as we react, and I do react fast. I am alive, well halfway, and still in one piece.

I really miss you. I love you and need you very much.

I am not really changing too much, but I am some. Joe noticed I swear more. I guess it's expected after seeing all the death and destruction.

I helped to take the stretcher out to a man who had gotten shot and brought him back in. I just couldn't sit back when someone needed help. I'm sorry but that's me, I'm not trying to be a hero. As we say over here, "There's only one place left for us to go, we've spent our time in HELL!"

I didn't have a change of clothes or socks for the first six days and slept wet. When the men went to the hospital, we had to carry their equipment with us. We never did figure out why it wasn't sent with the men. Like a lot of the guys, I ended up carrying about one hundred pounds for the last two days of the patrol. So you see, it's hard to think of very much to say except, I LOVE YOU!

The words keep me going even when I'd like to stop. I hope this puts your mind at ease. Yeah, right. Just remember, I promised to come home to you and I haven't broken a promise to you yet.

Love, Len, your husband and lover

* * *

One morning, after breakfast, LT asked us, "How's everything going?"

"We have a lot of work to do," I said. What I wanted to say was, "If you'd ever come out to help, you'd know what's going on." But I didn't.

"I can see that; what's the problem?"

"Well, we've been workin' hard to get our mortar pits in shape. It's really difficult to level the dang things in this red slimy glop," Bill complained.

"We're using sandbags to try to stabilize the mud, but we don't have any sand and this excuse for dirt just won't do; it's too wet and sticks together," I continued.

"You're just going to have to make do, because it's all we've got. Command is not going to send us out a fuckin' truckload of sand! Got it?" The LT walked away.

"Roger, LT," Wild Bill yelled. "I knew that son of a bitch wasn't gonna help. Why in the hell did he even ask?" He jabbed the toe of his boot in the mud left by last night's rain. "Okay, y'all, let's start puttin' this crap into those dang fool green bags."

* * *

The army engineers had bulldozed back the jungle for about a hundred yards beyond the perimeter. Keeping our field of fire space open was a full-time job. The jungle constantly reclaimed the open land. We burned off the new growth weekly to keep up.

It was quiet on the base one afternoon. The mortars weren't firing nor were the 105s. Then a loud explosion shattered the silence. There hadn't been any high-pitched whistle of an incoming round, but it sounded as if we had taken artillery fire. Everyone hit the ground.

"Where the hell did that come from?" Mugs yelled.

"Don't ask me," Joe screamed back, "but it was damn close."

"The smoke is right over there," I said, pointing not more than fifty meters from edge of the jungle. We realized flames were engulfing a jeep.

Someone at a guard bunker yelled, "Medic!"

Since there had been no more explosions, everyone was off the ground and headed toward the berms to get a closer look at the fireball. As we approached the main gate, two medics ran past us heading for the jeep.

"Get out there and protect those guys," Top shouted.

Of course there wasn't a GI who didn't have his M-16 in hand. The jungle hid the enemy; therefore he could be only meters away.

As ordered, we surrounded the burning vehicle to provide a security force so the medics could do their job.

"Damn," Doc hissed in frustration. "Too late, we'll have to wait until the fire's out."

One GI had brought a shovel and started tossing dirt on the jeep in an attempt to smother the flames, but the jeep blazed on. Finally, the fire burned itself out and what we saw made even us old-timers ill. There in the jeep were three charred bodies.

These young men had been spraying gas from the back of the jeep onto the grass. We never knew if a spark from the jeep's exhaust caused it or if one of the guys wasn't thinking and tossed a match while the gas fumes were still in the air. Either way, it must have sent a back-flash into the gas cans on the jeep, resulting in an explosion and the deaths of three fine men.

The vast jungle was not going to give up easily. It was a tough lesson for all of us.

* * *

Everyone knew the sweetest words in the whole damned war were, "Mail call!"

"Hey, Rough, did you get one of those perfumed letters from your girlfriend?" Rat asked, grinning.

"Yeah, but they're from my wife, and they're not perfumed, you idiot."

"I envy you, Rough. There's nobody at home waiting for me. What did she have to say, if I'm not being too nosey?"

"Let me read you this part. She won't mind."

"You just keep telling yourself that, but one of these days it's going to come out, and she's going to really be mad at you," Joe reminded me as he walked over to listen.

"Well, anyway ..."

Hi Lover,

Gee, I really miss you a bunch. I think a lot about you and our lives together before you were drafted. It seems years have passed since you left. I pray for you and all of the guys in that "stinking hellhole." (your words)

I appreciate your letters telling me about where you are, what you're doing, and the guys in your unit. They sound like a special group of men. I only wish you could feel comfortable making real friends, although I understand your reasons.

I'm so very proud of you, and all of the guys in Bravo, for doing your duty to our country.

I love you and I will always love you no matter how much you say you've changed. I know war can do that, but you're a strong person. Your personality and upbringing will win out over anything the war can do.

We have so many plans. We will have a better lifestyle if I'm teaching and you're on the police force. I can hardly wait to get back to a normal life with you.

Everyone in the family is fine....

I looked up and there were about a dozen guys sitting around listening to Lu's letter.

"The rest is about family and personal stuff. I just thought you'd like to know she always says a prayer for all the guys of Bravo Company. In her own way, she has come to think of you as part of her extended family."

"Aw, that's nice," Rat uttered wiping a tear from his eye.

* * *

The base had been scraped clean of jungle vegetation. This caused it to become slick and muddy when it rained. The goo stuck to everything, caking our boots and filling the tread so we had no traction. It was like walking on ice.

We all knew Libby was an enemy target, so we wanted the thickest bunkers we could build. We used dirt-filled wooden boxes reinforced with two layers of sandbags.

We had a lot more room there, so the three mortar pits were in a row about four meters apart. We built a thick blast wall between our sleeping hooches and the mortars, with the ammo bunker next to the blast wall and close to the mortar pits.

We were able to construct small individual sleeping quarters. It was a lot better than the old Hotel we'd had back at the bridge. There we had most of the mortar platoon sleeping under the same roof at one time, a bad idea. It would have taken only one well-placed enemy mortar round or RPG to wipe us out.

We were now an extra foot platoon when the company was out patrolling, but still a mortar platoon while in the firebase.

Libby was just a place to leave our mortars and our personal stuff while out. The short overnight Tiger Alphas were a thing of the past. Now we were on missions lasting from one to two weeks.

* * *

"Rough, y'all know what's takin' place come Monday?" Wild Bill asked during a break in our morning routine.

"We get to go home? No? Well, do we get out of this damn war for a few days?" I knew what he really meant.

"Shit, don't y'all remember nothin'? Most of us have been waitin' for this event for what seems like forever!"

"Dammit, tell me before you bust a gut."

"The LT's finally rotatin' home."

"No shit, you mean he's going to make it out of this lousy war alive?"

"Yeah, but I figured you already knowed that!"

"I sure hope we end up with a lieutenant who isn't on our case so often. Hopefully Abitchie will take his brooms home with him."

"Could y'all believe having to sweep the damn dirt at Jeanie and the bridge when we were through practice?"

"That was real dumb. Then at other times, he sounded like he was taking our side."

"Y'all must have seen a side of him, the rest of us missed."

"Hey," I changed the subject, "how'd you get the name Wild Bill anyway?"

"Y'all really want to know? Well, it's like this. I kinda got a temper."

"I hadn't noticed," I said with a straight face.

He just glanced at me and continued. "One night on a Tiger Alpha, we got set up, and wha'd'ya' know, some dumb shit started to light up a cigarette. Can you believe that? Even a FNG knows better 'en that. I just about came unhinged and tackled the asshole right there on the

TA. I wanted to beat the shit outta him. He was puttin' our lives in danger."

"That was a wild and dumb thing to do, Bill. So the name Wild just stuck, huh?"

"Yeah, I've been Wild Bill ever since."

"I'll bet you're glad it wasn't Dumb Bill."

"Yep," he said with a grin.

"Let's just hope the next platoon leader will be willing to listen to some advice from an old-timer like you," I said.

"Rough, y'all're an old-timer yourself, and I know ya ain't afraid to let the LT know what ya think. In fact, I remember you telling off the CO one time. Now that's really dumb!"

"Shit, Bill, I didn't know who he was at first. He interrupted when I was reading parts of Lu's letter out loud to the guys. He yelled at us to keep it quiet and I told him to shut up and listen. Which, he did. Then I realized who he was and apologized."

"I also remember ya got shit can burnin' detail for the next week!" Bill chuckled.

* * *

"Rough, Professor, Mugs, the LT wants to see the squad leaders in zero five," Bill called out one morning.

"What kind of shit's in store for the platoon now?" Mugs asked.

"It won't be good, I'll bet a month's pay on this one," I responded.

We were off, very slowly. We were in no hurry to get to the LT's HQ.

I would have lost that month's pay …

Chapter 26 - Jungle Operations

The LT had called this meeting to announce he was rotating home and that our new lieutenant was Lieutenant Bratton from First Platoon. I knew him. I'd worked with him on a patrol while at Fishnet. This was really good news.

LT also told us we would be leaving on a long patrol, but without him. Our new LT would lead this one.

Lieutenant Bratton gave us the details. "The choppers will be here at 0630 tomorrow, so get your stuff together. I know everyone is still tired from the long patrol getting here, but there's nothing I can do about it. I've already commanded Rough and his squad from Gun Three. I know you're a great platoon, and I'm looking forward to working with all of you."

"Wilco, Lieutenant Bratton," we all responded.

"Just call me LT."

"The men'll have their shit together and ready to go on time, LT," Wild Bill said.

"Bill, I'm counting on you to help in the transition between me and Lieutenant Bratton."

"Have a safe trip home, LT," Bill replied.

"Thanks, I hope all of you get home, too."

"Anything else?" Bill asked looking to our new LT.

"No, that should do it. Dismissed."

"Welcome to Fourth Platoon," I said.

Bill gave everyone the good news about the new LT and the bad news about going out on another patrol.

The first order of business while packing was finding the cartons of C-rats so we could pick out enough meals for at least four days.

All of us had our favorite C-rat carton. They were numbered, and we had learned what food was in each package. Number B-3 was my favorite, as it usually contained cans of ham, peaches, and packets of hot chocolate, crackers, and peanut butter. Most of my meals consisted of these items added to the stuff Lu sent from home.

We found beef jerky and something called instant breakfast were lighter, making it easier to pack enough food for a long patrol. The packaged breakfast drinks were supposed to be mixed with milk, an unknown item at a firebase and never in the jungle. So we had to improvise with water and the coffee creamer packets from the C-rat boxes. We carried the extra water on belts around our waists. We tried to make the sixty-pound loads comfortable, an impossible task.

We used our leg pockets to carry small things like blocks of C-4, which weighed a quarter of a pound each. We did, however, put the blasting caps in a different pocket. We didn't want any accidental explosion caused by getting the two too close together. Grenades were hung on our belts and other parts of our clothing.

At least the platoon would be spared carrying the heavy, cumbersome mortars through the jungle.

I was glad we had this new LT. The week I'd worked with him had given me a whole new perspective on officer-to-grunt relationships. There was respect on both sides.

* * *

At 0600, five birds set down and were each loaded with a platoon and the command group. These were the smaller Hueys. It was easier for them to find an LZ in the jungle.

Two men sat in the open doorways, one on each side of the door gunner. We wouldn't fall out as the speed of the moving chopper glued us to the floor.

The guys sitting in the door had to move back from the edge if the gunner opened up with his M-60. It wasn't the danger of ground fire; it was being pelted with the hot brass casings from the machine gun as it spewed forth its death and destruction.

The door spots made for great seats to see what was passing below, and the rush of the cool air felt great. But they were the first ones off. When we put down in the jungle, the chopper's M-60s fired over our heads into the foliage to secure the LZ.

When we offloaded, we ran away from the choppers bent at the waist to be sure the blades and the machine gun rounds were over our heads. We were also closer to the earth, so if Charlie was in the jungle and started firing, we would have less distance to go to hit the ground.

The company made it into the dense jungle and the choppers were gone. It had been a cold LZ. No enemy fire.

Because of the impenetrability of the area, the CO decided a single-file patrol would be best. First Platoon would take point with Third Platoon pulling rear security. This order of movement would change after lunch.

The point team moved out. They had the compass direction, and led the company slowly snaking its way through the jungle.

* * *

Fourth Platoon was on point when Rat and Mac sent word they'd found a trail showing signs of recent use. The CO decided we would find a spot away from the trail for our NDP, so we could set up an ambush.

There was still some light, so we had time to fix dinner before dark. "Hey, why do you guys always have a small pile of dirt next to the C-4 you use to cook with?" Slim asked.

He was the newest man in the platoon and on his first patrol. He was a smart kid and real nice, tall and lanky; he kind of reminded me of my brother-in-law.

"We use the dirt to cover the red glow of the C-4 when we finish cooking. It continues to burn even with the dirt, but its light could give away our position," I explained.

"It won't explode?" He asked.

"Not unless you stomp on the stuff while it's burning; then it will explode. You sure as hell don't want to do that! It would cause major damage to your foot!" Joe answered.

"Oh, I see. The stuff burns if lit with a match and doesn't explode, but if you hit it or stomp on it, it explodes!"

"You got it, kid." It seemed strange for Joe to be calling him a kid, as they were about the same age. Maybe our time here made him feel older.

Ole had been monitoring the radio and passed along some good news, "Hey, guys, Second Platoon has the ambush for tonight. Ricky wants the company on fifty percent alert however, so I guess we aren't going to be getting a lot of rest tonight."

"Shit! Ole, who's going to be sleeping this close to an active NVA trail anyway?" Rat asked rhetorically.

The artillery's FO called in our NDP and requested a marking round a distance away from the trail. We didn't want Charlie knowing we were near. The marking round landed at the specified coordinates off to the south of us. In keeping with the American Army's practice of firing night harassment and interdiction into the jungle, some HE rounds were fired just to help confuse the NVA about what was happening.

We found cover in case a firefight broke out. In groups of three or four, we set up our tarps to provide us with some shelter from the rain.

Once again, the thought of a firefight with the NVA gave us a sickening feeling. Death was real, even though a little voice kept whispering it wasn't going to be you. We all knew it was a possibility. No one wanted to think about it, but we did.

Ricky was disappointed. Charlie didn't move along the trail. It was another night of no sleep waiting for the enemy to show.

At dawn, the company packed it in and prepared for another day of patrolling. The trail coordinates were reported to our artillery company for possible H & I firing in the future.

The direction we were given was to some unknown area the Intel reports had indicated might be a good spot.

* * *

"Hey, Rough, you've worked with this new LT b'fore. What do y'all think of him?" Wild Bill asked on our afternoon break.

"I like the guy. He plays fair with the men and treats us like we have some intelligence, not just a bunch of stupid grunts who need someone to tell them when to pee."

"I'm a short-timer so it can only get better, right."

"How much time left, Bill?" I was glad for him, but envious of his pending flight on the Freedom Bird.

"Thirty-two days in the field, thirteen days and a wake-up at BMB, and I'm on my way to the World!"

"I wish I was that close to going home! I still have one hundred and ninety-four days to go—way too many!"

As we plodded on through the afternoon, my little voice kept telling me this new LT was going to be important in my life.

* * *

The swarms of mosquitoes were so thick at times the air around us was almost black. It was difficult to breathe without inhaling some of these nasty little buggers. Slapping them would give away our position and, as much as we wanted to use the whole bottle of bug repellent, we knew it wasn't a good idea either. We were in enemy territory and the odor carried for miles.

When it rained, the mosquitoes left and the leeches came out in force. A cigarette was useless in the downpour. Then we discovered they could be removed with our mosquito repellent. The awful smelling stuff didn't keep the mosquitoes away, but one or two sprays made the damn bloodsuckers back out of our skin. We'd rather a little smell than the leeches.

It may sound stupid, but we played games with them. We would wait for these creatures to come creeping across the jungle floor searching out our bodies. Then we'd give them a squirt of bug juice. Some of the guys started a body count of the leeches they juiced, and watched shrivel up and die. Gross, but this was war between man and pest.

That night, we sat soaked, cold, miserable, and without sleep, but Charlie didn't come. We suffered in the monsoon. They were some place holed up in a warm, dry bunker complex.

Ha! Who won this battle? It sure wasn't us!

We policed our area leaving nothing Charlie could use. No open C-rat cans, no flares, no Claymore mines, not even an unused M-16 round, and especially nothing personal. All papers and letters were burned to ashes and buried.

The lunch break was upon us before any of us realized how quickly the time had passed. Just as we halted, dropped our packs, and began to relax, the radio came alive with excited whispers, "We've made contact with Charlie." We all grabbed our rifles and circled in our defensive positions. We heard a few shots, some machine gun fire and then quiet.

Everyone sat frozen in place, waiting for the gooks to arrive and a major battle to ensue.

Nothing—no sound, no movement, nothing.

We waited.

Nothing.

Finally, Third Platoon, who'd been on point, announced excitedly on the radio that they'd come upon a small patrol of NVA and opened fire, killing two and wounding another. But, when they went to check, there wasn't anything, just some blood trails leading into the jungle. Charlie had taken his dead and wounded and any evidence he had been there and disappeared. No confirmed kills could be made. No bodies could be added to the already short numbers for the CO. He was not pleased.

This set the routine for our patrols in and around Firebase Libby. There would be endless days of crisscrossing the jungle with little or no contact. Bravo Company was getting a reputation for the smallest body count throughout the 199th. Did we really care? Hell, no! We just knew the fewer times we had contact with the NVA, the better our chances of going home when our time was up.

We came across a small patrol once in a while, and we had several small firefights while humping through the jungle. But, what frightened us the most was Ricky and the top brass in the 199th. They were starting to move us out farther and farther from Libby, forcing us to make contact. One way or another, we'd eventually come up against a large group of the NVA. It was our worst nightmare.

Chapter 27- Off to the Hospital

Something was wrong with my body. It wasn't just tired, it was alternating between being hot and cold. I needed to talk to Doc.

"Doc, I seem to have a problem."

"Yeah, what's that?"

"I've been getting chills, but right now, I feel like I'm burning up."

He reached out and put his hand on my forehead.

"Shit, Rough, how long have you been running this fever?"

"A couple of days, but this part only started last night."

"Let me take your temperature." He reached into a jar of alcohol sitting on the table and pulled out a thermometer. Jamming it into my mouth, he said, "You know the drill, keep this under your tongue."

"Right," I mumbled.

A few minutes later, Doc checked the reading. "Damn, 102.6°! I'm putting you on twenty-four hours of bed rest and aspirin every four hours starting right now. We'll see how you feel then."

"The company leaves again tomorrow morning. Will I be with them?"

"It will be up to me. It sounds like the CO is going to slow things down. We're even supposed to be getting an hour for lunch, which I'll believe when I see it. So if you're back to normal tomorrow morning, probably.

By the next day I felt 100 percent better. My temperature was down, so Doc pronounced me fit for duty.

"All right, Rough, enough of lazing about in bed. Let's get ready to go, we leave in ten mikes," was all Top said when I checked in the next morning.

* * *

Our patrol headed west, looking for the bad guys on the Ho Trail. The day started out miserable, as the rains came early, soaking us to the skin. It didn't get any better.

We got warm rains during the day, but at night the rain came in a torrent and was cold as ice, chilling us to the bone.

By the afternoon of the third day, I could feel my body burning up again. I figured I'd better let Doc have another look at me. So there I sat, on the wet jungle floor with this dumb piece of glass stuck under my tongue, looking for the leeches I knew would be inching toward my body.

"Let's see what we have here," he said, reaching for the thermometer. "Shit, Rough, it looks like you're headed back to the rear on the next re-supply chopper with FUO."

"I've got what?"

"Fever unknown origin. Most likely it's malaria. Top has to confirm your temperature before you're sent back."

Top was called over and my temperature checked with Doc and his magic wand.

"Dammit, Rough, I don't have a lot of choice in the matter," he grumbled. "Your temperature of 103.8 puts you on the next chopper. You are not going to die on me in this fuckin' jungle!"

"Shit, Top, I didn't plan this," I replied.

"Don't worry, Doc. I'll tell the CO there's one Echo Mike who needs to go to the hospital." Top continued. "You're damn lucky, Rough, a re-supply chopper's due in the morning."

"Top, I think Dan would be a good man to take over as squad leader while I'm gone," I said, worried about my guys.

"Sounds like a good choice to me. I'll inform the CO and the LT that we'll be losing another man to the growing number of hospital casualties, and pass along you're suggestion for squad leader. Get your ass well, and get back out to the company ASAP. We need all of you old-timers on these damn company sweeps!"

"Roger, Top."

"I'll be talking to the brigade's first sergeant, so don't be gold brick-ing," said Top. He seemed more worried about me taking advantage of time out of the field than my health.

"Sure, Top, I'll be back as soon as the doctor says I'm cleared to go," I replied.

But there was going to be one more night. Sure, I was sick, but I still had two hours of night guard. It passed slower than usual. The rain seemed colder and fiercer. It was like the jungle was getting back at me for being able to escape it for a time.

Wild Bill gave me a nudge at first light. "Rough, the chopper will be here in about one–five mikes."

By that point, I felt so miserable, I just wanted to die. I could hear the transmission from the incoming chopper. It would be able to land in this large clearing, not just hover and push supplies out the door. They had a man to pick up—me.

"Everyone, get your asses to the LZ and set up security," the lieuten-ant ordered. "Rough, I hear you're on your way to the rear hospital."

"Roger, LT," I croaked through my dry lips.

"Your suggestion of Dan is a good one. Don't worry, things will be fine. You just get well."

"Thanks, LT."

"Bravo-One-One pop smoke, over."

The CO's radioman popped a green smoke grenade.

"I see jolly green, over."

"Roger, jolly green, bring it on down."

I was to guide the chopper down safely away from any tree limbs or other obstacles.

Three of us unloaded the supplies then I threw my heavy pack through the door and crawled in.

"Hold on," the door gunner yelled in my ear as we started to move up and away from the jungle floor. I quickly found a place against the back wall.

There below me, the hated jungle was passing. It didn't look as daunting or dangerous from up here. It looked like a benign, never-ending green carpet. But I knew the truth. I had cut my way through it, foot by agonizing foot, exhaustion my constant companion. I had encountered its snakes, its leeches, its thorns and sharp leaves, its mosquitoes, its wetness and humidity, and so far I had survived. The real jungle was a very hazardous place.

It seemed like we had just lifted off when we put down at brigade's main base. As the crew began their shutdown procedures, I grabbed my rifle and pack and slowly moved out the door. I looked around for someone who might direct me to the hospital. I spotted a medic walking away from another one of Bravo Company's landing pads. "Hey, Doc," I called out.

The medic stopped and turned to where I was standing. "Is there something I can do for you, buddy?"

"Sure, if you can tell me where the hospital is."

"Of course, I'm headed there myself."

I fell in at least ten feet to his rear.

"You must just be in from the field. It's okay to walk next to me so we can talk. There are no booby traps here."

"Sorry, some things are habit. I just want to find out what's wrong with me. Our medic called it FUO."

"Yeah, we've had a lot of that lately, possibly malaria. Too many are guys not taking their pills."

I didn't remember Doc giving us any, but in this crazy war anything was possible.

It only took about five minutes to get to the hospital. I told him thanks and stepped up to the desk just inside the door.

The first thing the clerk did, after finding my name on his list and admitting me to the hospital, was have me sign my rifle over to the armory. Here, in a safe place away from the war, I didn't need my weapon.

I was assigned a bed, an army cot really, and issued hospital pajamas and shower shoes. I was told to take a shower before changing. I guess I was kind of dirty and smelly. It was weird not feeling my feet squish in wet boots. Good, but weird.

My temperature was down to only 102.9°, but high enough for them to believe our medic had gotten the 103.8.

The first night, just before lights went out, the guy in the bed next to me started moaning and thrashing around. The one medic on duty went over to check on him.

After looking at his thermometer, he said, "I need you to help me get this guy's temperature down fast."

Was he speaking to me? I didn't see anyone else.

"You," he said, pointing in my direction, "follow me." He headed across the ward, his volunteer right behind.

I wondered, how I could help, I was only a patient. It wasn't long before we reached an ice machine.

"Fill this bucket with as much ice as you can carry and bring it back to the ward. I need to go start an alcohol-soak immediately."

By the time I returned, the medic had the sick GI covered with a sheet and was soaking it with rubbing alcohol. He took the bucket of ice and poured it over the body under the sheet. One thing about an army cot, all the weight sinks to the middle, so when we dumped the ice it didn't fall over the edge. The medic then folded both edges of the sheet up and over, covering the ice.

"Go get more, and be quick about it!" was his urgent request. We continued until the patient was completely covered. When the doctor arrived, the high fever had dropped.

My last thought before I went to sleep: *I hope my FUO isn't this malaria stuff. I don't ever want to be packed in ice like a fish.*

* * *

Hi honey,

I'm sick and in the Seventh support hospital at BMB for observation. I'll be here until they find out what I have. That's why my letter is on this American National Red Cross stationary.

Would you believe clean sheets? I'd forgotten what they feel and smell like.

The doctors think it might be a light case of malaria and are holding me here while they do some tests to find out for sure. I don't think it is, though. I'm just worn out. My temp is back down today, so please don't worry about me. I'll be fine, I just needed some rest.

I love you very much and I really need your support. If it weren't for you, I know I wouldn't be able to keep on going.

It's great. I'm out of the field for a few days. I could get used to clean sheets, clean clothes and dry boots. I'm doing my best to stay well. I'll write tomorrow when I know more about this FUO (fever of unknown origin) thing.

Love, Your husband and lover, Len

* * *

There were TVs in the recreation areas of the hospital. We all watched the moon landing in July 1969. It was amazing to us, the US could put a man on the moon, but couldn't stop the senseless dying and suffering in Vietnam.

I was able to stay in the hospital for three days, but at the end of my third day something started nagging at me. My platoon was out there fighting and here I was in this safe environment. My decision was made. Tomorrow, I would ask to be released back to Brigade.

The next morning, when the doctor made his rounds, I said, "Well, Doc, it looks like there isn't any lasting problem. I feel just fine today. I need to get back to my platoon. Maybe it was a simple fever and won't come back."

"That's a possibility. Sure you don't want to rest a few more days?"

"No, I'm fine."

Looking at my chart he said, "You seem to have a low body temperature. Is that unusual?"

"It always runs a degree lower than the expected 98.6, but normal for me," I answered.

"Okay, I'll process you out this afternoon, and then you're on your way back. Have your medic keep an eye on you in case your temperature spikes, and take your malaria tablets."

"Wilco, Doc." I knew none of us in the field took the tabs. I don't know why more of us didn't get that damn bug!

Later that afternoon, the clerk stopped by my bed. "It's time you got back to your unit. Oh, yeah, I brought your uniform. We'll need those pajamas for someone who really needs them. You guys act sick just to get out of the field."

He was making me angry. He had no idea what the men in this room had been going through every damn day. The term REMF became the perfect description of this bastard. He'd never seen one minute of the real war in Vietnam, and yet he would go home and tell anyone who would listen how he suffered over here. I wanted to say, "Fuck you, asshole, you need to get out in the jungle and find out what fighting in this mess is really all about!" But I didn't. He wasn't worth my energy, the creep.

He had a bundle of clothes under his arm—my old uniform, boots, and socks. They smelled even worse than I remembered.

I gritted my teeth and asked him, "You couldn't have brought me a clean uniform?"

"Get one yourself, slacker."

He needs to leave now or I'm going to punch this jerk in the nose. The clueless REMF will probably put in for a purple heart, get one, and then really have something to brag about. I was pissed.

He must have gotten the message from my enraged glare. He dropped the bundle, picked up the papers I'd signed, and left in a big hurry.

I dressed quickly and headed off to Bravo's HQ. On the way, I ran into brigade's first sergeant.

"Hey, soldier, where are you headed?" he asked.

"I was just discharged from the hospital and was going over to headquarters ..."

"Then you had best report. And do something about that uniform, soldier."

"Wilco, Top, on my way."

When I entered the office, the clerk looked up. "What can I do for you?"

"Get me out of this war!" was my response. "But, I guess you can't do that."

"No, besides, I'd send me home first. What do you need?" He had this pained look on his face.

"I was just released from base hospital and I'm supposed to be on the next re-supply chopper for Bravo Company. I understand you can tell me when it's going out."

He turned to a board behind his desk to check and took a deep breath. "You'll have to wait until tomorrow at 0600. It'll give you plenty of time to go over to supply. Smells like you need a clean uniform," he said scrunching up his face.

I'd worn this one for over a week before I was sent to the hospital. There it sat in some corner balled up for four days. Rancid, didn't even come close to describing the stench. I could hardly stand myself it was so bad. My uniform must have really attacked his nostrils.

"Where's supply?"

"Just go out the door and turn left. You can't miss it." He said pointing and holding his nose.

I followed his instructions. There were lots of crates and boxes stacked all around the building. I approached the GI sitting behind a desk reading the latest *Playboy*.

"What the hell do you want? Woo-wee do y'all stink!"

"I need a clean pair of fatigues. These are worn and dirty and probably should be burned."

He was trying not to breathe very deeply and had his hand over his mouth and nose. He waved me back away from his desk and disappeared out the door. "I'll be right back," he mumbled through his fingers.

This would have been funny, if I weren't the joke.

His "right back" was more like ten minutes, which gave me a chance to peek at the centerfold of the month. *Mmmm, not bad.* He returned carrying a clean set of fatigues and dry socks. "Damn, no boots."

"This is the best I could do. You looked like a large, so these should fit."

I took them from the young man. There didn't appear to be a changing room so, looking around and not seeing any females, I started to change right there.

"You don't mind me using your office, do you?" I asked after the fact. I couldn't get out of my old uniform soon enough. I stripped to bare ass, no underwear in Vietnam.

A few weeks in the war helped shed some inhibitions. When nature called in the jungle, you stepped behind a tree, did what was necessary, and caught up with the platoon. We didn't have much privacy while on patrol.

Once I was presentable again, I headed to the mess hall. I'd only have dinner and breakfast here, then it was back to C-rats. I got an icy-cold Coke, ordered dinner, and found an empty table. This was a real treat. We didn't have anything cold in the jungle. We had no 7-Eleven, no McDonald's, no Taco Bell, no ice, just C-rats and tepid water. I figured to take advantage while I could.

I still had my bed in the hospital where I'd sleep until time to leave in the morning. I wrote a letter home and hoped my mail was back at Bravo.

* * *

Hi honey,

The doctor is sending me back to duty tomorrow. Their magic has fixed me up and I feel better, but my stomach still bothers me and I've had a few headaches, but no fever.

They're not sure what it was. I think most of it was due to exhaustion. Whatever it was, it kept me out of the field four days.

I haven't gotten any mail here. With my luck, they'll start sending it here now that I'm leaving.

I forgot to tell you about the Apollo flight. I got to see it when it landed. It was really a fantastic sight. Amazing how it came off so perfectly.

Don't send any film until you receive this last roll. I'm not sure if the camera is working right. It got a little wet, but I hope it's okay. I want to get more pictures so let me know how many came out.

The photos you sent of you are about shot. I guess I take them out and look at them too often. Please send me new ones.

I've had so much time to think about our life together. I really love you. I miss our early mornings walking on the beach. I picture you laughing and talking. You're always so happy. I remember getting dressed up to go to dinner and a movie like we were rich. Well, honey, I was rich, I had your love. I can hardly wait to step back into that life as your husband and the father of our future children.

I need to get some sleep before I head back into the war. Just remember my promise to you. I won't break it. I love you with all my heart and I will come home.

Love, Your lover and husband, Len

* * *

Zero-five-hundred came early. It seemed like I had just closed my eyes. I checked out of the hospital, had breakfast, and got my old trusty M-16 and my helmet. I picked up my backpack, which seemed heavier since my stay in the hospital. I found the chopper on a pad just where I'd left it. The engines were running and the blades turned in preparation for takeoff.

I walked over to the door gunner. "You must be Rough. Been expecting you. We'll be leaving in about one-zero mikes. We still have to load the water. This will be a quick stop at the LZ, so be ready to get your shit off and help unload."

"Roger," I replied.

My short time out of the war was like a vacation, but now it was over. I was on my way back into the jungle. Why I volunteered to go back early instead of staying another day or two, I'll never figure out, just dumb I guess. But, I did feel a lot more alive on this trip back. It was amazing what a few days of rest and relaxation could do.

Chapter 28 – Damn, I'm an RTO

The flight out to the company felt like seconds. Once again, I was looking down on the hated jungle. As we started our approach to the open LZ, I could see the detail waiting for the chopper to land. Ole, our RTO, was waiting there, too.

The chopper hit the ground and I threw my pack out through the side door. I was right behind it. I turned around and started catching supplies, passing them to the guys on the ground.

"Ole, you came to meet me," I yelled over the whine of the engines.

"Hell, no, I broke my leg last night and I'm headed back to the hospital. Guess who gets the radio?"

"Don't tell me, it's me? Damn!"

"You guessed it, Rough! Top thinks you should have it since you're all nice and rested."

"I guess it's his way of getting back at me for leaving," I yelled, as I helped Ole through the door.

He turned around and grinned at me as the engines revved preparing for liftoff.

We moved back into the jungle away from the ascending chopper, and there, standing next to the damn Prick-25 was Top.

"I've got a little present for you, Rough. Now, get it on your back, we're moving out. We've been waiting all morning for you."

I looked at my watch; it was only 0620. I would need a few minutes to repack. I had to make room for the radio and its two extra batteries, increasing the weight by more than thirty pounds.

"Well, Rough, now you have the responsibility of carrying the radio," Dan said as he walked over to welcome me back to the platoon. He would keep the job of squad leader for now. I had no problem with that. He was a good man, and we got along fine.

Then it hit me ... Ole broke his leg! A broken leg doesn't heal overnight or in a few days. Son of a bitch, I was going to hump this fucking radio for a lot longer than a couple of days.

If I'd only stayed one more day ...

"Glad to see you're back. Are you set to move out?" the LT asked.

"Roger, LT, the radio is packed, and I'm as ready as I can be."

"Rough, I know you don't like it, but you're my RTO now."

"No problem, LT, I remember how you want the radio handled. I've been out of it for four days, so give me time to get back in the swing of things."

"Fair enough, Rough."

* * *

At least I wouldn't be part of a point team. Then again, maybe it would be better than carrying this damn radio. It was heavier than it looked. I was definitely hoping Ole would make a quick recovery and would once again become the platoon's RTO.

I remembered how to carry the radio's hand mike so I could hear incoming transmissions, and at the same time leave my hands free to carry my rifle and push the jungle out of the way. I clipped it on my shoulder harness close to my ear. It was wrapped in plastic so it wouldn't get wet. The volume was turned up, but not so loud that it could be heard very far from the radio.

As the company moved out, the LT was in his spot, six feet in front, where he could turn and grab the hand mike to be on the radio fast.

Hours passed before I heard those welcome words, "All Bravo stations, three-zero mikes for lunch."

"Thank you, God," I muttered under my breath. I was out of shape.

The day seemed to last forever and my pack got heavier as we traveled another two thousand meters after lunch. Finally, the CO's RTO broadcast good news, "Attention all Bravo stations, stop and set up NDP, out."

The radio kept me informed about what the company was doing and any activities going on in and around our AO. As RTO, my spot in the platoon's NDP was close to the middle, which made it easier to pass the radio as the guard changed during the night.

After heating my dinner, I made my first radio check. The CO's RTO called, "Bravo-Three-Two-X-ray, commo check over."

I responded, "Lima-Charlie, over." If the radio transmission hadn't been loud and clear, I'd needed to fix the problem before the night watch started.

We all quieted down for the night.

* * *

Hi honey,

I got back to the company yesterday afternoon. Ole broke his leg. I don't know how and I never think to ask. So at the present time I'm a Radio Telephone Operator or RTO. That puts an extra thirty pounds on my back, ugh. I guess I'm just a pack mule.

In a few days we head back to the firebase.

This is going to be short as we are ready to leave. I just had to let you know where I was and tell you I love you and miss you.

I've got to go. I love you with all my heart.

Love, Len, your husband and lover

* * *

Time passed; days turned into weeks. I'd been carrying the radio for thirteen days. If I didn't have it on, I felt lost, alone, and exposed. I knew all I had to do to get help was make a call over the company net. The radio could bring artillery, choppers, or reinforcements.

My weight was below 170 pounds. On these patrols, I was expected to carry ninety pounds of supplies and equipment. Humping through the sweltering jungles, with all the creepy crawly things, not even considering the enemy, could kill a man. All the RTOs who served here managed to handle the radio and so would I. I had to survive. I'd made a promise to Lu. I would come home.

Chapter 29 - The Bunker Complex

On one patrol, our point team came upon a plateau where the jungle had thinned out. They started moving faster and before we knew it we were in the middle of an NVA bunker complex. The guys cutting point were experienced and should have recognized the signs. We all should have. Thank God nobody was home.

We walked straight through, watching for booby traps. The CO called a halt about hundred meters on the other side. Our location and situation were called back to headquarters and Arty.

The surrounding area needed to be secured before we started our search and destruction of the bunkers. The CO sent out five teams to hunt for Charlie. Mac was carrying the radio for the day, giving me a rest, but being behind him, I heard each patrol check in.

One team made a find, except someone forgot a very important rule. In a free-fire zone there are *no* friendlies. It means you shoot first and ask questions later.

They had radioed, "There are a couple of kids in the area, so be careful not to shoot them." He'd almost finished his statement when these kids dropped into a spider hole and came back up firing AK-47's. They were NVA soldiers.

One man took a round in the stomach.

"Medic," yelled someone over the radio.

Doc was up and running towards the wounded man without thought to his safety. He called for a couple of men to bring the stretcher.

Rat, Mr. Cynic, who never volunteered to do anything, went with Dan. We had started taking machine gun fire from the NVA out from the perimeter. They had Doc, Dan, Rat, and the guys with the wounded man pinned down.

This new LT seemed to have a death wish. He decided the two of us were going to take a LAW out past them to destroy the machine gun position.

Rat had left his pack when he went to help bring in the wounded man. He always packed a LAW. I grabbed it on the run and headed out with the LT.

As I ran I thought, *Shit, he's going to get me killed! Who does he think he is, John Wayne?*

The LT stopped; we were out in the open. I couldn't see any cover, unless we were six inches tall and could hide behind a blade of grass.

He asked, "Rough, you remember how one of these works, don't you?"

"Ah, I think so. Where the hell are the gooks?"

"From my best estimate, they're about four hundred meters out, near that small clump of elephant grass."

About then, they opened up with a burst of gunfire. The LT had been right. Getting low to the ground, I went to work. *Come on Rough... remember how to fire a light antitank weapon.* We had practiced during AIT and again at Redcatcher. But this was different; now I was dodging machine gun rounds. I was petrified, and my hands were shaking.

"Let's go, Rough."

"I'm ready, LT."

"Okay, get it done!"

"Fire in the hole!" I yelled just before touching the trigger.

Smoke and flames belched out the rear of the LAW as the warhead was propelled the four hundred meters in the direction of the machine gun fire. A cloud of smoke, dirt, and other debris flew into the air at about the right spot. It must have worked; the firing stopped.

Even as the roar of the LAW died from my ears, I could hear the silence of death. I looked up to see the LT racing back to Mac, yelling over his shoulder, "Go help, Doc!"

He was on the radio requesting 105 support in seconds. He checked the map. "Drop your rounds on grid: golf-five. This is to be HE rounds."

"Roger, Bravo-Three-Two, HE rounds on grid golf-five," I could hear Arty repeat the order.

"Heads up, guys," the LT bellowed to the company.

Arty radioed and relayed, "Shot!"

Then "Splash!" was heard a short two minutes later.

The first round was just about on target, four hundred and fifty meters from us and just behind where we thought the gun had been.

"Nice shot, Arty, now add fifty and fire for effect."

Arty was right on target. There was a salvo of three rounds, which rained down on grid G-5. The explosions had barely died away when the lieutenant was back on the radio. "Bravo Company needs one medevac chopper. Be advised of a possible hot LZ."

"Bravo-Three-Two this is Angel-Zero-One. We'll be there in zero five mikes. Have package ready to dump through door with takeoff ASAP. Over."

"We're ready. Bring it on down, over."

"Roger Three-Two, will call when we start our run. Out."

"Thanks, Angel-Zero-One. It's a stomach wound, hurry."

"Roger, gut-shot, over."

Good to his word, less than five minutes later we could hear the whop-whop sound of the medevac hovering over the treetops.

"Bravo-Three-Two, pop smoke. Is it still a hot LZ? Can you cover us? Over."

"Roger Angel-Zero-One, we are taking some AK fire. Over."

"Bravo-Three-Two, I see ruby red. Over."

"Roger, Angel-One. Will put down covering fire, over."

"Thanks, Bravo, over."

"Wilco, Angel-One."

The company was prepared for the inbound chopper, which hovered about three hundred meters out from our landing zone. We weren't taking a lot of fire from the NVA, just enough to be a danger to the chopper.

"Bravo-Three-Two, coming in, over."

The chopper dipped its nose and dove for our LZ hugging the tops of the trees. At the last second he pulled the nose up and dropped to the ground. Doc and the two men with the stretcher were waiting to put the wounded man on board. They threw the GI like a sack of potatoes through the open door. As soon as the soldier hit the floor, the pilot gunned the engines and headed for the safety of open sky.

The medevac took no ground fire. We could tell the pilot was determined to get our wounded man out no matter what, and to hell with the NVA. "Thanks, Angel-Zero-One, I'll have to buy you a beer sometime," the LT said as the chopper disappeared over the horizon, taking our wounded man back to the hospital and out of the war.

The CO gave the job of seeking out the snipers to Platoons One and Three. This left the dangerous job of looking through the bunkers to the Second and Fourth.

This was a good-sized complex. We figured it was a stopping off place for those traveling the Ho Express.

We discovered seven bunkers large enough to sleep eight to ten NVA soldiers each and another larger bunker used as a hospital. We found *beaucoup* vitamin K, a cache of provisions, medical supplies, and important maps and documents. We were ordered to bring back the papers for translation and destroy everything else.

There was a lot of rice in bags along the walls. We cut open the bags and dumped it in the mud on the floors. We could clearly read the UNICEF markings. It had been stolen from the people of South Vietnam, but we had no way to return the precious rice. We could only destroy it, so the enemy couldn't use it.

The medical stuff was mostly vitamin K. Later, Doc explained to us about how the gooks would pump themselves full of the vitamin making them more willing to fight. Vitamin K made their blood clot faster when they were wounded, giving them longer before the wound slowed them down.

"Oh, oh, here comes Rat. He's really pissed at you," Joe informed me.

"At me? What did I do?"

Before Joe could answer, Rat stuck his nose in my face and yelled, "Why in hell did you use *my* LAW? I've carried that fuckin' thing for over 150 miles and never got a chance to fire it! And what did you do?"

"Aw, Rat, the LT …"

"I'll tell you what you did, you son of a bitch, you stole it from my pack and used it!"

"Rat, let me tell …," I tried again to explain.

"That's what you did! Now it's useless. It's a one-time deal and now that *you've* fired it, it's finished. I never got a chance, you fucking bastard!"

I wasn't too sure how to handle this situation. As I was getting ready to say something, I heard Joe as he stepped between us.

"Now, Rat, Rough was only doing what he had been ordered to do by the LT. He didn't have a choice. If you blame anyone, blame the new LT. But you may want to think about the fact that they saved your life. Remember you were carrying the stretcher for the injured guy, and the machine gun was spraying fire towards you. By my way of thinking, you should be thanking Rough and the LT, not yelling at them."

"Yeah, but it was *my* LAW!"

"Which was used to save *your life*! Wasn't that why you carried it in the first place?" Joe continued.

"But, I wanted to fire it." He sounded like a petulant little boy.

"Well, you didn't, so shut the fuck up. You can get a new one when we get back, now let's finish checking out these bunkers."

"You're right, Joe, but I'm still pissed at Rough," he glared in my direction.

"Come on, Rat," Joe coerced him towards a bunker.

"Are we going to use some CS grenades so the place can't be used for a spell?" asked Rat.

Joe wanted him to use some of his anger on the NVA. "I understand that's the CO's plan if our C-4 and grenades don't do the job."

"Man, that stuff's nasty. The stink and irritation of tear gas lingers a long time. No one'll be able to live here for months."

"Yeah, that's the idea!" Joe said, "Now let's go."

We looked through the bunkers very carefully. We had been hearing "fire in the hole" for the last five minutes as, one by one, the other bunkers were blown apart.

Joe disappeared into the black hole of yet another one. He stopped just inside to let his eyes adjust to the pitch-black interior. "Damn. It's dark in here. I could use with some matches or a cigarette lighter," he spoke through the portal. We could hear him mutter as he kicked something.

It only took a couple of minutes for Joe to check out the inside. "There's not a damn thing down here but darkness and some empty cans."

"Find a couple of good spots to put the C-4 and y'all get the hell outta there," Bill called to Joe.

"Toss me in two more blocks of C-4. I have just the spots, but I only have two left."

Bill passed the explosives down to Joe. "Y'all got blastin' caps?"

"I've used my last one."

"Rat, you got any?"

"Hell, no. I guess I forgot them in my other pants," was his smartass answer.

"Doesn't anybody have blastin' caps?"

"Hey, we can use a Claymore to set off the charges," I suggested.

"I could use an extra man to hold a match. Send Rat."

"Rat, y'all take this mine and get in there to help Joe."

"Shit, you want me to go? Joe, any rats down there?"

"Nope, they wouldn't fit."

"Come on, Rat. The CO wants this job done so we can be far away by the time it gets dark." I prodded and he glared.

Rat took a Claymore mine and disappeared into the bowels of the bunker. "Just remember who gets to blow this fucking thing!" He yelled for my benefit, "I never got to use *my* LAW."

A loud explosion in the main bunker followed, "Fire in the hole!" Dirt, smoke, and dust blasted skyward. The strong smell of gunpowder hung in the air, but to the dismay of the entire company, the bunker was hardly damaged.

"Shit, Top, we used five blocks of C-4, and this thing jumped at least an inch off the ground, but it stayed intact." One of the men from Second Platoon yelled in frustration.

"Then we'll leave it unusable. Who's carrying chicken shit grenades?" Top asked.

Two guys spoke up, "We've got a couple."

"Pull their pins and on my count of three, toss them inside as far to the back wall as possible."

"Wilco, Top."

"1 … 2 … 3. Fire in the hole!"

The grenades exploded, sending gas and smoke billowing throughout the log bunker, seeping into all the corners and crevices. The acrid smell of gas was there to stay.

"Rat, are y'all finished yet?" Bill yelled through the doorway.

"No need to yell. We're right here," Rat said as he and Joe crawled out the door. Rat carried the detonator, which was hooked up to the mine.

I threw the remnants of the LAW into the cavern to be buried under the rubble.

Everyone backed away and checked to be sure no one else was near. I stood behind the trunk of a large palm.

Rat yelled, "Fire in the hole."

When the mine detonated, it caused the blocks of C-4 to ignite, creating a huge explosion. Smoke, dirt, and splintered wood went every which way, flying into the air and the surrounding jungle.

"Great balls of fire! I think we finished off that bunker!" Wild Bill exclaimed, brushing the dirt and debris from his uniform.

"Dammit, Rat, what did you use in there, a small A-bomb? We could have used one on our bunker," Glass from Second Platoon asked.

"Of course not. It was just a Claymore and four blocks of C-4, Drill Corporal."

"Yep, that'll do it. Well, ah, nice job, fellas," was all he had to say as he walked away shaking his head.

"Bill," the LT said, "get Fourth ready to move out in zero-five."

"Roger, LT."

It was going to be dark soon and we were nervous about staying in the area much longer. We all shared the uncomfortable feeling the NVA would be coming back soon, and we wanted to be far, far away.

We'd been moving about twenty minutes when the CO called our 105 Battery to fire on the area .We heard the screech of the rounds as they passed over our heads, raining their destruction down upon the bunker complex. The NVA might come back and try to repair it, but we knew Arty would now use it regularly for target practice.

We'd done something to help out in this war. All of our patrolling, all the endless miles we had hacked through the jungles, all the backbreaking ordinance we'd carried, and yeah, all the complaining, had finally done some good for a change. For one of the few times since I'd arrived, I felt good about the day that was coming to an end.

* * *

Hi honey,

For the first time I feel better about why we're here. I know you're really proud of what we're doing. Now, I am, too.

Remember I told you the CO and the major were doing their best to have us catch the NVA. Well, yesterday it almost happened. We wandered into a bunker complex. No one was there except a few men.

We got in a short firefight and a man from another platoon was wounded. We destroyed the large complex and their supplies. Charlie will never be able to use it again. We did the job we're here to do.

So, how is my number one girl doing? Okay, I hope. I know you will be better when this nightmare separation is over and I can come home to your arms. I love you and I miss you so very much.

Always remember you are the most important person in my life. Without you, your love, and support, I would never have been able to make it through this hell.

I'm sorry, I've run out time. I need to get this on the chopper.

Love, Len, your husband and lover

P.S. Hawaii can't come soon enough for either of us!

Chapter 30 - The Chopper Disaster

The new LT thought everyone should know how to handle every job, so for this patrol we switched off working the radio every other day. I would again be the RTO for the next two days, carrying the PRC-25, the Prick-25, or the ass-kicker. By whatever name, it was damned heavy.

This was scheduled as our re-supply day. We were due to have a Kit Carson scout from brigade sent out to help guide us. Before being captured, he'd been part of an NVA company, which at one time had worked this area of jungle.

Our designated LZ, according to the map, was an open area only a good day's patrol away, if everything went right. That didn't happen very often. We'd learned to expect the unexpected.

The CO gave the point team the direction, and we slowly sliced through the jungle toward the LZ. A few hours later the radio crackled to life.

"Bravo One-One-X-ray, this is One-Three-X-ray, over."

"One-Three-X-ray, go."

"Tell One-One there's no terrain fitting the map, over," the point team reported.

"One-Three-X-ray, how could you get lost?"

"One-One-X-ray, we must have been given the wrong numbers, over!"

As the RTO, I could hear what was being said.

"Attention all Bravo stations, take zero-five."

The company slowed to a halt. We stopped, checked for leeches, ants, or pointy objects, then dropped our packs and our exhausted bodies to the jungle floor.

"What the hell's the matter, and where's the LT going in such a hurry?" Mugs asked.

"The CO called for all platoon leaders ASAP. It seems we're lost. We're stopped while they sort it out. First Platoon or the CO really screwed the numbers," I answered.

"Shit, and I thought we were stopping to get a few minutes' rest."

"If we spend too much time getting back on track, the re-supply chopper will be at our LZ, and we won't fuckin' be there to meet it," Joe reminded us.

"Damn straight! It's not gonna just land and leave our supplies, either."

It wasn't long before I heard, "Arty, this is Bravo One-One. Requesting fire mission, one marking round at grid Foxtrot-Seven, over." These were the coordinates for our assigned LZ.

"Roger, Bravo One-One, marking round at grid Foxtrot-Seven, over."

"Attention all Bravo stations: Shot," came the word over the radio.

"Heads up! Round's on the way. Let's find the damn thing," I yelled.

A couple of minutes passed.

"Splash," reported Arty.

The marking round exploded a good fifteen hundred meters to the north, not the direction we were heading. Damn, we had a long way to go to reach our LZ. We had important documents that had to get back to HQ. Kit would be dropped off and one of our men, Ryan, picked up. He was down to two weeks and would be going back to BMB and out of the war.

Most of us weren't happy the CO required him to be on this patrol. Everyone made sure he was in the safest spot in the company and not walking point. He'd already survived fifty weeks and we all wanted him to get back to the World, alive.

The silence of the moment was broken. "Break's over guys," LT said as he returned.

"Dan, you and Rat are the point team for now. Do not get us lost. Got that?" his voice oozed irritation.

"But, LT," Rat started, "It had to be the CO …"

"I don't give a rat's ass what happened. Now get us going and in right direction! We're the flippin' point team the rest of the day!" the LT hissed.

Rat continued to bitch as he passed the other platoons heading to the front. "… can't find their way out of a damn paper bag without the Fourth …"

Now, I knew why LT had looked angry. He had a good reason. Fourth Platoon was to step in and clean up the CO's mess and get us to the LZ in time for the chopper.

"How'd we get so lucky?"

"Strange as it may sound, Rough, the CO thinks Fourth has the best point teams, and I agree."

The LT was a nice guy, but even while I carried the radio, we never became friends. We always remained LT and his RTO, Rough.

The jungle had gotten thicker and the point team had to make a few wide swings around some thick bamboo. We definitely weren't going to be at the LZ early. We just prayed now we'd be on time.

Evening was fast approaching. A grumble from my stomach reminded me I didn't get much lunch and only managed a sip of water on our last five-minute break.

"LT, do you ever have a feeling something bad's going to happen? I have one about today. We're pushing too hard."

Before he could answer, the radio came to life. Dan and Rat had reached the LZ.

"Attention all Bravo stations, this is One-One-X-ray, we'll break for dinner after the re-supply bird is unloaded, out," radioed the CO's RTO.

"Damn, LT, there won't be enough time to check the area before the chopper lands."

"We haven't seen any sign of gooks today. We'll have to hope it's a cold LZ. Besides, the CO's not worried."

At the LZ, the company made a loose formation around the clearing. We had no time for a good sweep of the area. Ryan was to be the chopper's guide, since he needed to be close to climb on board when it landed to drop off Kit and the supplies. He would carry the NVA documents back to headquarters.

"Bravo One-One this is Supply Zero-Two, pop smoke, over."

The CO's RTO popped a purple smoke grenade.

"One-One, I see goofy grape over."

"Roger that, bring it on down."

We waited for the chopper to land in an open area the jungle had provided us. Then it happened. Above the whine and "whop whop" of the chopper's engines, we heard a noise we all knew and feared. It was the sound of an RPG being fired. Every head quickly turned looking for the spot where the rocket had been fired, but we all knew the bastards would be gone before we could retaliate.

A second or two passed. Time seemed to move in slow motion. We watched the smoke trail from the rocket as it made a beeline for the chopper. Everyone was helpless. All we could do was watch the impending catastrophe.

My radio was useless. I was paralyzed. No one could call the chopper in time. It didn't stand a chance against the RPG. There was a bright flash and loud explosion as the rocket grenade and chopper collided.

"Damn," the LT groaned.

We all watched in horror as the chopper listed to its right and started down through the jungle. Its blades slashed a path through the foliage, as it fell toward Mother Earth. The roar of the dying engines assaulted our ears, smoke and fire billowed from the tail section. We heard the screech of metal as the bird was pulled apart.

"Shit." I tried to burrow myself into the jungle dirt and mud. I was unable to take my eyes away from the disaster happening before me.

The chopper sliced a path through the jungle as it fell towards the man waiting to board. Ryan just stood there as if his feet were glued to the spot. He must have been so shocked he couldn't move out from under the falling chopper. He finally dove for cover, but to no avail. The blades continued whirling before they imbedded themselves in the ground. In that instant, I knew Ryan wouldn't make it back to the World.

I continued to watch as blood and body parts flew through the air and scattered throughout the jungle around the dying chopper.

Something spewed from my gut, burning my throat and mouth as it erupted.

The chopper finally came to rest, lying on its side. Through the bloody, cracked glass covering the cockpit, we could see two men moving. All of us were frozen in place at the sight except Wild Bill. He managed to climb through the open, twisted doorway. He grabbed one pilot by the neck of his uniform and pulled him out of the cab before the gas tanks could explode. The other followed Bill. He'd saved both their lives. But he was unable to rescue the Kit Carson scout.

"Medic," Bill yelled as he climbed out of the burning chopper. Doc was already running toward Bill and the injured pilots. They had suffered cuts and bruises. One had a broken leg, the other a dislocated shoulder. Their flak jackets had saved them from deeper wounds on their torsos.

There was an explosion, and a huge fireball singed the hair from the arms we had thrown over our faces for protection. The Kit Carson scout became a part of the inferno. We had the gruesome task of picking up Ryan's body parts. While expecting the NVA to return, we kept our rifles in hand as we put everything we could find in a body bag. It was a difficult job. There was a lot of upchucking as pieces were found.

"God, this was Ryan's helmet, and it's still attached to his head," Dan moaned as he brought the helmet to Doc. Doc wasn't looking too good either. He gulped and then added it to the bloody pile of pieces, which had once been a person.

We would have to carry the two pilots and the ominous black bag to a different LZ. Brigade wasn't going to take a chance with the medevac chopper landing here. Another open space had been located three hundred meters from this calamity.

We headed to the new LZ, leaving Kit and the chopper where they'd died. The fire had been so intense there was no way to extract a body from the wreckage. The grave would be the scarred jungle, but the foliage would soon grow back, covering the evidence. It was Mother Nature's way of correcting man's errors in judgment.

Everyone was silent, as we wound our way to the LZ. We reflected on the destruction we had witnessed and thanked God it hadn't been us.

We made the new LZ early. The CO sent four squads to search the area for any threat before the chopper was cleared to land.

It brought water and C-rations. Though we weren't in the mood to eat, we knew we should. The jungle extracted a lot from our bodies.

We loaded the injured pilots and Ryan's body. The black bag reminded us of how fragile our lives were, crushing our hopes and dreams of returning home. The chopper left, taking its cargo and leaving behind a deathly silent jungle.

We were angry with the CO for making Ryan come on this patrol. We were angry with ourselves for not having the time to sweep the area around the LZ. We were angry with the slant-eyed bastards who shot the re-supply helicopter out of the sky. We were even angry with Ryan for dying so close to his trip home on the Freedom Bird! Yeah, Bravo Company was *angry*!

* * *

We still had a couple more days of the patrol left, according to Top and the CO. We were going to stay at this location for the night. It was as good a spot as any.

Most of us would have felt better if we'd been extracted and had gone back to Libby for a couple of days of rest. We all needed to figure out how to handle Ryan's death.

"Dammit, LT, we should have known better than to call for a chopper until we'd swept the area."

"Roger, Rough. We made a mistake. We learned a very expensive lesson today that cost two men's lives. We won't make that error in judgment again."

"I can only think about how my wife and the rest of my family would feel if it were me!"

"I know what you mean, but file it away."

"Wilco, LT, I'll do the best I can. I saw the chopper cut Ryan into pieces. It won't be easy to 'file it away', sir."

I don't think it will ever be filed away. Damn Ricky and Top. We could have gotten by for one more night without supplies and done things the safe way. It wouldn't have been the first time any of us went hungry or thirsty. Ryan shouldn't have been on this patrol and he shouldn't have paid the ultimate price! It was senseless!

I turned to the lieutenant, "It doesn't get any easier watching someone killed, and I hope it never does. Witnessing a fellow GI's death without feeling would take away our humanity."

"You have to forget it for now. We have to go on with our lives and do our jobs. Right now, your job is to carry the hated radio and be alert for the enemy. I don't want any more men to die!"

I still had six months to go in this damn war! Anything could happen, so I needed to mentally get back into it. I didn't want to end up like Ryan. I wanted to go home on the Freedom Bird. I'd promised Lu. Thinking of her was my way to keep sane in all this madness.

Chapter 31 - The Day After

The morning after Ryan's death was a somber one. And yet, we were all thankful deep inside that it hadn't been us. We were undamaged and alive. We quietly did our duties, ate breakfast, and got ready for another monotonous day of humping through the green monster.

The NVA were in the jungle somewhere. Bravo's men had been sent to find them.

The day became really hot and steamy, and by lunch we felt as if we were in a sauna. People actually paid good money to get this kind of treatment, and here we were getting paid about three dollars a day for the privilege.

Thank God it was quiet, perfect for humping and thinking. We were beginning to look and act like zombies. If we ran into more than a few NVA, we would be in serious trouble.

While it was still light, the CO called a halt. We finished our usual NDP setup, and settled down for the night.

"Rough, get your meal fixed before dark."

"Right, LT. It doesn't take long to heat my ham and hot chocolate."

"What, no coffee?"

"You'd have to be a lifer to call that stuff coffee. It would even give battery acid a bad name."

"Yeah, you're probably right. Looks like you'll be needed on perimeter guard. Tell Bill you're available."

"Roger, LT."

I wandered over to where Bill was eating. "What time do you want me for guard?"

"Rough, y'all can have the first shift. That okay?"

"Sounds good to me, Bill."

"Rat, Joe, Mugs, I guess we'd best put up some rain shelter, or we're gonna be cold and real damn wet. Give me your ponchos," Wild Bill said.

Two of them were snapped together to make a ground cover. The other two were used as a roof.

"I gave the LT mine to use as a ground tarp since he was sitting by himself," I said grinning. "I'm pulling guard with you turkeys, and figured I'd use your cover."

"You really like that guy, don't you?" Joe asked.

"He has a good idea of how to run the platoon and how to treat the men. Yes, I like him. We could be friends if not for this stinking war."

I was in the midst of four other guys, trying to keep dry under one corner of our combined poncho-liner roof, with the radio, the grenades, the Claymore mine hand-firing devices, and my rifle.

I made sure that the grenades were easy to find in the dark. I had the pin pulled slightly out of the handle, SOP for night defense.

The first thing used in an ambush were the Claymores and then the grenades. Both weapons could take out more of the enemy without exposing our position. With a grenade, you pulled the pin, let the handle pop off, and threw it in the direction of the enemy. It exploded, giving you time before the VC pinpointed your location. The mines were also easy to use; we just pushed a button.

Our rifles were the last fighting weapons to be used, since the muzzle flash gave away the spot we fired from. We didn't want to give Charlie a target.

As night settled, our friends, the jungle night creatures, came to life. Their noises, the chirps, the buzzes, and the hums were a friendly sound to our ears. Absence of the night sounds meant danger; the enemy was near.

The CO, in anticipation of NVA in the area, had sent out two LPs. During my watch, the LP to the north called in for a light. They thought they had heard a patrol east of them a hundred meters or so.

"Bravo-Arty, Bravo-One-One-X-ray, we require one illumination round a hundred-fifty meters due east of our position, in grid F-6," advised the CO's RTO.

"Bravo-One-One-X-ray, Bravo-Arty, one illumination round in grid F-6, roger."

We watched as the night sky to our right lit up.

"Bravo-One-One, do you need other rounds? Over."

"Bravo-Arty, negative, out."

They knew where we were and could bring the max on the area if needed.

"Was the CO just trying to scare the gooks with one airburst over their heads?" Sam, one of the new guys, muttered to Joe.

"Now watch what comes next," Joe answered.

Not long after the artillery was called off, we could hear the sound of a chopper in the distance. I was still manning the radio so I was able to monitor the CO's transmission.

"Apache-Alpha-One, this is Bravo-One-One. Over."

"Bravo-One, this is Apache-Alpha, how do you read? Over."

"Apache-Alpha-One, read Lima-Charlie, over."

"Bravo, say our fire mission, over."

"Apache, need you to check area for any unfriendlies about one-fifty meters due east."

"Roger, Bravo-One, one-fifty meters east. On our way, heads down, pop smoke your position."

The CO's RTO popped a white phosphorous grenade. Our colored smoke couldn't be seen in the dark, but a WP grenade put out a small, bright light.

"Bravo-One-One, I see Willie-Peter, over."

"That's a roger, Apache; Willie-Peter it is. Give them hell, out."

After a few low passes by the Apache gunship, I heard, "Bravo-One, no bad guys in sight, over."

"Roger, Apache, take out some jungle. We have a feeling they're still there. Over."

"Wilco, Bravo-One, glad to oblige, some jungle it is, over."

"Thanks Apache-Alpha-One."

With those last words, the gunship backed off and found the spot the CO had requested to be fired upon. In minutes, the jungle was being cut to pieces as it first strafed the area with its mini-guns, followed by rockets. As each weapon was used, the pilot would back off a short way and then fly in to rake a different area, a short distance from the first. He hoped to catch the NVA as they moved away from the area.

The attack had taken all of ten minutes, but if the enemy was anywhere near the place, it must have felt like a lifetime.

After this short strafing run, it was time for the Apache to head home.

"Apache-Alpha-One, thanks for the help. Have a safe run home."

"Thanks, Bravo-One, we are out of here, out."

"Wow!" Sam yelled to Joe.

"Yeah, wow!" was all Joe said.

With the chopper gone, things got deathly quiet. The darkness closed around Bravo Company like a scratchy blanket. Nerves were on edge, so it was difficult for anyone to sleep. Everyone had the uncomfortable feeling the NVA were still near. We had to be ready.

A blinding white flash followed by a very loud "ka-boom" shattered the stillness. Every man in the company dropped to the ground. We tried hiding behind anything that might mean cover from incoming.

"Fuck, that was too damn close," Joe yelled to Rat as we all slowly scraped ourselves off the jungle floor.

We were on our feet waiting and listening. Was it retaliation for our gunship?

"Hey guys, it was only lighting and thunder, not incoming," Rat grinned.

"Rat, you asshole. One of these days ..."

"Yes, Mugs ..."

"Enough from y'all! Now listen!"

We could hear the rain pounding the jungle not far off. The monsoon rains were like standing under a waterfall. There was no way to stay dry. The racket it made as it pounded us made it impossible to hear anything else.

The rest of the night was uneventful. No more contact with the NVA. As it slowly turned from dark to light, the company brought in its night defenses and got packed up.

While we were eating, I just had to ask, "LT, do you think the CO will put Bill in for a medal? Pulling those pilots out of the chopper before it exploded was a brave thing to do!"

"Keep this to yourself, but I plan to recommend Bill for the Silver Star. It was a heroic act on his part. He could have been killed."

I asked the LT who was going to carry the radio since my two days were up.

"Rough, can you handle it for one more day? It would only be for the morning. We're scheduled to be picked up by 1100."

"Okay, LT, but you owe me; someday I might need a good deed."

We made it to the new LZ in plenty of time to set up security. The company wanted to make sure this chopper wouldn't get shot down when it landed. A shithook was being sent to take us out of the jungle. Bravo Company was very glad to be going home after this disastrous patrol.

Chapter 32 - Back in the War

Hi honey,

Guess who's back in the hospital? Yep, me. The FUO came back. I was running a temperature of 103.4°. This time they're treating me for the flu. I'm down to 164 pounds. That's not too good, I know. I've been here for two days, but I didn't feel well enough to write. I'm feeling much better now so please don't worry. It seems like I'm always telling you not to worry, but I know you do it anyway.

My promotion to SP 4 went into effect the end of July and I finally got my MOS changed. I'm now an 11C20, mortar man. If we ever get to a firebase like Jeanie, in the Delta, I'll stay in the mortar platoon.

My LT told me I was put in for bronze star with "V" device. Probably won't get it, but at least I was recommended. Honest, I wasn't trying to be a hero. I just did what had to be done.

The CO hasn't let up. We're still below strength and most of the guys are new. Men are still being walked into the ground, including me.

Well, enough complaining. The good news is that I should be rested and in good shape when I get back to my company. I'm fine, really. It was just a little flu bug I could have picked up even if I'd been home.

I was able to listen to the football game between pro all stars and college. The college guys did a great job. Better than expected.

I found out why our company was pulled down near BMB. It was because of President Nixon's visit. How about that, a President of the US of A in 'Nam! I didn't think that would ever happen.

Oh, I'm sending you this poem called, "Yet Filled With Grace," it's from the *Stars and Stripes* today. The words fit my life while in the jungles, something I would have written if I could.

I'll rejoin my unit tomorrow. See, I said I'm fine and fit for duty.

Honey, I really love you and I'm trying to take care of myself. I want to be able to join you for R and R. That's the dream keeping me going when I'm not sure I can take another step. I should know the dates sometime next month.

Please take care of yourself. I want a healthy, sexy wife when I see you. I miss you so much. It will be heaven to hold you and listen to your voice for real. I hear you talk and laugh in my head so often. You whisper, "I love you" on the evening breeze. The sunrise reminds me of your long golden hair lying on our pillows. You are my wife, my life and my reason for living. I love you with all my heart.

Love, Len, your lover and husband

* * *

I returned to the platoon on the afternoon re-supply chopper and was immediately informed that I was still the RTO. They'd passed the duty around waiting for me to come back. Damn! Top then informed me I was to be out on a trail ambush with my squad. Welcome back!

When the NDP had been set up, I found myself with the crew of Gun Three stomping off into the jungle to set out our protection for the Tiger Alpha. It was a quiet night without contact.

In the morning, I had just finished repacking to accommodate the radio and extra batteries when we got word, "Get it on." So I slung the radio and pack over my head. *Shit, this thing is heavier than when I left for the hospital.*

How I managed to hump through the jungle and stay on my feet, I'm not sure. I wasn't going to let the rest of the platoon know how badly I was out of shape from doing nothing in the hospital. I'd die before I let anyone know how much I was hurting.

By the time our mid-morning break rolled around, I was positive my back was broken, my arms were about to fall off, and my rubber legs wouldn't hold me up. But the patrol went right on patrolling, and all I could do was keep right on moving with them.

* * *

The next two days dragged by. Every step meant pulling my boot out of a quagmire and placing it in front of the other one stuck in the same muck. It was probably imagined, but I felt like I was moving in slow motion.

Finally, our last night in the jungle was over! Morning creaked upon us. The radio came to life with those hated words from the stupid bastard at BMB. We could go our entire lives without ever hearing about a "super fine morning in Vietnam" from some asshole who had the easiest job in the damn war. What a crock! We were cold, wet, exhausted, and hungry. The only thing fine was the fact we made it through another night alive.

We were headed back to Libby. We all hoped it would be for a while, but knew it wasn't likely. The best part of returning was the welcome batch of letters from Lu. Between being in and out of the hospital and out on patrol, I hadn't received any for almost two weeks. It seemed like a lifetime. One made me want to cry.

> Hi love,
> I guess by now you've heard Neil Armstrong and Buzz Aldrin were the first men to walk on the moon. As Armstrong's foot touched the soft moonscape, he said, "That's one small step for man; one giant leap for mankind." Those words will live forever. What a fantastic accomplishment.
> It's been on TV most of the day. I watched what I could after work. Thank God, word about Vietnam has all but vanished. I can use a break!
> I am so sick and tired of watching protestors march and pictures of the bloody fighting over there on the news. I get really angry. It's hard to be optimistic about what's happening where you are. I'd like to thank the media, however, for finally showing some good stuff about walking on the moon.

You would think if we can put a man on the moon, someone could figure out how to end wars. Especially the one you're fighting. I really want you home. I miss you a whole bunch.

How are you feeling? Leeches, ringworm, and other stuff in the jungle sounds pretty serious to me. Hey, you're supposed to be taking good care of yourself. Remember your promise to me. So let me know how you are as soon as you can. It's such a long time, two weeks, on the turn-around between letters, but just keep me informed!

Everybody is doing fine here at home. Your brother and Kathy took me out to dinner and a movie last Saturday. It was a lot of fun, but I don't like being a third wheel. It made me miss you even more.

I can't wait to hold you in my arms. I might even do other stuff with your sexy body! I'll bet you can guess what that means. Ha! Ha! Ha! I hope you're not planning on any rest or relaxation while on R and R! That's what the two R's are for, right?

I can't wait to start a family … maybe on R and R? You mentioned it before and I think it's a great idea. You know, we aren't getting any younger. Ha! Ha! We'll both be twenty-four by then. You did say something about being 'the old man' of your platoon. Just kidding …

Well, I need to get this ready to mail before heading off to work. I love you, I miss you, and I want to hold you so much. Please be careful.

All my love, Lu

* * *

Hi honey,

We came back to Firebase Libby this afternoon. The platoon strength is down to eighteen men counting Doc. We should have thirty or more. It seems most of the remaining men are new. I haven't even met some of them. The CO still hasn't let up. Hopefully, someone will see what's happening and he'll no longer be a CO.

I was out in the jungle for my birthday on August tenth. One of the guys took my picture for you. I'm trying to catch up with everybody's letters. I have a candle so I can see after dark to write to everyone who wrote and wished me a happy birthday. What did you do, give them orders?

I loved the brownie cake. All the guys said to tell you thanks, too. I really like my new watch. It replaced the one that died of sweat, rain, mud, and jungle rot. Since it glows in the dark, I can see the time while on guard. I wished you were here to see it. No, I wish I were home to show it to you!

We've been separated for your birthday and now mine. Next year we will be together for both and we'll have to do a double celebration. God, I can't believe we're twenty-four. That means next year it will be a quarter of a century for us both, or are you still counting them? Ha! Ha!

Honey, you are so beautiful and don't look a day over twenty! I love you so much and I can hardly wait to hold you again. Come on R and R!

Love, Len, your husband and lover

* * *

Top stopped me on the way to my hooch.

"Rough, we need to talk."

"Sure, Top, what's up?"

"By now you've heard about the little fuck-up one of the men in the company pulled while you were in the hospital. I want a name of the asshole responsible for the fraggings!"

"I'd help if I could, but I just heard about it from Joe. To tell the truth, I'm not sure who'd pull a stupid stunt like that. Dammit, Top, you know none of us are happy with the new CO. It could have been anyone."

"Fuck! It's going to be one tough job, but I'll find him."

"I'll put the word out and do my best to be sure it doesn't happen again. I honestly don't believe Fourth would do it."

"Thanks for your candor," Top said as we reached the Fourth Platoon's area. He went off, grumbling under his breath.

I spoke with Bill a few minutes later. If he told them to stop, it would go over better. Everyone listened to him; they liked and respected him. Fragging could bring major repercussions.

Bill was rotating back to Redcatcher in a couple of days, then home two weeks later. I'd miss the man and his Texas humor. We'd have been good friends if we'd met somewhere else and another time.

* * *

Lieutenant Don might give us a bad time once in a while, but it was done with humor. He earned our trust and our appreciation. The men of the Fourth Platoon came first, and he would fight for our well being. He wasn't afraid to butt heads with the CO.

One morning, the LT began his meeting by saying he had good and his usual bad news.

"We're heading out on another two-week patrol. We should be re-supplied every three days, so don't carry a lot of unnecessary weight. You guys have been at this long enough to know what you'll need."

"Roger, LT," we all grumbled.

"Now for the good news. We're going to be operating as a platoon independent from the company. We'll be doing short sweeps, only moving about two thousand meters, all easy walking, with an hour for lunch. Then we'll move about one hundred meters into the jungle to set up an ambush and wait until dark. The objective for our working on our own and taking shorter, slower walks along the periphery of the jungle is to try to draw Charlie out of the woods."

"Hey, LT, does that mean we're to be the bait on this patrol?" Joe asked.

"Yes, but I doubt we see any NVA in this area. I know how you guys feel about being exposed. Being wounded once was enough for me."

Most of us remembered Good Friday at FB Jeanie when he was injured by a booby trap.

"Sometimes I wonder about our intelligence guys, but we'll go with their plans. I'm sure there are small patrols, maybe four or five NVA each, but not the large concentration intelligence and the CO are expecting. We've covered it too many times for that."

"So, you don't think we'll have any major firefights?"

"We'll see some action, Rough, but we'll have the backup of Arty and the rest of the company. It should be an easy patrol for us. Inform the other guys and get ready. We leave at 0700 tomorrow."

"Roger, LT," we acknowledged.

* * *

The end of the monsoon season was coming, and we were getting shorter and fewer rain showers. What I wouldn't have given for a shower and a clean uniform. Someone must have heard my plea. How it happened, I don't know, but the next morning we were moved by truck to a compound for a shower, clean uniforms, and hot chow.

I never figured out where we were, but it felt like heaven. We left at noon to go back on patrol and set up an ambush for the night.

We all knew it wouldn't be long before we picked up the jungle smells again. It was part of our defense, but for a few hours, it had been great being clean!

The days moved fast. We had lots of contact with Charlie, but it was, "now you see them, now you don't." They would just vanish into the jungle, especially after a small firefight. No bodies, just some blood trails, and then they were gone. We never found evidence of compounds or a large concentration of NVA as had been reported.

"Things have been fairly quiet so far. That worries me," Joe said one afternoon.

"Not much happening, that's for sure. We walk all day and set up at night. Actually, I like this kind of a patrol," I replied.

"We haven't seen anything for a while. Maybe they know Fourth Platoon is on patrol and have scattered in fear!"

"Rat, sometimes I worry about you. Do you really believe that shit?" Joe asked.

"Hey, man, don't fuck with the Rat!"

"Well, whatever it is, I like it!" I said again.

"This has been one of our better patrols, especially without the CO hovering. That bastard is a royal pain in the ass!" Joe said.

"We've been out for eleven days now, but we're supposed to head back to Libby day after tomorrow, right?" Mac asked.

I answered. "At times it seems like I've been here for years. It begins to feel like our whole existence has been spent in this fucking jungle. Sometimes it's hard to remember we actually had other lives."

"Man, Rough, that's really deep. Are you now a philosopher?" Joe asked.

"No, but when I take out the picture of my Lu it all comes back to me vividly. She's my world and my escape from this hellhole."

"As I've said before, you're one lucky bastard! Someday I'd like to meet her. I feel like, through her letters to you, I already know her."

"Let me read you part of her letter I got today."

To my husband and lover,

What's going on with R and R? I need to put in for my vacation at work pretty soon, so keep me posted. I can hardly wait to see you and hold you in my arms. I don't know if I'll let you go back to Vietnam. Maybe I'll bring a big suitcase and just smuggle you home with me.

It is a little scary watching the news about the war. I keep listening for anything about the 199th. I have mixed feelings, I want to know, but I really don't want to hear what's going on. The media always shows the worst; which, of course, gets the protesters going. I'd like to take a club and beat both groups until I got their attention and then tell them that I'm very proud of my husband who is doing what his country asked of him. How would they like living under the conditions you've described? Sometimes freedom of the press and freedom of speech are overrated!

Oh, how did I get on my soapbox when all I wanted to say was I love you with all my heart! I really am proud of you and all the guys fighting over there. I know that someday we can look our children in the eye and tell them you served our country with honor and dignity.

I want to spend the five days loving you and....

"Well, the rest is personal. Lu is the gentlest lady you'd every meet, but she can be quite a fighter when she's being protective."

"Does she have a sister?" Joe asked.

"Yes, but I got the pick of the litter. Besides, I think Lu said she has a boyfriend."

"Just my luck!"

* * *

Finally, it was our last night on patrol. The weather seemed to know we would be leaving the area, and it was going to throw its worst stuff at us all night long. The monsoon storm was on its way toward us with thunder and lightening crashing all around. There was nothing we could do but hunker down and try to keep dry.

We got back into Libby at 1600 the next day, and after a whole five hours, we went back out on an ambush. We sat outside the perimeter all night waiting.

Hi honey,

I know it's hard for you to sit at home and listen to all the news about Vietnam, but I'm really all right. Our battalion isn't where all the action is so it's not really that bad.

The best thing you can do for me is pray. Pray for me and all the GIs fighting in this war.

Guess what? Our company got three new mortars. They were complete with the new sights and everything. All of us are so happy! We're like kids at Christmas.

We'll be at the firebase for a while, I hope. No word on when we'll be going out again. I've even shaved two days in a row.

Honey, the sky was clear last night and I saw your star. I told it to watch over you and protect you. I asked the angels in heaven to watch over my angel on earth. I know Gram is watching out for both of us for she wants to see her great-grandchildren from heaven.

It's late and my candle is about shot, so I'll end this for tonight. Actually, good morning as you're on your way to work about now. I love you and I need you a lot. Be a good girl and I'll see you soon on R and R!

Love, Your lover and husband, Len

Chapter 33 - Rubber Tree Plantation

"Hey, Rough, what were you doing to the radio earlier?" Joe asked a few days later.

"I was cleaning it, hoping to get rid of some of the corrosion caused by the constant dampness."

"Yeah, but it looked like you were throwing it up against the wall of your hooch. Is that some new method of cleaning things that I'm not aware of?" Joe asked, being a smart ass.

"That is a time-honored method used by all RTOs for loosening corrosion on the coils. Even the poor old PRC-25 doesn't like the jungles."

"I can sympathize with it."

"Only, because you're not an RTO. Shit, I've got to get my pack together, attach the damn radio, and find a place to cram my stuff. Then find four other men to carry extra batteries."

"Yeah, it's tough, Rough. Hey, I made a rhyme. You know 'tough' and 'Rough.' It was funny, you know?"

"Thanks, Joe. You definitely need a chance to carry this thing. By the way, how did you get missed last month when we were all taking turns?"

"I, ah, well, you see, ah, I kind of made the LT think I'd already had my turn," he confessed then changed the subject. "Why so many batteries?"

"Each battery is only good for about forty-eight hours. When they die, I hack them up with a machete and bury the pieces in the jungle. For a long patrol I need a lot of spares. There's no way I could carry them all."

"Oh, but I have to carry the sixty." He said then turned around and wandered off.

* * *

We waited until near dawn before taking care of the tubes since we could be called upon to fire illumination rounds or possibly HE before the night was over. The mortars would lay idle during our patrol and would be covered with sheets of plastic to keep them dry.

* * *

Hi honey,

Our CO is in hot water. There have been too many complaints about him from men in the company. We've had two dog teams that have had their dogs walked until they couldn't move anymore. The last dog came out of the jungle on three legs. The CO wouldn't call a dust-off chopper in, even though the dog's trainer asked for it.

Our new FO wrote the CO up and sent the complaint in. We've had three men go see the Inspector General and two more are going after this next operation. So you can see things are looking bad for the guy. In fact, there have been two attempts on his life. You'd think he would get the hint.

The army is trying to make this place livable. They're bringing in rock and gravel to put on the red sticky mud so it won't get too mushy and slippery. They're even trying to fix the roads so when it rains vehicles don't slide off. I've never lived where it snows and gets icy, but I've heard this is worse. More power to them. Hope it works.

The rainy season is almost over. The last part of August and the first part of September should end it for us here.

The 199th flag might be coming home soon, but that doesn't mean the men will be with it. So don't get your hopes up if you hear about the 199th leaving Vietnam. I'm sorry.

I had to go to Redcatcher the day before yesterday by mistake. Some clerk screwed up, but by the time they figured it out, I had to spend the night. Aw, shucks. Ha, ha, ha.

There are still a lot of guys arriving. I saw about three hundred getting ready to start Redcatcher training and there were roughly that many who just graduated the week before, all for the Brigade. We can sure use them.

Well, that's enough about stuff here. How's my girl? I really miss you. Only six to eight weeks until R and R. It seems like forever right now. Just so you know, I'm very healthy and in the best physical shape ever. Just wait and see. You won't recognize me. I'll be the tall, skinny, tan, muscled guy with the big grin on his face.

By the way, how is your tan coming? You don't want to go to Hawaii without some color and burn as usual. You blonde chicks with your fair skin. Oh, how I love my blonde! You just wait until Hawaii and see how much I love you. You may not even get in the sun!

I do love you with all my heart. See you soon.

Love, Len, your husband and lover

* * *

The morning broke as usual with a light fog hugging the earth around Firebase Libby, but it would soon burn off. Libby's LZ was located outside of the main entrance next to the road, making it easy to protect. We dragged our feet as we headed to the LZ.

After we boarded the choppers, each man sat alone with his own thoughts. A tap on my helmet brought me back to the job at hand. The chopper was starting its descent toward a hole in the jungle, our starting point.

I ran a final inspection of my rifle: a round in the chamber, check; safety on, check; selector switch moved freely, check. My thumb would be on this switch until I was safely away from the chopper, and needed to prepare the weapon to fire. I didn't want to accidentally destroy the helicopter.

If we started taking ground fire, I'd only have to flip my thumb and start returning fire as quickly as possible.

The choppers buzzed the LZ trying to draw any possible ground fire before they started the final descent putting us on the jungle floor. There was no incoming. We'd take a cold LZ anytime.

I hit the ground and ran from the chopper, prepared for anything, but nobody was home. Whew!

As the sound of the choppers disappeared over the hill, the quiet that followed was almost deafening. We formed up in our platoons. The CO gave the order for the company to move out and we began snaking our way into the jungle.

I figured out why the term "snaking" was used. We never made a straight line while walking through this type of terrain. The area had never been penetrated and there were clumps of bamboo which had been growing forever and were as big around as tree trunks. It was impossible to cut through so we had to go around, giving us a meandering path much like a slithering snake.

As the point team was cutting through the foliage, there was a loud scream ahead of us. With the shriek, the company came to a halt. We quickly maneuvered into our circular defensive positions around command. All our rifles were pointing out toward any possible attack areas.

There was a call for the medic. Speculation ran rampant. There hadn't been any weapons fired so it most likely was a booby trap or *punji* sticks.

A few minutes later, which seemed like hours, Rat, who was in front turned, and whispered, "Rough, pass the word that now we have watch out for some fuckin' huge red ants. One got the point man. Their bite is really painful."

I turned and said, "Pass the word, now we have some real nasty large red ants." The warning drifted back to the rest of the platoon, man to man, in a whispered hush.

So now the jungle was throwing us another hazard to go along with the snakes, leeches, mosquitoes, thorns, and other maladies common to hot, humid, damp locations. The place was now crawling with some of biggest red ants we'd ever seen. When we moved out again, we looked out for this new danger.

The CO sent word that we would be stopping in about two-zero mikes. This would give us time to set up a good NDP before dark.

The point team broke out of the jungle and into rubber trees. They moved easier in this terrain since they no longer had to cut a path through the foliage. They still had to watch for booby traps.

There were dirt levees throughout, making it easier to set a defensive position. The command group would be in the center on high ground with the rest of the platoons circled around it.

After being in the jungles where the trees were packed in tightly, being in this sparsely-treed grove left us feeling very exposed. There wasn't a lot of cover to protect us in case of an attack. The NVA was out there, and no way would we forget it.

This area made another problem for us. It would be impossible to build a cover against the inevitable rains. In the jungle, there were a lot of small trees and bushes we could tie ponchos to, giving us a roof. Here in this grove, the trees were too far apart and too big around for our tiebacks.

We also realized levees were built to catch the rainwater, and the flat ground would become a series of small ponds when it rained. It wouldn't be fun to sleep in.

We also had another new problem: spiders! They were as big as a man's open hand. Were they dangerous? None of us knew and we sure weren't going to let them get close enough to find out. Everything else in the jungle was harmful to us. Therefore, anything that large must be bad.

"Shit, did you guys see those damn spiders in the webs between the fuckin' trees?" Rat asked.

"You bet your ass I did. There must be hundreds of them," Joe responded. "Between monster spiders, the damn red ants, and the rain, I'm not getting any sleep tonight."

"Doc, are those fuckin' spiders dangerous to us? Do you think sleeping in a water-filled area will keep them away?"

"I don't know, Rat, but I would treat them like they're poisonous until someone finds out otherwise," Doc replied.

We all decided the rainwater would be welcome for tonight. We hoped it would keep the spiders in their webs and the red ants off the ground.

Dark came upon Bravo Company and the rubber tree plantation. We settled down for the night.

"Quit the chatter and get some sleep," LT said quietly.

Some smart ass in the group whispered, "Okay, Mom." He received a few chuckles, breaking the tension.

All our preparations were set. The LPs and ambushes were out, the platoons were in their defensive positions.

The rain didn't even wait until midnight to drop its cold, wet load on us. Our meager attempts at staying dry proved unsuccessful. We had thrown our ponchos over our heads and tucked them around our bodies, leaving our faces uncovered. There was only one good thing about the rain, it kept the mosquitoes away and, we all hoped, the ants and spiders, too.

Thunder rumbled in the distance. It slowly moved closer to the rubber trees. Then all hell broke loose. The first close bolt of lightning streaked into our location. The boom that followed was ear-piercing. A tree fell somewhere in the distance as it was shattered by another bolt.

This would have been the perfect time for the NVA to be moving. The heavily falling rain made a lot of noise as it crashed onto the foliage and the ground. We couldn't have heard or seen a thing. A whole herd of circus elephants could have marched through, and we wouldn't have known.

Joe was on my right with his M-60 machine gun between the two of us. I had teased him earlier that he wasn't going to get any girl when he got home if he insisted on sleeping with that thing. I thought he was going to hit me before he started laughing.

"Shit, Rough, do you call this living? I'm not sure if it's even considered existing," Joe mumbled, as he tried to keep dry. "At least in the rice paddies the water wasn't so damn cold."

So we just sat there under our ponchos in two to three inches of water. We were all awake, staring out into the night. There was nothing to see but blackness. The rain pounded on the trees and our heads.

The night dragged on, as if it were moving through the mud we were sitting in. Finally, darkness started changing to morning gray. The rain stopped, and the water had mostly soaked into the ground. It seemed quiet and peaceful.

We took a good look at where we'd set up our NDP. We saw row upon row of trees, neatly spaced about eight feet apart. The trunks were a little bigger than telephone poles in thickness. They stood about twenty to twenty-five feet tall, with the branches jutting out at least nine to ten feet up the trunk. They were a dark reddish-brown color with long, almost flat, dark green leaves.

Each tree had a circular slash mark around the trunk, about four feet off the ground where the sap could seep down into a bucket against the trees. The sap dripped so slowly we couldn't even see it move. The thick tree branches kept sunlight from penetrating, so it was dark in the grove. The whole area had crisscrossing dikes like the rice paddies. The ground was the rich dark red dirt of Vietnam.

We could all hear the low rumble of a truck as it plowed down the muddy road towards the rubber trees.

It was an old, well-used military deuce 'n half which came to a halt right in front of us. To our surprise, the back of the truck held about ten Vietnamese women. It had hardly stopped before the door on the passenger side flew open and a very distinguished-looking gentleman of about fifty years old jumped out and started toward our position.

We all stared. We could not believe our eyes! He was wearing a white suit, with a spotless white shirt, white shoes, and a straw hat. We were all trying very hard to keep from laughing. Since he was obviously the owner of this plantation, we didn't want to insult our host of the night.

The CO started his way. We could hear the man call, "Oh, I say there, officer," as he approached. He spoke with a clipped British-sounding accent. We were pretty sure he was Australian.

"I wouldn't come any farther, sir. My men haven't brought in all our night defense ordinance," the CO explained.

The gentlemen stopped in his tracks then addressed the CO, "Sir, we will wait until you finish. Then my girls will need to begin working the rubber trees."

The LT moved over to us to be closer to the CO and the Aussie.

"LT, is this still a working rubber plantation with the war so close?" Joe asked, whispering.

"It looks like it. These ladies will be in a lot of trouble if we don't get the area cleared soon."

The two men were in a discussion. Neither looked happy. The CO was pointing to some of our night defenses. The planter kept looking at his watch and pacing. But the Aussie wasn't having any of it. From all the stomping around during the discussion, the white shoes and pants were no longer spotless. Red mud was splattered from his mud-encrusted white shoes to his knees.

The CO turned away from the Aussie. "Bravo, I want to be out of here in two-five mikes, and the place will be clean when we leave, and I mean clean!"

The LT turned to us. "You heard the CO. Get to work."

"Roger, LT." And move we did. In less than twenty-five minutes, we had the night defenses put away, and we were on the road, heading out.

As soon as the CO gave the Aussie the "all clear," the women went right to work. No silk dresses here, mostly long black pants with long-sleeved blouses of varying colors. These clothes were made for working in the fields, not the dresses the GIs saw in Saigon.

So, for a short time, the American Army had guarded this rubber tree plantation so the workers could go about their daily business, war or no war.

Chapter 34 - Just Another Routine Patrol

Hi honey,

Tell your brother I received the information on joining the police force. It will be a while before I get a letter off to him, so tell him thanks.

I forgot to tell you, my football is at BMB. It will never make it home, but that's all right. It got used a lot over here and everyone had loads of fun. That one ball helped take our minds off the war even if only for an hour or two.

We moved out yesterday, and we'll be gone about ten days to two weeks. I know it's hard on you when you hear the news, but don't worry. We all want to get home alive so we're real careful about what we're doing.

We left Libby by chopper. We're in a marshy jungle with no open spaces, so our re-supply was dropped from about one hundred feet up. No mail going out. We might not be able to get a letter out for the whole nine or ten days we'll be on this patrol. I will try and write some every day and get it out when I can. I hope to God you are prepared for this. I will be all right, don't worry.

8-26-69

We aren't walking as much. The colonel is out here with us. It makes us wonder if we aren't going south very soon. I sure hope so. I've had enough of this jungle. At least we're sleeping dry since we set up before the rain hits. It's better now as it only lasts a short time.

We have hurt the NVA on this mission, mostly by finding supplies. Also, we destroyed five NVA and captured two. None of our men got hurt.

We set up an ambush last night, but nothing happened. While I sat there waiting, I got to thinking about coming home. About the day I'll walk off the plane in LA and know it will be the last time I will ever have to leave you. I will hold you in my arms and never let you go.

The first thing I want to do, after I change out of my uniform for a pair of shorts and a shirt, is go walk on the beach with my love. I have dreamed of that for so long. Miles and miles of sand, NO stinking rice paddies and NO damn jungle! That will be heaven! I love you.

8-29-69

We're at BMB right now getting a short stand-down. It's what we need. After a week, everyone is worn out. I'll get a couple of letters off while I'm here. We leave on August the thirtieth to go back out. Because of all the contact here, we won't be going south for another month or so. Damn.

It sounds like the 199th is going to be disbanded and sent home. The men with less than ten months in Vietnam will be sent to other units.

Hey, send me some of those multi-vitamins in your next package. It might help since we are eating C-rations most of the time. I'm back up to 170 pounds, but won't get much over that as long as I'm an RTO, just too much weight and too much walking.

This stand-down is nothing like the last. They keep us busy most of the time. I really need some rest. I'm getting sick again, no fever, yet. I can't go see Doc until I run a fever of 102 or higher.

Right now our Kit Carson scout is playing his harmonica for us. He once was an NVA soldier, but defected. All the company likes him, and he does a good job for us.

I love you so much. This war is hell, but I will be all right. I promised I would come home, and I intend to keep it. God, R and R is in six to seven weeks, I hope. When I get back from this patrol I should have the dates.

I hate to end this when I'm talking to you, but sleep is a necessity. I will finally get this mailed in the morning. Sorry I didn't get it out last week, but it was impossible.

Always remember, no matter what may happen over here, I love you with all my heart.

Love, Len, your husband and lover

* * *

I woke in the middle of the night. A small voice in my head whispered this was going to be a bad patrol. There was no way to explain it. It was just a gut feeling which scared the hell out of me.

Another day was finished. No matter how long we'd been in the jungle or acclimatized ourselves to our surroundings, Charlie still ruled the nights. They were better at moving through this terrain. Of course, this was their backyard and they'd had a lot more practice.

It took us a while, but we've learned to live more like creatures of the jungle than the civilized humans we had been back in the World. Our personal habits needed some refining before we could be reunited with family and friends. Our mommas would be ashamed of us, but this was war in a very inhospitable country.

The radio crackled, "Bravo, we are setting up our NDP."

"Hey, Rough, it's still light. What say we fix hot chocolate to go with our beef jerky?"

"Sounds like a plan. Do you have any C-4?"

"Of course, but I only have a half a block."

"Shit, Joe, it would heat enough water for the whole platoon if necessary."

"No damn way. Let them use their own. I've been screwed enough this last couple of months."

As we sat talking, the new guy on my right said, "Hey, Rough, I'm not sure how to set the trip flares, Claymores, and stuff for our night defenses. You, Joe, or Rat, someone with experience, always puts them out. I'd like to know how it's done. You know, someday I'll be an old-timer, like you."

"It's easy, Tank." We didn't have a good nickname for the kid yet, besides what would you use for someone named Tank, "Sherman"? "Let me explain. We use a Claymore clacker, attached by wire, to set off the mines. They are set and covered, and then we run the wires back to the defensive circle, where we can set them off by squeezing the trigger if needed."

"So it's like a first line of defense against the enemy if he should stumble on our position?"

"Well, no, our first lines of protection are the listening posts out in the jungle. If Charlie gets by them, then we begin defending ourselves with the Claymores and the grenades."

"What about the trip flares? How are they used?"

"They're set around the perimeter, out about twenty meters. It takes a steady hand. They have a handle and a cotter pin, just like a grenade. But we attach the pin to a wire across a path or between two trees, wherever some gook might pass through. To really make them effective, we pull the pin out—just enough to keep the handle from separating and setting it off, but enough so it'll come out if someone trips the wire. When that happens, you think you're looking directly at the sun shining overhead in the middle of a blazing desert. It's blinding."

"What do we do if that happens?"

"All hell breaks loose. It'll only go off if it's tripped by the NVA. Everyone in the company will open fire on that spot. You don't want to be anywhere near a tripped flare!"

"Now I see why you experienced guys set them, I'd probably pull the pin out too far and the damn thing would go off, resulting in mass destruction of my body."

"Well, actually, when we're setting them out, everyone is aware, but mistakes do happen. They could give the NVA our position. Those damn flares are so bright they can be seen a couple of hundred meters into the jungle."

"Wow! Thanks for all the info, Rough, Maybe I can go with you tomorrow night when we set up and learn how an expert does it. I have to help Dan tonight."

"Sure, kid, anytime."

* * *

"Joe, Rough, Rat, the CO wants more Claymores and trip flares set out. He just knows there will be a large group of NVA coming through here tonight, and he doesn't want them to get by."

"He wants us to set up more defenses in the dark? You know that's not smart when we can't see what we're doing, LT," I complained.

"I know, Rough. I argued with him, but his mind is made up and we'll have to do it. Just be careful. I don't want any accidents. I figured you three are the most experienced and can do the job safely."

"Thanks for trying, LT," I said.

"Yeah, we'll get right on it," Joe grumbled.

"Goddamn Ricky and his gung-ho orders," Rat added, under his breath.

"Okay, guys, lets just get it done."

"Roger, LT."

About five minutes later, I heard Joe mumble in my direction, "You almost done, Rough?"

"Yeah, I just have this last trip flare and I'm through."

"See ya under the tarp," he said as he headed back.

I gently set the flare on the ground and eased the cotter pin out a short way. I slowly opened my hand turning loose of the trigger. I started to stand. Suddenly night became day.

"Ah, shit!"

BOOK TWO –
THE AFTERMATH

Life is a Why

Why was I allowed to get this far, to almost see the end of my struggle
   To be thrown back a distance
   And see the end might not be attainable after all?
Why?
Life is a why!

Why was I allowed to rise from that green hell
   Broken and battered hoping to find
   My life was about to begin again
But be cast upon my bed
   With a body that is trembling and shaking,
   Thinking, to die might have been better after all?
Why?
Life is a why.

Is there no reasonable answer?
   No! You say.
   Wait, yes.
Life is a why
   And there is hope.

-Len Rugh, 1983

Chapter 35 - The Telegrams

Lu

Sunday, September 7, 1969, 7:10 AM, California

Why is the telephone ringing so early? It isn't time to get ready for church. Oh, I was having such a wonderful dream. Darn phone, stop ringing, I want to finish my dream. Len and I were in Hawaii playing on the beach ... Okay, okay, I'll answer!

"Hello!" I was a bit angry and still a little groggy from sleep.

"Lu, this is Bill, is there anything we can do for you?"

Why is my brother-in-law calling? And why is he asking a stupid question at this time on a Sunday morning?

"What do you mean, Bill?"

I could hear him talking to his wife, Kathy. He'd put his hand over the phone, but I could make out a few words: "get," "telegram," and "Len." With each one, my panic rose.

I yelled, "Bill, what's going on? Bill? Tell me what's happened? Bill ..."

By the time he came back on the line, my family was standing in my bedroom doorway. Between the phone ringing and my shouting, they'd all been awakened.

"Lu, we received a telegram a few minutes ago. Len has been wounded," Bill explained. He and Kathy lived in the apartment behind Len's mom's house. He must have been summoned when the telegram arrived.

"Oh, God! Not Len! Bill, tell me what it says."

He read the telegram sent to my mother-in-law, Helen. With each line, I began to die. Len had been critically wounded. Nothing else he said could penetrate my foggy brain. I whispered, "Len ..."

This can't be happening! It must be a nightmare. I'll wake up soon and it'll all go away.

Mom rushed in and sat on the bed next to me. She put her arm around my shoulders, trying to understand what was happening.

"Lu, it really sounds serious. We'll be home all day. When your telegram arrives, let us know if you learn more details," Bill pleaded.

My mom had taken the phone from my trembling hand and said, "Bill, this is Betty. We'll keep you posted. I think Lu is in shock right now. I'll have her call you later, all right?"

I guess Bill apologized.

Then Mom said, "I know, Bill. We went to dinner last night to celebrate our anniversary. They probably tried to deliver her telegram then, but no one was home."

Dad, sitting on my other side, held my hand. He probably didn't know what else to do.

"I have to get ready," I said, in a daze.

Dad gave me a hug. "We'll be in the kitchen if you need us."

"Thanks," I mumbled.

"I think this is why Len wanted you to live with us while he was in Vietnam. He knew we'd both be here, just in case ... Now get dressed. We'll see you in a minute," Mom said as she closed the door, leaving me alone with my fears.

Bill's news was becoming real. It wasn't some horrible dream. Len *had* been badly wounded ... *Would he live? Oh, Lord, what do I do now?*

I had to be strong. Len would need me while he got better. *He'll recover. We have plans. Len promised he'd come home.*

I could hear him say the words. They ran over and over in my head, like a mantra. *Len, don't you break your promise to me! Don't you dare!*

I stood looking into the closet but couldn't remember why. *It's just a day like any other day*, I reminded myself. I had to decide what to wear. *If I stick to my usual routine, I can survive this. Just take one second at a time.*

God, how could life ever be normal again?

I was numb. I felt I was in another place, apart from the me suffering the pain and anguish. I knew my husband was fighting for his life in a hospital somewhere in Vietnam, but nothing could pierce my comfortable cocoon.

Deep inside, I knew one of us was a fake. I didn't want to care or face reality right then. I wanted this world of no feelings to continue.

Mom knocked on the door, calling to me. Then I heard the doorbell. It was time to face reality.

"I have a telegram for a Mrs. Luanna Rugh," I heard a man's voice. "Is she here?"

"Yes, I'm here," I answered as I walked to the door.

"We tried to deliver this message last night, but no one was home. I'm sorry. Are you her father?" he asked Dad.

"Yes, I am."

"Good," the man replied. "We're not allowed to deliver telegrams unless a family member or a close friend is present. Sign here please, Mrs. Rugh."

"Thanks," I mumbled as I stared at the buff-colored envelope. With trembling hands, I opened it and took out the three-page message.

Reality hit. It was true; Len really was seriously wounded. It wasn't a dream. It was a living nightmare. *What am I going to do now?*

The telegram slipped from my hand and fell to the floor. I needed to sit down. My legs obeyed and carried me to the couch.

Dad picked up the telegram and handed it to me. I read it to my family. It had much the same information as Helen's. The essence was that Len had a penetrating head wound in the left frontal lobe. What that meant, I wasn't sure, but I knew it wasn't good.

I called Bill, but the rest of the day was a blur. My mind had shut down against more trauma. I was going through the motions of existence, but my life as I'd known it had ended.

I remember our minister, who had married Len and me just two and a half years before, coming by. We sat quietly and talked and prayed for Len and his full recovery. He asked me to come and see him later in the week. I said I would, and then he left.

Finally, the day was over. I lay down on the bed and closed my eyes, but sleep was elusive. Now, when I needed my brain to shut down, it began working overtime.

I dozed off and on during the long night, but kept waking with a start. The images playing in my mind were horror-filled. I envisioned Len in his uniform the day he left. Then it changed to the scenes from the nightly news of men fighting and Len with his head blown off, lying on the jungle floor. It was awful. Blessedly, morning came and I sat on the couch and kept my mind blank while my family hovered around me.

My father had called the bank where I worked to explain what had happened. He was told I could take as much time off as I needed.

So for the next few days, my life was in a kind of a Neverland. Then the letter arrived.

Hi honey,

This is our last day for this stand down. We leave tomorrow morning for another operation. So it could be between seven and ten days before you hear from me again. There is just no way to get our mail out.

Let's see, there isn't much from here. We did get some of our gear fixed, but it's all in pretty bad shape. Most of the guys got drunk and sort of tore up the EM club last night.

We were supposed to take some classes about the jungle while we were here. Ha! What I don't know, I don't need to know so I ditched them. Most of us did. After two months in this hell, we've learned more than we ever wanted to know. I don't want to be in jungle ever again. When we buy our home, there will not be any plants even resembling stuff that grows here, it would be a nightmare.

Well, I've got to get some sleep. I'll mail this tomorrow before we leave. I love you very much and I wish I could be near so I could tell you in person. Be a good kid. Good night my love.

Love, your lover and husband, Len

"Dad, it's all a mistake. I just got a letter from Len. He's okay! They must have thought it was him, but it has to be some other guy!"

"Honey, look at when it was written. It's dated August 30, five days before Len was wounded."

"Oh, Dad, when does the hurting stop? I guess I should face the truth. Len is critically wounded and might die. I need to go back to work and climb out of this protective false life I've created for myself."

I could almost hear him cheering and thinking "finally!"

The next evening, the second telegram arrived …

Len was still in critical condition and had been transported from Vietnam to the 106th General Hospital in Yokohama, Japan.

I called Len's mom and brother with the information. They'd received word just before I called.

* * *

A few days later the phone rang.

"Hi Lu, this is Bill. How are you?"

"I'm just hanging on. The tough part is waiting for another piece of information about his condition. One of my customers at the bank gave me the phone number of the Army Casualty Department in Washington, DC. As his wife, I can call and get updates any time, day or night. They've been very helpful, going out of their way to answer my questions."

"Let us know what's happening. Mom's worried. Hell, we all are. Now, really, how are *you* doing?"

"I'm in a kind of fog. My mind's accepted it, but my heart still thinks he's coming home to me whole as he promised. It's a nightmare. I just want to wake up and have it all go away."

"Yeah, me, too. I can't imagine him being hurt. He's always been so strong and athletic. From the information we've gotten, he'll never be like that again."

"I'm still receiving letters from him, written before he was wounded. It confuses things. One minute I know what's happened, and then a letter comes and it's like he's here with me and everything's okay."

"What's hardest for me is trying to make sense out of what's happened. Why did it have to be my brother? Why was he there anyway?"

"I can tell you how he felt about the war and his involvement in it. I received a letter today. It's probably the last one he wrote since it's dated September third, the night before it happened. It explains a lot."

"You want to read his last letter to me?"

"Yes. Maybe it will bring you some peace. Here goes."

Hi honey,

We're back out on one of our stinking patrols again. I'm doing fine, well, for what's happening. I carry the radio and lots of other junk, so it's really tough going in this marshy jungle.

I get the feeling from your letters that you are worrying too much about me and not enough about yourself. Please, don't. I told you I would come home, and I will. I'm taking good care of myself. Everybody looks out for everyone else over here.

I want to tell you how much I love you and how very much I miss holding you in my arms. It's only another few weeks until R and R. I can hardly wait.

I was thinking the other day about why I'm here and all I could think of was how we have lived our lives together. Remember the night we drove up to Chantry Flats and stopped at the pullout to look at the lights? It was like we were on top of the world. I guess in a way we were.

It will be so good to take a ride up into the hills again and look out and see our land. A great land, one that provides us with the freedom so many people take for granted. It didn't come to us on a silver platter. It was bought with the sweat and blood of our men in the service. And what makes men fight for their country? The ones they love: the wives, the children, or the sweethearts each man is doing his best to protect!

Yes, one day I can look at our country and say, "I've done my best to keep it free. Now I'm home to enjoy it with my wife."

I thank God for sending you to me. I thank God for the chance to do a small part in helping my country, even if it means going through one year of hell. Soon it will be in the past. Our children will be able to enjoy our country and I will be able to hold my head up as a man.

Well, I need to get back to my job for the next five months and fifteen days, but who's counting. We're on the downhill side and moving faster to that ride home on the Freedom Bird.

I need you by my side and in my life. I love you with all my heart and soul. I will always keep my promise to you and see you in Hawaii on our R and R. Be a good kid and remember I'll always love you.

Love, Len, your husband and lover

"Wow! My brother wrote that? You do bring out the best in him. Thanks for sharing it with me. It's helped me understand."

"I know what you mean. It's given me perspective on this past week. Well, actually, on the last seven months."

"I need to think a bit about what he said. I'll talk to you later. Bye."

"Good-bye, Bill," I answered to a dead line. "I guess he was really affected by the letter and didn't want to show any unmanly emotions." I said to no one in particular.

Chapter 36 - Home the Hard Way

Len

The flare is in the wrong place and it's too damn intense. In my pain-racked brain, what I thought was the flare was actually a bright light. I tried to look around to find someone from my platoon who could explain why the flare was still burning. *Why doesn't Joe, or Ole, or Rat, or Wild Bill cover the thing with dirt before the NVA spot us? I'd better call in the gunships and put the 105s on standby. We're going to be attacked for sure and all hell is going to break loose!*

"Don't worry, you're safe in my hospital," I heard someone say. I didn't recognize the voice speaking to me.

He must be one of the new guys. Wait a minute! Did he say hospital? Has my fever come back, again?

I tried to ask where I was, but even to me it sounded like so much gibberish.

What's going on?

Somewhere, hidden by the blinding light, which added to my confusion and pain, a stranger was trying to explain where I was and what was happening.

I'd never experienced so much agony. I felt like my skull had been cracked open and someone was hammering directly on my brain. Never before in my entire twenty-four years, through migraines and a dislocated left shoulder, did I hurt so much. I couldn't concentrate on what this person was saying to me.

"Just who the hell are you?" was the last thing I remember before the lights went out and my body went into a deep sleep. He had given me something to take away the brightness and the excruciating pain.

When I finally woke up I tried to call for our company medic, "Doc!"

He might be able to give me something for the pain and explain why the guys let the flare burn for so long. Had the choppers or the 105s been called? I was sure LT had taken care of it. Our lieutenant was too good a platoon leader not to have us covered, even if the CO didn't.

I felt around, but nothing seemed familiar. Everything was smooth and soft, no hard, wet jungle floor.

Now I remember. There was a faceless, nameless voice who said something about being in a hospital. I must be back at BMB, but what does that mean? Why am I here? What's wrong with me?

Something important was missing. *Where's my damn radio? The LT will need the radio to call for help. I was carrying the radio, wasn't I? Shit, I've also lost my M-16. How will I explain that one to Top? He's really going to be pissed!*

Then the lights went out and the pain went away once again, complements of the voice. In my confused brain, it was taking on its own identity.

Where the hell is Doc, I need him, like right now! He was nowhere to be seen or heard.

"Doc!" I tried to call out again, but nothing I said came out like it should. If I couldn't understand it, how could anyone else? *Why am I speaking nonsense?*

I tried again, "Doc! Where the hell are you, Doc?"

He wasn't answering my thoughts or my call.

"Hey, soldier, your buddies aren't here. They were left back in Vietnam."

They didn't make it to a hospital? God, does that mean they're all dead?

"You are really a survivor. You suffered a bad head wound."

None of the others survived? What happened when that flare went off? Did my mistake cause everyone else to be killed?

"I understand there was a lot of death and destruction when you were hit. Man, that must have been some firefight!" Mr. Voice exclaimed. "I would have liked to have been there to see a real fight!"

"No you wouldn't, buddy!" I tried to say.

Had a whole company of damn NVA fired on my unit, killing every-one?

"From the report, you were the only wounded they brought in that day."

They're all dead! How will I ever be able to live my life knowing I caused their deaths?

"Hey, pal, don't get so upset," the voice pleaded as he added some-thing in my IV. Again, everything went blank. While I was in this deep sleep, it started—my nightmare:

The flare goes off, and I run back to the company's NDP. Suddenly, my radio's at my feet and my M-16 is in my hands. I'm on rock and roll, putting out as much firepower as I can. Red and green tracers are buzzing all around me. I look to my right and see Joe, Wild Bill, and Dan lying down.

I stand there yelling, "No!" I try to go to them, but my feet won't move. I feel myself starting to fall and join my buddies on the jungle floor.

Then a hand grabbed my shoulder and shook me.

The voice I had come to recognize said, "Wake up, Mr. Rugh. You're having a bad dream."

I tried to open my eyes. I just wanted the horror I was confronting in my sleep to go away. I wanted to find the face belonging to the voice, but the lights were too bright.

The medication took over once again. The lights went out and the pain went away. I slipped into that blissful deep sleep. At least this time my nightmare didn't come back to haunt me. I slept quietly, for how long I don't know.

Then there was that voice calling to me. It had taken on a familiar sound during the last few times I'd been able to stay awake.

"It's time for you to get up and do some walking. We need to get you ready to go home."

Walking? I'm not even awake. How can I walk?

Someone transferred me to a wheelchair. I was taken to the physical therapy room.

A wheelchair? What in hell do I need that for? I've been walking most of my life. I've probably humped several thousand miles since being in 'Nam. Walking shouldn't be a problem.

"Mr. Rugh." The name sounded like one I should know. "We're not going to take any steps today. I just want you stand up. I'll be right here behind you, so don't worry about falling down."

Fall down? Now why would I fall down? God, what's wrong with me?

I tried to push myself up, but nothing worked. The medic lifted me so I could stand. The blood drained from my head. My body felt cold, heavy, and clammy. *Damn, don't let me fall down! And, for God's sake, don't let me pass out!*

"Look out, here I come," I tried to say as I fell backwards toward the medic and the floor. He caught me. The voice had become a human with a face. He had become my guardian angel.

"I guess you're not quite ready for walking just yet," he said as he sat me down once again.

No shit! I hurt too damn much right now. Just let me lie down and rest for a couple of minutes. Then we can catch up to the company.

I thought I was still in the jungles of Vietnam, not in some damn hospital out of country.

* * *

For six weeks, the doctors monitored my recovery, waiting for me to become strong enough to make the trip from the hospital in Japan to California and the World. The morning before I was to return home, I woke up to find several doctors standing around my bed.

"Mr. Rugh, you've suffered a severe head wound and have been fighting a bout of meningitis. As a result, you've lost a lot of weight and most of your strength. You are paralyzed on your left side due to the injury. We feel we've done all we can for you here. Since you're finally stable enough, you'll be released tomorrow to the air force for the trip home."

I tried to acknowledge them, but my speech was still garbled, so I just nodded.

Six weeks? I've been here six weeks! Oh, my God, Lu! Where is she and what is she doing? What have they told her? She must be going through hell. I need to see her. Why isn't she here with me? I know she would be if she could.

I tried to ask about her. I guess someone must have figured out what I wanted, because I remember someone telling me I'd been in the contagious ward. No visitors allowed … so, no Lu. Damn! I really needed her now.

* * *

Time had passed in a haze as I drifted in and out of wakefulness. But most often I was in a deep sleep due to the pain medication. Sometimes the nightmare returned to haunt me and I could see my buddies lying bloodied on the jungle floor. Hearing and feeling nothing were the best times, no pain, no war, no nightmares, and no death. I was safe from all harm.

The following morning, my familiar voice spoke to me as his hand shook me out of my deep sleep.

"Mr. Rugh, it's time to get you ready to go home."

I must be this Mr. Rugh guy. It's what he keeps calling me. But my name is Rough. I remember Joe, and the rest of the platoon calling me that, but never Mr. Rugh.

Questions went through my mind as this medic was getting me dressed for my trip back to the World.

Why can't I walk or even dress myself? I know I'm weak, but it shouldn't be too difficult to get dressed. What was it those doctors said about me? My mind seems so muddled. God, what's going on? I can't focus or remember the words they uttered only hours ago.

Maybe when I get home, Lu can explain everything to me so I can understand. Lu, I remember her. She's my wife and she's important to me. I need to concentrate so I can remember.

They're going to make me wear military pajamas on this flight home? No uniform? Dammit, I don't want to see Lu for the first time wearing pajamas. I had it all planned. I was going to walk off the plane at LAX in my uniform. She would greet me with open arms and I would hold her and hug her and never let her go. It was not supposed to be this way!

"Where is my uniform?" I kept trying to ask, but no one understood me. "Hey, medic, I don't want to go home for the first time in almost a year looking like a fucking gook in pajamas! Dammit, listen to me!

Where is my uniform?" I still received no response from this stupid medic. He just continued his job of getting me dressed.

I guess it really doesn't make any difference what I wear. I don't know where I'm going except it's not back to the damn war.

Bravo Company won't be here to see me off. Oh, God, that's right, I killed Fourth Platoon. There'll be a whole new mortar platoon now. How am I going to live with their blood on my hands? I'm going home. Maybe there I can sort this whole thing out. I need to see Lu, I'm sure she'll have the answers.

* * *

I was moved from my hospital bed. I saw the ceiling as we rolled down the hallway. Then we were outside and there was a very bright blue sky above me for a short time. *So this is Japan, not much to see from this gurney.*

I never did learn the name of the medic, Mr. Voice. I just remember him telling me "good luck," as he pushed me outside. In a matter of minutes, the sky was replaced by the inside of an army ambulance. It lurched off to an unknown destination.

Shit, take it easy, that hurts like hell!

Our next stop was my appointment with an air force medevac. It would take me and other wounded GIs back to the good old US of A. It was not what I'd pictured as my Freedom Bird back to the World.

I was given a shot, and again the lights went out. I spent most of the flight in sleep mode as pain medication kept me knocked out.

I awoke when we landed in Hawaii, but was unable to leave the plane like other patients who could walk. Someone had arranged to have a small Hawaiian musical group board the plane to entertain us on our way home. They might have been good, but I hurt too much to enjoy it.

Go away and just leave me alone!

The medics realized I was agitated and after another shot, my body went into a deep, deep sleep. I was out the rest of the trip until we landed at Miramar Naval Air Station just north of San Diego.

Then I experienced the most frightening part of the entire trip. I was rolled off the plane and the medics pushed me into the back of a damn hearse!

"Wait, I'm not dead!" I remember trying to say, but they kept moving me into this vehicle of death. All I could see was the gray ceiling.

Shit I'm not dead! Let me out of here! I'm on my way to see Lu. God, they're going to bury me alive!

I tried to yell loud enough that someone would know I wasn't dead, but no one was paying any attention. The hearse rolled forward toward my meeting with a grave, I was sure. Then it happened again: a flashback hit me.

I'm standing in the jungle and I see Joe hit by green tracer rounds and fall to the jungle floor. His life's blood seeps into the dirt not far from my feet. His blank stare freezes me into place. An explosion goes off to my right. I turn, trying to see what has happened, but something sticky is dripping across my vision. I try to wipe it away as the smell of copper and gunpowder assaults my nostrils. What I see through the red haze is Wild Bill and Dan lying on the ground with shrapnel holes in their bodies.

"No!" I yell as I try to help them, but my feet won't move. The faces seem to be telling me it's time to join them. My squad is all around me looking through sightless eyes as they lie there.

They're all dead in that damn stinking jungle!

* * *

A voice began speaking to me, but not the voice I know. It was a different voice, one more professional, deeper and older. "Mr. Rugh, it's time for you to wake up. I need to talk to you."

I fought my way back to the surface. I could see the person speaking. I knew it wasn't any of the Fourth Platoon; they would have called me Rough. Slowly, the sleep drained from my head and body and I became aware of my surroundings, even if they were still hazy. I opened my eyes just a little at first as if probing for a booby trap.

"At last I can see part of your eyes. Now try to open them all the way."

Shit, and let all the pain come back? No way!

"Okay, son, just try and stay awake for a few minutes."

"Son?" Is this my dad? It can't be. He probably doesn't know I'm in this hospital.

270

I had to get my eyes open, pain or no pain. I had to see this person calling me "son." I opened my eyes a little bit, letting in more light from the room. I saw a very distinguished-looking man dressed in a white hospital jacket over a khaki uniform. I looked at him through fuzzy vision. His features were unclear to me, but I could make out enough of his face to know he wasn't my dad. This person had a big black mustache. *My father never wore a mustache, did he?*

"Let's sit him up a little," this new voice said to someone I couldn't see.

"A short talk is what you want?" I mumbled in the garbage I'd come to expect.

"Do you know where you are?"

Of course, I'm in a lot of pain!

"Let's put what you are thinking into words so I know the answers. Let's start with your name."

"My name is Rough," I tried to tell him. At least it's what I thought I was saying. My brain was too scrambled. I was unable to put two words together that made any sense.

This person asked me for the phone number where my wife could be reached.

I tried to tell him, but I couldn't put the numbers in any kind of order.

"We'll let you sleep for now and try again later after the effects of the sedatives have worn off."

I slipped back into oblivion once again. *Where am I? What happens now?* Questions I had no answers for kept swirling through my mind. *Am I home? Where's Lu?*

I didn't know it then, but my wife had been notified by the Army Casualty Department and was on her way to the hospital to see me.

Here I was lying in a hospital ward on my back with tubes and needles running into my body keeping me alive. I couldn't walk or dress myself. I had to be fed through an IV and I couldn't seem to put two words together that made sense to anyone. The only good part: I was home at last and alive, for now.

Chapter 37 - Len's Home

Lu

I called the Army Casualty Department several times a week for the latest updates on Len's condition. They knew the news first and were responsible for sending the telegrams out to the families.

The latest information was very disturbing. Len had been reassigned to the Air Force and was being *shipped* home to southern California.

All the telegrams I'd received through this long ordeal had said Len would be home in two weeks and would be transferred to Letterman Army Hospital in the San Francisco Bay Area, not southern California.

I made another call to the hospital in Japan. The nurse quickly said, "Mr. Rugh is no longer here. He was *shipped* home today." She couldn't answer any other questions.

To me it meant only one thing—he was dead. *Oh, God! What am I going to do now? How can I live without him? I should let everyone know, I guess. How do I tell them this news? We've all been praying so hard for his recovery. I can't believe he's gone; I didn't get a chance to tell him I love him!*

I bit my lip trying to keep the tears from falling. After seven weeks, I was going through it all again. Only this time it was the end. Len was dead. *How can I keep myself together while my whole world is crashing about me?* I sat on our bed, where we'd spent so many wonderful hours, clutching my torso lest I fall apart.

* * *

"Morning, everyone." I tried to be cheery as I walked into my parents' kitchen half an hour later.

"Okay, Lu, what's the matter?" My dad saw the tears in my eyes. He could read me like the newspaper.

I explained to Dad, Mom, and my brother, Walt, what I'd learned. I then announced my conclusion that he must not have survived.

"Lu, they didn't say he was dead, did they?" Walt asked with the bluntness of a twenty-year-old.

"No, but what else could it mean? They wouldn't tell me over the phone he'd died. They'd send someone in person." I was trying to be brave, but my voice cracked. "I'm sure it's the reason the nurse wouldn't give me any information."

"That's not a good basis to make you think he's gone," Dad stated as he stood up to enfold me in his arms.

"You know that all the information we've received so far said he'd be going to the Bay Area, not here. Now they tell me he's being shipped to southern California. I'm afraid he's coming home via the air force in a flag-draped box." Saying my worst fears out loud caused me to panic and my heart began to race.

"Now, sis, have some faith and don't think the worst until you have confirmation," Walt said as he put his hand on my shoulder.

"How can I continue to hope when I don't know what's going on?" I couldn't keep my body from trembling in frustration and fear. "First, it was waiting more than the promised two weeks, and now he's being shipped to a different area? No, it's the end."

Mom took my shaky hands in hers as she said, "I'll be home today in case anyone comes to the house ..."

"Thanks, Mom. When they arrive, send them to the bank. I need to know right away. In my heart, I feel he's still alive, but I knew this could happen." I forced the words through my tears. "I've tried to prepare myself since I received the first telegram. Actually, I've been afraid he could be killed since he left for Vietnam. I didn't want to think about it, but I faced the reality I could lose him over there."

"I know, honey. It's something we've prayed about," my dad whispered with tears in his eyes as he gave me a hug. He was a man of few words, but he was demonstrative.

273

"I need to go to work to keep my mind occupied. Waiting around would drive me crazy. I'll try to keep hope with me all day."

"Hey, kiddo, just be strong a little while longer and think positive thoughts. We should know one way or the other by the time you get home."

"Thanks, little brother, I don't know how I could have gotten through these last months without everyone's support. I love you."

Dammit, Len, you promised! I thought for what seemed the hundredth time in the past weeks.

* * *

"Any news?" I asked as I rushed in the door after work.

"No, sweetheart, we haven't gotten a word on where he is or his condition."

"Thank you for being so patient. I must have phoned at least twenty times."

"It's okay, sweetheart; I knew you were anxious. Go make your call to Army Casualty. Hopefully, they'll have more information by now," Mom suggested.

With dread, I dialed the number. A young man gave me terrific news and gently chided me for worrying. It would be the last time I'd need to call them. Len was home and he was alive!

"You've been wonderful, thank you so much. Knowing I could contact you at any time made it easier. I can never thank you enough for your time, your understanding, and your patience. God bless you all."

"Ma'am, we were just doing our duty, but thank you. You go take care of that husband of yours. Good luck to you both."

* * *

"Yahoo, he's alive!" I screamed, bounding into the kitchen, smiling through the tears. "The army decided to transport him to Camp Pendleton Naval Hospital because it's closer to home."

"What great news! Oh, there's the doorbell," Dad announced as he headed to the door.

It was the man from Western Union. I thanked him as Dad slipped him a couple of dollars.

I opened the envelope, took a deep breath, and began to read silently.

"Well, what does it say?" everyone asked at once.

"Len's alive and at the hospital on Camp Pendleton. I've seen the entrance off the I-5 freeway in Oceanside."

My dad nodded his head and said, "It's at least ninety miles from here."

"Well, I'm driving down to the hospital tonight. The telegram has directions on how to get there." I was feeling so elated. I was finally going to see Len. I wanted to leave right then.

"You are not going by yourself," Mom announced. "I'll go with you since the guys have to go to work early. Dinner's ready. Let's eat quickly and then go."

"I'm either too nervous or too excited to eat, but you go ahead."

"Honey, this is going to be a long night and you need to keep up your strength. You've lost too much weight already and you don't want to look like skin and bones when you see your husband. Now sit down and eat."

"Okay, Mom, but I want to get on the road as soon as possible."

"See, sis, I told ya' everything was going to be all right!"

"Yeah, you did. Thanks," I said as I gave my biggest supporter a hug.

* * *

The one hundred miles from my parents' home to the naval hospital on Camp Pendleton Marine Base was the longest drive of my life. So many things kept running through my mind. *What will I find when I finally come face to face with this man I love so much?* I was frightened and hopeful at the same time.

We found the main office of the hospital and received directions. Large Quonset huts were connected by long hallways and covered several acres. Without directions, we could have walked for miles and never found the correct location.

There are no words to describe the feelings I had as we approached the ward. A large man with a black mustache met us. He introduced himself as Dr. Jackson and said he'd been trying to locate me all afternoon. Mom and I were taken into his office where he updated us on Len's condition and prognosis.

"Mrs. Rugh, you've already been informed that your husband suffered a severe head trauma—so severe, in fact, he's still considered critical. He may not live."

I gasped. Today had been a roller coaster ride of emotions. First, I woke up thinking good thoughts about Len, then the news from the hospital, the call to the Casualty Department later, and now this. *How much more can I take?*

He continued, "Be prepared. Seeing your husband for the first time will be a shock. He's missing a one-and-a-half-inch wide strip of his cranium from an inch above his right eye back to the crown, created when the bullet passed between his skull and brain. His brain is almost totally destroyed on the right side, and his mental capacity has been acutely diminished."

Is that what the doctor in Japan had been trying to tell me? How much worse could it get?

"He's very weak and has lost a lot of weight, down to just 138 pounds. He's being fed intravenously, but we need to get him on solid food soon. He can't feed himself, so we may ask you to do it when you're here. I don't have enough corpsmen to work one-on-one."

He only weighs twenty pounds more than me? How can that be?

The doctor continued with his analysis of Len's condition. "He's not speaking clearly and can't be understood. He's not aware of his surroundings. Prepare yourself. He most likely won't know you."

What's happening? How could he not know me?

"He is permanently paralyzed on his entire left side and will never walk again. We tried to get him to sit up earlier, but he didn't have the strength to stay upright. He'll need to get stronger so we can operate to insert the plate to replace his missing skull. That may take weeks."

I had been staring in a daze at his very large hands folded on his desk. My only thought was: *How could this large man with these huge fingers perform delicate surgery on my husband's brain?*

"He'll need constant care, so in a few months your husband will be sent to a VA facility where he will remain for the rest of his life."

Oh, God! How can I live my life without him? I thought again as the tears streamed down my face.

Dr. Jackson handed me several tissues and went on. "While in Japan, he suffered high fevers from meningitis and most likely will not be able to father any children if he were to recover enough to resume your marriage. I know this is a very bleak prognosis, but you needed to know what to expect. This will be a difficult situation for you. I don't see much improvement from where he is now. In cases like these, the wife may obtain an annulment if no children are involved. You don't need to make a decision tonight. Mrs. Rugh, do you have any questions?"

I sat there in stunned silence. I had expected the worst, but this was far beyond anything I could have imagined. Not in my most terrible nightmares had I dreamed an outcome so horrifying. We'd been married for two and a half wonderful years full of love and life and hope for the future. Now I was being told there wasn't any hope for a future with Len. *How can I give him up?* I had to see him.

"Dr. Jackson, I haven't seen my husband in nine months. I need to see for myself, so please take me to him. I'm sure I'll have questions, but they'll have to wait." My voice came out as a rusty squeak like it hadn't been used for weeks.

"Of course, Mrs. Rugh. I know this has been difficult, but you needed to be prepared for your first visit."

"Lu, I'll be right behind you," Mom said as she touched my shoulder.

"Thanks, Mom. I seem to say that a lot, don't I?" It could never be enough for the support through this ordeal.

* * *

I followed the doctor through the ward. It consisted of forty beds, twenty on each side with a desk about halfway down. I wasn't aware of much of anything on the first trip through the building. I only wanted to know where Len was.

I felt as if I were walking down a deserted alley through hell. The only thing I could hear was Dr. Jackson's words echoing through my head. I couldn't reconcile my strong, healthy husband, the man I loved as life itself with this mindless, senseless body described by the doctor. *This can NOT be happening! I WILL wake up soon and the nightmare WILL be over.*

I was led to a bed just past where the corpsmen were stationed. Dr. Jackson pointed. If I'd come on my own, I would never have recognized the person lying there. He was battered and broken. They had him connected to bags of fluids.

Just before I reached the foot of the bed, the occupant struggled to raise his head. A quiet and somewhat garbled voice said, "Hi, kid, they told me you couldn't come to visit me. I love you."

He knows me! Oh, God, maybe they're wrong! I turned around to see my mother crying and even saw a bit of moisture in the eyes of this big bear of a doctor.

I heard Dr. Jackson breathe, "I can't believe it! Those are the most recognizable words he's said."

After what I'd been told, I couldn't believe it either. Was this a miracle?

I ran sobbing to Len's side. He held me with his right arm as he kissed me hello. This was not easy because of the IV and other apparatus attached to his body, but it was the most wonderful hug and kiss ever. Len was home and he knew me! Everything was going to be all right, I just knew it.

As I stepped back and looked at him, my first thought was a picture of holocaust survivors. He was so thin with big, deep-set eyes. His hair was a bit of stubble only covering parts of his head. The size of the indentation in his skull was a shock, even though Dr. Jackson had tried to warn me. This man didn't begin to resemble the one I had married, but he was still a most wonderful sight.

A corpsman brought me a chair, and I sat down next to him and tried to carry on a conversation. Len was doing his best, but he seemed exhausted. Dr. Jackson placed his big gentle hand on my shoulder and assured me that he'd just had a long day and would be better the next trip down. It was a much different outlook than only a few minutes before, and gave me hope for a future with the husband I loved so much.

* * *

Since Len was still in critical condition, I was allowed to visit him at any hour day or night. During the first few weeks, I drove the two hundred mile round trip down to see him three times a week. Most often I made the trip alone.

When I walked onto the ward, there were several greetings. I'd gotten to know a few of the other guys. Some didn't have visitors and were very lonesome, so I tried to bring flowers or cookies to cheer them up.

There was one nice black man with a spinal cord injury from Vietnam. His name was Scotty, and he was in the bed across from Len. He always smiled and told me to have faith things would work out just fine.

One weekend, when I came to visit Len, Scotty's bed was empty. I figured he'd gone home for the weekend. Later in the day, Len explained what happened to Scotty. He'd developed a sudden virulent infection. In his weakened state, he couldn't fight it and had died the day before. I stared at the empty bed all day long. I cried that night. I would miss the sweet, smiling young man.

Now, I also lived with the fear with each trip down to see Len that I would find another empty bed.

* * *

During my visits, we got to know each other again. There were some changes, but he was pretty much the same guy I'd married. He had a lot of physical problems and I could see some differences in his mental capacity. He was quieter and not very confident in himself. Not the strong Leo, A-type personality telling the sun when to rise and shine.

I remembered the offer from the military about annulling our marriage, but after that first night, I never considered it. This was my husband "for better or for worse, in sickness and in health, till death do us part." I'd made that promise and I wasn't going back on it now. We'd make the most of our life together and live each day as if it was our last.

There were lots of questions to be answered in the next few months. I listened to Dr. Jackson's ideas and suggestions. He became more encouraging with every improvement Len made.

He had been slowly but steadily gaining weight and strength. His speech was still difficult to understand, but I'd gotten better at making out his intention, if not the words. We realized part of the problem was his hearing. He was deaf in his left ear and his right had a constant ringing, making things even more complicated.

Our conversations were lots of fun, me trying to understand him and him trying to hear me. I'm not sure what we sounded like to others, but we didn't care. It was just good to have him home from the war.

Len had been at the hospital about three weeks when I got the scare of my life. I walked in one evening and found him asleep. He was thrashing from side to side and mumbling to himself. I could make out words like "dead," and "blood," and "flare," and something about being his fault.

I was trying to decide if I should wake him when a corpsman came over and gently shook his shoulder. He woke with a start and then he saw me and smiled.

It took a while and a lot of starts and spurts, but he finally got these words out. "I need to tell you what happened. I've pieced together what I remember and what I was told while in Japan. I'm pretty sure of the circumstances of the day I was wounded. I've been having this same nightmare ever since."

He described as much as he could remember: setting off the trip flare, the gunfire, the blood, and his buddies falling.

It was frightening to me, and I wasn't the one who had to live with it. Len had endured so much in Vietnam. How could anyone survive the pain and anguish and guilt he was suffering? Len would need me for as long as we'd have together. I promised him in my heart that I'd give him my love and support for the rest of our lives.

Chapter 38 - Recovery

Len

Lu's first visit to the Naval Hospital at Camp Pendleton began my recovery. I was there for two reasons. It was close to where Lu lived, if you call a hundred miles close. And one of the top neurosurgeons in the country was stationed at this hospital. Dr. Jackson, while with the navy, had helped develop a new type of plastic. It was far better for repairing missing skull from major head injuries than the old metal plates.

I'd been shipped home via the air force, was stationed at a naval hospital on a marine base, and I was still in the army. At least I thought I was. Who said our military can't work together? But, it all seemed a little confusing to me.

There I was, lying flat on my back in another hospital bed. All I could do was look at the ceiling or the bottles which hung nearby. They contained life-sustaining liquid slowly dripping through tubes connected to my body.

Lu's walk into the ward must have been a long one. I'm sure I wasn't what she expected. There'd been a lot of physical changes since I left for Vietnam.

When I looked up into her frightened face and wide blue eyes, I knew I had something to live for. I'd almost forgotten in my pain and drug-induced state. Lu was my life and my strength. She'd gotten me through many days and nights in Vietnam and she would get me through this ordeal, too.

* * *

Time passed slowly. My only bright spots were when I had visitors. Since Lu came whenever she could, my medicine was put off until after her visit unless I was in extreme pain. I didn't want to be asleep or incoherent while she was there.

I needed to recover so I could be with her. I had to figure out a way to get back on my feet again. We had a lot of plans for our life together, and I couldn't do anything about them in the hospital. I wanted out so badly. Oh, sure, I was getting better, but not fast enough. *I want to get going, NOW.*

I began to tell the corpsmen I didn't need any pain medication. I had to clear my foggy brain.

"You're sure? Dr. J. says you can have meds for the pain any time you ask," the young man said.

"I'm fine. It's just about gone," I lied more than once.

Truthfully, it had lessened, and having had migraines most of my adult life, I could tolerate what pain there was.

I just wanted to say, "Let's get me up and walking so I can get out of here! I need to go home and start my life again."

Everyone seemed to be cautiously optimistic about my recovery and planned to take things slowly. Not my schedule at all.

* * *

During the war, the hospital was short of corpsmen and nurses. These men and women gave much of themselves to help the broken and battered GIs arriving day and night. It was a hectic life.

For those of us restricted to our beds, the small light at the desk was a beacon. It meant someone was around, help was near.

Many on this ward couldn't do much for themselves. Our biggest concern was also our most embarrassing. We couldn't get out of bed to go to the bathroom.

All day and long into the night, I could hear calls for the corpsman. Often these calls would come too late. This problem was no one's fault really. Due to our injuries, Mother Nature continued to function on her own without our knowledge or ability to prevent it. All of us had our share of humiliating accidents.

The few men on duty tried their best to keep us comfortable and dry, not an easy task. They often ended up washing our bodies, changing our bedding and our pajamas.

I knew I had to relearn to control this function if I ever wanted to go home. It would take a lot of will power and concentration, but I would do it. I had to have this licked before I would be allowed to leave. I was a twenty-four-year-old man and I didn't plan on wetting the bed for the rest of my life. Try explaining that to your wife!

* * *

One day, an Army Liaison Officer awakened me. My first incoherent thought had something to do with my not being in uniform and that he was here to get me back to my unit. When I realized where I was, I was really baffled.

I think I asked him what he wanted. I'm not sure what he actually heard.

He came to attention and saluted. In my mixed-up brain, it made no sense at all. He was an officer and I was a lowly E-4. Why should he be saluting me?

Then he started speaking. "Specialist Four Leonard W. Rugh, for being wounded on the field of battle I present to you this Medal of the Military Order of the Purple Heart. It is given to you on behalf of a grateful nation …"

I could only understand a few words and lost track at that point.

He shook my hand and placed the box containing the medal on my night table. He saluted me once more. Making a sharp turn, he marched back down the ward leaving me somewhat confused.

I wasn't sure if it really happened or I only dreamed it. When Lu came in later, she picked up the medal and, with tears in her eyes, kissed my cheek. I could tell she was very moved, I only wished she had been here for the brief ceremony.

* * *

I'd been at the Naval Hospital about four weeks when Dr. Jackson told me he'd be inserting a large plastic plate into my head to reconstruct my skull where the AK-47 round had blown a large chunk away.

283

I don't remember much of the day of the operation. For Lu, it was probably one of the longest of her life. And, like so many since I left for Vietnam, I wasn't available to comfort her.

The doctors told my family it would only take three to four hours. They found a lot more cranial fragments left in my brain tissue than expected. The MASH unit in Vietnam had not been able to remove many of the minute particles left when the bullet passed between my brain and skull. The bone that had kept my brain protected for the first twenty-four years of my life had been pulverized. The operation lasted a lot longer than expected.

* * *

Lu

The morning of the surgery in late November dawned crisp and cold. Len's mom, brother, and sister had been constant visitors and were there. My mom and dad were also with me for support.

I sat waiting … waiting for news about Len's condition. Did he survive? Dr. Jackson had explained that in his weakened condition, his chances of making it through this grueling operation were about fifty-fifty.

Like flipping a coin: Heads, he lives. Tails, he dies.

I needed to stop thinking so morbidly and concentrate on good things, positive things. *I'll be really mad at you if you die on me, so don't even try, Leonard Rugh! Oh, he's so dang stubborn, he's not about to give up.*

I'd told Dr. Jackson how much faith I had in him and his team, but I knew Len's life had always been in God's hands.

It was such a relief when I was finally told he had pulled through. I'm tough, but how much mental anguish could I take?

No one could see Len in recovery, and the doctor suggested we all leave and return the next day. Since I had my car and Dad had to work the following day, my parents and Len's family all decided to head home. As I walked toward the door, one of the corpsmen came running up to speak with the doctor. Len was very agitated and calling for me.

I said good-bye and hugged everyone then followed Dr. Jackson into a small room. Len was thrashing on the bed and corpsmen were checking to see if he had dislodged any of the stitches or IV tubes. The doctor suggested I speak to him and hold his hand. I did both, and he began to calm down. I was told I could stay as long as I wanted.

I got the feeling they thought Len still might die. But, I wouldn't consider that.

I stayed by his side for many hours and prayed for him to live, trying to give him my strength and my love. I held his hand while he drifted in and out of consciousness. He was plagued by his nightmare and cried out in anguish for his buddies. He pleaded with me to just let him go. He said over and over that he didn't deserve to live since he'd caused so many deaths.

Between the pain, the medication, and his garbled speech, I could only guess at what he was trying to say most of the time. But it was clear he wanted it all to end. I couldn't let that happen.

"Honey, I need you to live. Please don't die," I pleaded with him. I talked of our previous life and our plans for the future. I tried to paint a rosy picture of the two of us in our own home. Of us sitting on the beach, watching the sunset while our children played in the surf. I wanted to give him a reason to live.

On many occasions, we'd discussed his feelings of guilt and remorse. I tried to put things in perspective and remind him it was an accident, but he wouldn't be consoled. He was positive he was to blame. His nightmare was chilling and real to him.

All afternoon and into the night, I sat by his side. A corpsman brought me a sandwich and something to drink and later something for dinner, I don't remember what.

Everyone encouraged me to leave and take a break, but Len would become restless, so I stayed. Around midnight he fell into a deep sleep. I finally went to find my bed at the hostess house about one o'clock. The crisis had passed, and I knew in my heart he'd make it.

* * *

Len

The medic must have heard me cry out during my nightmare. He quietly entered the room and added something to my IV. Then deep sleep took over and there was nothingness for a time.

When I next awoke, all I could see through a drowsy, pain-filled haze was the face of an angel. It was my Lu, sitting by the bed holding

285

my hand. She'd spent a long time at my bedside with no sleep and a lot of worry.

She talked to me about our future together. With those thoughts in mind and another dose of medication, I drifted back into my cozy sleep. I was in a world with no pain, no problems, no bad memories, and no nightmares.

When I woke again, I was back on my bed in the hospital ward and Lu was nowhere in sight.

"Where's my wife?" I whispered.

The medics were getting better at understanding my garbled speech and one answered. "We talked her into returning to the guest house for some sleep."

Good! I thought. *She'll come back soon.*

Lu returned a few hours later. The bank had given her two days off, so she could spend time with me.

I was confined to bed for recuperation and couldn't yet start physical therapy.

Damn, Christmas is coming. I have to be ready.

My major problem: I couldn't get out of bed to go to the head.

Mother Nature still ruled my body. My system was not responding to my commands. I was as helpless as the day I was born.

Is this to be my life from now on? I'd rather be dead. But Lu said she'd kill me if I died. And she'd find some way to do it, too!

"Medic!" I called to take care of my humiliating problem.

No, it's not medic. It's corpsman.

"Corpsman!"

"We're going to have to change his sheets and pajamas," a voice said to a blurred face standing near the foot of my urine-soaked bed.

They were too late. *Oh, Jesus, just let me die.*

* * *

Lu

I came down on Friday night to surprise Len. All day, I'd felt he needed me. As I entered the ward, I saw blood seeping up his IV tube. When I got close to his bed, the heat radiating from his body caused me to panic.

I yelled for the corpsman.

He left to find Dr. Jackson or Dr. Pratt. One of them was almost always on duty.

Dr. Pratt gave him a quick examination and ordered an alcohol rub, antibiotics, and two units of blood. He wasn't sure what had happened since Len had been fine when he'd checked an hour before.

"What's going on, Dr. Pratt?" I couldn't hide the fear in my voice.

He spoke gently, trying to calm me, "He's developed an infection."

I remembered Scotty, the nice soldier who'd died of an infection a few weeks before. It seemed to be one crisis after another. I was sure it would never end.

"I don't think it's too serious," Dr. Pratt told me a nervous hour later. "His temperature has already started to come down. Why don't you go to the hostess house and get some sleep. There's nothing you can do here. I'll have someone monitoring him all night. He should be fine by morning."

"Thank you, but I'll stay for a while."

"I knew you'd say that. The corpsman is bringing you a chair. If you want to stretch out, feel free to use the cot in our office. You'll see, come morning, he'll be better. I promise."

"I'll hold you to it."

When Dr. Pratt came to check on him several hours later, he was doing much better. His temperature was way down.

"I've decided to go get some rest. Good night, Dr. Pratt."

"Sleep well, Mrs. Rugh."

He kept his promise. Len's fever was almost back to normal when I returned the next day. He was very tired and spent most of the two days sleeping, but I was there each time he awoke.

* * *

Len

With the operation out of the way, I started getting stronger. It was finally time to begin a physical therapy program to get me on my feet. I soon realized it would be a long, frustrating, and degrading process.

I spent a lot of time in the physical therapy room discouraged. My left leg muscles weren't responding to my commands and wouldn't support me. I couldn't take even one small step.

Just trying to stand was a major task. I'd get lightheaded and was sure I was going to pass out. None of the guys in rehab looked big enough to hold me up if I started to fall. I was scared!

Then one day instead of going into PT, the corpsman took me to a small room just inside the main entrance.

Now what do they want me to do?

I'd been past this room but didn't know what it was for. The little cubicle contained an examination table and a gentleman I hadn't seen before.

He began explaining as I entered, "We have a work order for a long leg brace for your left side. This will make it possible for you to get out of your chair and walk."

Sounds good to me.

"Let me get some measurements. I'm sure you want your freedom," he said.

Freedom! What a wonderful idea.

The technician took a large piece of drawing paper and outlined my left leg. He then took measurements at different points, making notations on the paper.

"With physical therapy, concentration, and lots of practice with this brace, you should be able to stand and walk after a couple of months or so."

"Yes, sir! I was hoping it would be next week."

"It will take me three or four weeks just to get all the parts and build the brace. Continue with PT. The stronger you are, the better your chances of walking."

"Wilco, sir!"

If I can walk instead of spending the rest of my life in a damn wheelchair, I'll do it. Wheels are not my style.

* * *

For months, my nourishment had consisted of liquids dripping through the tube attached to my body. I'd been on an IV for so long the corpsmen couldn't find a working vein in my arms, so I was being given fluids through a needle in my chest.

To supplement the IV, they put me on a soft diet: Jell-O, broth, applesauce, and stuff like that. Yuck! Lu and everyone else who came to visit was put to work feeding me.

When I could finally eat *real* food, I was in heaven. Lu's mom stayed in the camper a few days at a time to cook for me. I was finally starting to gain weight and get my strength back.

The hospital food all tasted bland, not much better than C-rations. The only thing edible was the breakfast cereal which came in small boxes with real milk. They couldn't do much to ruin it. Breakfast soon became my favorite meal of the day.

The food in the hospital canteen was better than what the mess hall offered. Lu ate there when she visited. She said it was, "Okay, but not as good as Bob's Big Boy!" I didn't care! I'd try anything.

So whenever Lu or anyone else came to visit, I conned them into getting me something from the canteen. I was eating cheeseburgers, fries, and cokes or milkshakes, or grilled ham and cheese sandwiches as often as possible. I could hardly wait for the day I would get out of that damn hospital bed and walk down to the canteen by myself. But for now, I'd talk the corpsmen into helping me into the wheelchair and have my visitors push me there.

My sister, Dixie's coming. She'll take me. After all, I am her favorite brother.

I looked at the clock. Damn! It was only ten in the morning. A guy could starve waiting until lunch!

* * *

I was determined and worked very hard to stand so I could move from the bed to a wheelchair. I also had to be able to sit in a chair for an extended length of time. I'd been on my back for over three months, and relearning to sit upright wasn't easy. I felt like a newborn infant. I had to get stronger and more self-reliant if I wanted to be a part of the family again.

Four weeks and what seemed like hundreds of hours of hard work and tears paid off when, just before the holidays, Lu and her dad came to pick me up for my first trip home. It was one of greatest days of my life.

I had the pass in my hand. I'd get five whole days with the family at Christmas. My dream had come true! I was going home!

The wheelchair I left the hospital in was more modern than the old wooden one I'd been using. Lu and I had joked about it being the one President Roosevelt had utilized. (Get the picture?) This one was practical, easier to push, and actually folded up, making it easier to transport.

A corpsmen lifted me into the back of the camper. The table area inside had been converted into a bed for me to lie on while we made the long trip home. Lu sat in a chair in the back to keep an eye on me. It was very different from the last time we were in the camper before I shipped out to Vietnam.

At home, Lu's dad and brother, Walt Jr., lifted me out into the wheelchair. They had a one-story house with wide hallways and doors, perfect for getting around. There was a ramp up the steps, which I was sure Lu's dad had built.

Their home never looked so good. It was decorated and smelled like Christmas. I'd forgotten the wonderful aromas. After spending almost a year with the stench of Vietnam and hospitals, this really was heaven.

Our bed was already there since Lu had been living with her folks while I was in Vietnam. Everyone was teary at my being home for the first time in ten months. I was so excited!

I'd worn hospital pajamas and a robe home, but I wanted to wear real clothes. I'd lost so much weight; everything I owned was way too big and hung from my frame. Lu finally gave me some things of her dad's, a closer fit. It felt good being dressed in civies.

At times I'd be confined to bed during the day since my body was still quite weak. The doctors didn't want me to take any chances. I could injure myself if I fell. I didn't care as long as I was out of the hospital and with my Lu.

Much to my frustration, I couldn't do anything for myself. I was like a 150-pound limp doll, totally helpless. This was not how I pictured my first visit home or the rest of my life!

Dr. Jackson had explained to Lu what I could and couldn't do, what I needed and how to help me. She was shown how to raise me up so I could be moved in and out of my wheelchair to a bed or chair and back again. I was unable to get up or stand on my own yet. I couldn't wait for the magical brace to be finished.

* * *

I had one burning question which needed to be answered. I was a man and I was home for the first time in almost a year with my wife. Could I make love with her? If so, how? I was pretty sure, even with my paralysis, everything was working, but how could I do anything about it? We would be limited on the logistics of making love.

I was nervous knowing I had to talk to Lu about it. Would she even want to try? I wasn't the man she'd married and enjoyed making love to. Maybe my mangled body would turn her off. What then? I was different in so many ways, but I really wanted to hold her and love her and make her mine once again. What was I going to do about it?

When the subject finally came up, Lu told me she had many of the same questions and had given it a lot of thought. We did a bit of experimenting and came to a mutually satisfying finale.

"Oh, honey. I was so worried you wouldn't want me to make love to you," I tentatively whispered.

"Silly, why would I feel that way? I love you and I always will," Lu whispered back.

There was one disadvantage to making love under my in-laws roof with a house full of people, being quiet enough so no one else would hear.

"You'll be doing most of the work since I'm like dead weight and not much help."

"Hey, I've always wanted to lead on these expeditions and now I have the opportunity."

"Lu, I don't believe you just said that!"

"Actually, me either," she said with a laugh. "You know I always do my best talking on this subject with the lights out."

"Yeah, we've had lots of discussions in the dark about making love and a whole bunch in the light of day."

"You are not gallant, talking that way to a lady."

"Well, then you won't want to hear me when I say, 'That's the best damn sex I've had since leaving for 'Nam'!"

"No, buddy! What I'd rather hear is, 'It's the only damn sex I've had since leaving for 'Nam'!"

"You know me better than that! There wasn't a female there I would have spent one minute with or do anything else with for that matter. You were with me every minute of the day and night. You pulled me through some tough times and I would never have done anything to break our bond. All I could think of was walking off the plane at LAX and into your loving arms. I had it all planned, but you know what's said about 'the best laid plans.'"

"I know that. I was only kidding. Say, army guy, are you physically up for another go at this love making stuff?"

"Just move your hand a little lower and you'll get your answer. Only, this time I'll lead …"

We could be man and wife together with a little work and lots of enjoyment. I was a man who was married to a wonderful and understanding woman. God, I really loved my Lu. I knew at that moment we were going to be all right.

* * *

My family came to visit me at Lu's folks' house since it was a hassle for Lu's dad and brother to load me into and out of the camper. I really enjoyed seeing them outside of the hospital.

Christmas was wonderful. My mother-in-law, Betty, helped me purchase a warm fuzzy blanket for cold nights and a beautiful pendant, a silver cross with a diamond in the center, for Lu. It was the first time in many months I saw her eyes really light up and sparkle like they used to.

Lu and her family gave me a color TV to watch during the many hours I'd be in bed back in the hospital. I couldn't get down to the TV room by myself, and the long days were difficult with nothing to do.

Christmas Day we had a delicious dinner of roast turkey and ham and all the trimmings. I ate more food than any grown man should, but it all tasted so good.

Christmas of 1969 was the greatest. I'd remember it forever. The best part was I would be coming home again the next week for New Year's.

* * *

My first trip home was a mixed blessing. I was overjoyed at the things I could do and frustrated at the things I couldn't. I wanted to feel like a whole man and a true husband to my wife. I knew it was impossible, but I wanted to get back as much as possible. I realized there'd be a lot of work to do before achieving that goal.

Home again, I could handle it! It would be tough for Lu and it would take a lot of patience and hard work for me, but someday we'd be together for the rest of our lives. Only God knew how long it would be. We promised each other to take every day He gave us and make the most of it. Life was precious, and mine with Lu would be the best!

Chapter 39 - My Nightmare

Happy New Year! It was 1970 and I was home again! Lu and I started the new decade with a kiss for good luck. We were both exhausted, so we celebrated early and went to bed about 10:15 PM.

I was awakened by sounds like guns firing. The neighbor's teenaged boys had decided to celebrate with cherry bombs and firecrackers at midnight. The noise sent me back into my nightmare.

The flare erupts. It's so bright, night's become day. Why doesn't someone cover the damn thing with dirt before the NVA spot us?

I run back to the company's NDP grab for my radio's hand mike to call in the gunships and put the 105s on standby, but my radio is corroded. We're going to be attacked for sure and all hell's going to break loose!

I kick the damn thing trying to get it to work, but nothing. I hear RPGs and grenades explode throughout the jungle mixed with the sounds of M-16s and AK-47s firing. I snatch my M-16 and start to rock and roll, putting out as much firepower as I can. Red and green tracers whiz around me like angry hornets.

I stand in the jungle firing. Then I see Joe running toward me laughing his fool head off about the flare I'd accidentally set off. I'm never going to live this one down.

I watch as green tracers drill holes in his flak jacket and his body. He suddenly stops with a funny look on his face. No, it's more a look of shock just before he crumples to the ground. Blood fills the holes in his jacket. The air is filled with the screams of men.

"Joe!" I yell as I run to where he fell, his blood seeping into the dirt at my feet.

I drop to the jungle floor and call, "Medic!" I hold him in my arms, trying to comfort him. Joe looks at me in confusion as he rasps his last breaths.

No! This can't be happening!

I turn to look at Dan and Bill. They're racing towards Joe and me. An RPG explodes at their feet throwing them into the air and back onto the jungle floor. I leave Joe and run to find them sprawled in grotesque positions. I stare as red stains their dirty uniforms. Their eyes gaze unseeingly at the carnage.

Oh, God, I caused this.

There's another explosion to my left. I turn trying to see what happened but something sticky blinds me. I try to wipe it away. The smells of copper, gunpowder, and death assault my nostrils. I see through the red haze as Ole and Mac deflate in a slow-motion death. They lie on the jungle floor with gaping holes in their torsos. A black liquid discolors their fatigues, emerging red to mingle with the jungle dirt and muck.

I stand there, my feet unable to move, something drips down my face into my right eye. What is it?

I swipe my hand at the red film, but I can't seem to wipe it away. I look at my hand. No! It can't be. But it's blood, *my* blood! Oh, God, what's going on?

I've never experienced so much pain. It feels like my skull's been cracked open and someone is hammering directly on my brain with a sledgehammer.

Doc might be able to give me something for the pain and explain why the guys let the flare burn for so long.

Where the hell is Doc? I need him NOW!

"Doc! Where are you?" Why isn't he answering?

Doc is also down. How did that happen? Medics are here to help the wounded. They can't get hurt!

"Medic!"

Has someone called in the choppers or the 105s? I'm sure LT took care of it. LT's a good man.

Shit, it's the LT, or most of him anyway, blown to bits. Blood, there's too much blood. It's on the bodies, on the ground and in the trees. Everywhere I look, I see splattered blood.

Before the flare extinguishes, all of my squad are lying on the jungle floor, dead; but I'm still standing and screaming, "NO!"

The faces of my men lying all around me seem to tell me it's time to join them. I feel myself start to fall. My mind makes one final cry to God. "Why them?" I don't get an answer.

Then there's nothing but darkness and pain ...

Someone was shaking me.

"Len, you're having a bad dream, wake up."

I forced my eyes open. I just wanted the horror to go away.

"I'm awake," I muttered groggily. I couldn't stop trembling.

"Are you all right? You're shaking!"

"No. This is the same nightmare I always have; only it seemed worse this time. I could actually see the guys die."

"I should have realized and spoken to you when the firecrackers exploded, but you said you were okay so I just went back to sleep. I'm sorry."

I took Lu's hand, "You have nothing to be sorry for. I'm the one with the problem."

"Maybe you should tell me again what you think happened."

"I killed them. I let the NVA know where we were. I wish you had let me die, too. I wouldn't have to live with the guilt or this nightmare."

Lu sat up and shook me. "Well, that's not going to happen, buddy! I have you back and for better or worse you are stuck with me. So, just don't get any ideas of dying on me, you hear that?"

"Loud and clear."

"Well, I should hope so."

"We tried not to become buddies over there, you know, but we did. The damn war had a way of doing that even when we all fought against it. We didn't want to be close to anyone, it was too painful when we lost a friend." I couldn't keep the pain hidden in my words.

"Len, you've always had lots of friends; you're just that kind of guy. I wouldn't have expected any difference in Vietnam. I know it hurts, but time will make the pain lessen."

Lu tried to reassure me, but frustration enveloped me in dark futility.

"We fought and lived together and we all wanted to get back to the World alive. Dammit, they should have gone home sitting up on a Freedom Bird not in flag-draped coffins. They were only doing their lousy jobs. Shit, none of us liked it but it was what we got paid to do."

"Len, I know the war was a living hell for all of you, but you're home now and we have a future together. I won't let the war take you away from me again. I will not let it ruin our lives." Lu's voice started to crack.

"But it was my fault."

"You don't know that for sure. You only remember what someone in Japan told you when you were under medication. You were delirious at the time. How can you trust your memories?"

"My 'voice' in Japan told me what happened. I was the only survivor. I will never forget the look in Joe's eyes when he died in my arms. How could that not have happened?"

"Not one of your buddies would blame you for being alive. They'd want what's best for their friends. You would."

"The dreams must be real. They all died in that damn stinking jungle!"

Lu's voice rose. "Honey, it was an accident! I hate to see you in such physical pain and mental anguish."

"I survived! They didn't!"

"We have to live our lives as best as we can. You've come so far. Dr. Jackson refuses to put a limit on how far you can go."

"I guess I was just too stubborn to die."

"You, stubborn? Never!" Lu said with a laugh.

Her humor broke through my darkness. It was hard to stay in a black mood when she unleashed her cheerfulness.

"Yeah, right," I grumbled.

"We need to put the past behind us. We'll have a wonderful life, I just know it."

I tried to hold Lu with my good arm. "I love you so much."

"I love you too, you big lug."

"I'd never have had the desire or determination to make it this far without you by my side. I'm okay now, really. Go back to sleep. We're starting a new decade and a new life. Who knows where we might be at the end of the next ten years?"

"There'll be a lot of changes for us, but we'll make them together," Lu said, wiping the tears from her eyes.

"Good night again, love," I said with a kiss.

"Good morning," Lu mumbled as she drifted off to sleep.

I stayed awake thinking. It's amazing how much of the future we can see while staring at the ceiling in the dark. We would have a good life now that I could come home and be with my Lu. We'd be fine. I knew it deep inside.

Chapter 40 - The Struggle to Walk

Len

My speech still left a lot to be desired, but Lu was learning to make out most of my slurred words. I still had lots of trouble putting my thoughts into phrases and getting the words in the right order without stuttering and mumbling, trying to complete my sentences. Dr. Jackson mentioned this problem would be worked on at a later date with the help of speech therapy.

A surprise waited for me when I returned from my second trip home. My new brace was finally finished. I wanted out of that damn wheelchair ASAP!

Now the true rehabilitation began. I would walk again!

I admitted that I was a bit wobbly, and my left side would probably make it more difficult, but I was confident. I could do this! I just needed practice walking with this new piece of equipment, that was all.

* * *

God dammit, son of a bitch and fuck it all to hell! I couldn't think of enough swear words for the piece of metal junk strapped to my leg. It was impossible to control the fucking thing on a damn leg that wouldn't respond to my commands. It was like strapping a twelve-pound weight to an immovable object and trying to force it to move with sheer will-power. Impossible!

I'm never going to be able to walk again! I'll never have the independence of getting around without a fucking wheelchair! I'd rather be dead than be a dependent cripple for the rest of my life. Having someone around all the time to help me into and out of that contraption is NOT my idea of freedom.

"I don't care what the people in rehab say, it's not going to work. It hurts to stand. I have to hang on for dear life so I don't fall. I can't move my leg. My right leg is so weak it trembles trying to hold me up. I get lightheaded and I keep losing my balance. It just isn't going to work and it's a mistake to even try. I'm going to bed and lying there for the rest of my life and praying to die very soon."

I was talking to myself, but everyone else on the ward could hear my tirade. I didn't care, I was angry.

*   *   *

The next Saturday, Lu drove down to visit me for the weekend. She always spent all day, stayed the night in the military hostess house on base, sat with me most of Sunday, and then drove home so she could go to work Monday morning.

Lu told me several weeks later about this conversation:

Dr. Jackson stopped me as I entered the ward. "Mrs. Rugh, may I speak to you?"

"What happened? You have a look that says something's wrong."

"Nothing's physically wrong with your husband, but we are having a problem with his attitude. He's become uncooperative and is refusing to go to physical therapy."

"When I was here Wednesday night, he was very enthusiastic about getting his new brace and walking again. What happened?"

"His rehab team and I feel that he thought just because he had this brace, he was magically going to get on his feet and take off running. That's not going to happen. It's going to take many months before he'll be able to strap on his brace and walk on his own with a cane. He decided after two sessions it was hopeless and is refusing to continue."

"What can I do?"

"You have such rapport with your husband; try to get through to him. You'll have to be tough or else he'll just give up and spend the rest of his life in bed."

"He's always been so active, swimming, playing basketball, whatever sport he could find. The prospect of him never being able to do any of that again is the most difficult reality he's had to face."

"You know, two months ago I would never have given him a chance of surviving or even of getting out of bed, but he's come so far. He challenges my original prognosis every day. I'm writing him up in the medical journal as an example of how much a man can improve with his type of head trauma. And now this setback? It's like he's given up. I hate to see him stop now."

"So you're sure he can walk again?"

"My team was impressed with his progress. He's only been to two sessions, but went farther than we originally thought possible for a first try."

"Well, I'll talk to him and see what I can do to put him back on the right track."

"Most wives would have walked away by now realizing life in this situation would not be fun or easy, but here you are. You are one strong lady!"

"Thanks for the compliment, but I'm just being a wife to my husband who needs me."

"Well, I'm sure you didn't drive all this way to look at my ugly face, you'd better go see him now."

* * *

Lu

"Hi, honey, how's everything going?"

"Just go away and leave me alone."

"Excuse me? I just got here and I'm not leaving yet so you're going to have to put up with my company. What's your problem anyway?"

"I'm never going to walk again. Why would you want to be with a bedridden cripple?"

"Gee, I thought we were married. Wives usually want to spend time with their husbands, or is this a new concept for you?"

"Well, that was when we thought I'd be able to walk!"

"You've only gone to rehab a couple of times, what gave you the idea you'd never walk again?"

"I tried it and it isn't going to happen!"

"You can tell all that with two sessions, huh?"

"Yeah, I can tell, so just get used to the idea that your husband will spend the rest of his life in a bed unless two big strong guys struggle to put him in a wheelchair, and then you'll have to push me everywhere."

"So you gave up. My big brave man is just going to go back to bed and die. What about me?"

"What do you mean, what about you?"

"Remember the plans we made for our lives over the holidays? You were going to be walking in those plans. Granted it was with the aid of a cane and a brace, but nevertheless you were going to be on your feet."

"Yeah, well reality hit and smashed those stupid dreams to bits! I'm not living a fairytale; I'm living a fucking nightmare!"

"You will not use that word in any conversation with me! Do you understand?"

"It's my fucking word and I'll use it any fucking time I want to!"

"Okay, that's your prerogative, but I don't have to stand here and listen to it! This is our life for better or worse, so just get used to me being a part of it and clean up your damn language!"

"I'll bet this wasn't what you expected when you said our marriage vows."

"We were never given any guarantee that we would be living a rosy life without any bumps in the road. We have to make the best of what we've been given. You're home, you're alive, and we will make a good life. You need to promise me that you'll go back to rehab on Monday and do your best."

"Honey, I've already told you it's a waste of time. It just isn't going to happen."

"Well, let me tell you this, Mr. Stubborn-I-Know-It-All: I'm only twenty-four and if you think I'm going to spend the rest of my life with a person who would rather crawl into a hole and pull the cover over the top than to come out fighting for what he wants, you have another think coming! You can just spend the day sitting here stewing. I'm going to take time just for my self and go shopping! When I return, if I return, you had better have a new attitude or I'm out of here for good!" With that said, I turned around and marched out of the ward.

"That was a wonderful performance. I hope he really thinks about what you said and decides to go back to rehab on Monday!" Dr. Jackson met me at his office door.

"That was probably the hardest thing I've ever said to him. Even telling him good-bye the day he left for Vietnam was easier."

Dr. Jackson handed me his handkerchief, "Here, dry your eyes. Take a day to relax. You deserve time for just yourself. I'm prescribing it as your doctor. You can't go on pushing yourself the way you've been. It's a beautiful, sunny, warm winter day so go enjoy it. He'll be fine."

"I'll be back by dinnertime and thanks," I said as I headed out the door for my first day in months without an obligation to be anywhere.

* * *

That evening, I strolled back onto the ward rested and determined. I had spent the day watching the waves breaking over the jetty in Oceanside Harbor and taking a long nap back at the hostess house. I felt ready to take on the world, or at least one very stubborn husband.

Before I even reached Len's bed I heard, "T ... Th ... Thank God, you c ... c ... came back. I ... I ... was a ... afr ... afraid I ... I'd ... lost you."

He must have been watching for me. I hoped he'd done some thinking about our future.

"I've given a lot of thought about a life without you and it really scared me. I would do anything to prevent it. I'll learn to walk with that f ... I mean damn brace if it kills me. I've never given up on anything yet and I'm sure, by God, not going to start now. Thanks for coming back and for the verbal kick in the butt, I really needed it."

"I love you, you big lug. It would take a lot more than that to get me to leave. I think you'll be surprised what a lot of hard work and determination will do for you. I'll bet you're up and walking by our anniversary six weeks from now."

"I'll give it my best. I want to walk out of here and take my wife to a nice place for an anniversary dinner."

"It's a date."

* * *

Len

Monday morning I started what was to become a great triumph. I struggled and groaned and put up with a lot of pain, and I uttered a lot of cuss words. There were still days when I wanted to call it quits and give up, but I never lost sight of my goal. I was going to walk when I took my wife out. There wouldn't be champagne and dancing, but it would be a night to remember.

I wanted to surprise her so I downplayed my accomplishments. I was improving faster than I let on. She was right as usual. It went better after I got through the first few sessions.

Lu got off work early to get me ready for our big night. When she walked in, I was already dressed in real clothes and standing on my own two feet. The silly girl began to cry, messing up her makeup. She was so beautiful. I felt better than I had in a year. Her smile lit up her face like the sun. Her look of wonder was etched in my mind forever.

I began our fourth year of married life standing on my own. I needed help from a corpsman to walk the few steps to the wheelchair. It would be several months before I could do an extended amount of walking, but it was a start in the right direction. We were one step closer to our dreams.

Chapter 41 - Getting My Life Back

Len

I was released from the naval hospital on Camp Pendleton to the Veterans' Administration Hospital in Long Beach, California, in March of 1970. I still needed hospitalization while I was going through speech and physical therapy. The VA added occupational therapy to keep me busy.

Even after two months with my leg brace, I was still confined to the bed most of the time and used a wheelchair to get around. I was frustrated because I couldn't put my leg brace on by myself, and discouraged because learning to walk again was such a slow and agonizing process. I had balance problems and leg muscles that didn't respond to commands.

No one seemed to know how long I'd be in the hospital. I still wasn't able to go home except for an occasional weekend. But I was closer to Lu and the family, only about forty miles.

Lu came to visit several nights a week. Sometimes we'd go to the Denny's across the street for a beef dip sandwich. *Mmmm, it was so much better than hospital food.* We could also drive a mile down the street to a Bob's Big Boy for a spaghetti and chili, my favorite. It took a while for us to get going since I needed help getting my brace on. Often there was no one to help, so I'd take a wheelchair down to the hospital's cafeteria and eat. The food wasn't the best, but we could eat together.

We'd have a nice visit, but way too short for me. Life wasn't moving quickly enough towards my goal. I wanted to go home to stay!

* * *

My speech was slow and garbled. Lu did a good job of figuring it out, but it was difficult to carry on a conversation with other visitors. I tended to stutter and stammer, having the word I wanted come out as something else, or so garbled I had to repeat myself several times to make the person understand. It was aggravating, both for me and for the listener.

I remember my first morning in speech therapy. After I was escorted to the speech office, the receptionist pushed my wheelchair into another room with four men sitting around a table.

"This is our new patient, Mr. Rugh. He comes to us from the army after being wounded in Vietnam," the nurse said before she left.

"She called you Mr. Rugh, but what is your first name? I'm Mr. Bill. Everyone calls me Mr. Bill," said the guy who was obviously in charge. "I know it's your first time here so you may be nervous. To my right is Dave, then Frank, and George is next to you." He said all this in a slow, professional, and deliberate manner.

Each man attempted to say hi and tell me his name. Dave's attempt was hesitant and garbled.

"Hi. I ... I ... I'm ... D ... Dow ... Dope." I managed to figure out what he was saying and it wasn't Dave. I wasn't alone in having speech problems.

"No, lets try that one more time. You're Daaaavvve," Mr. Bill said as he slowly pronounced Dave's name.

"I'm Do, no Da ... av ... ve."

"Almost there Dave, try it one more time. Nice and slow repeat, Daaavvvve."

"N... Ni ... ice a ... und s ... s ... slow D ... Daaave."

"Good job. Dave, say it one more time, just Dave."

"Ju ... ust Daavve." Mr. Bill looked frustrated even to me.

I was thinking about saying Dave myself, but knew that sometimes the words I wanted to say didn't come out the way I wanted them to either. Saying their names was as difficult for the other two men as it had been for Dave.

Mr. Bill turned and asked, "Now, what do we call you?"

I started to say my name is Len but Len didn't come out without a struggle. I ended up using my old nickname from the war, "The ... ey ca ... call me Raa Rough."

Mr. Bill could see this frustrated me. "Now, tell us who you are again."

"M ... My na ... am his is L ... Len," at least it was what I was trying to say, but even to my ears it came out slurred and hard to understand.

"I think your first name is Leonard. Well, guys, we'll call him Len. You are one of the few Vietnam GIs to come through here so far. As you can see, you're the kid in this group. George and Dave are WWII vets and Frank was in Korea. They're here due to strokes, but have many of the same problems as with your head injury. Now say your first name again."

"Le ... Le ... Len."

"Great. I know it's early, but I think your first name is enough for today. I'll have our receptionist call for your escort to take you back to your ward. We'll see you again tomorrow morning."

"O ... okay." I managed.

DAV volunteer escorts took patients from place to place within the hospital. They were my legs and arms, pushing my wheelchair until I was able to walk and began finding my own way. I still got confused and turned around easily. But even Lu managed to get lost once trying to get from my room to the cafeteria. This was a huge hospital.

* * *

I, like a number of other vets on the head and spinal cord injury ward, wasn't allowed to even try to take a shower without a nurse present.

"Now, Mr. Rugh, we've told you before you must tell someone at the nurses' station before you get in the shower stall," I was scolded one day.

"I was n ... not to take uh ti ... time doing t ...this easy." In my mind I was saying 'I was only trying to do something simple and not take you away from your duties,' but I could tell she didn't understand much of what I was saying.

I couldn't even get clean without someone being close, what a pain.

"It's my job to see that you don't fall."

"Oh, sh ... shit." I was thinking, 'Okay.'

"I hope that was a mistake. I'm only here to help," the nurse replied to my 'oh shit' comment.

"Okay." It came out right this time.

"I'll send in a male nurse to assist you. Don't forget your modesty cloth," she said as she handed me a washrag.

I muttered, "Thanks," with a chuckle. *A modesty cloth, an eleven inch square of terrycloth; what a joke.*

I didn't want to anger the people doing their jobs and helping me and hoped speech therapy would help.

* * *

On April seventh, 1970, I was officially retired from the US Army. The doctors still felt I couldn't function on my own. They had no hope that I'd be able to work or take care of myself, or live any kind of a normal existence.

I couldn't picture myself in a medical facility for the rest of my life. No sir, not me! I wanted out of that hospital, and I'd have done anything to accomplish that end. I just wanted to get back what I had before Vietnam, with some minor adaptations, of course. I had high hopes of living a life with Lu away from doctors.

The army issued me a complete set of military uniforms from top-coat to skivvies for the occasion. They must have made a mistake, though, as they gave me slacks with a size twenty-eight-waist. I hadn't worn that size since I was in eighth grade. They made several other mistakes as well. There were also five or six medals in the stuff. For what, I had no idea. I had my Purple Heart. Now there were more. When Lu came to visit that night, I hoped she'd figure it out. I wouldn't be wearing any of it in the hospital. Lu could take it home.

* * *

"Hi honey, how was your day?" she asked as she breezed into my room that evening.

"I'm exhausted. I don't know why, but I have a whole new wardrobe. Are they keeping me in the army? Don't they realize I'm not fit for duty yet? Dr. Jackson told me he had everything arranged for me and I didn't have to go before the retirement board to be retired. So, why do I need a uniform?"

"Probably just SOP for new retirees. What's in the little boxes?"

"Some medals or something, I don't know. The guys that came in with the stuff talked too fast for me to get it all."

"Oh ... my ... God! Honey, these three boxes are Army Commendation Medals! One has a 'V' for valor and one has an oak leaf cluster. You're really a hero!"

"No, I was certainly no hero; I was just doing my job the best I could. I don't know anything about any medals."

"Well, the army seems to think you're one, and so do I! The Army Commendation Medals come with explanations. One was issued for the day you were wounded. There is also one for National Defense, Good Conduct, Vietnam Campaign, Combat Infantry Badge, one for being an excellent marksman, and of course the Purple Heart. You will always be my hero!"

"Yeah, well, I ... ah, guess so. Would you take this stuff home? I won't need it here."

"Sure, now back to your day ..."

* * *

Frustration was my constant companion all day, every day. I expected to take care of my family as a husband should, but here I was barely able to get out of bed on my own. I had a long way to go. Lu told me it would take time and to be patient. Well, this hospitalization shit was going on eight months. I needed to get on with my life.

I wanted more. I wanted to get up, dress myself, and get going without help. I wanted to think for myself. I wanted to order a meal out without a translator. Dammit, I just wanted to be independent. I wanted to be a man.

* * *

A typical day started with physical therapy intended to strengthen the weak muscles in my right leg and arm, and to try to get my left arm and leg to move when I told them to. I was unable to do something as simple as make my left hand into a fist. I needed to move my fingers so I could grasp something. The therapists and I worked day after day trying to accomplish this simple task. They'd ask me to move one finger at a time.

"Okay, Mr. Rugh, move that pointer finger today."

"S … Sure," I'd respond.

And every day I hoped he was right. I prayed that today would be the day when I could finally move some part of my hand.

"Let's get to work."

Dammit, no matter how hard I concentrated on telling my hand to move, it didn't, not even one twitch. My hand was dead, no feeling, no movement, nothing. *Oh, God, why did this happen to me?*

After a frustrating twenty minutes, my therapist for the day would say, "Enough of that. It's time to stand up to strengthen your legs."

Again, I was optimistic. I was going to walk on my own. For some idiotic reason, they wouldn't let me use my brace during this part of the therapy.

"Let me help you stand between the parallel bars. While I hold you, put your weight on your right leg. We'll stand here for a few minutes and build up your strength. We can't begin moving until your right leg can hold your weight. It will be a few more weeks before we can try taking steps."

Shit, I wanted to start walking right away! This was taking way too long. I had to try it.

"Whoa there, where do you think you're going?"

My therapist wasn't too happy with me when he had to catch me as I stepped off and nearly fell.

"I told you, you're not ready yet."

I was ready, just my damn legs weren't!

"I j … juss had t … to try."

"Don't rush it. You could cause more damage, delaying your progress. Besides, you don't want me to get in trouble do you?"

"O … kay, I … I'll do it y … y … you ray."

"You'll see; it won't be long now. You're getting stronger every day. Just be patient."

God, I really hate people telling me to be patient.

* * *

My nights were haunted with dreams of the day I was wounded and my platoon was killed. I started having a lot of pain, and my headaches were often worse than migraines. The doctors put me on heavy medication again. Physical therapy was agonizingly slow. I couldn't see any progress. Speech therapy was impossible, not much improvement there either.

At times I couldn't find many reasons to go on living. And then Lu would walk into my room and the sun would shine. She could change my gloomy day to one where I was happy to be alive.

* * *

My days at the VA hospital had become a routine. I was awakened at 0700. Someone got me cleaned up and dressed for the day. Breakfast was at 0800 and physical therapy started at 0900 for about an hour and a half. At 1100, I was taken to occupational therapy. I'm not sure why it was called that since I was doing arts and crafts, not anything I'd do as a real job.

I did make a really nice clay vase and a cutting board I painted with a picture of a seahorse. I gave them to Lu for her birthday in June. She was pleased and surprised. I'd done them by myself with just a little help.

My day continued with lunch in my room at 1200. At 1330, I went to speech therapy and at 1430 I was back in rehab for PT. Dinner was at 1800. Then I had the rest of the evening to watch TV or read a book. Lu visited a few times a week.

Lu or her mom would come down to get me on Friday afternoon or Saturday morning. We learned to put my brace on. By now I could walk very slowly with my cane for support. I was allowed to go home for the weekends as long as I was back by 1800 on Sunday. It was a slice of heaven. For a short time, I was out of the hospital and able to sleep with my wife by my side. It was hard on both of us when I had to return. This was definitely not how I saw my future.

* * *

The months moved along and I was finally making progress in all areas. The nightmares were less frequent, and my feelings of despair lightened every day. The pain diminished and I was starting to get around on my own.

I needed help putting my brace on and getting dressed. I would become confused, and something as simple as putting on my shirt was a trial. I would get part of it wrong-side-out, the buttons wouldn't match, or I couldn't slide my left arm into the sleeve.

I had to wear my dead-weight left arm in a sling to keep it from pulling out of my shoulder socket. It hadn't healed correctly from a high school football injury. By the end of the day without the sling, my shoulder would be in excruciating pain.

Tying my shoes was impossible. They tried to teach me how to do it one-handed, but the ability eluded me. I think my confusion was due to the injured part of my brain, or at least it was what I had been told by a doctor.

I sure missed the one-on-one care I'd had with Dr. Jackson. Actually, I missed the man himself. I could never thank him enough for all he and his team had done for me and Lu during the four and a half months I was at Camp Pendleton.

After I was up and ready to go, I could get to the bathroom by myself. What a liberating feeling to not have to depend on someone else to tend to my bodily functions!

When I was home on the weekends, everything went smoothly. On those brief visits, I could actually feel what it would be like to be there permanently. I needed help, but I could sort of walk and kind of talk.

Speech therapy three days a week was doing wonders for my thought processes as well as my speech. I learned how to put words together, and how to say the words so they could be understood. I was getting better at communication, and fewer people were asking me to repeat words.

I was now able to do some simple math. It was never my best subject in school, but now even the easiest problems became real challenges. I asked my therapist one day why it was so difficult. The reply had something to do with the right side of my brain and the trauma knocking out my ability to figure things out, especially math problems. That info matched what I'd already been told. Well, I could work with that. How much math does a man with a wife who's a math whiz need anyhow?

My abilities were far beyond what my original prognosis had been that day when I arrived back in the States. Even so, I had a long way to go.

* * *

I was released from the VA hospital in April 1971 and put on outpatient status. After all the therapy and rehab, I was finally able to get up and out on my own. It had been a slow and aggravating process, but I could stand and walk very slowly with the use of my cane.

Lu had obtained a transfer to a local bank branch and had moved to Long Beach to be closer to me several months earlier. The apartment was across the highway from the hospital. This made it easier for her to visit me and for me to get home on the weekends.

Now I was on my own. All my thoughts of freedom and getting up and around were warring with one very large mental problem. I didn't want to be seen in public.

I felt my body was deformed. I had a very disgusting scar running the entire length of my head from forehead to crown and down behind my right ear. No amount of hair was going to cover it. My left side didn't work. I was afraid people would notice and feel sorry for the poor cripple. I didn't want to subject myself to the pitying looks of strangers.

I was content to just stay inside the hospital or the apartment. This wasn't fair to Lu. She didn't complain, but I could tell she was worried about me. Something had to change.

Again, it took Lu to get things moving.

One evening while we were sitting in the living room watching TV, she turned to me and asked, "How about going out to eat and to a movie Sunday afternoon?"

"No, I don't want to go anywhere this weekend."

"All right, how about next weekend? We'll plan a day out together with a nice lunch and then something fun."

"No, I'd rather stay at home. I don't want to go out."

"Is this what you want our life to be like? Spending every day and night hiding in our apartment?"

"I'm just not ready to go out in public yet. You know I still need lots of help and more practice before I'm ready."

"This from the guy who couldn't wait to get out of the hospital and back into life. Well, sitting on a couch in our apartment isn't much different from sitting in a chair in the TV room at the hospital."

"I'm here with you, and that's all I need."

"You need to think about what you want out of life and let me know very soon. I work inside five days a week and I'd like to get out in the fresh air on my days off. I thought you wanted it, too. How do you see our life together?"

I let my muddled brain try to think through this simple question.

Life had been so much easier before the war and the AK-47 round which took out the right side of my head. I could think faster, and I'd have known the answer.

I knew I would have been one of those people looking down on this poor cripple in my former life. I'd always been a big strong athlete, not this puny shell of a man. I had to admit, I'd been hiding from the world and from myself. *What do I want our life together to be?* God help me, Lu was right. I'd only traded one confinement for another.

If only I could talk so people could understand the words I was attempting to say. I was getting better, but many words still came out garbled.

Lu and I had been watching a program about sharks.

"I know that one, it's a hammerhead shark," I thought I was saying. It was what I'd wanted to say, but what came out was "ham-head shit."

"No it's not a 'shit,' it's a 'shark'. A ham-mer-head shark."

"That's what I said, a shit."

"Let's try it again … shaaarrrk."

"O … tay it's a shi … shi … sha … r … r … shit."

"Oh, boy, is this going to be fun or what?"

"F … F … Fun, what's f … fun if I say 'ham … ma … head shit?' Now y … you k … know why I d … don' want g … go out."

"Honey, it's coming along. Just give it time and be patient."

I really hate that word, patient! It's bullshit!

I knew what Lu was thinking. I could see it in her eyes. I'd thought I was the only one suffering. I realized she endured the same pain and doubt that plagued me. She was just better at hiding it. She'd always wanted what was best for me, so it was her frustration as well.

314

* * *

In November of 1971, twenty-six months after I was shot in Vietnam, the VA released me from all hospital care and rehab. They couldn't do anything more for me. I had improved as much as I could, and much more than was ever thought possible. I was sent home with a pat on the head and orders to not attempt working, going to school, or doing anything too strenuous. In other words, exist but don't live.

I had learned to dress myself. I could hobble with my cane to the bathroom, get a shower, and put my brace on, by myself. The brace shop at the hospital had remade my shoes with Velcro fasteners so I could even "tie my shoes," by myself. I was almost independent, but still reluctant to go out in public.

Lu and I were really on our own. We were still living near the hospital and throwing good money down the drain paying rent. My finances had finally been straightened out, and the VA owed me some back pay. We felt the best way to spend this extra money was to buy a home.

When we were first married, we used to borrow the camper from Lu's parents and go down to San Clemente State Park to camp. We had talked of living there some day, so we headed that direction.

Our search started in San Clemente, but we couldn't find anything within our budget that wasn't a real fixer-upper. I was in no shape to fix-up anything.

Someone was looking out for us because we found a new housing development. We could actually afford these homes. They were single level without steps. For a small down payment, we could own a beautiful new home in Dana Point, California.

We moved in on our fifth anniversary in February 1972. We were really on our own since we were now about seventy miles from the rest of the family. This started the two of us down a new path and a new way of life. Lu had quit her job so she could be home to take care of me, not that I needed it. It was nice to spend every minute with her, although there were probably times when she'd have been happier with some time to herself.

We started taking walks together around the neighborhood in the mornings and evenings. Our home was in an area without any other housing nearby. We were among the first to move in, so we saw very few other people. This was great. We began to know our new neighbors

315

as they moved in. Everyone was friendly and greeted us without my expected looks of disdain or pity.

I found out two of our close neighbors were Vietnam vets also, but we mostly stayed away from the subject of war in our talks. We became friends. Life was good.

The family, especially Lu's dad, came down and helped with the landscaping. The neighbors got together and put up fencing. It was beginning to look like a real home in a real community. Now this was what I wanted out of life. How much better could life get than this? As it turned out, things were going to get a lot better.

Chapter 42 - It's Time to Make a Life

Lu

I gave Uncle Sam a strong, healthy, sexy, hunk, but I wasn't exactly sure what I got back. Len had been outgoing, an incredibly strong Leo with an A-type personality, but the guy I was now living with didn't want to be seen in public. He was unsure of himself and unable to do so many things.

I had to assume countless duties in our marriage that had been exclusively his before Vietnam. He was not the man I married. I felt disloyal to my husband. I felt unfaithful living with this new Len.

Oh, he still had the same smile, if now a bit crooked. The same voice, if now a bit garbled. The same sweetness, if now a bit timid. And the same love for me, if now a bit tentative. He seemed to fear my reaction to him and his disability. I tried to show I loved and supported him as often and as much as I could, but he didn't seem to believe I felt the same as I did when he left for Vietnam.

It was as though someone had taken the best parts of my husband away. I could no longer count on him for strength, leadership, forcefulness or protection. I had to make all our decisions and plans alone.

I was as frustrated as he was with the changes. Probably more so, since I could better see and feel the differences. I missed the romantic side of him, now gone forever. I had to learn to adjust to the changes.

I loved Len completely, and yet my heart broke every time I saw him struggle to do many of the things I could do with ease. We'd taken so much for granted and never realized just how lucky we were.

In time, I evolved from a quiet, shy introvert to a strong, decision-making, leader of the family. It was as much of a battle for me as Len's learning to walk and talk again. Our personalities changed to meet our new roles.

The first time I saw him in the hospital, my decision was made. I'd stay with the man I loved more than life itself and make the most of every day. I knew it would be difficult for both of us. But it was the path I chose and I wouldn't change my mind.

* * *

Len was now home on a full-time basis. There would be no more walks across the busy street between our apartment and the VA hospital, much to my relief.

He had nothing to do all day, every day, seven days a week. He would wake up in the late morning, get dressed, eat breakfast, and sit on the couch watching TV. He never ventured outside while I was at work. The weekends weren't much different. He had to break this pattern. Then something happened which would change our lives for the better.

The bank branch where I had been working closed. The building was being torn down to build a new high-rise. I could have transferred, but I felt the need to be home with Len. So I turned down the transfer and quit my job.

Several weeks later, the VA finally straightened out Len's finances and we received a check for the difference in his back pay. After talking it over, we all decided to use this money to by a house.

Len and I had always dreamed of buying a home near San Clemente, California. So we packed a bag for a week, rented a room in a little motel, and went to find a home.

What a scary process. First, we located a realtor to show us around. We couldn't seem to communicate with this rather portly gentleman. We didn't want anything with stairs, which meant *no* split-levels! We did not have a large amount of money for a down payment, so ocean-view homes, though nice, were not in the budget. Finally, after several frustrating days, we said thank you, but no thanks.

We started looking through the newspapers. We thought we wanted an older established home with landscaping and fencing already in place, but we weren't having any luck. Most of the homes were just too expensive.

One day we made a wrong turn and ended up in a new housing development.

"Lu, I'm sorry I meant to say go left to the harbor for lunch, but I said right instead. Now we're here in this building zone," Len apologized.

"Well, what do you want to do? We could see the models since we're already here. It's still early for lunch."

"What the heck, let's take a look."

All of the models were single story and had nice floor plans. We were pleasantly surprised when we saw the prices. We were sure we had found our new home. However, we wanted a second opinion. So I called my dad. He had built homes in the past, and we figured he'd give us good advice.

Dad's birthday was the next day, a Sunday, so we invited him and mom down for lunch in Dana Point Harbor and to see the houses.

After lunch, we drove up the hill to the place we hoped to live. Mom was impressed and suggested we buy the big four-bedroom since it had a large master bath with a walk-in closet. We had passed the easy part.

We were very nervous as Dad walked through the homes in various stages of construction. He rattled doors, looked at wiring, checked out foundations, inspected roofs, and scrutinized the ground. He told us they were well-constructed and was pleased with our choice.

So on January 7, 1972, we purchased our first home. We filled out the necessary paperwork and wrote a check for the down payment. Escrow would close about the same time the house was finished.

We picked the color of the appliances, carpeting, and front door. Our appliance choices were avocado green, burnt orange, or harvest gold. Ugh! I decided I could add lots of blue, my favorite color, to the green, so the decisions were made.

The next five weeks were hectic. We packed and gathered our furniture from various family members where we had stored it. We signed papers and more papers. *Have we just signed away our lives? Can we do this?* We rose above the many moments of doubt. The day before our fifth anniversary, we moved into our new home.

We were just far enough from the family, about an hour's drive, to have privacy, but close enough in an emergency.

There was a lot to be done to make it a home. I was hoping Len would now have some projects to keep him occupied and off the couch. He had several jobs besides taking out the trash. He could water the new plants, take walks around our neighborhood, and help paint the colorless walls.

We weren't very far from Camp Pendleton. We could shop in the exchange, buy groceries in the commissary, and use the medical facilities at the naval hospital.

It seemed strange not to see the old Quonset hut buildings of the old hospital, with their long hallways. They had been torn down with the completion of the new building. In a way, we'd miss them. Our lives had changed a lot within those walls.

We often dropped in to see Dr. Jackson. He was still shaking his head at Len's progress. He had him tested in 1973 by the same clinical psychologist who had tested Len's mental abilities in 1969. When the two tests were compared, the improvement was phenomenal. Dr. White couldn't reconcile the differences. Len had him scratching his head. My husband seemed to have that effect often on people in the medical field.

* * *

When I learned about Len's injury, I didn't think this life was possible for us. God does work His own plan in our lives. We'd come a long way and were really living now. How much better could it get?

Chapter 43 – What, Me a Father?

Lu

<u>Dear Diary – Dec. 8, 1972</u>

Am I pregnant? Should I tell Len my suspicions or wait for them to be confirmed? It would break his heart if I were wrong. I'll have to give it more thought.

<u>Dear Diary – Dec. 10, 1972</u>

Well, I told him, but cautioned him to wait until we knew for sure before getting too excited. Yeah, right, Len not be too excited! Oh, well, he deserves something good happening to him and a baby, well, it's more than I'd hoped for. I pray to God it's true.

Len

<u>Journal Entry - Dec.10, 1972</u>

Lu thinks she might be pregnant. We made an appointment with the doctor to find out for sure. I'll be the happiest man in the world if I'm to be a father. The doctors had no hope of me ever fathering a child three years ago. This will be a real miracle for us.

Lu

<u>Dear Diary – Dec. 15, 1972</u>

I *am* pregnant! We're very excited. Now we have to wait a very long seven and a half months. I just want a healthy baby, but Len says it's a girl. I hope he's not too disappointed if it's a boy.

Len

<u>Journal Entry – Dec. 15, 1972</u>

Well, we got the good news. Lu is six weeks pregnant! We should have the baby about July 27, 1973. Gee, we had nothing better to do on the night of Nixon's re-election. I'm betting on a girl. It's what I want, a nice healthy baby girl! We decided on a girl's name almost six years ago before 'Nam. Sandra, yep the baby will be Sandra Rugh.

Lu

<u>Dear Diary – Dec. 25, 1972</u>

Sometimes my husband really amazes me with his thoughtfulness. He gave me a little heart and diamond pendant today for being pregnant with his baby. I cried and then he told me how much he loved me, which of course made me cry harder. It must be hormones. Len just laughed, the stinker.

Len

<u>Journal Entry – Jan. 1, 1973</u>

This is the year I've waited for my whole adult life. I'm going to be a daddy. I gave Lu a small heart necklace for Christmas to honor her for being the mother of our child. I told her she could pass it on to our daughter when she grows up, if she wanted to. She got all teary-eyed, silly lady. *Oh, how I love her!*

<u>Journal Entry – Feb. 18, 1973</u>

Wow, we've been married six years! It doesn't seem long for so many things to have happened. It's finally starting to dawn on me what changes are still to come. I need to learn how to be a father. I have to admit, it's scary having the responsibility of caring for a little person. Lu will make a great mother and I'm sure she can teach me what I can't figure out for myself.

Lu

<u>Dear Diary – Feb. 18, 1973</u>

Our sixth anniversary is here. I wasn't sure Len would live until our third. The year 1969 was a year like I hope we never live through again. We've managed to put most of it in the past. In a little more than five months, I'll be holding Len's pride and joy in my arms. I've never seen anyone so excited and so petrified at the same time. This will be interesting.

Len

Journal Entry – July 1, 1973

Today was really funny. Lu's birthday was two weeks ago, and for eight weeks she's older than me until I catch up on August tenth. Well, she realized when the baby comes in about four weeks the birth certificate will show that she's a whole year older.

Of course, I said the wrong thing when I told her it didn't make a difference. She's eight months pregnant, big, uncomfortable, swollen ankles, hormones all out of whack, and she started bawling. The more I said, the more she cried, and the funnier I thought it all was. Oops, was I in trouble now!

She finally calmed down and made some remark about waiting until after my birthday to deliver this baby! I don't think I can wait that long.

Lu

Dear Diary – July 1, 1973

Today was not a good day and I made rather a mess of it. I started crying and Len thought it was funny, which made me cry all the more. I'll never live this down.

Len

Journal Entry – July 26, 1973

Well, tomorrow is the day our baby is due! It's been the longest nine months! I'm not sure just what to expect. I'm concerned I won't be able to do what fathers are supposed to do for newborn babies. Oh, God, I need your help!

Lu

Dear Diary - July 26, 1973

Well, tomorrow is supposed to be my due date, but I don't think it's going to happen. The doctor doesn't think so either, but I'll know more the day after tomorrow when I see him again.

Len's afraid he won't be a good father with his disability. I keep telling him this baby will be the luckiest ever. It will have its father around to give it love twenty-four hours a day, seven days a week. He keeps correcting me when I say "it," to say "her," or "she," or even "Sandra." He is so convinced we're having a girl, he even bought a pink dress to bring her home from the hospital. This ought to be interesting.

Len

Journal Entry – August 10, 1973

It's my birthday and Sandra hasn't arrived yet. She's two weeks over-due and her daddy is about to have a nervous breakdown. I know Lu is under a lot of stress and very uncomfortable. Come on baby get born!

Lu

Dear Diary – August 10, 1973

I remember making some comment about waiting until after Len's birthday to have this baby, but I didn't mean it, honest, God! I'm tired of being pregnant. I'm tired of not being able to see my feet. I'm tired of carrying all this extra weight around. And I'm really tired of having people ask me, "Isn't the baby here yet?" I'm just tired of it all! Come on baby!

Len

Journal Entry – August 14, 1973

Lu is finally in labor! Hooray! It shouldn't be long now! It's 4:00 PM and I've got to go …

When we arrived at the hospital in San Clemente, the doctors put Lu in the labor room. We sat and waited and waited some more. About one in the morning, I was nodding off, so Lu and the nurse sent me out to the waiting room to sleep. All I can do is sit and wait and try to get some sleep. Damn, it's taking a long time. Why isn't my baby girl here yet?

Journal Entry – August 15, 1973

I'd fallen into an exhausted sleep on the couch. My worried mind began the old nightmare once again. I was back in Vietnam with gun-fire and the bright light from the flare. The guys were falling around me. They looked up with their sightless eyes, accusing me of being their killer.

Someone shook me awake. *Where am I and who is this person?* A nurse. *I must be back in the hospital.*

She told me, "It's time." *Time? Time for what?* Finally, through a fog, I realized what was happening; my baby's coming, NOW!

I looked at my watch, that's what fathers are supposed to do, right? It was 6:38 AM. It took me a minute to get the kinks out and stand up. The nurse led me to the delivery room door. I got there just in time to see another nurse take our daughter to the clean-up area. Yes, I was right; we have a healthy baby girl. *I can pass out the pink bubblegum cigars. What a long fifteen hours Lu was in labor.*

I asked the nurse for the dimensions: eight pounds exactly and twenty-two inches long. I'm a father. My daughter Sandra is finally here!

Oh, God help me; now what do I do?

Lu

Dear Diary – August 17, 1973

We brought little Sandra home today in her new pink dress. I don't think there has ever been a prouder papa. All he can say is, "She's so pretty." I'm so lucky I have them both. This is a day I only dreamed of and now it's come true.

Even though everyone has been trying to convince Len he'll make a great father, he's scared to death. My mom placed Sandra in his arms and he did just fine. He did say something about her being so small. I'm not exactly sure what he expected.

Len is such a wonderful, loving man. He'll be a great daddy to our little girl. We are the luckiest couple with the most beautiful baby in the world!

Len

Journal Entry – August 17, 1973

We brought my daughter home today! I got to hold her for the first time. She's so small and helpless. She's so cute with her black fuzzy hair and her big blue eyes. I think she has my nose and chin and her mom's smile. I wonder what she'll look like when she's all grown up. I know she'll be beautiful.

She holds her little hands together as she looks up at her dad. I think she must be saying a prayer for the two of us. I can use all the help I can get.

What if I do something wrong? What if I drop her? Lu assured me that babies are pretty resilient and Sandy will be just fine. I'm not so sure about me. Being a father is going to be a challenge

Lu

Dear Diary – August 22, 1973

Len is amazing. He just loves to hold our little Sandy and sing to her. He talks incessantly to her. I can see she loves her daddy's voice. Even with all his hearing problems, he can sense Sandra fussing before I'm aware she's made a sound. *Thank you God for giving us this wonderful child. Amen.*

Len

Journal Entry – August 22, 1973

Something I learned in Vietnam as a part of my protection has stayed with me. I can still feel when something is wrong or I hear a change in the normal sound of the area I'm in. I can hear Sandy move and start to fret before Lu, even with her new mother's built-in alarm system. There isn't much I can do but be sure she's up. I can't help with that part of raising our daughter yet.

Journal Entry – Sept 15, 1973

Sandy is one month old today. She is, without a doubt, the most beautiful and the most wonderful baby girl in the world, and I am the luckiest daddy alive.

I have one concern that I can't discuss with Lu. I'm concerned about my mortality. I have a family now and I need to be around to take care of them. Lu asked Dr. Jackson how long I might survive. He had no answers and, until now, it wasn't a question I'd concerned myself with. What would happen to Lu and little Sandy if I died? Would she be able to take care of the two of them without me? I had to give this some serious thought. *What is my life expectancy? Does anyone really know?* I guess it's a question every man faces, disabled veteran or not. *God help me!*

* * *

Time passed quickly after our daughter was born. It had been two months and sixteen days, but who was counting? I was starting to feel more relaxed taking care of my daughter. It wasn't as bad as I'd feared. I could handle a lot of the duties daddies are supposed to. Of course Lu was right there most of the time in case I ran into a crisis.

Babies are very active little critters and Sandy could wriggle with the best. Trying to hold onto a baby is often difficult for parents with two arms and legs. It seemed impossible for a parent with only one of each working, but somehow we all managed to survive. I left most of the care to Lu and I got the easy part of keeping little Sandy busy while her mama did other things like cook, clean, wash, etc.

I'd been using my right side to do so many things for the previous four years, and my right arm and hand were strong. Sandra still didn't weigh more than a feather.

Sandy's pediatrician said she'd be okay even if I picked her up like a football. I didn't think so. She still seemed fragile to me. I could support her small body on my arm. She fit perfectly with her head in my hand and her body along my arm, with her legs on either side of my elbow.

I hadn't tried to walk while carrying her. My balance was shaky, and I didn't want us to fall down. I couldn't use my cane and hold her at the same time. This would be as difficult as learning to walk again.

I first needed to learn to get around without my cane. Then I tried it while carrying Sandy. No problem. Around the house where everything was one level with few obstacles, I was extra careful and watched the floor. I have no left peripheral vision and have a tendency to ignore stuff on my left side, so it was still a challenge.

One other small problem Sandra and I had to cope with: trying to change the diaper of a wriggling infant. It's nature. Babies mess their diapers, and Lu couldn't be home all the time, so I had to do the job when the time came.

A few weeks later the time arrived. I knew it would. Man, I wasn't looking forward to this at all. Lu had gone on some errands, and Sandy and I were at home waiting for Mom to get back. She started fussing.

Oh, shit! Yep, it smells like shit!

Sandy and I couldn't wait until Lu got home to change this diaper. Whew! I had to get her into her bedroom and onto the changing dresser. Over the previous weeks, I'd learned to carry her and keep my balance. I picked up my sweet little daughter, only now she smelled like an outhouse. *Oh, well, here goes.*

I'd watched Lu do it numerous times. It looked easy enough when she did it.

You can do this, I kept telling myself. Thank God I didn't have to worry about safety pins. We had the new self-sticking pull-tabs on the disposable diapers. I only had to change it and then toss the dirty diaper away.

"Okay, Sandra, please hold still so Daddy can fix this damn diaper. Oops, sorry, Mommy keeps telling Daddy to watch his language. With a little cooperation, we'll get this mess cleaned up and you'll be more comfortable."

Was she paying attention to this plea? 'Sure, Daddy, anything you want, Daddy.' Yeah right, it was like trying to hit a moving target. My little darling was way too active to just lie there quietly. She was used to Lu playing with her during this time and now she wanted to play with Daddy.

I finally got the stinky, dirty, wet diaper off. That was the easy part. *Oh, yuck! I've got to clean the poop off my daughter's butt. Burning shit cans in Vietnam would be preferable.*

I got most of it off, I think. Somehow I had to get a clean diaper on this daughter of mine. Doing this with one hand wasn't easy, but I stayed with it. *Now how does this thing go on? Oh, yeah, it goes under the baby with the wide part across the butt. Fold up the front and attach the tapes. No sweat, Dad!*

Wow, I did it! Wait a minute! This doesn't look like the one that came off! It's good enough for now. We just have to hope Lu gets home before it's time to pee or poop again.

We settled down on the couch to wait for Mom. I really looked at this new life I'd helped to produce. She was so perfect. Did I deserve all this happiness? No!

My mind wondered back to my buddies from Vietnam. I didn't know if we'd have remained friends after the war. We were from all different parts of the US. I'm sure we'd have run into each other at reunions or something. But then I remembered they were dead. I'd never see them again. They'd never have the experience of fathering a child, of having a beautiful, loving wife, of living in a dream home.

Okay, Rough, snap out of it. You have a daughter to take care of! You're supposed to be babysitting; Lu's not home, so assume your responsibility, now!

Wow! What am I doing here in this fantastic dream? How did I get so lucky? I know I don't deserve to be the only one alive, but now I have a family to protect and that's what I'll do.

* * *

"Hi, how did Daddy and his little girl make out?"

"All right … I guess."

"Oh, oh, what happened?"

"Just come take a look. I think Sandy and I needed your help."

"What do you call this?" she asked as she picked Sandra up off the couch, trying not to laugh too hard. The diaper slowly slipped off her little bottom and fell in a heap at Lu's feet.

"Okay, it needs a little work and I need more practice," I mumbled. "But not poopy ones just yet."

"Well, at least you tried. Thanks for giving me a break. You'll get better." Then with a giggle she continued, "You can't get much worse!"

"It was like trying to pin the tail on a donkey while the donkey was moving."

"I know. I change her numerous times each day."

"At least you have two hands to do it."

"Do I hear some frustration, Daddy?"

"Me frustrated? Damn right, I'm very frustrated. I can't do something as simple as change my daughter's diaper."

"So your first experience wasn't a total success. As I remember, four years ago we were told you would never have a child of your own. This precious darling is your flesh and blood. Both of you are my miracles and in case you haven't noticed, you're both like two stubborn peas in the proverbial pod. She's so much your daughter."

"Yeah …," I said with a grin.

"And I also remember the doctors said you would never walk again. Who's out walking around the block most every day when he has time?"

"If you call what I do walking!"

"Just what do you call it? It looks like walking to me. At least you're not riding in some 'dumb wheelchair' as you call them."

"Well, it's different."

"So how is it different?"

"It just is!"

"Someday you and Sandra will go around the block together. Can't you just picture it? I can. I see both of you walking along, her chattering and asking questions and you ambling so proudly, introducing her to everyone you meet."

"Thank you for the mental picture. I needed the reminder of just how lucky I am. How would I have made it so far without you? I love you!"

"I love you too, you big lug. Now let's put a fresh diaper on this naked child of ours. I'll give you some pointers on how to work with this little charmer."

Chapter 44 - Me Go to School?

Len

Time seemed on a fast track after Sandra came along. We were busy with all the parenting needed in the first year of our child's life. She was running everywhere and constantly babbling trying to communicate. We celebrated her first birthday. I couldn't believe how quickly time was moving in my life.

Meanwhile, I was becoming a couch potato. It was easy to sit back and let the world pass me by while watching TV.

One day while going through the mail, I came upon the catalog for the local community college. I glanced at the classes and made some comment to myself about one that seemed interesting. The next thing I knew Sandra and I were being shuffled into the car. The three of us were off to some destination, but I didn't have a clue where.

"Honey, where are we going?" I asked.

"You're going back to school," Lu answered.

"Ah ... this is a joke right?"

"I don't think so, but we'll soon know. It's about time you got off the couch and out of the house. I've been trying to think of something to get you back into life. You found a class that sounded interesting, so let's find out about it."

"Lu, you were there when the VA patted me on the head and told me to literally go home, sit by the fire, and do nothing. No work, no therapy, no school, no nothing. I can't do anything! That definitely means no college classes."

"That's a lot of hooey and you know it! I also remember a conversation the first day you got home about never walking or speaking clearly.

And look at you now. You've been like a caged tiger with nothing to do."

"We have Sandra to keep us busy. We go for our walk almost every day and I read to her in the afternoons."

"Oh, sure we have Sandy and she keeps us busy, but there's nothing to stimulate your mind. You're becoming bored, so let's try this."

"Sure, me go to school talking and walking the way I do?"

"We can ask if it's a problem. Classes start in about three weeks. Now which class seemed interesting in the catalog?"

"I was thinking about a speech class. I need more practice. Oh, no, you don't! I am not going to go to college, so just turn this car around and go home, now."

"Not on your life, buddy. Speech sounds like a good class to start with. Now what else did you find?"

"Lu, let's be reasonable. I cannot function at college, my doctors told me so."

"Just humor me, okay? I'm sure there's someone on campus who can answer our questions. Now, what was that other class?"

Man, she can sure be pushy when she wants to be!

"Political science sounds fun."

"Political science sounds like fun to you? Boy, you do need to get out."

We stopped in the parking lot of Saddleback Community College and went through the schedule. Lu wanted us prepared just in case.

"We should talk to a counselor first. We'll explain your circumstances and see what's best for you."

We found the main office. The counselor I needed to see was in.

"Mr. Rugh, Mr. Bergman will be able to see you," his secretary told us.

I never knew if he really did have time that day or if he just made a hole in his schedule to see me. The four of us sat down in his office to talk about my taking a class or two.

"We encourage our Vietnam vets to get back into the educational system, and this is a good place to start. Now, what classes did you have in mind?"

I hesitated and Lu nudged me, giving me the look, letting me know she was there if I needed her.

I stuttered and stammered the names of the two classes I was thinking about. Talking to people I didn't know was harder than talking to
family. He didn't seem to mind my starts and stops and nodded his
head as I spoke.

"Good choices. I have just the right person for your speech class.
In fact, I just saw her. Let me see if she's free for a minute. I'll be right
back."

My stomach was doing flip-flops. I hadn't been in school since 1965.
Then I had normal speech and I wasn't walking with a brace and cane,
and I definitely hadn't had a brain injury. Here I was talking about going to college, knowing the VA told me I couldn't handle it. *What am
I doing?*

"Lu, I think this is ..." This thought was put on hold when Mr.
Bergman returned with another person.

"Miss Bennett, this is Mr. Rugh and his wife and daughter. Mr.
Rugh is interested in your speech class this semester."

Miss Bennett made a good first impression. She'd taken time for
me and I was only thinking about taking her class.

"What would you like to know, Mr. Rugh?"

"I ... I th ... thought it only f ... f ... fair for us both if yo ... you
k ... k ... knew where I w ... was c ... coming from."

"And where would that be?"

"I g ... guess I need to know if you th ... think I might be able to
h ... handle your cl ... class."

"Why wouldn't you handle it?" she asked smiling.

"I'm a d ... dis ... disabled vet and even after s ... speech therapy at
the VA, I ... I still have p ... problems with my speech, especially w ...
when I'm n ... nervous. I'm also deaf in m ... my left ear and have hearing l ... loss in my right."

"I grade my students on their work. Would these problems keep you
from doing the work required in my class? Would you refuse to give
your best when it's your turn to give a speech?"

"No, I'll do the best j ... job I can. I just wanted you to kn ... know
there might be some di ... difficulties."

"Mr. Rugh, I'm sure we can handle any small problems."

"Small problems?" I asked, somewhat bewildered.

"Be in class the first day, and we'll take it from there. I noticed your speech improved each time you spoke, I'm sure you'll do just fine."

"Thank you for taking time to speak with us," Lu added.

"It was no problem. It was nice to meet you folks. By the way, you have a very cute and well-behaved daughter," Miss Bennett said as she walked out the door.

Mr. Bergman gave me papers to fill out for registration. He told me he'd get them processed so I wouldn't need to stand in the long lines.

And then he dropped a bomb, "By the way, I want you to take one more course."

Shit, I thought, *that's three classes! What have I gotten myself into?*

He must have read the expression of fear on my face. "It's okay, Mr. Rugh. The third class is very easy. I teach it. It's recommended for all students who aren't sure what they want to do, or students like you who've been out of college for a number of years. We discuss goals and do vocational and aptitude testing. I have two reasons for wanting you to take it. I can keep closer watch on your progress and there is also the financial part of it. This class gives you enough units to qualify for your GI Bill benefits."

"This has all h ... happened so fast we n ... never gave a thought to that p ... part."

"Well, you're entitled to the benefits."

"Heck, I ... I can always use a little extra m ... money, especially with a wife and d ... daughter. It would be n ... nice to have help p ... paying for books and s ... school fees."

"Good luck, Mr. Rugh. You'll see, everything will go just fine."

"It's Len."

"All right, Len. Here's my card if you have any questions."

He also explained I would need to talk to the vet rep on campus sometime in the next week. We went by but their office was closed for the day.

* * *

"Now see, that wasn't too bad, was it? I like your speech teacher, I think she'll be a big help." Lu said as we walked out to the car.

"That was the easy part. The hard part starts when I have to come back to school for real."

"Are you getting cold feet already and after the way Miss Bennett and Mr. Bergman treated you? Give it a try; you can always drop a class if three get to be too much."

"I had to open my big mouth and say something about one class! That was all, one, O-N-E."

"Yes, I can also spell: T-H-R-E-E."

"You are such a smart as ... aleck. Why do I put up with you?" I asked laughing.

"Because you love me and can't live without me." She continued on a more serious note, "I know you're nervous about getting around campus and going back to school after ten years."

I don't know how Lu understood my fears, but she always seemed to be able to read my mind.

"You were quiet during the time in Mr. Bergman's office," I commented.

"Honey, I won't always be around, and you need to handle matters for yourself. You did just great! Things will be fine once you get into a routine. You know, I'll always be here."

"This means you'll have to drive me to school the days I have class."

"No problem. Hopefully your first class won't start until nine as we requested."

"I noticed the political science class is in the library, so I'll have to walk up the hill. I should be able to make it if I allow extra time. We asked for classes on the same days with time between, right?"

"Yes, classes in the mid-morning and early afternoon."

"It's only three classes; I can handle that," I said, deep in thought.

"You've never given up on a challenge yet. I don't expect you to start now."

"I see they have a small cafeteria on campus, so I'll most likely eat lunch there."

"See, you've already figured out some things."

"Yeah, sure, I'd rather face the VC, if truth be told. I wasn't very successful when I went to college after high school."

"This time, you'll have lots of family support and you won't be working forty to sixty hours a week at two jobs. And the crack about facing the VC, that's bullshit and you know it. You'd never willingly do that again!"

"Watch your language, small ears pick up everything, or so I've been told."

"Look who's talking."

"Just repeating what some tall blonde once told me."

"Mr. Bergman suggested buying your books before school starts to beat the long lines. We have to come back to see the vet rep anyway, so we'll get them then," my tall blonde suggested.

"As soon as I know for sure I've got my classes, we'll come back."

"Do you really think you won't get your choice? As a vet, you have priority registration."

"No, but I can hope, can't I."

"Leonard Rugh, that's a lousy attitude and you know it."

"I guess, but it won't be easy. How am I going to juggle books and notebooks and use my cane at the same time?"

"I'll think of something."

"You're really trying to get rid of me."

"Not get rid of you, but get the husband I sent off to war back. You've become a recluse!"

"A what?"

"A recluse is some nut who sits in his house not going anywhere."

I had no answer for that. The rest of the drive back to the house was silent. This gave me some time to think about what Lu had said and search myself.

Am I going to get back into life or am I going to remain a hermit safe in my own little world? I wondered. *Damn, Lu needs a husband and Sandy needs a father, not a recluse.*

It *was* time to get on with living again. So I made the decision, the one Lu had started me toward. Going back to school was the place to start.

* * *

In the next couple of weeks, Lu and her mom came up with a way to carry my books and still be able to use my cane. I couldn't use my left side to carry a briefcase, and a backpack was out. They made a bag out of denim cloth with a long strap I put over my head, resting on my left shoulder. The bag hung off my right hip for easy access. This allowed me free use of my right hand for my cane. Lu's mom even sewed a place for pens and an outside pocket for my class schedule.

My paperwork came in the mail letting me know that I was now a student at Saddleback College. My three classes were on Tuesday and Thursday, each for an hour and a half: speech at nine, the special class at eleven, lunch at twelve-thirty, and political science at one-thirty. Lu would pick me up by the library at three.

We visited the vet rep's office and signed up for benefits. Then we bought books and took a walk around the campus to find my classrooms and figure out the best route between them. I kept telling myself, *I can do this.*

Even though I'd made the decision, the thought of college still turned my stomach. It was almost as bad as waiting out a trail ambush in the jungle. At least, here, no one would be shooting at me with an AK-47.

Thinking about Vietnam reminded me of Dan, the professor. He would have enjoyed going back to a university. I'd bet he wouldn't be scared to death. Hell, he'd have been teaching by now. But I knew that would never be because he was dead, like all my platoon from my time in hell. Their names and faces were always with me. They'd haunt me forever.

* * *

Slowly, ever so slowly, my first day of classes approached. I spent the night before in a restless sleep as all the challenges of this new adventure swirled in my head. I finally gave in to exhaustion and fell into my recurring nightmare.

The damn flare erupts with the light of a million moons and suddenly the air is filled with the sounds of mines and grenades exploding, machine guns and rifles firing, and the screams of men dying.

Red and green tracers whiz around me like angry bees. I see Joe, Wild Bill, and Dan crumple like broken matchsticks with their arms and legs at odd angles, but I'm still standing. I cry out, "No!"

Lu shook me. "Len, wake up. You're having another nightmare. Are you all right?"

"Man, this hasn't happened in a long time."

"We've discussed this before; it wasn't your fault. Go back to sleep; it's only 2:30."

"I love you."

"I love you, too," Lu said as she put her head on my chest and her arm around me. "Get some sleep. Tomorrow will be a big day."

* * *

Morning came with Sandra tugging on my blankets, yelling "Da! Da!"

"Hey, honey, it's time to get your lazy body up and ready for school. How are you feeling?" Lu asked as she picked our daughter up off the floor.

"I'm up, but I don't feel very well," I mumbled incoherently.

"I know it was a rough night, but you'll be fine as soon as you get going. You're now a college student and classes start today."

"It's too late to back out now," I muttered as I pried myself off the bed and slowly plodded to the bathroom.

She had my clothes laid out, like a kindergartner on his first day. All I had to do was shower, shave, dress, and eat breakfast. My stomach felt like a herd of butterflies was using it as a flight school, and my head spun like a top just let loose off a string.

I took extra time over my breakfast, stalling.

"It's not going to work, you know. You will be in the car in five minutes so Sandra can take her daddy for his first day at school, right?"

"Right!" I said with as much enthusiasm as I could muster. I had my new book bag along with everything Lu thought I needed. This would be the first day of a new me.

Sandra was teething and a little fussy, so Daddy had to hold her in his arms on our way to school. (This was before the age of mandatory car seats.) I talked to her, trying to settle Little Miss Wiggle Bottom down. For Sandy, there was no reason to stop moving. Her teeth hurt, so I let her chew on a finger as her teething toy.

We arrived at school with plenty of time for me to get to class and find a seat not too close to the front, but close enough to hear. While waiting, I looked around at all of the kids arriving. *Shit, I'm twenty-nine, and most everyone else is seventeen, eighteen, or maybe nineteen. I feel old enough to be their father. They're at the age where they could have been in my platoon. What the hell am I doing here?*

I was beginning to think this was a mistake. I was going to pick up my stuff and leave, but I didn't get the chance. Miss Bennett walked into the room, smiled at me, and I felt compelled to stay.

She began by explaining the class and what she expected from us. While speaking, she walked around the room. On her second pass, she stopped right in front of me. I'd been trying to be inconspicuous, a very difficult trick for a man in my physical condition. She reached into my arm sling and pulled out the object I'd placed there earlier. I was in the habit of using the sling like a pocket, but I'd completely forgotten about this item.

"Mr. Rugh is going to give us our first impromptu speech by explaining what this is," she said as she held my daughter's teething ring up for the whole class to see.

What an embarrassing moment. I felt like a rabbit caught in a snare with nowhere to hide.

"T … This is my d … daughter Sandra's t … tee … teething ring," I stammered.

"Now that is about the shortest speech ever given in my class. For your information, I will ask each student here for an impromptu speech. Mr. Rugh has passed his first. However, I will expect more from each of you than just one sentence."

Everyone laughed at that, including me.

Welcome back to school and your new life, Rough.

I was still using my nickname a lot when talking to myself. I'd been called Rough for many days before the bullet took me out of the war.

My speech class went fine, once the teacher moved on to her lecture and I settled into taking notes.

Mr. Bergman's class was informative and gave me much to think about. What was I going to do with the rest of my life? Which direction was I moving in and how far could I really go? What was I doing? My mind whirled in many directions.

Saddleback Community College, a two-year school, was still in its infancy. It sprawled out over a hill leading down into a valley. My first two classes were on the lower campus, but the new library and its classrooms were up the hill.

Getting from my speech class to Mr. Bergman's Introduction to College was easy enough. I only had to dodge a few students during my short walk between buildings. The problem came when I had to walk up the hill for my political science class.

I had plenty of time after lunch to make the quarter-mile walk. I'd been practicing a lot around the block at home, but this was climbing. Actually, the bushes and trees on both sides were the worst part of the pathway I had to travel.

Damn, it reminds me of the paths I hacked through in the fuckin' jungles of Vietnam. Knock it off, Rough. This is a college in southern California, not a war zone far away in another lifetime. It's not going to stop me from living this new life!

It was a difficult trek, and I felt winded, but alive, when I accomplished it for the first time. *I made it! Whew!*

I was nervous walking around campus as many students used skateboards to travel between classes. I couldn't move as fast as they did. I knew they were wondering what some old geezer like me was doing here on campus. Moving out of their way would have been almost impossible.

My cane was a steadying force as I held it in almost a death grip. Passing through my mind was the question, *"What the hell am I doing here?"*

When I walked into the room, I sighed with relief. I'd made it. I found a spot where I could see and hear the instructor. I knew after speech, I wasn't going to be inconspicuous in any classroom. At least Mr. Bergman had only nodded to me when he entered the earlier class. What would happen here?

I had not met this instructor before. *What will be his reaction?* After taking roll, he quickly scanned his new students and briefly stopped on me, but kept going. After class, I'd give him a bit of my background so he'd understand my circumstances.

He spent the first day going over the synopsis of this class. Mr. MacDonald was interesting and encouraged us to discuss our feelings about politics and government. *Boy, this I could really get into. I have a lot to say on the subject.*

Just before the end of class, Mr. MacDonald caught our attention by saying, "We have a gentleman who is a part of living history in this class. Mr. Rugh is a Vietnam veteran. We'll have much to learn from him in the weeks ahead."

I sat there stunned. I had no clue he had any idea who I was. My counselor must have talked to him about me. Several students took a minute after class to come over and shake my hand. It was the nicest welcome I'd ever received.

Okay, I can do this. Besides it's only going to be for a semester or two, just until I find myself. I talked to myself a lot.

The day went without incident, and I was feeling better about this new adventure by the time Lu picked me up that afternoon.

"Well, how was your first day?" she asked as soon as we were on the road.

"All right, I guess." I kind of felt like my mom just picked me up from my first day of kindergarten."

"What's wrong?"

I explained what happened in speech.

"Good for her, and good for you," Lu said with a smile.

"Me?"

"Sure, you survived, didn't you?"

"I knew you'd see it that way. Man, I feel really old and out of place."

"I'm sure you're not the first older person to go back to college. Not all students are fresh out of high school you know! Think of it this way, you're getting an early start on how to talk to teenagers for when Sandy reaches that age."

That brought a smile to my face. Only my wife would find something humorous at a time like this. I'll always thank my speech teacher. My impromptu speech set me on this new path. I survived the first day, and I could smile about it.

* * *

Time moved by swiftly after that first very long day. I settled into a routine for Tuesdays and Thursdays. Lu and Sandy brought me to school in the morning and picked me up in the afternoon. In between, I was on my own. It gave me a sense of independence and freedom. I

341

was up and off the couch, doing lots of walking, but most importantly, I was doing lots of thinking and my mind was expanding.

It wasn't all roses and smiles. There were days when I became very frustrated and even a little confused. One day during my third week, I received a shock.

I saw a student who looked so much like Joe from my other life. Same build, same hair, even the same walk from the back. I'd walked many meters following him through the rice paddies and jungles. I would recognize him anywhere, but how could that be?

I called out to him, but he didn't answer. I tried to catch up to see his face, but he moved much faster than I could.

Oh, God, please don't tease me. Let it be; let him be alive!

He was gone!

Dammit!

The campus isn't that big and there aren't a lot of students here, I'll watch and I'll find him again. I have to see for myself if it really is Joe.

I watched every day for the Joe look-alike so I could see his face. The following week I was lucky. I stopped the young man. He didn't have Joe's face at all, and he was only eighteen, way too young. The kid was patient with this nosey, disabled, older man when I explained why I stopped him. He was Italian like Joe, which probable accounted for the similarity in build and walk.

The young man, Tony, and I nodded hello from time to time and we even had a few short conversations. He was a smart, personable kid and had questions about me and the war. It was nice to have a friend on campus.

* * *

I had to write several papers for the poly sci class, another difficult trial. I could gather the information I wanted, but I had no idea of how to put it together, let alone type the damn thing.

"Lu, I need help! Can you type?"

"Ah … yes, sort of, why?"

"I have to write and type a term paper for school. I can't do it by myself."

"Okay, first thing, we'll need to buy an electric typewriter."

"Ah, man, this is going to be a major project and expensive, too."

"Honey, relax. This won't be the only paper you'll write. So let's invest in a good one. With your GI Bill money, we can afford it."

This began an interesting time for me and a frustrating time for Lu. She spent hours and hours organizing my notes and information. She then spent many more hours typing, making carbon copies for my files. I don't know how many times she had to retype pages to get them presentable. She mumbled something about, "There must be an easier way."

I wouldn't have made it through the class without her help. I had an easier way, but she wouldn't let me quit. She ended up typing three papers for that class. I couldn't have accomplished the task myself.

At the end of the semester, the grades came out. I passed all my classes. I got a C grade in political science. It was a hard class with lots of writing and tests, difficult for me. I received B's in speech and Mr. Bergman's class. I felt really good about myself and I could see pride in Lu's eyes.

The semester was over and I had survived being out in the world. I couldn't go back to hiding in the house any longer. I had a taste of freedom.

Second semester started in January. I signed up to take two classes, another political science class and English. They'd mean a lot of work and more writing, but I felt confident I could handle them, with Lu's help, of course.

I'd faced the ghosts from the past. I thought I had seen Joe and it was frightening, but I survived and was better for it. Lu had been right, as usual.

Chapter 45 - Life with Lu and Sandra

For the next few years I couldn't have been happier. Sandra was grow-ing, walking, talking, and Daddy was spending lots of time with her. Lu was around all the time and I couldn't get enough of her smiles and laughter. Oh, she scolded me occasionally as any wife would, but we had a good life together. Our home was almost perfect, with lawns and bushes, flowers and trees outside, and a real hominess inside with Lu's special touch.

Then tragedy struck. My doctor, my mentor, my hero, Dr. Jackson was killed in a plane crash in Arizona. I was devastated by the news and I cried for my friend.

"Lu, why was a guy like me, a cripple, not good for much of any-thing, allowed to live and a great man with so much to give to so many, taken away?" I asked in anguish.

"Who knows why things happen the way they do? We could ask that question until the end of time before it would be answered. I'm sure God had a purpose."

"I wouldn't be here if not for Dr. Jackson. He was kind and compas-sionate. I owe him so much. What do I do now?"

"You go on with the life he gave you and live it the best you can. Make it stand for something. He'll be watching you from above, and I know he'll still be shaking his head in wonder over all the things you'll accomplish in the years to come."

I knew she was right. Dr. Jackson had been amazed at the birth of our daughter and delighted by her visits. He was always anxious to hear about us and how we were doing in our home. He seemed impressed with my college successes and my ability to get around. Our lives were truly better over the years for having known him.

The pain of his loss stayed with me, especially with each visit to the hospital. It seemed as though the lights had dimmed somewhat with him gone. My only consolation, at least I hadn't been the cause of his death.

* * *

My going to college inspired Lu to go back and finish her BA in biology. Between what she had taken before we married and the few classes she took while I was in 'Nam, she'd finished almost three years at Cal State University, Los Angeles.

It presented a problem. We lived about seventy-five miles from her school. What to do now? What about Sandra? She was only two. We looked into the same major at Cal State, Fullerton, only forty-two miles away, but it would mean an extra year to finish. The required classes were different for the same major, and the two schools didn't have the same class titles for similar courses.

"I'm going to forget going back to school for now. There's no way until Sandra is in school all day," Lu said one afternoon in frustration.

Her parents were down for the day and heard her. Her mom came up with a solution. We'd live with them Monday through Thursday. She'd take care of Sandra while we were in school. CSULA was an easy drive from their home. It would only take four quarters for Lu to finish.

"We have your schooling figured out, but what am I going to do?" I asked later in the day.

"You'll take classes there, too."

"Lu, it's one thing to go to Saddleback where on a good day there might be a few thousand students. You're asking me to attend a four-year college with an enrollment of over forty thousand. I'm not sure I'm ready for that." I was frustrated again.

"I think you are, but I'll make a deal with you. Let's try it for summer quarter and if it doesn't work, we'll come home and you can go back to your regular routine. Does that sound fair to you?" She asked.

"I'll give it a try. It will only be for summer and all of next year, right? I'll do my best. I want you to finish."

"Len, you'll be fine. Now you can really spread your wings."

"What about your teaching credential? I know you really want to complete the fifth year."

"I've checked, and I can finish at Fullerton. We'll work on that after I get my degree."

We both enrolled in California State University, Los Angeles, and moved back into Lu's parents home four days a week. We went back to Dana Point on Fridays to resume our lives there.

Actually, it worked out better than we'd hoped. I amazed myself at how well I did. There was a larger selection of classes. I got good grades in all of them in the four quarters I attended CSULA.

I learned my most valuable lessen while there: Never, I mean *never* take a class with your wife, especially if she's a lot smarter than you. It could lead to divorce. We tried it. I worked my butt off studying, reading, taking notes, and anything else I could think of to pass the class, and got a C. Lu went to class, but hardly looked at her notes, did very little reading, and got an A. *It just wasn't fair! Dammit!*

Lu graduated with a degree in biology in June 1977.

* * *

After the adventure in Los Angeles, I decided I'd attend CSU, Fullerton, instead of returning to Saddleback. Lu was supportive. She and Sandra drove me back and forth for a month or so.

"Honey, this isn't working. You and Sandra wait or go to the mall or whatever for the five hours while I take my classes and then we drive home in traffic. There must be a better way for me to get there," I said one day.

"I've been concerned, too. We've worked around Sandy's preschool on Monday, Wednesday, and Friday, with you in school Tuesday and Thursday. Next year Sandra goes to kindergarten five days a week," Lu reminded me.

"What about the bus?" I asked.

"What about that bus?" Lu said at the same time.

We were staring at the Orange County bus making a swing in front of the school to let off its passengers.

It took a bit of scheduling and making several transfers, but I could do it. The only problems were: the early hour leaving in the morning, late afternoons coming home, and the over two hours each way. It had only taken Lu only an hour to drive each way.

Once I started, bus riding was grand. I had a greater sense of freedom. I could get around by myself without depending on Lu. I went to school and back. I got to the VA hospital in Long Beach. I could shop for birthdays, anniversaries, to buy books, and whatever when I wanted. I'd gotten better about talking to people, so my bus rides turned into interesting experiences.

* * *

Sandra was finishing first grade. Time had slipped away from me again. One day in April, she came home with a flyer about a summer swim team. This precocious six-year-old had decided she wanted to become part of the team.

Lu and I read the information, then asked, "Sandra, honey, it says you have to swim the length of a twenty-five yard pool. You barely swim the length of our pool and it's only seventeen feet." We'd put in a small back yard pool two years before so I could exercise.

"Mommy, I can do it. I've been practicing. This is what I really want to do, please …"

"Tryouts are on Saturday morning at the high school. We'll go see about it then. I don't want you disappointed if you don't make the team. Okay?"

"Okay, Mom!" she said in her big girl voice.

Listening to this conversation between mother and daughter, I wondered, *Where has my little baby gone? Who substituted her for this child before my eyes?*

Saturday morning dawned sunny and warm instead of the overcast normal for that time of year. We ate breakfast early so it wouldn't interfere with Sandra swimming. At the appointed time, we walked to the pool.

There must have been fifty little boys and girls waiting to try out. We signed her up and waited until it was time for her to get in the pool. They gave all the kids time in the shallow water to practice. In the case of the less serious swimmers, it was a time to play. Sandra got right in and struggled through the many bodies to swim from one end to the other.

When the whistle blew for everyone to get out, we were concerned. She hadn't been able to finish even one lap.

Tryouts started alphabetically by age group. Sandra was in the five-to-six age group since she wouldn't be seven until the middle of August. When her turn came, Lu and I had our fingers and toes crossed. We said a little prayer she'd accomplish her goal and cheered her on from the side of the pool.

"I have no clue where she gets her stubborn streak or her determination," I mumbled.

Lu heard me. She looked at me and said, "Look in the mirror, Daddy. Talk about stubborn and determined!"

She made it! Our little girl made the team. *Now what?*

I'd always envisioned my child playing sports. You know, baseball or basketball, one I knew how to coach, but swimming? I knew how to swim, but that was about it. This would be a whole new world.

We were handed an information sheet, a schedule of practices, and another schedule of swim meets. The first would be in three weeks.

Swim meets? I hadn't given it any thought. *What has Sandra gotten us into?*

She bounced her way home. I decided I'd better have a serious talk with this little munchkin about the responsibilities of being on a sports team. The more I thought about it, the more I realized it was also a big commitment for the parents, too.

* * *

Sandra faithfully went to all the practices and worked very hard. Finally, the day arrived for her first meet. This would be the beginning of yet another phase of our life.

It was a small meet between two summer league teams at our home pool. We got her signed in and found a place to sit. The swimmers were grouped near where the coach was sitting.

I heard a call for timers. Then I saw a few men and women sitting in chairs at one end of the pool. They received stopwatches. *Hey, I used one of those when I was coaching. I could do it, but who'd want a person in my condition to time?* So I sat back and watched.

The first set of swimmers walked behind the blocks and, following the starter's instructions, stepped up and got ready to dive into the pool.

Bang! It was the signal for the swimmers to begin the race. To me it meant something entirely different. The VC were shooting at us. I must have jumped ten feet into the air and came down running for cover.

Lu realized what was happening and grabbed my arm. She was speaking, but I didn't understand her words. I finally calmed down enough to figure out where I was and what happened just in time for the beginning of the next heat.

Bang! I think I only jumped seven feet this time, but I didn't head for cover.

"Len, do you want to go home?"

"No! This is important to Sandra I want to be a part of it. I'll have to learn to live with the starting pistol."

"All right, but I'm sure she'd understand …"

"I'm staying!"

I'd retrain myself not to jump as the gun went off and become a calm, cool dad, like the rest of the fathers. I handled everything else thrown at me over the years, and I would master this.

Sandra got two first-place ribbons in the two events she swam. I was so proud of her. I really did enjoy the meet. Now, if only I could get used to the damn gun!

* * *

The following weekend we went away to another meet. I'd met many of the parents of our little team. One fellow, Nate Varney, had become a good friend. He was a timer and wanted me to become one, too. I decided to try it. I knew how to use a stopwatch and there were usually two or three people per lane in case someone screwed up.

So when the call for timers came, I was ready to go. Nate and I worked the same lane so he could explain the procedure to me. He was a quiet, soft-spoken man with a slight stammer. I knew all about speech problems. I still had a few myself.

The first few starts were the toughest, partly due to the sound of the gun, but I eventually got the hang of it.

Sandra did well on the summer team and ended up joining a more demanding year-round team, the Mission Viejo Nadadores. Their practices were farther away and required hours on the road. We became real team parents as the meets grew longer and more intense.

Nate and I were now timing buddies and good friends. His son and our Sandra would become like family. We went on to time many meets together, and I continued to improve. Over the next few years, I'd work meets of all levels, even Olympic trials. What a thrill that was!

I'd come a long way from the terrified coward who jumped at the sound of the starter's pistol. I wasn't a cripple sitting on the sidelines. I'd found a niche I could fill and do a good job. I was important in my daughter's life.

Chapter 46 - Rough vs. the VA

It was my job to retrieve the mail. One day there was a letter from the Veteran's Administration. It looked important. I opened it and shook out the paper to read what they had to say.

Lu and I had stretched my GI Bill money out over six and a half years. I'd taken two classes each semester since transferring to Cal State Fullerton and was ready to start another semester. This notice declared I'd used up all my funds. I was no longer going to receive any assistance for schooling.

"Dammit, I guess it's time for me to drop out of this college thing. I was only going to Saddleback for a semester or two. How long ago was that? It seems a lifetime."

Lu heard me grumbling and came to see what the problem was.

"You knew this was going to happen, but you've come too far to give up now. I think Dr. Jackson would have been surprised and very proud of you."

"Yeah, I really miss him. When he died, it was like a part of me died, too. No matter how busy he was, he'd make time to see me when I dropped in say hello."

"Hey, we have to make the most of what we still have. I'm sure Dr. Jackson is up there smiling down on you—actually laughing and shaking his head, as usual. You threw his prognosis of your limitations out the window. He'd want you to continue going to school, I'm sure." She had a valid point.

"Honey, I can't see wasting money for classes. It would be too much of a drain," I argued.

"Well, I don't think so. Your education is too important. Let's check with the vet rep and see what he has to say."

"I should have thought of that first," I muttered.

"You were too angry to think. We'll go to school tomorrow morning and see what they can do."

"Damn, the VA told me not to go to college in the first place. So, why would they help me continue?"

"Len, we knew when you first started, the GI Bill was only for forty-eight months of full-time schooling, and we've used that up."

"I'm sorry, but this letter feels like the end. I have to admit, I enjoy going to college."

"We'll find the money somehow. I could always take a part-time job while Sandra is in school. We both want her daddy to continue. What do you think Mr. Bergman or Miss Bennett would say if they heard you're ready to give up?" Lu asked.

She was really laying it on me. Lu was right. I had to continue, even if it meant a fight.

"Oh, and honey, when we talk with the vet rep guy, please keep your temper under control," she continued.

"Who, me? Lose my temper?" I asked incredulously.

"Yes, you." Lu had a determined look in her eyes.

"All right, I'll wait until I get the bad news. Then I'll lose my temper."

"You're incorrigible. That's why I'm going with you tomorrow."

"Don't worry. I know how to talk for myself. I learned it at the VA hospital in Long Beach. I'll be good. I don't have many choices."

"Yep, you're right." She always had the last word.

* * *

The next morning after Lu got Sandra off to school, we drove to Fullerton and the veterans representative's office on campus. I'd been in this office many times.

"Good morning, Mr. Rugh."

"I guess it's a good morning for you; you're still getting paid."

"Oops, sounds like we have a small problem this morning. Let me see if someone's available to help you."

"I don't see anything small in having my benefits end while still I'm attending classes," I said as I turned to Lu.

She gave me a warning look, but I was in no mood to calm down. I was mad.

About then, one of the vet reps came out and said, "I understand your school benefits are going to be curtailed."

"Yes, according to this damn letter!" I grumbled, trying to control my anger.

"Let's go to my office, and we'll get everything straightened out, okay?"

"Yeah, I guess so. This is my wife, Lu. May she come too?"

"Of course she can. My name is Steve." He offered his hand and I shook it. No point in starting out badly.

After we sat down he continued. "Now let me see the letter. This just states that you have used up your benefits under the GI Bill. I'm sure it was explained to you that there were specific limits as to the length of time and total amount of money."

"No, it wasn't!" I growled.

"Yes, it was," Lu said at the same time. "I was aware of the specifications. We've made it go as far as possible. Are there any other programs available?" She put her hand on my arm, trying to soothe me.

"Oh, I should just drop out of school and go away. That's what the VA would like me to do, right?" I asked sarcastically, ignoring her silent objection.

"Wait a minute. You're a 100 percent disabled vet, aren't you? Did you have a full-time job before being drafted?"

I nodded in the affirmative, not trusting my voice.

He continued. "There might be another way. Give me a day or two to see what I can find. Don't give up just yet."

"Sure, the VA wants me to disappear just like when I was in the hospital."

Lu took over at this point, fearing what I might say next. "You see, Steve, the VA told Len when he was released to, in essence, go home and do nothing for the rest of his life. That included college. They decided he couldn't handle it mentally, physically, or emotionally. He's come a long way since that prognosis."

I'd had enough and struggled to push myself up and out of the chair. My body automatically stretched and my left knee popped as it always did after sitting for a while.

"Good old snap, crackle, and pop," I said in frustration. I finally got both feet under me and into a standing position. "Well, this meeting hasn't resolved anything. I think it's time to go."

"You do need to go since your class is about to start. But Len, give Steve a chance to find out what's possible," Lu spoke again, trying to smooth over my outburst.

"Mrs. Rugh, we want our vets to get every possible benefit. I hope to have good news when you return," Steve said to Lu as I started to leave.

"Nothing's going to happen. I'm screwed, I just know it." I left the door ajar when I walked out.

I heard Lu say, "He normally isn't hard to get along with, but when it comes to the VA, I can never tell how he's going to react."

I started to walk back in when Steve answered, "I know what you mean. Even I get frustrated with the red tape, but we'll try to work within the system. I'm really sorry he's upset. I probably would be, too. I promise I'll do my best. I'm on his side."

"Len doesn't have class tomorrow, so we'll be back on Thursday. Will that be long enough?"

"It should be."

"Do we need an appointment to see you?"

"No, just come in anytime. I know of one program. I'm not sure if he qualifies, but I'll check."

"Thanks for your help, Steve," Lu replied.

I met them at the door. "Yeah, thanks, Steve. I guess I wasn't thinking too clearly when I got the letter. Sorry you caught my anger." With my apology, we left.

Lu waited for me to finish my morning class. We had lunch, and she went to the mall while I attended my afternoon class. She picked me up afterwards, so I could avoid the two-and-a-half hour bus ride home.

* * *

On Thursday morning, we returned for our meeting with Steve. He told us he had good news. There was a vocational rehab program through the VA for guys who couldn't go back to their old jobs. He felt we had a good case and should appeal directly to the board in Los Angeles. Steve gave us the phone number of the office. We had to initiate the process for my appeal ourselves.

"I guess I'll have to fight the VA in LA now," I said as we left his office.

"It's not fighting them, it's presenting your case to them," Lu insisted.

"It's the same damn thing, only in nicer words."

"Dammit, Len, why are you so defensive when it comes to the VA?" Lu asked.

"Just a habit I guess. You have to admit we've been butting heads with them since day one."

"You're right, but let's think positively."

"Okay, we'll call this afternoon and see what they say."

"At least now we have a place to start," Lu reminded me.

When we got home that afternoon, Lu called. I was not very good at talking on the phone, especially since I was hard of hearing. Besides, I don't think Lu trusted me not to lose my temper again, so she explained my problem. She talked for about ten minutes and looked satisfied when she ended the call.

"Well, what's the decision?

"You have an appointment with a Mr. Collins for next week."

"An appointment doesn't mean we're going to get anywhere!"

"It gives us time to get copies of all your college transcripts. We want to be able to show this guy what you've accomplished."

"Okay, wife, you win."

Lu went to the kitchen to fix dinner and I sat down to think. *Yeah, right. The VA's going to come up with money for me. Dammit, help or no help, I'm going to finish school and maybe even graduate some day. I want to now. It might take me another six years, but I'll show the VA what I can do!*

* * *

The week passed slowly. I went to class and got my transcripts. I had evidence that I could pass college-level courses.

We arrived at the VA office, and a secretary greeted us. "Good morning. Do you have an appointment?"

"We're Mr. and Mrs. Rugh, and, yes, we have an appointment at 11:00," Lu answered.

"If you'll take a seat, Mr. Collins will be right with you."

He was in his late fifties, tall, nicely dressed, and suave looking. His wavy, graying hair was neatly styled and he had a smooth, relaxing voice. After introducing himself, he led us into his cluttered office. The décor was a shock. This formal-looking gentleman was a surfer. I recognized him in the many photographs on his desk and hanging on the wall.

"Mr. Rugh, I'm sorry about your problems with the GI bill, but rules are rules," he stated.

"I told you it would be a waste of time and money to get my transcripts and drive through traffic to get here," I whispered none too quietly to Lu.

Mr. Collins continued. "I don't think I can help you. I found a problem in your file." It was open on his desk. Lu and I could see the VA's diagnosis of my case in large red letters: UNRETRAINABLE.

"So I was right! This was a complete waste," I said getting ready to walk out.

I'm sure Lu was surprised at my restraint to that point. There were lots of words bubbling through my mind at that instant. They'd have made a drill sergeant take notice.

"Wait a minute. Did I hear you say something about your school records?" Mr. Collins asked.

"Yes, we have copies of the thirteen semesters he's been in school," Lu said very quickly. She didn't give the frustration she knew was building in me time to explode.

"May I see those?" he asked.

"Of course," I said sarcastically as I handed him my transcripts.

"And just for your information, all the work required for those classes was done by Len, except, I typed his papers. He did all the library research and rough drafts, I just did the mechanical stuff for his political science classes."

"Yeah, I even spent hours at the law library one semester for a law class," I added.

"May I have my secretary make copies for our files?"

"That's what I brought them for," I said, stating the obvious.

Mr. Collins ignored me as he looked at my records. "I see you have enough credits to just about finish your junior year."

"You can thank my wife for that and not some jerk in the VA system that doesn't seem to know his head from …"

"Okay, Len, I think he has the picture. It's time for you to relax."

"I am relaxed!"

"Mr. Rugh, what exactly are you looking for?"

Lu spoke up before I could blast him. "He's used up his GI Bill and we were told about a vocational rehab program which he might be able to draw on to finish up. We're not sure we could pay for school without outside help. I hate to see him drop out and go back to sitting in his chair watching TV all day."

"Since you were designated unretrainable, I'm not sure how much we can do. I have to admit, I'm totally amazed that someone with your injury could have gotten this far, and with a 2.65 GPA! You say you've done all this work yourself?"

"Yes, sir, those are *my* classes and *my* grades."

"Well, we'll be holding an evaluation meeting on Friday morning. I'm sure my colleagues would like to see these transcripts. We'll thoroughly consider your case. I can see what you've done so far hasn't been easy."

"No, it's been a lot of hard work for him," Lu agreed.

"I can't guarantee anything, but you've convinced me. Now, if I can just persuade the rest of the board, well, we'll see. Be sure my secretary has your home phone number before you leave, and thank you for coming in today. I'll give you a call the first of next week."

We stopped by the secretary's desk and gave her our information. "Mr. Rugh, let me validate your parking ticket. You don't want to get charged for parking today."

"Thanks."

Then we fought our way home through the LA traffic.

After we left the office, I turned to Lu, "I'm really pissed at being told I'm … what was that word? Oh yes, unretrainable. What the hell does that mean anyway?"

"I think it has to do with the VA's original prognosis—not going to work, school, or anything else. You've proved everybody wrong for the last ten years. Why stop now?"

"What do they want me to do, just give up?"

"I don't think they said anything about giving up," Lu growled at me.

"No, they just implied it. Everywhere we turn it's 'give me a couple of days.' I'm tired of hearing it. Too bad the goddamn VC didn't give me a couple of days to think about it before they put a fuckin' bullet in my head.

"Hey, watch the language, mister!"

"I'm sorry. It's just the frustration."

"Come on, Len. You can wait until next week," Lu stated.

"I know, honey. You're right."

"I usually am," she said modestly.

* * *

It was a long week. I kept to my regular routine: going to school, doing homework, taking Sandra to swim practice, and worrying about the VA's decision. I noticed even Lu seemed preoccupied. We didn't talk about it. I guess we didn't want to jinx it.

Finally, on Monday, Mr. Collins's secretary called. He wanted to see us in his office as soon as possible. We scheduled an appointment for the following day.

All the way to LA, Lu and I discussed possible reasons for this meeting. She was sure it was good news. I'd been granted money to continue and we'd sign a contract or something. I, Mr. Pessimist, was positive it was going to be bad news and they just didn't want to tell us over the phone. Mr. Collins wanted to explain to this unretrainable *(God, I hate that word!)* veteran why I didn't qualify for the vocational rehab program. It would be a totally wasted trip.

We were shown right into the office where three men waited.

"Uh-oh, this is going to be *really* bad news," I whispered to Lu.

"Mr. and Mrs. Rugh, this is Dr. Larson," he said indicating a tall, friendly-looking man in his early sixties. He continued, "And Dr. Hall."

Dr. Hall was a surprise. He was young and must have been right out of grad school.

"They are clinical psychologists and wanted to meet you."

"We couldn't reconcile the diagnosis on your medical records with the college work you've completed. Sorry about making you come back, but we had to see this remarkable individual for ourselves," announced Dr. Larson.

We never came close to guessing this as the reason for our trip. We'd both been wrong. But now what?

Dr. Larson, who seemed to be the "Top" in this group, continued. "We've decided it would be an injustice not to let you finish what you've started. Therefore, we welcome you to the vocational rehabilitation program until you complete your education."

Man, you could have knocked me over with a whisper! I was in shock! *Did he just say what I thought I heard him say?* I was accepted. Yeah, I was "welcomed into the vocational rehab program until I complete my education."

I think I muttered a thank you. The rest of the meeting was a blur. I was glad for Lu. We were given facts about the program and then completed the enrollment papers. I would finish the semester on the GI bill, but starting in the fall, I'd be on the new plan.

We told the men thank you and good-bye, had our parking ticket validated, and headed out to the car. I was totally baffled by the events of the meeting, but finally realized I would have the money to pay for the rest of my education.

This was the best incentive for me to continue. Sure, I would have finished since Lu wouldn't have let me give up. But the faith and support of these men gave me a welcome boost in the right direction.

On our way home, Lu and I discussed what I needed to do. Her suggestion was to make an appointment with my college counselor about completing the classes I needed for graduation.

* * *

I met with the counselor a few weeks later. What a surprise! I had accidentally, with a few suggestions from Lu, taken all the classes needed to meet graduation requirements. I only had the thirty units for my senior year to finish. The biggest problem was the damn math requirement. I had taken the class twice and gotten a D both times. *What am I going to do about that?*

I could hardly wait to get home and tell Lu the good news. I was sure she'd be surprised. And I hoped she might have some ideas about the math class.

"Hi honey," I called as I came through the door.

"I'm in the kitchen. Sandra is having a snack before swim practice."

"You'll never guess how close I am to graduation!" I said with as much pride as I could muster. I told her about the day's conversation.

"Oh, really? That's wonderful!"

She had this funny "I know something you don't know" look. After fourteen years of marriage, I knew that expression.

"Okay, what's up? Never mind; I just figured it out. All those times when you suggested I take a science class or an English class for variety in my schedule, you were leading me towards graduation. You sneak, what am I to do with you?"

"Just love me! How about that? You're going to graduate from college with a BA in political science!"

"Well, I might have a problem with that. I still have to pass the stupid math class. Mr. Dull has given me a D for trying both times I've taken it. But it's not a passing grade! How will I get around that?"

"I have an idea. Let's meet with your counselor and the head of the math department and anyone else necessary to make a decision about this requirement. We have your medical diagnosis. It states that the part of your brain which was destroyed was the math-processing portion. If we can convince these people you're unable to pass math, they may grant a waiver."

"It might work. I'll talk to my counselor next week. I'll also see Mr. Dull, the math teacher. If I explain my problem to him, he might be supportive at the meeting." I was really getting into this.

"Good idea! I hadn't thought of that. I'm proud of you," Lu said, then gave me a great big hug.

* * *

I talked to Tom, my counselor, the following week. He explained the process of requesting an exemption. I showed him my medical records, and he made a copy for his file.

"Len, with this data, I'm sure you'll qualify when we petition to waive the math requirement. I'll get everything in motion and notify you when it's set up."

"Thank you. I'm still worried, though. I was surprised when you told me how close I am to graduating. It's never been my goal. I always considered attending college as a way to get out of the house. However, my wife quietly steered me in this direction. Now it's like a dream. But passing math is the hurdle I have to overcome to finish."

"Don't worry. You're the most interesting person on my caseload. Your story's amazing. I'll do my best not to let you down."

Tom was in his early forties, but already balding. I told Lu he probably pulled his hair out working with students like me. She laughed at that and told me she couldn't wait to meet him.

He was an athlete. I liked him, but I envied his ability to participate. That's one of the things I missed most being disabled. I'd always been involved in sports. Basketball, baseball, or football, it didn't matter; I'd been good in all of them. Now I could only sit on the sidelines and watch.

It hurt each time I went to watch my brother Bill's games. It was difficult to be relegated to the bleachers. I wanted, with every ounce of my being, to be in there with him.

My one saving grace was Sandra's interest in swimming. I participate by timing, watching her swim, cheering her on, and sometimes even coaching her. I was a part of the process. We were getting more and more involved. I'd finally found a place where I felt like me. There, I wasn't an invalid; I was a dad.

During the next few weeks, Tom kept me informed of his progress in arranging the faculty review. Finally, he let me know that the meeting was set for the following Monday morning at ten.

I was a little apprehensive and nervous. Lu picked up on my feelings when I shared the news later that afternoon.

"Hey, big guy, I know you can handle this by yourself. But I'd like to be there if you don't mind."

"I was going to ask you to come anyway. Not because I might lose my temper, but because I want you with me," I answered.

"So, what are you planning to say?"

"I'm going to explain about my head injury and how it affects my ability to handle math beyond the very basics. I'll point out that I've tried the class a couple of times and couldn't get a passing grade. Then I'll refer them to my medical records, and explain that I can get more than one doctor to certify the information, including the doctors from the VA. Do you think that might work?"

"You've convinced me," Lu said as she fell back on the couch in a pretend faint. "All the evidence is overwhelming, and you present it so passionately."

"You think it'll work, huh? I really want to graduate now."

"As I recall you were only going to go to Saddleback for a semester or two, and then you wanted just one more, and now you want to graduate. Congratulations Mr. Rugh, you really will show those guys in the VA. I knew you could do it all the time!"

"Yeah, after you finished your degree, I couldn't quit, could I?"

"Nope," she said grinning.

"Man, I really hate having to fight to go to school. It's something most people in America can do without the hassle."

"I think Fullerton will be easier to deal with than the VA. You just wait and see."

* * *

On Monday, we took Sandra to school before we drove to Fullerton. I felt as nervous as I had that first day I went to Saddleback seven years before.

There were six people in the room when we arrived. They had received the reports from Tom and Mr. Dull before the meeting. They'd also been through my medical records and were ready for me. I was given the opportunity to explain my side, and then they would make a decision and give me the result. *I could do this.*

"Good morning, Mr. and Mrs. Rough." *Wow! Was this a good or a bad sign?*

"Please have a seat. We have read through the evidence presented on your behalf and would like to hear from you. Just tell us what you want us to know about yourself and your goals," said the head of the history department.

I'd seen him before but never had the chance to actually meet him. His stare made me feel like I was on the hot seat. I glanced at Lu for support, then began by correcting the pronunciation of my name.

I spoke slowly and as clearly as I could. Lu and I had practiced what I would say and how I would say it. It was a tough speech for me, but I knew Miss Bennett would have been proud.

Once I got started, everything went just fine. I finished by telling the board about my recent visit to the VA, the business with the unre-trainable label, and the unexpected outcome of being admitted to the vocational rehab program.

I must have given the speech of my life. They approved my appeal to waive the math requirement. Tom told me later it was a unanimous vote. I was on the road to graduation. We calculated the date to be May of 1983; only two years away.

* * *

One of my most important achievements while at Cal State Fullerton had nothing to do with classes at all. I found the office for handicapped services and spent many hours there studying and getting to know the program. They offered help for those of us in need, but I found I could also be of service.

I spent four semesters reading textbooks, assignments, and tests for one of the legally blind students. Mike was also a bus rider and lived in the same direction. We spent many hours riding to and from school together. My reading and speech improved when I helped other students. I felt useful. I could make a difference in someone else's life. The whole mentor–tutor relationship went both ways.

* * *

On May 21, 1983, before all of my family and friends, I walked across the stage, shook hands with the head of the history department, and received a diploma for my bachelor of arts degree in political science.

My life was amazing! I had a truly remarkable wife and a smart, funny, and wonderful little swimmer for a daughter. I lived in a beautiful home in a scenic seaside town, and I had actually graduated from Cal State University, Fullerton. Not too bad for a guy who in 1969 was given a dismal prognosis.

I'd come a long way down a difficult road, but I'd made it. The most important thing I'd gained was self-respect. There were still challenges to overcome and my nightmares and guilt to live with, but I had so much to be grateful for. I felt like the luckiest and most blessed guy in the world.

Chapter 47 - I'm a College Grad, Now What?

I'd actually graduated from college! According to the doctors at the Veterans' Administration, it was impossible, but here I was at my graduation party, surrounded by a hundred or so of my family and friends who'd believed in me.

The unofficial theme of this party was "The Impossible Dream." Several gifts alluded to it. One was a music box, which played the song from *Man of La Mancha*. I guess it really was all about my reaching a goal which had seemed far from my grasp.

The party was the best part of the nine years it took to achieve that goal. I now enjoyed being around people again. Lu remarked to me one day that she felt I was about 80 percent back to my old self. It felt good and I was really having fun!

"So you're a college graduate, huh? Now, what are you going to do with the rest of your life?" my brother asked.

"Heck, if I know! I haven't given it any thought, Bill," I replied.

What am I going to do? I have a bachelor of arts degree in political science. Wow! Big deal! What now?

* * *

In the following weeks and months, I slipped into my old routine. There was nothing in my life to get me up and going, so I began sleeping late. I spent my days watching TV.

I was frustrated. Work was questionable. Oh, sure, an employer might give me a job. After all, I was a disabled war vet, and the American public was finally tolerating those of us who fought in Vietnam. But I might take that job from someone who needed it more. Since my war had ended and many men and women were leaving the military, the job market was tight.

The big question was: what kind of job was I qualified for? In my former life I'd worked on a telephone ground crew. That was definitely out. I could barely walk, so how could I climb a telephone pole?

I'd worked as a cook and an assistant manager for a restaurant. I was no longer qualified for those positions. Hell, I couldn't even meet the requirements to be a busboy.

The truth was there weren't a lot of jobs for someone like me. So I sat home trying to figure out my purpose in life. I was useless, just another screwed up, crippled Vietnam vet!

I tried not to let the frustration and despair show. I forced a smile when others were around, but inside I felt hopeless. What could I contribute to my family? Both Lu and Sandra had busy schedules. So where did I fit?

Lu had gone back to school to finish her teaching credential and was away most of the day, five days a week.

Sandra was in the fifth grade and was at school most of the day. When she came home, she said, "Hi, Dad," gave me a kiss, then disappeared into her room to finish her homework before swim practice.

We attended swim meets every other weekend where I still timed. But I had nothing to do on weekdays.

* * *

In the November following my graduation, I began having serious seizures. I'd had one every few months since being wounded, but I'd learned to live with them. Mine were called Jacksonian seizures, or motor seizures. During them, I was usually conscious and aware of my surroundings. My eyes locked, staring at brightly-colored lights, while my body rocked back and forth in a rhythmic motion, as my motor control shut down. I'd learned to sit down wherever I was until it passed, get up, take about four aspirins for the headache to come, and continue with whatever I'd been doing.

One night, however, I began a series of seizures that didn't stop. Lu and I were scared. She rushed me to Camp Pendleton where I spent several days in the hospital. Evidently, the Phenobarbital and Dilantin I'd been taking for fourteen years were no longer working. I was slowly weaned off those two medications and a new one substituted, Tegretol.

This was a new setback in my life, and from somewhere deep in my soul came the words for a poem, "Life is a Why."

The new medication worked, and I was released. Before, I'd felt tired and disorganized, but now I felt more like my old self.

* * *

Lu completed school in May of 1984 and received two teaching credentials. She could teach kindergarten through high school, but chose to substitute teach, instead.

My father-in-law, Walt was around quite often and always ready to take me places, like to my doctor's appointments and other places I couldn't get to on the bus. The two of us had a lot of good times together.

My sense of uselessness grew. Lu was around more often and it got harder to keep my feelings hidden. I needed help out of the quagmire of depression.

* * *

During the summer, Sandra joined a new swim team. She had been with Coach Pat at her previous team and followed him when he became head coach of SCAT, the South Coast Aquatics team in San Clemente, California.

She had to purchase a suit and other swim gear with the SCAT logo. The parent who had ordered and coordinated the team's equipment couldn't continue, so the swimmers and their families were looking for a replacement.

One evening after practice, Lu and I were sitting at the dinner table when she asked the question that would alter our lives for the next eight years.

"Len, didn't you work for the sport shop at the Boys' Christian League (in Arcadia) before we were married?"

"You know I did, why?"

"Sandra's swim team needs someone to obtain and sell supplies for the swimmers. It should be a person who'd have time to order the equipment. I think it's something you could do, and it would be a big help to the team."

I sat there stunned. "I couldn't do anything like that. Come on Lu, look at me. I'm not good for much of anything."

"Who are you? You're sure not my husband who fought so hard to recover after I was told he'd spend the rest of his life in a facility. And you're not the guy who spit in the faces of the doctors when he was told he couldn't walk! And you're certainly not the man who struggled for almost a decade to finish college against the VA's label of unretrainable! And where's the fellow who wasn't supposed to father a child, the same one who needs her daddy's help with the swim team? You've been moping around here for over a year, looking for a purpose. Now get off your 'I'm-a-useless-good-for-nothing-cripple' kick and start living again! I don't think we can handle much more of this shit!"

Lu was angry. She sounded serious about this project with the swim team. The least I could do was check it out and see if she was right.

"Okay, I'll talk to Sandra's coach and see what they need. I'm not promising anything since I'm not convinced I can handle it."

"Of course you can! Someone needs to do the job, and I know you're that someone. It's time to get back into the world again, buster."

"I guess I'm going into the sporting goods business," I answered hesitantly, still doubtful.

The next night after swim practice, Lu and I talked with Pat about what the job would require.

"We need suits for everyone on the team. If you take this on, it would really help," Pat said.

I only took a couple of minutes to decide. "I'll give it my best. It's not like I don't have the time. I think I can manage, with Lu's help."

"Thanks. I'll work with you until you get comfortable," he offered.

A few weeks later, Sandra needed some practice suits. We went to the local sporting goods store. They were very expensive.

"Dammit, Len, I don't think it's right for the kids to have to pay so much for workout suits and all the other equipment at retail stores," Lu said as we walked out to the car. "We used to get them from the Nadadores' swim store at the pool. Couldn't we do that, too?"

"I'll start looking for a better source of good quality, less expensive gear," I answered. "I bet if we went to suppliers directly, they might sell us stuff in bulk at a reduced cost."

"Now I know why I thought you were right for this job," Lu said with a smile.

"Of course, the team's going to have to invest some money. Instead of ordering suits as needed, we'll keep larger quantities on hand, selling them at cost. The team won't make a profit, but it'll sure help the kids and the parents."

"It sounds good to me, but you'll need approval to spend the extra funds," Lu replied.

At the next board meeting, I spoke to everyone about my idea. Lu had been a member as secretary/treasurer for about four months and thought she knew how they'd respond.

"What a great idea! It'll help all our swimmers. But are you sure you want the extra work and responsibility?" Pat asked.

"It was my idea, and, yes, I'm ready to take it on," I answered confidently.

One evening about a month later, I was fitting a new little swimmer with his suit. He couldn't have been more than five years old. After we got the fit right, he turned to me and said with a lisp, "Thansh, Mither TSCAT Tshop man."

I realized I was doing something important, at least for one little guy. I wasn't useless. I had a purpose. Lu had been right. This was my job. I developed a relationship with each swimmer on the team. I couldn't hide behind a stopwatch any longer.

They called me the SCAT Shop Man.

* * *

The first year Lu and I carried the SCAT Shop in the back of our van. The team continued to grow for the next few years, and by 1987 they used three different pools. Lu and I, or most often Lu's dad, Walt and I took the SCAT Shop to each at least once a week. We were now outfitting over three hundred swimmers.

Our list of supplies grew, too. We now sold practice suits, goggles, sweat suits, warm parkas, caps, and countless other things with the SCAT team logo.

We also opened the shop at our swim meets and sold stuff to other swimmers. This became a full-time business. Yes, it was a hectic schedule, but I had found my niche. I was definitely back out in the real world, and I was working with kids again.

My one problem continued to be using simple math. I could handle it as long as I wasn't rushed. The parents and kids understood and accepted my handicap.

I was busy ordering and picking up supplies. I could take the bus to some of my distributors and pick up small items. I carried them home in my trusty book bag. It was faster and cheaper than having them shipped. I was constantly looking for new suppliers with products at better prices.

I became quite the businessman and was known throughout Orange County's swimming community, not only as Sandra's dad, but also as a timer and an equipment supplier. I was in heaven, I was needed, and I was working.

My pay? I received ten dollars a month for gas and the thanks of all the swimmers and parents. Wow! It was worth a million bucks to me.

* * *

Another change in my life came from an unexpected source. We had purchased a second-hand computer from Lu's cousin. Lu used it for secretarial and treasurer stuff for the team. She also kept a roster of every swimmer and their families.

I'd been keeping records of my inventory and tracking the finances of the SCAT Shop by hand. Lu felt the computer would help. I confess, I was afraid of it.

Through a complete lack of understanding on my part about this complicated machine, I wanted nothing to do with it. Lu could do all her work on it, thank you very much. I was just fine. I wasn't going to even touch it. Not me! No way!

Lu finally convinced me that since we were getting more supplies and more swimmers, I needed a better system. Sandra worked with me enough so I could turn it on, find the right program, and do some work. However, I was sure the computer would lose everything when I turned it off. She helped me save my data so it didn't go away.

"Dad, I've told you many times how to do this. You do it this way," she would say as she showed me once again the workings of the computer.

I usually responded, "Don't tell me, just do it for Daddy, please."

She'd heave that thirteen-year-old sigh and say, "Okay."

One evening, she asked innocently, "Dad, why don't you take a class and really learn how to use our computer?"

"Honey, you know my head injury makes learning complicated things almost impossible."

"Yeah, well if you can graduate from a four-year college, you can learn to use a computer!"

Dammit, she's right. Here I am turning forty-two, and my thirteen-year-old daughter knows how to use this stupid machine. Maybe I can learn, too.

"Hey, Lu, I'm getting frustrated. Where could I take a basic computer class?" I asked at dinner.

"I think Saddleback College should have a class. The semester starts in a few weeks. We'll check it out."

Lu drove me to the school the next morning.

"There've been a lot of changes since my first time here twelve years ago," I observed.

"Look, building's going on everywhere," Lu agreed.

"There are a lot more students here now than I remember."

At my first stop, I talked with my old counselor, Mr. Bergman. He was as happy to see me as I was to see him.

"We now have a special services department for the disabled, and they have computer classes for physically-challenged students." He suggested I talk to the department secretary.

She explained, "We have just the class for you, Mr. Rugh. We keep it small so our lab assistants can work one-on-one with each student, and there's still an opening."

"Thank you. May I sign up here?"

"Sure, just fill out these papers."

I got back into my "get up early and go to school" routine.

Lu did a lot of substitute teaching, so I needed to find my own way to Saddleback. After seven years of riding the bus to Fullerton, it was easy. Now a bus route swung right onto the campus. I took two buses and about an hour to get there. No sweat!

I didn't know what to expect, but I did know what I wanted out of the class. My goal was to become computer-friendly and get over my fear of turning it off, and especially of losing stuff. *I can do this,* I kept telling myself.

* * *

"First, I should tell you I'm afraid of these smarter-than-me machines. When I graduated from college, we used typewriters. I'm not sure I want to be a part of the computer age, but what can I do? My daughter challenged me to learn," I heard myself explaining to the instructor.

"Don't worry, you'll get used to it, and before you know it you'll wonder how you ever lived without it," she replied.

"Yeah, well I don't think it'll go that far, Mrs. Allen. I'll just be happy to do the very basics."

"We'll see, and call me Mary," she said smiling.

"I was shot in the head in Vietnam, which left me paralyzed on the left side. It's affected my thinking processes, sometimes making learning difficult," I said, explaining my disability.

"This class is designed for your type of brain injury, Mr. Rugh," she informed me.

"My name is Len, by the way. I hope you're right. I'll need all the help I can get to tame this computer."

Mary and Diana, the assistant, were kept busy moving from student to student, checking over our shoulders and answering our questions.

"What happens if I push this key?" I asked one day. I was really getting into this computer stuff, and I just couldn't seem to learn it fast enough.

"That's a hot key for spell check. Be sure to study the handouts. They'll answer a lot of questions. Do you have a computer at home where you can practice?" Diana asked.

"Yeah, but my wife, my daughter, and I share. We've worked out a schedule. Sandra's homework has priority, but I have a few hours in the afternoon before they get home."

"The department has a computer lab. The hours are posted on the door. You're lucky, only the students enrolled in our computer class are allowed to use it," she continued.

"I'll take advantage of it if I need to."

"So, what do you want to work on today?" Diana asked.

"Would you go through saving data step-by-step, and then watch me to be sure I'm doing it correctly?"

"Of course, that's easy."

Diana went through the process, slowly. When we were ready to turn it off, I asked, "Won't we lose everything?"

"No, we saved the data into its memory. It disappears from the screen, but it's not lost. You can retrieve it the next time you go into this program."

"If you say so. You're the expert."

"Well, I'm not sure I'm an expert, but I do know my way around computers," she said as she saved my work.

She turned it off.

The screen went blank.

"I thought this would happen. Everything's gone!" I said, frustrated.

"Len, are you going to be one of my problem students?"

"Who, me? A problem?" I responded as if she'd hurt my feelings.

"Yes, you ...," she answered.

Thus began a long friendship. I would make many other friends, both staff and students in the special services department.

I spent a lot of time in the computer lab, and also on our computer at home. I was overcoming my fear. What had once been frightening was now a pleasure.

* * *

Before Lu and I were ready, Sandra began high school. Spring semester she would start on the varsity swim team as a freshman. The problem was what to do for the fall semester. She had to take a PE class to meet the six-semester requirement. Her counselor suggested another sport, water polo. But the school only had a boys' team, none for girls.

She met with the high school water polo coach and asked him if she could participate in the summer league program. She planned to try out for the team in the fall. The coach looked at her strangely, but gave his approval. He didn't have much choice. Lu and I figured he thought she would drop out long before he'd have to face fall semester. He didn't know my daughter, yet.

"I have no idea where she gets her stubborn streak! Just tell her she can't do something she really wants to do, and she plunges in with both feet. No pun intended," I said as we all walked home from the high school Sandra would attend.

I heard Lu mumble something about "peas" and "pods." I didn't have a clue what she might mean by that. Yeah, right! My Sandra was definitely her father's daughter!

Sandra took to water polo quickly. She surprised everyone by playing exceptionally well and made the freshman team. Was she ready to play on the boys' high school team? We weren't too sure, but she was. Our daughter had really found her sport in this new game.

I also had to learn a new skill, watching out for yellow water polo balls flying through the air. It's not an easy task when you can't see or hear on the left side. I had to put my old war warning system to work.

Most of us GIs had developed the internal warning system to stay alive. I hadn't lost this ability to sense when danger was near and managed to dodge the ball more often than not.

It was a new experience for Lu and me to just sit on the sidelines watching. We were just spectators now who traveled to every high school meet to watch Sandra play.

* * *

I was involved with Sandra's swim team, spending a lot of time at swim practice, timing at swim meets, and running the SCAT Shop. I had my class at Saddleback and my practice on our computer, using it to maintain inventory and sales for the team. I was involved with the high school water polo and swim teams. I didn't have time to sit and do nothing or feel sorry for myself. Once more, I was content and very busy.

Chapter 48 - My Class Assignment

The following year, I took the computer class again. This time it was to have an extra benefit for me. My instructor, Mary, suggested I also take her English class as the two went hand-in-hand. Most of her assignments could be done with our newly-acquired skills. It was on the same days, an hour before the computer class.

"I'm not sure I need another English class, but it sounds like a good combination," I admitted.

She just smiled and said, "I'll see you on Thursday at nine for English."

* * *

About halfway through the semester, Mary was working with us one-on-one when she asked a question which was going to have greater impact than I could have imagined.

"I want you to use your knowledge of computers and find some project to work on for this class. Is there anything you'd like to write about?"

Just jokingly, I said something really crazy. "I've always thought of writing a book about my experiences in the Vietnam War."

"Great, you start tomorrow."

"You're joking! Me write a book? You know about my writing skills. I can design the world's longest run-on sentences, my paragraphs are a joke, and besides, I'm the world's worst speller."

"That's why there's a spell check dictionary in the computer program, or have you not been listening in class?"

"Oh yes, it's F-2 as I recall," I said flippantly.

"It looks like you're going to get a lot of practice with that key the rest of the semester."

She couldn't be serious! I wasn't sure I was ready to handle going back into Vietnam and that damn war. The nightmare still haunted me, maybe not as often, but it was still there between me and a good night's sleep.

I left Joe and my platoon dead in the stinkin' jungle. Do I really want to stir up those memories? I sure don't want to relive that horrible day again. Oh, sure, there were the good times and the comradeship, but to put it all on paper? Could I do that? What would be the repercussions?

"Len?" Mary pulled me out of my contemplation. "I can see you're doing some hard thinking. Is there a problem? I think you know I'm more than just an English and computer instructor. I'm also trained to listen. Do you want to talk about it?"

"I guess it's writing about the war."

"I understand, but sometimes it helps to face our fears. Maybe writing about it will help."

"I need to talk to my wife. If, things get too bad, I can stop at any time, right?" I asked in a prayerful whisper.

Mary leaned over and put her arm around my shoulders then spoke in her soft, reassuring voice which put me at ease. "I'll let you make the decision of how long you want to continue with the project. It was just a way to have you practice your computer skills."

"Thanks, Mary. Maybe I need to do this so I can put the war to rest, if that's even possible."

On my bus trek home that day, I dredged up memories I had long forgotten. I remembered the day I received my draft notice, my time in basic and AIT, my arrival in Vietnam, and the smells, the sights, and sounds. They bombarded my brain. I had now opened the box marked "Do Not Open ... Ever," containing all the feelings and pain. I couldn't seem to shut it again. By the time I got home, I was drained.

"Honey, what's wrong? Did you have another seizure?"

"No, nothing that simple," I replied.

"Sit down and talk to me!" Lu insisted worriedly.

"I opened my big mouth today and mentioned I'd considered writing a book about the war. Mary took me seriously. She wants me to start right away. I'm just not sure this is a good idea. All the way home, my mind has been spinning with thoughts of life in the army, especially the guys I left in 'Nam. What should I do?"

"Well, you've often mentioned writing a book about the real war. Maybe now's the right time. It might even be good therapy to finally get all the ghosts out of your brain and put your feelings on paper."

"I think it's what Mary was trying to say, too. She also told me I could stop at any time if it was too much. The major reason I've never started or given it any serious notion is my writing skills. You know how bad they are."

"Gee, I haven't a clue what you might be talking about."

"Sure, wife! You know very well I'd be a really lousy author, and I hate English."

"Well, you're not signing a contract to write the great American novel. Why don't you give it a try? You know the old saying, 'nothing ventured, nothing gained ...'"

So began the odyssey which would become something of an obsession. I spent a lot of time in the lab and at home sitting in front of my computer, as I put my feelings, my blood, my sweat, my fears, and even some tears on paper in a feeble attempt to write my story of the war.

The assignment brought back recollections of my time in hell. Once I really got into the project, the story started to pour onto the screen. The flashbacks and nightmares started again, but they only haunted me for the time it took to write about them.

As the days went by, it became easier to dredge up the events from that hideous war, but they were never easy to write down. I struggled over the words I would use. Eventually, it became a sort of healing to finally express my feelings. I had never really talked to anyone about what I saw and did. At last, I was releasing it all from my system, even if it was only transferred to the computer.

* * *

One day after writing about a particularly difficult memory, I was on my way home when a man got on the bus. He sat across from me and kept staring at my leg brace and arm sling. He was short, fat, and balding. His clothes were dirty and wrinkled and he smelled like he hadn't showered in a long time. I thought he was rather disgusting and possibly drunk. Then he opened his mouth and proved it.

"What happened to you? Your wife beat you up?" he asked with a nasty laugh.

Lu and I'd heard stupid questions like this all the time from thoughtless and rude people. We'd been asked everything from if I'm "a victim of women's lib" to "What's the other guy look like?" These idiots think they're funny, I guess. I sometimes wished they could be on the receiving end to understand how much questions like that hurt.

Lu, the greatest wife in the world, would never do anything to harm me. She stayed with me when almost any other woman would have washed her hands and walked away. *I hate it when she's insulted by asinine comments and stupid questions.*

I really don't mind questions like, "Were you hurt in a skiing incident?" or "Is that from an automobile accident?" or even, "What happened?" At least those questions are intelligent, not hurtful.

"Hey, I asked you a question, buddy!" the slob bellowed.

I tried to let it drop without an answer, but no way. He yelled at me again.

I'd finally had it and really laid into the guy. I looked him in the eye and told him the facts about how, when, and where I was wounded. I went into all the gory details.

It worked. He sat there with his mouth open and his eyes bulging.

But he had to make a dumb remark about my wife abusing me. I let him know what a wonderful wife I had and that I didn't appreciate his slurs against her.

Usually when someone asks stupid questions, I just ignore them, turn around, and walk away. If I go into a store and someone working there makes a stupid, insulting comment, I leave without making a purchase.

The jerk on the bus mumbled an apology as he quickly exited at the next stop.

I didn't know if I wanted to laugh or cry over the events of the day. By the time I got home, I just wanted to sit down and watch TV until my sanity, in the form of my wife and daughter, returned for the day.

* * *

Writing about Vietnam was tough as I tried to put the difficult words into the computer. It felt good to get the horror out of the private box in my mind and got easier as time went on. I worked for years on this epic. It would cost me a lot of frustration, confusion and mental pain, but there was also joy, satisfaction, and release. The worst of the memories had been filed away and not allowed into the daylight. Now they were there for the entire world to see.

The words came crashing out of my brain, tumbling over and over. I couldn't write them fast enough with my one-handed typing. I often agonized over the right words to use. At that point, I didn't concern myself with the mundane parts of writing, like sentence structure and spelling. I made a new paragraph when I felt like it, which I'm sure wasn't often enough. Once I began, I had this overwhelming need to keep going.

What had started out as a class assignment was now a big part of my life. I worked before I went to school, in the lab there, and after I got home.

During all the years I worked on my book, Lu never read one word. This work was to be my memories and thoughts alone. She didn't want to influence what I wrote. We made a deal. After I had everything in the computer and was finished, she would then, and only then, help me to edit the text. I'm sure she was dying to read it, but she stuck to her part of the agreement.

I kept going. I was writing pages and pages, but it would take her organizational skills to put them in order.

* * *

I decided to expand my schooling beyond the computer. Special services told me about an adaptive PE class. Students wanting to be physical therapists took the class to work with those of us needing therapy. I was using my muscles again. I hadn't had any therapy since November of 1971, when the VA had turned me loose.

I had to keep my body strong, to be as healthy as possible so I could continue walking. Not easy for someone in my condition. I called this class "physical torture," but it became my lifesaver. I attended for an hour, four days a week.

I decided to repeat my speech class with Miss Bennett since I was now at Saddleback extra days. I'd heard she was getting ready to retire. One day, I approached her about signing up again.

"Of course I'll be glad to have you. Just remember I expect you to do different speeches than the first time you took my class," she said with a laugh.

Like she'd remember my speeches.

"I wouldn't have it any other way, but you won't be able to find my daughter's teething ring on my first day," I answered.

"Oh, that's right, you're the one! I pulled the baby's teething ring out of your sling for the whole class to see. I noticed you're still wearing the sling."

"This is as good as I'll get. I'll use this sling until they put me in the ground."

"How's your daughter?"

"She's now a junior in high school and doing very well. She swims and has found a new love in water polo. There isn't a girls' team, so she plays on the boys' team and hopes to make varsity next year. She's really good, although I might be a bit prejudiced."

"I've noticed your speech has come a long way since our first class together."

"I had speech therapy at the VA hospital long ago, but I think a lot has to do with your class. I learned to speak in front of a classroom full of people, not easy for me at that time. You made me face my fear of being in public. Since then, I've had a lot more confidence in myself."

"My class is still on Tuesday and Thursday mornings at nine."

"Great, it will fit into my new schedule."

"I'm glad you decided to take my class this year since it's my last. I'm finally retiring. I now have young people whose parents were in my classes. It's time to let someone else teach our future generations."

"You'll be missed."

"That's nice of you to say, Len. Thank you."

"I said it because it's true. When I walked in that first day, I was beginning to think it was all a mistake. I was positive I didn't belong there. I nearly got up and left. Then you walked in, held up Sandra's teething ring, and made me stutter the one-sentence speech."

"It was one of the highlights of my teaching career, and you handled it well as I recall. I sometimes tell that story to my classes. It helps break the ice and gets them relaxed."

"It's a little late, but you have my permission," I said laughing. "It broke the barrier I'd built for protection. I can never thank you enough. That one incident started me on a new path, and I'll always be grateful. It was exactly what I needed."

She smiled.

"I feel if it hadn't been for your positive attitude, I most likely wouldn't have gone back for the second semester. I'd probably have spent the rest of my days sitting on the couch watching TV."

"If I remember correctly, your wife would never have let you get away with that."

"Yeah, you're right there!" I acknowledged.

"So, what have you done since you left Saddleback?"

"I transferred to the Cal State system for seven years and earned my BA in political science in '83. Then I worked with Sandra's swim team while she was growing up, which took a lot of my time. I've been back here for two and a half years taking computer classes."

"You've been very busy, I see. Not bad for someone who, as I recall, was only going to be in school for a semester or two."

"Well, that was my original plan, but as things progressed, the idea of staying in school took hold. I couldn't stop until I graduated. Here I am still going to college sixteen years later."

"In that one semester in my class, I saw someone overcome some real problems and stand before my class to give one of the most powerful speeches I've ever heard."

"Thanks! It was because I had an instructor who believed in me and gave me a chance."

* * *

I was now in school during the mornings and early afternoons, Monday through Thursday. This gave me time to be the SCAT Shop Man in the evenings. I worked on my writing every free moment I could squeeze out of this busy schedule. Now my mornings started before the sun was just a pink line across the horizon, and usually didn't end until well after the sun's colors had turned into night black.

* * *

Lu went to work full time as a high school academic advisor in August of 1990, and in June of 1991, Sandra graduated from high school. Two very important events in my life, yet they didn't affect my daily writing schedule.

I couldn't believe it, my little girl was all grown up and leaving for college. *Where has the time gone?* Lu was right, as usual; I was the luckiest dad in the world. I'd gotten to spend so much time with her, was always there for her, and did so many things with her. *God, I'm really going to miss Sandra when she moves four hundred miles away to Sacramento and UC Davis. Why is her school so far away?*

Lu said it was a part of life when our child left the nest, but I noticed she had teary eyes when she said it. She was just as upset as I was. Life goes on. I settled back into my routine.

In June 1995, my father-in-law and best friend, Walt Brush died of cancer. Even though we had known it was coming, it devastated my family and gave me pause to rethink my own mortality. He was a wonderful man and I would miss him.

Chapter 49 - Life Changes Again

For the next few years, Lu worked at the high school and I took my computer and PT classes at the college. I'd given up the SCAT Shop and turned it over to another parent when Sandra graduated and went away to college. Working on the book was taking more and more of my time. It kept me busy.

Sandra met the love of her life and became engaged. They decided to be married during the summer of 1999 on a large yacht in Newport Beach, California. The night of the rehearsal, the boat was tied up at the marina, but the night of the wedding we were sailing around the bay.

I was in position to walk my daughter down the aisle. We'd practiced and I was ready, if not a bit nervous. We stepped off and I was doing just fine. Then the boat lurched, and I lost my balance about halfway to the altar. I'm not very stable on my feet and usually use my cane to steady me. Here I was, clinging to my daughter in her beautiful wedding gown. I was so afraid I was going to fall and take her with me.

My brother-in-law was on the aisle next to me. He realized what was happening and reached out for support. Sandra held on tighter and whispered, "Daddy, I've got you, just hold on."

The maneuver went so smoothly, I don't think many of the guests realized what had happened. We made it to the altar where I proudly gave my daughter in marriage. Steve is a wonderful addition to our family and has made my daughter happy.

* * *

Life was good. But every time I'd felt this way, something happened to make it better, or something really bad happened to wake me up.

My sister, Dixie, died of a sudden heart attack. It was a wake-up call.

Lu and I sat down and took a good look at our lives. We talked of the things we wanted to do and decided now was the time to make some important changes.

Lu made plans to retire from her job effective March 1, 2000. We bought a truck and fifth-wheel trailer and planned a great adventure. We're both native Californians and wanted to see what the other forty-seven contiguous states looked like from ground level.

We planned to take three months to travel around the US, driving through twenty-six states. Were we crazy? Quite possibly. Neither of us had ever done anything like this before. I was handicapped. What could I do to help? Lu had ideas and made a list of my chores while on the road. We made arrangements for mail, paying bills, and had someone from church staying in the house. We were ready to leave.

* * *

Lu's brother had a colleague with the Pasadena police named Bruce, who had been in my unit. We were introduced one day when we were visiting Walt at his job. I was the first vet he'd met from the 199th since his return from 'Nam.

We talked a few minutes but realized we didn't know any of the same people. He was there the year before me and in a different company. We both knew the area we had fought in very well, however. It was an interesting visit.

A few days before we were to leave on our trip, Bruce recognized my name in an article on the Internet Web site Redcatcher, written by a former buddy of mine from 'Nam. Marty Glasgow was searching for guys he had lost track of from the war. Bruce passed along Marty's request to find me to Walt.

We'd planned to have dinner with Sandra and Steve, Walt and his wife, Sherrie, and several other members of the family the next evening before we left for our three-month trip. They brought the page of "Marty's Memories" to me then. While waiting for our table, we sat down to read the email. There were a few lines about me …

Things heated up when we got up north. It made the time go fast. There was lots of contact and the first of many lost friends. We set up a day ambush by a trail and two VC walked up on the patrol. Joe spotted them first and opened up with his 60. He literally held the first VC up with his fire. Rugh was hit in the head in the exchange. The second VC didn't get his AK off his shoulder. I don't know what happened to Rugh after extraction. The AK round was still in his helmet between the steel and the liner. We spent the night uphill from the bodies waiting for any attempt to retrieve them but there was no further contact.

* * *

I don't remember much of the conversation during dinner that evening. My mind kept swirling about the words on the page. Boy, it was sure weird to find out someone had been asking for information about me on the Internet. I didn't even know there was a Web site about the 199th.

Wow! Glass was alive! But how could that be? Didn't he die along with the rest of the guys on that day so long ago?

He'd been in another platoon in Bravo Company, so I figured it must have been only the guys from Fourth Platoon who died when I was wounded.

Marty remembered the events differently than what I'd been told. I might have been a little confused, but the voice in the hospital had explained I was the only one left alive, didn't he? I'd been so badly wounded I'd been left for dead. Didn't he say they were all dead? How could there be any other survivors from my horrible mistake?

After dinner, Sandra asked me if I wanted to email Marty since his address was at the top of the paper. She and I discussed what I wanted to say and we made contact that evening.

Marty was stunned to hear from me. He'd wondered for nearly thirty-one years what had happened after I was taken away on the medevac chopper. I'm not sure he truly believed it was me.

Wait a minute, a chopper. I didn't realize I was flown out of the jungle. Who put me on it? Now, there were more unanswered questions.

Sandra and I discovered this Redcatcher Web site was all about the 199th. We found it rather interesting. There was so much information about the unit and the men who served in it.

Lu and I left two days later. This trip now became a quest to find the truth—the real truth about what had happened that day long ago. I thought I had it all figured out, but now I was baffled.

We stayed in contact with Marty while on the road. Our itinerary included a stop to visit Gettysburg in mid-May. We arranged to meet him at the campground there. He said it wasn't too far from his home in Pennsylvania. I was anxious and impatient to see Marty and have my questions answered.

Lu was right when she said it would be easier to talk in person, so I should sit back, relax, and enjoy the trip. We'd spent many hours planning our route, and I wanted to follow our original plan. It would be worth the wait to finally learn what had really happened.

* * *

We took off on March 9, 2000, on our expedition of discovery. With Lu's retirement, we'd have time to see and do everything we wanted. We weren't getting any younger, and I didn't know how long I could put off using a wheelchair.

Lu admitted to being a little apprehensive, but assured me she was fine with hitching and unhitching, pulling and parking the trailer. I knew she could do it. I had more faith in her than she did in herself. There wasn't a lot I could do but give her encouragement.

Our itinerary would take us about ten thousand miles. We'd journey east across Interstate 10 to Florida to see Disney World and visit friends and family. Then head north up the coast, through DC into Pennsylvania, on to central New York, visiting Steve's family there. We'd then make a left turn towards the west and home through Niagara Falls, Ohio, Oklahoma, and the Texas Panhandle, arriving back in California before Lu's birthday in June.

I felt compelled to make this journey. I had to face the Wall and see Marty. I had a burning desire to know the truth. Nothing was going to stop me now.

Chapter 50 - One Scary Night

One event almost made us turn around and head back home. We were trekking across Texas. Lu had been driving through forty-mile-an-hour winds all day and she was exhausted. We needed to stop, but we were in the middle of nowhere.

In our camping guide I found the only RV park for miles. (The book was about the size of the Los Angeles telephone directory, and just as heavy.) Lu and I often read the information, then selected a place for the night. In this part of Texas, we had only one choice.

We followed directions to the RV camp. There was just an off ramp from the highway, not even a place to purchase supplies. Lu found it, drove through a large set of chain-link gates, and registered at a little building with an office sign. The attendant told us to pick any spot and set up for the night.

My wife was raised on a dairy farm and her family had grown all their own cattle feed. Her first impression of this park was one of disbelief. It had been an old alfalfa field, complete with levees and stubble from the last crop. The owners had laid out conduit for electricity and pipes for water, but that was about it.

We were the only ones registered for the night, which was a little disconcerting, but we were too tired to go on. After finishing our setup, it began to rain.

The sky looked rather ominous. Being southern Californians, we'd never seen anything like it. The clouds were moving and seemed to be circling. Since we watched the Discovery Channel, we recognized the conditions. The same notion immediately popped into our heads: tornado!

We had just watched the movie *Twister* a few weeks before, and it was still fresh in our minds. The clouds were beginning to look like they did in the movie the night the big one hit the drive-in.

Lu tried to find out about the weather on the radio—nothing; on the TV—no stations; the weather channel—again nothing. No cell phone service. We were nervous.

I had the sudden urge to kick or throw something. Any good radioman knew the tricks of making the equipment work, but jungle rot wasn't the problem this time. We were just too far out in the boonies to bring in any type of transmission.

Lu suggested we check with the fellow in the office. So, while Lu started dinner, I put on my jacket and walked the fifty yards to find out what was going on.

Lu saw an alfalfa field, but I saw dry rice paddies.

What the hell am I doing in the rice paddies again? I'm back in the World and a long way from Vietnam, right?

Take it easy, Rough. You're a point man again, and just need to check with HQ, then it's back to the NDP. You can do this just like you have so many times before.

Be careful. The VC might have a booby trap out here some place. Remember what Top said about staying off the paddy dikes. I can hear his voice telling us to check them out before sitting down and never, ever walk on them.

The office was dark and locked up for the night and I was back in the present with a very uncomfortable thought. What if the owner had gone to find shelter from the storm and forgot to inform us?

I headed back to the trailer. The light rain had turned into a thunderstorm.

Shit, I'm really getting wet, but I've been through the monsoon rains in Nam before.

At that moment, Lu looked out the door to see what I was doing and yelled, "Get your butt in this trailer, now! You're a walking lightning rod with that brace!"

I noticed my circumstances and came to the same conclusion. I put on as much speed as I was capable of getting back to safety.

Lu hugged me when I came through the door. She'd really been worried about me. The walk over and back had only taken ten minutes, but the whole weather picture had changed drastically.

Now we were really in a quandary. We could leave, but where would we go? We were tired and hungry and had absolutely no idea if, when, or where a tornado might hit. Not knowing where to go, we might drive directly into one. No, we were probably better off staying right where we were. Surely the man we registered with would have come to warn us of any danger, wouldn't he?

We decided there wasn't anything more we could do, but this was going to be a very long night. Lu made my favorite soup. It warmed us up on this blustery night and, for a few moments, took our minds off the weather outside.

The thunder crashed, the lightning flashed, and the wind howled. It was quite a storm. We were scared to death of meeting our imagined tornado. I'd gone many times without sleep under stressful situations in the war, and now I wanted to stay awake to hold and comfort Lu. I knew she hated the wind. I thought: *Will we live through the night?* And realized only God knew the answer.

We finally went to bed where we huddled under the covers and waited for the inevitable, whatever it might be.

* * *

The rain, our worry about a twister, and the terrain of the RV park all contributed to that night's frightening dream. It was similar to my recurring nightmare, but with the added element of the storm. I'm sure Vietnam doesn't have tornados but it did that night.

I watch my buddies fall in the rain and wind. I hear the thunder of gunfire taking lives on the battlefield. A tornado lifts their bodies and spirals them up, up and away. What's happening? I'm so confused.

* * *

We woke up to an eerie silence. Not knowing what to expect, we peeked out the window. The sight that greeted us was the very antithesis of what had gone on the night before. We couldn't see a thing through a thick blanket of fog. Lu called it a "tulle fog." This was unsettling and unexpected in Texas. I didn't like it one damn bit! It was too sinister and disturbing and gave me the creeps. I couldn't wait to get back to civilization.

We'd survived the night and the imagined tornado never materialized. I wondered, was this an omen? Should we turn around and go home? I'd been dreading the trip to the Wall knowing what I'd find. I looked for an excuse not to face the names of my buddies listed there. Was my subconscious telling me this was a mistake or wishful thinking on my part?

Lu and I discussed my dream and my worries. She knew I had to face my past. So, in the end, we decided to continue with the trip as planned. I had so many questions. Maybe the answers were to be found by finishing our journey.

When we were ready to leave, the fog was still too thick to find our way out. Lu and I checked the road and decided I would walk point to lead her through the gates.

Hell, I'm walking point through the damn rice paddies again. The flippin' war just won't go away. I look for Joe. He should be between me and the main element. Of course, he isn't here! I got him killed, with a lot of my other buddies on that fuckin' night so long ago …

Come on Rough, get back on track! You need to guide Lu out of this mess.

Wait a minute, I'm no longer Rough, I'm now called Rugh.

I was leaving this RV park hoping never to return. This one time was one too many as far as I was concerned.

Later that morning, the fog burned off and the weather turned beautiful with bright blue sky and white puffy clouds. It was a great day to be alive!

Everything was all right; we had survived unscathed. Lu and I never found out if there'd been any tornados that night. We really didn't care. We just wanted to get back on the road and away from there. It's truly amazing what an active imagination and your fears can conjure up with just the right set of conditions.

Chapter 51 - The 199th Light Infantry Brigade

Lu

Marty's sudden emergence back into Len's life had gotten both of us thinking about the war, his buddies, and his military unit.

Other than the stuff Len could remember, we knew very little about the 199th. We had discovered information on the Redcatcher Web site, but on the road we couldn't access the Internet. We learned about an infantry museum located at Fort Benning army base in Georgia, so we decided to check it out.

Len told me, "I guess I must be getting old. My army brigade is now found in a place reserved for the past, a museum. That's where you should find things about WWI or WWII, even Korea, but Vietnam? I guess it has been twenty-five years since my war ended."

"It's difficult to realize we're getting older," I observed. "Several younger generations have been making the world safe since your war."

"At least we haven't lost the number of men we did in my war. Hey, it's time for Sandra's weekly call, right?"

During the conversation, Len told Sandra about the museum and his shock at being on display there. She reminded him with a laugh, "You know, Dad, your war was in my school history books."

"Don't remind me, I feel old enough already."

"All of that happened before I was born, so to me it's ancient history."

"I know. Time's gone by quickly these last thirty years, but does it have to move at the speed of light?"

"Oh, Dad ..."

"Just don't say I'm getting old, daughter of mine."

"Never! I wouldn't ever think such a thing about my dad."

We could just picture her saying this with a straight face and mischief in her eyes.

"Yeah. Yeah. Yeah."

Len always tried to have the last word with our daughter. Once in a while he actually succeeded.

I sat there listening to this conversation between father and daughter. Then it hit me full force: these two very special people were my miracles from God.

Len survived his extensive head wound and was capable of doing so much more than Dr. Jackson and his team ever dreamed possible. His prognosis all those years ago was so scary for me. Day by day, I saw him emerge from the shell the military sent home to the strong, though disabled, man he was now.

Sandra was definitely her father's daughter even though the doctors thought it impossible. They're alike in so many ways. This special bond between them is powerful. She's so good to him and for him.

Sandra has often challenged her dad. Only she could have convinced him to take his first computer class. She'd been there to help him understand what he'd learned at school. Our daughter had kept him going, both mentally and physically, since she came into our lives over twenty-six years before. I'd given thanks every day of my life for these two amazing people who made my life so special.

Len and I missed her and our son-in-law immensely while we were gone, but there would be many more phone calls to keep in touch.

* * *

We arrived in Columbus the middle of April and spent one day at the Infantry Museum. It was housed in a large three-story building and included everything and anything we'd ever wanted to know about the American infantry, from pre-Revolution through Desert Storm.

Each area of the three floors was dedicated to a different war. The displays included uniforms, weapons, maps and battle plans, personal items and memorabilia from the soldiers, and artifacts from the period.

It was all interesting, but we were looking for the Vietnam display. We found it on the third floor. For me, it was enlightening. I could finally see some of the equipment Len had described in his letters home.

There were weapons of every kind and caliber: hand grenades and mines, the M-16, the M-60 machine gun, the LAW, and the mortar tubes used by Len and his platoon. There was even an AK-47 used by the enemy when Len was wounded.

"Oh, you've gotta see this. For all these years you've heard about my mortar tube. Well, now you're going to get a first-hand look. This is almost like the one we used at Firebase Jeanie. See that piece? That's the part ..."

He spent almost half an hour explaining each piece of it, what it was for, how it was used and, of course, how much it weighed. He spoke of the guys in his platoon and told stories about their adventures.

There was one moment when I could see that one of the objects had triggered a painful memory, but he pulled himself together and let it pass. He didn't want to talk about it, but I assumed we'd discuss it later.

He continued with one of his recollections about having to carry a third of the mortar on an excursion through the rice paddies. It was almost as if he was back in the war, his descriptions were so vivid. There was a lot to talk about, bringing back many memories for him, good and bad. I kept watching to see if this was upsetting for him, but he handled it like a tour guide.

There was a display of a typical firebase. Len just laughed. "If this is a 'typical firebase' it's not from the war I was in. Maybe it's typical for the REMFs, but not in any jungle area where Bravo Company fought. We didn't have wooden buildings or nice, neat sandbagged bunkers, as you might remember from my pictures. None of ours were big enough for more than one or two men to crawl into, and we certainly couldn't stand up in the damn things."

"Oh, is that what you called those cave-like hovels you lived in ... bunkers?"

"Yeah, Miss Smarty Pants! This is supposed to be a 'typical' field kitchen? Boy, is that a joke! The only time we had one was at Firebase Libby in the middle of the damn jungle, of all places. It was under a canvas tarp with the cook stoves along one side. There were no tables or chairs inside. They would have gotten in the way when we had to leave in a hurry. We ate off one-by-twelve planks on tall sawhorses."

"What, you ate standing up?"

"Something like that. You know, I remember at BMB there was one similar to this. It was in the rear, far from the fighting and the real war. Our few days there were the best days in that stinking country."

"Well, have you seen everything you want to see in here?"

"I'm ready to go. I think this exhibit was very well done," Len acknowledged as we left the room.

In the windows of the hallway leading from the Vietnam display were stained glass insignias for each infantry unit that fought in the war. There were unit flags, draped with the citations given during their active duty, a very impressive presentation.

Outside the building, we found a lot of military equipment too large to fit inside. As we wandered around, we notice there were memorials to the different infantry units across the street from the museum.

The memorial for the 199th, Len's unit in Vietnam, was very moving for both of us. It sat out on a grassy knoll by itself. It amazed us to discover the 199th was created especially for Vietnam in 1966, and was deactivated in October of 1970 at Fort Benning, Georgia.

We spent several hours on that beautiful day sitting at the memorial to the unit that Len had called his own for all those months of hell.

"I hope my old unit never has to be activated again," Len whispered as we walked away from the monument. I could only put my hand on his shoulder in comfort. We both knew it would take an all-out war for it to happen. What a solemn moment it was for us both.

Later that evening, after dinner, Len explained what had happened in the museum. He was describing the mortar setup and what each of the guys in his squad did to fire the weapon. He was there again with Joe, Rat, Ole, and Mac, when he realized they were gone. They'd been killed because of him.

Tearfully he muttered, "We planned a reunion when we got back to the World, but that will never happen. We'll never be together again. I left them on the jungle floor."

I held him while he cried for his buddies. War was hell, but being the only survivor is even worse.

Exhausted, Len finally fell asleep. Thankfully his dreams did not return during the night.

Chapter 52 - The Wall

Finally, I faced my biggest fear. Lu had been coaxing me to visit the Vietnam Veterans' Memorial in Washington, DC, since October 1982 when "The Wall" was finished. She wanted to see it, and since we were going to be in DC ten days, I really couldn't find any valid excuse not to go.

Was I ready to see the names of my buddies? Yes, I had to. I needed to apologize to them for getting them killed. Over the years, I'd found so many reasons not to travel across the country to face my ghosts, but I couldn't put it off any longer; the time had come.

I'd lived with the guilt every day for thirty-one years. Sometimes it seemed like I was being haunted, not by them but by my own remorse. Standing in front of that black granite edifice inscribed with over fifty-eight thousand names, looking for the few I could remember, was one of the most difficult things I'd ever had to do. Thank God, I had Lu by my side. She was my strength.

I'd gone over and over in my head the events that had led me to this place. I'd searched and searched for the words to say to these men who were as close to friends as I allowed myself in that damn bloody war. Again and again, I'd had my nightmare of those events I was so sure were real. How could it have happened any other way?

Oh, I knew God had forgiven me by the great life I'd enjoyed for three decades. I had a wonderful wife, a terrific daughter and a beautiful home. Now, at this memorial wall, I was seeking the forgiveness of Joe, Rat, Mugs, Dan, Mac, Wild Bill, and all the other guys from the Fourth Platoon of Bravo Company, 199th Light Infantry Brigade, who died on 4 September 1969.

* * *

May 15, 2000, dawned clear, but the weatherman had predicted thundershowers. Lu and I steeled ourselves for the visit. I managed to put it off until our very last day in DC. The day I had been dreading had finally arrived.

"Hey, the weatherman said showers for today, are you sure you want to go?" I think Lu was giving me a way out. She was aware of my reluctance and fear.

"I know it might rain, but I've been in worse. I've finally resigned myself. I feel it in my whole body. I have to make this journey today or I'll never go."

I was shaking. My insides were in knots at the thought of seeing the names. But, I had to bring some closure to that damn war and, hopefully, the ghosts would finally be laid to rest.

"I know what this means to you, to be able to end your torment. We've been together through all the nightmares and flashbacks. I've held you while you cried and berated yourself for your mistake. Hopefully this will help you put it all in the past where it belongs." Lu's hand was firm in mine.

"I'm sorry for burdening you with my guilt and frustration. You mean everything to me. I'll never be able to thank you enough for staying with me these past thirty plus years."

"I'm with you all the way. I promised you when I took my vows on our wedding day in 1967."

"I know it hasn't been easy, but I never would have made it without your love and understanding. I love you with all my heart."

"I know. I love you, too. Now, let's go. We won't melt, even if it does rain." Lu was always my voice of encouragement.

* * *

We took the sightseeing bus and got off in front of the Lincoln Memorial. It was just a short walk to the area we were seeking.

The first thing I noticed was the statue of the three GIs in the familiar uniform I'd worn every day. The guys could have been anyone from my company.

Then I looked up and the Wall was there before me. I stood in front of this impressive long black granite monument, so plain and yet so heart-wrenching. I gazed upon all those names carved on its face, knowing each one was for a brave soldier who gave his life for his country. I had to find the few I knew, my buddies, among the thousands listed there.

There were directories of the names. Actually, they looked more like telephone books in waterproof stands. People could locate the men they were searching for and know where to find them on the panels. I realized each of the panels had a year engraved. The men lost during that year were listed on the panel.

I began my search.

"Honey, they aren't here! Why aren't they listed in the directory? Where were they? Am I wrong? Please, God, let them be alive! They didn't deserve to die that day."

Lu laid her hand on my shoulder upon hearing my prayer, spoken with a shaky voice and a heartfelt sigh.

"Don't get so upset, there's probably a logical reason why you can't find them. Are you sure about the last names?"

"My memory isn't the greatest, but I knew some of those names like they were my own."

Now I was really confused …

The predicted rain began to fall and, along with it, my hope of being forgiven. My mind drifted back to those days of hell on earth.

Come on Rough, shake it off, it really is thunder, this is the year 2000, and you're standing in front of this black monolith. Lu is right. There must be some explanation as to why the names aren't here.

I turned around to carefully walk back down the rain-slick granite path to the 1969 panel for one last look.

Then it happened, my feet began to slide from under me. I couldn't seem to find traction with my cane, and my balance failed. Before Lu or anyone else could catch me, I fell on my butt, and my pride.

It had come to this. My humiliation was complete. I sat there in the rain and began to cry. I don't think I'd ever been so discouraged.

Several people ran to my aid, trying to lift me out of the puddle of water and back to my feet. I waved them off. I just needed to sit and gather my courage and my strength before attempting to stand.

For a minute, I didn't know where I was. I looked up at the Wall. I was staring at the panel for 1969. My reflection was superimposed over the names from the year I had spent in hell. There were tears flowing down my face joining the rain from above, God's tears.

Then the sun broke through the clouds and I could see a small rainbow like God's promise to Noah. At last, I felt He was forgiving me and cleansing my soul.

In that moment, I went from total despair to renewed hope. I was forgiven. I knew there had to be an explanation for why the names were missing. I would find the truth.

This trip to the Wall had been worse than I had expected in some ways, and better than I had imagined in others. I just had to learn what happened that fateful day.

* * *

We left the small valley where the Wall was located and headed back to the park and our trailer. I was very quiet on the ride, and Lu just let me think about all we had or hadn't learned from the day's trip.

After dinner, we sat down to watch the news on TV. But I needed to talk, so Lu turned it off.

"Sorry, I've been so quiet. I was just reflecting on today's events."

"I know. I figured you'd talk about it when you were ready."

"I thought I knew exactly what happened. Now, I don't. I'm so confused."

"Len, in three days we'll see Marty in Gettysburg. Maybe you were the only casualty that day."

"It'll be good to see him again after all this time."

"You two can spend the day sharing your pictures and memories. I'm sure you'll get your questions answered then."

"I've had the events in my head and my heart so long. Now things seem different. No matter how it turns out, I want to thank you for always being by my side. I wouldn't be here if not for you."

"Thanks, but where else would I have been all these years? I had you sort of trained. Why would I want to break in someone new?"

"You've been working at it now for over thirty-three years, and I'm not too sure you have it right yet. I think it'll take at least another thirty or so. I'm a slow learner, you know."

"Uh-huh, sure you are. Well, it's late and this has been a long day. Don't worry, I'm sure we'll get everything solved when we see Marty."

"Maybe. But how could I have been so wrong all these years?"

Lu had no answer for me. I would just have to wait the three days. It wasn't long, considering I'd already waited almost thirty-one years.

I was so exhausted I fell into a deep, mind-numbing sleep. There was no nightmare during the night. I guess my poor brain was muddled.

What is the truth? God, please help me solve this.

Chapter 53 - The Visits

Three days after we left DC, Lu and I sat waiting for Marty to arrive. I think I was more nervous and apprehensive than the day I'd gone to the Wall.

I remembered Marty, also known as Drill Corporal. We knew each other from Fort Ord, and he was in Third Platoon of Bravo Company in Vietnam. It had been a long time, and I wasn't certain what to say. I felt we'd be strangers since we had both probably changed in the years since we last saw each other. I was sure a lot had happened to us both.

And then he was there ...

We were older and I was disabled, yet the years seemed to fade away. We were back in the time neither of us wanted to remember, but couldn't forget. I'd known him then, but we were two different guys now. Sometimes our conversation seemed stilted as if he couldn't reconcile who I was in my present physical condition with the man I'd been in the war.

We looked at pictures, both his and mine, and talked about old friends. He had located some of the guys from our unit on the Internet, including my last LT.

It was a poignant day for me. I found out everything I remembered, or had been told, about the events of the day I was wounded were wrong. Marty answered most of my questions, but not all. I did find out the incident involving me and the trip flare was not even the same day. It happened several days earlier. Now I was really confused.

In the end, I had more questions than answers. Before Marty left, he gave me the email address for Lieutenant Don Bratton. He suggested we contact him as he had more first-hand information. Marty explained he'd heard from the LT, and he was anxious to see me if we were traveling anywhere near his home in Ohio.

I had to get this resolved for my own peace of mind. I'd carried the guilt for all these years. I needed to know what really happened.

Lu and I emailed LT that evening giving him our proposed travel plans, which included visiting the Football Hall of Fame in Canton, Ohio. A few days later we received a great email back from Don. He was really surprised to get my message, and of course, he wanted to see me.

> Hi Len,
> Marty forwarded to me the note you sent him. I am so happy to hear from you. I have thought constantly about you since you were wounded. I will never forget seeing you as you were penetrated out of the jungle. You waved to us. Doc Gibson and I tended your wound. I doubt you remember that.
> Marty has a picture of us on his Web site. Go to Marty's Nam Pictures album 1, picture 33. I am the guy shaving.
> I live in Medina, Ohio, which is south of Cleveland. I know you are going to the Football Hall of Fame. Will you be staying near Medina or Canton?
> My family is excited to meet and visit with you, too. Let me know your plans so we can arrange our schedule. We want to be able to spend time together. I am eager to hear more from you and visit with you both. I want to hear how you are doing. Whenever I think about Nam, I think of you.
> Take care and stay in touch, Don

* * *

So now we planned to include a meeting with Lieutenant Don. Over the next three weeks of our trip up through New York to see our son-in-law's parents and back through Niagara Falls, we kept in contact, setting up a time and place to get together. I looked forward to this visit with many emotions, fears, and expectations, hoping to finally find out what really happened on September 4, 1969.

I was so nervous and didn't quite know what to expect when meeting an officer. Even though I'd been out of the military for over thirty

401

years, grunts and LTs just weren't friends. There was always the barrier of rank, and this was an officer I had truly respected in 'Nam.

I later found out that he was just as anxious as I was. I don't think he knew what to expect from me, and I hadn't any idea of what to look forward to from him.

We were picked up at the RV park by his wife and taken to meet Lieutenant Don at his home for dinner. When I stepped out of the car and we saw each other for the first time, memories came flooding back. Don looked me in the eye and touched me like he couldn't believe I was real and not an apparition.

It was a beautiful night and we had a terrific dinner outside on their patio. We all sat around discussing our trip and Don's job.

Don, Lu, and I went into his den after dinner to talk about Vietnam. I excused myself to go to the bathroom. Later that night, Lu told me about their conversation while I was out of the room.

* * *

Lu

"I was so surprised when I heard from Marty that Len Rugh was alive," Don began. "When he asked if I was interested in hearing from him, I gave him a great big yes! I couldn't wait to contact you, although I wasn't sure what to expect."

"I'm sure it couldn't have been easy for you not knowing all these years what had happened to him. He's been through a lot, but he's a strong guy and too stubborn to give up," I told him.

"Lu, I have to tell you, though I know he's the same man I knew in Vietnam, I can't believe he's capable of doing what I've seen him doing tonight."

"The doctor's original prognosis was very grim and he's come a lot farther than they ever thought he would," I explained.

"I didn't want to say this in front of Len, not knowing how he would handle it. Now please bear with me, I need to tell you what I found when I first came upon him after he was shot. I hope this doesn't bother you too much."

"I'm fine. I've learned to tolerate almost anything relating to my husband's injury."

"When I first got to his position, he was face down in a pool of his own blood. The bullet had literally split his head open like a melon, and his brain lay there in the leaves and muck. Our medic lost it when he saw the damage. I cleaned it as best I could and bandaged his head back together. Doc and I tied him on the extraction hook. The last I remember as they pulled him up through the canopy toward the waiting helicopter, he was signaling to those of us on the ground. It was eerie. I kept thinking this man should be dead!"

"After hearing your description of what happened, I'm amazed he survived at all," I said. I sat there in a daze. Having it put in such vivid detail made Len's recovery all the more amazing.

"No one could have survived that ordeal, no one. But it's him. He is definitely the same man I knew. I just can't believe it!"

"Thank you for telling me, but I don't think you'd be able to tell him anything about what happened that he couldn't handle. I'm sure he wouldn't have expected any less."

* * *

Len

When I returned, Don finally gave me the answers I had been seeking. I explained to him what I'd been told in the hospital. I also described my nightmares and my feelings of guilt. I could see he understood my anguish.

He told me the night I remember accidentally setting off the trip flare and the actual day I was wounded were several days apart. I don't remember anything in between. I was glad to know Marty had been right, and there were no consequences from my blunder. I hadn't caused the death of any member of my platoon! It was the greatest news in my life. That was why the names weren't on the Wall. The guys were still alive!

Don explained what happened on the day I was wounded.

"Two NVA came down the path into one of our ambush positions. Joe was on his 60-caliber machine gun, firing as usual like there was a whole company of gooks. He began yelling for more ammo. You grabbed the requested ammo and headed towards him, and on the way, you were shot. Doc was the first one to you, but he froze. You were a real mess. He hadn't had to deal with anything more than a few minor wounds, nothing as extensive as you with half your head blown away."

"Then what happened?" I asked.

"I did what I had to do and called for a medevac chopper. They dropped the extraction hook down between the trees. I tied you on the hook and sent you up through the canopy. The last image I have of you is waving good-bye as they loaded you on board."

"So you never knew I was alive and well and living in southern California with my wife and daughter?" I inquired.

"I've always wondered if you survived. Oh, we were notified you made it back to the MASH unit alive, but that was our last report. None of us thought you'd make it. I figured you were long dead from that terrible injury. I was sure no one could live with that much damage, especially not in your present condition."

"Lu always says that I'm too mean, stubborn, and ornery to die. She's probably right."

"I've never said such a thing in my life, even if it is true on occasion, especially the stubborn part," she said with a laugh.

"That last image of you waving has stayed with me all these years. I've always wondered if I could have done more to save you. When Marty told me you e-mailed him, I couldn't have been more shocked. Doc and I didn't think you had a chance in hell. You are truly a miracle and I'm glad you're alive!"

"I can never thank you enough for saving my life and for taking away the guilt I've carried with me since 'Nam. Now I can face myself in the mirror every morning and know I didn't cause the deaths of the men of Bravo Company, Fourth Platoon."

"No, you were doing your job and giving it your all. I put you in for our highest medal for your selflessness and courage. You never did do anything halfway. Lu, your husband is a remarkable man and I'm proud to know him."

"Thanks for the information, Don. I'm proud of him, too!"

"You'll never know what a weight I've carried all these years, Don. Now I'm free to fully live my life," I said as I hugged him good-bye.

"If you don't have other plans, why don't you and your wife come to dinner at the trailer tomorrow night?" Lu offered.

"Sounds great. I'd love to see you guys again. We'll be there around 6:00 PM, is that okay?"

"Sounds great, we'll see you at six," Lu answered.

* * *

Later, when I got into bed, I made the mistake of thinking about what Don had explained. Lu repeated their conversation and the stuff he had left out in his rendition to me. My mind began spinning as I fell into an exhausted sleep sometime in the wee hours of the morning.

Another nightmare? I'm innocent this time. Surely the nightmare will go away!

This was totally different from the ones I'd been having for what seemed like all my life.

Joe's walking at the front of Fourth Platoon carrying his M-60. Of course, I'm still carrying the radio. Then things come to a head as we round a bend in the jungle trail. Walking right towards us are two NVA soldiers, the recon for a larger group.

Joe is fast and his M-60 cuts one of the enemy down and stands the other on his toes as the rounds from the machine gun tear into his body. Since Joe started carrying this powerful weapon, he's felt safe as long as he's on rock and roll. With the 60 on full automatic, he puts out lead as fast as he can. The 60 goes through a lot of ammo in this mode, and it isn't long before Joe calls for more. No one seems to be moving to supply him.

We're going to be in big shit if Joe doesn't get some ammo soon. Our M16s aren't the firepower, the 60 is. I just know there's a whole company of NVA coming around the bend.

I hear Joe yelling, "Ammo up." I don't stop to think about exposing myself. I just react. I grab a can of ammo and sprint towards Joe's position.

I'd called for Arty to drop rounds on the enemy while Joe cut down the point team. They were all blown to hell before any of our guys fell. I'd saved the platoon, and everybody was patting me on the back.

I'd finally put my horrible nightmare to rest. I had been vindicated, and I would be fine. I could go home without the guilt heavy on my shoulders and on my heart. I was a new man in this new century.

Epilogue

Lu

I'm proud of the people we've become in the years since Len's return home from Vietnam. We are incredibly close, and our marriage is enduring.

We've gone through so many changes, but perhaps the most difficult was the reversal of our personalities and roles. Through necessity, we grew and adjusted to meet our new requirements. It wasn't easy. I felt like a butterfly set free from the cocoon of my inhibitions. Len had to learn the restraints of his physical limitations. It was a long struggle for us, but required for our survival.

As the years have moved along, we've grown stronger. I had to grow up and learn figuratively to stand on my own two feet. Len had to accept his disabilities and re-learn how to just stand.

He came to realize he was stuck with me for the rest of our lives and accepted my love unconditionally.

I've finally recognized the man he became as my husband in my head and my heart, and the feelings of disloyalty have faded; but there will always be a special corner of my heart saved for the young man I married that February day in 1967.

* * *

Len

Lu and I came home from the trip with a renewed spirit. I finally knew the truth about what happened on September 4, 1969. My self-imposed guilt was lifted from my shoulders. I was free of the nightmares that had haunted me for what seemed like forever.

Knowing the men from my platoon had survived Vietnam was a great relief. I hope someday to look them all up to let them know I survived the hell, too.

Now I plan to really enjoy the rest of my life together with Lu.

In June 2005, our grandson, Edward, was born. Lu calls him "our miracle of miracles." This little man, my pride and joy, gave a whole new purpose to my life.

* * *

On February 17, 2007, with friends and family present, we renewed our wedding vows to celebrate our forty years of marriage. Our daughter and grandson stood with us before the most important people in our lives in our home church in San Juan Capistrano. Our pastor and friend of many years led us again in words of commitment, repeating the promises we made to each other a lifetime ago.

But perhaps the most special part of the day was having Lieutenant Don Bratton standing with us as best man. I wouldn't have been alive to celebrate this milestone had it not been for him.

All the promises we've made to each other through the years were honored in that memorable ceremony. And we rejoiced in the life we have shared together.

* * *

Jesus said, "… And the truth shall make you free." John 8:32 KJV

We would love to hear from our readers
Via email:llrugh@att.net
Or on our website
www.rughfamilywriters.com

Yet Filled With Grace

It's blistered feet, withering heart, and a fifty-pound pack that's on his back;
It's many a cut and bruises which no ointment ever soothes;
It's a monsoon which never quits.
      And thoughts of home which don't fit;
It's climbing cruel mountains, only to find, two in front for each behind;

It's thousands of insects of various kinds which deprive him of his peace of mind;
It's booby traps and punji stakes, leeches, mud, and deadly snakes;
It's cold C-rations, eaten in haste, but rest assured none goes to waste.
It's the constant strain of staying painful alert, of trying to sleep in mud and dirt,
It's unwashed fatigues, but he dare not spare his drinking water—it's often rare;

It's long and lonely nights of fear, while each sense asks, "Is Charlie near?"
It's treacherous tunnels and close-quarter fights
      And endless patrols to keep Charlie from hiding;
It's that minute that seems like two years, when enemy rounds crack close by his ears.

It's sudden stillness the jungles assume when a burst of fire signals his doom;

It's the terrible agony with which he's filled when hearing a comrade has just been killed:

For when bullets, rockets, and other hard knocks don't quite get Charlie out of those rocks

When planes and ships and tanks have failed—the man with the rifle will prevail;

It is his silent prayer at night, "Dear God, I did not ask to fight.

But I take comfort in knowing we're right.

I pray tonight will not take me in death.

      I pray that at dawn I still have my breath."

I ask that when we are through with this strife, at least some men will know a better life.

When the bombs have stopped falling, we shall hope to find

      A free Vietnam and a wiser mankind.

-S. Sgt. Willie E. Green
243 FLD SVC Co.
Pleiku, Vietnam

Pacific Stars & Stripes, Tuesday, August 5, 1969
Used with permission from Stars and Stripes. ©1969, 2008 Stars and Stripes

GLOSSARY OF TERMS

Military Alphabet
    A-alpha
    B-bravo
    C-charlie
    D-delta
    E-echo
    F-foxtrot
    G-golf
    H-hotel
    I-india
    J-juliet
    K-kilo
    L-lima
    M-mike
    N-november
    O-oscar
    P-papa
    Q-quebec
    R-romeo
    S-sierra
    T-tango
    U-uniform
    V-victor
    W-whisky
    X-x-ray
    Y-yankee
    Z-zulu

Terms Used by GIs Found in This Book

201 file - A GI's military history, containing everything from medical records to disciplinary action

AK-47 - A communist-supplied semi-automatic rifle

Alpha-Zulu - Azimuth

AO - Area of Operations

Arty - Artillery

Beaucoup - French word for many, a whole lot

Berms - Walls of dirt reinforced with sandbags

Boonies - Areas that were not in or near a populated area or major city, usually jungle and mountains

C-rats - C-rations; shortened term for field rations, canned food issued to men in the field

Charlie Oscar - CO, Commanding Officer

Cherries - GIs that have not come under fire by the enemy

Choppers - Term for almost any helicopter that was used in the war

Claymore clacker - The device used to send an electric charge to detonate the mine

Claymore mine - A command-detonated mine filled with C-4 explosives and packed with steel buckshot that can kill anything in its path for up to twenty-five yards when exploded; very effective for night defenses, on patrol, and for protecting a firebase

CO - Commanding Officer, or company commander

Cobra - A helicopter gunship that could saturate an area about the size of a football field with M-60 rounds, leaving nothing untouched

Cold LZ - A Landing Zone that is not taking enemy ground fire

CP or **Charlie Papa** - Command Post; usually the company commander's area

CS - Chicken Shit; a tear gas grenade, not deadly, only irritating to eyes, nose, throat, and skin, used to contaminate bunkers, bombs and other ordinance

Doc - The name used for a medic trained to handle basic medical emergencies

DZ - Drop Zone; area designated by ground troops for an air craft to drop supplies or **Eagle flight** - Fast movement of few men using choppers to give the appearance of many men in the field

Echo Mike or **EM** - Enlisted Man - Not an officer, this term usually used over radio

Eleven Bravo - Military occupation or specialty code for an infantry man

Eleven Charlie - Military occupation code for a mortar man

FDC - Fire Direction Control; men that were responsible for working up the figures and numbers for the gun crews so they could align their tubes correctly making the rounds go where they were supposed to

FNGs - Fuckin' New Guys; Old-timers' slang for GI's just off the plane and new to the war

FO - Forward Observer usually with ground troops

Free Fire Zone - Areas where GIs can shoot first and ask questions later, not usually in areas where civilian population or friendly troops were found

Grunt - A ground soldier, any GI in the infantry

Guide Man - One man appointed to guide each chopper into a landing zone

Hot LZ - A Landing Zone that is taking fire from the enemy making it dangerous for a chopper to land

HE - High Explosive; a mortar or artillery round used to blow things and the enemy to pieces

H&I - Harassment & Interdiction; artillery fired into suspected enemy areas of movement at the whim of headquarters.

Hooch - A small living/sleeping area, usually large enough for only one or two men

Huey - Name for one of the military's mainstay helicopters, used as medevac or gun-ships, built by Hughes Aircraft Company

Illumination round - A round fired by either the artillery or the mortars, an airburst flare that floats down on a small parachute

KIA - Killed in Action; when a soldier dies in battle

KP - Kitchen Police; duty to prepare and clean up before and after meals

LAW - Light Anti-tank Weapon; a one-shot small rocket

LCM - Landing Craft Military; used in WWII to do amphibious landings and used for transport up and down rivers in Vietnam

Lima Charlie - Loud and Clear; radio lingo

Lima Mike - <u>L</u>and <u>M</u>ine; a pressure-sensitive mine, set and forgotten until stepped on, hopefully by the enemy

LP - <u>L</u>istening <u>P</u>ost; two to four men made up an LP, situated away from the firebase or NDP as an early warning of the approaching enemy

LZ - <u>L</u>anding <u>Z</u>one; area where a chopper could put down to pick up or let off soldiers

M-16 - American-made semi-automatic rifle, which used a small 23-caliber round, but was very deadly

M-60 - A 60-caliber machine gun light enough to be carried and fired by one man

Medevac - A chopper used to pick up wounded men from the field

Mikes - This has two meanings: one mike equaled one minute of time, or one mike equaled one meter of distance

MM - <u>M</u>illi<u>m</u>eter; used in determining the size of a round of any type

Mortar Tube - A small artillery gun, an 81 mm, used by Americans or a 60 mm used by the ARVN

MOS - <u>M</u>ilitary <u>O</u>ccupation <u>S</u>pecialties

MP- <u>M</u>ilitary <u>P</u>olice

MPC- <u>M</u>ilitary <u>P</u>aper <u>C</u>urrency; currency printed by the government to keep US money out of the hands of the enemy and often referred to as 'funny money'

NDP - <u>N</u>ight <u>D</u>efensive <u>P</u>osition; a location to spend the night while on patrol, usually secured with trip flares and Claymore mines

NVA - <u>N</u>orth <u>V</u>ietnamese <u>A</u>rmy; regular ground troops, found mostly in the northern fighting areas of the war zone. Could be distinguished from his Southern counter part, the VC, as they usually wore regular military uniforms which the VC did not.

OD - <u>O</u>live <u>D</u>rab; the shade of green for all military clothing, vehicles, etc.

Oscar - Term used to designate an officer

P-38 - A military can opener, one came with almost every box of c-rations

Pop smoke - Request to detonate a smoke grenade for identification

Point Team - Term used for the two men at the front of the company while on patrol. One man was designated the point man, the second was to his rear about ten feet with a compass giving the point man directions.

Poncho - A rubber rain cover that could be snapped together with other ponchos to make a small tent

Poncho Liner - A small quilted blanket used for warmth inside the poncho

PRC-25 - The standard radio used by the field troops, it picked up the nickname of Prick-25

Shithook - Slang for the Chinook helicopter, used for supplies and to move troops. It could carry a full company of men, but needed a lot of room to land and takeoff.

Red tracers - The color, usually every third round lights up after being fired from a rifle. The Americans used red tracers where the communists used green.

REMF - Rear Echelon Mother Fuckers; not an endearing term for the men working at safe base camps and not out in the field where the war was being fought

ROE - Rules of Engagement; rules about when a GI could open fire, usually 'Don't fire unless fired upon,' different from a free-fire zone

Roger - Radio slang for message received and understood

RTO - Radio Telephone Operator; the person carrying the radio who stayed close to his officer so he could call or receive transmissions

Tiger Alpha - Trail Ambush; one of many ways of designating an ambush position

Top - Senior enlisted man in a company, a first sergeant

VC - Viet Cong

Wilco - Will Comply; acknowledging a transmission has been understood and the orders will be followed

Willie Peter - White Phosphorus used as a marking round and night time identification

Zero in - Finding where your round would go when fired, left or right, high or low of center, for semi-automatic firing

About the Authors

Leonard Rugh was born in Glendale and raised in southern California. In 1966, he began working at the Bob's Big Boy restaurant next to Pasadena City College where he met his wife, Luanna. About a year and a half after they married, Len was drafted and sent to Vietnam.

On September 4, 1969, Len was shot in the head while on patrol in the jungles north of Saigon. No one thought he'd survive. Even months later, the doctors were baffled not only by his survival, but his progress in spite of his massive brain injury.

In November 1971, he was discharged from the VA hospital in Long Beach and sent home to sit and do nothing for the rest of his life. That wasn't in his nature, so in August 1974, a year after the birth of their daughter, Sandra, he started college. With Lu by his side, Len struggled with classes and transportation for nine years. It was the answer to his impossible dream when in May 1983 he walked across the stage and received his diploma for a bachelor of arts degree in political science.

After spending over twenty years writing this book, he's now working on a series of short stories and a novel about his dog, Gina.

✐ ✐ ✐ ✐✐ ✐

Luanna Rugh was born in Modesto, California, and grew up on a dairy farm until her fourteenth birthday when her family moved to southern California. She attended Pasadena City College. After graduating with an associate of arts degree in biology, she began working on a four year degree and eventually a teaching credential at Cal State, Los Angeles.

In the summer of 1966, she met the man of her heart, Len. They were married in February 1967. Len's being drafted and subsequently wounded caused their lives to change dramatically.

When the daughter they were told they'd never have was two, Lu went back to college to complete her bachelor of arts degree in biology. Seven years later, she finished the year required for her teaching credential.

Luanna wrote a novella as part of an anthology called *Snowflake Secrets*, which was published in 2008 by Whiskey Creek Press. She's completed a children's book and is currently working on two new novels.

~ ~ ~ ~ ~ ~ ~

Len and Lu

Today Len and Lu live quietly in Laguna Woods, California. They are members of the Lagunita Writers Group with whom they meet every week. The information, suggestions, and encouragement from this group have been invaluable.

They travel in their motor home whenever possible. Their daughter, son-in-law, and long-awaited grandson Edward moved to New York in 2005, where their second grandson Nathan was born in 2008, so that is their usual destination.

They feel truly blessed to be together, surrounded by loving family and friends.